Noel Brown teaches at Liverpool Hope University. He is the author of *The Hollywood Family Film: A History, from Shirley Temple to Harry Potter* (I.B.Tauris, 2012) and co-editor of *Family Films in Global Cinema: The World Beyond Disney* (I.B.Tauris, 2015). He has a PhD in Film from Newcastle University, UK, and has written extensively on children's and family films in classical and contemporary British and American cinema.

'From forgotten silent films through to globally popular animations, this wide-ranging cultural history tells a fascinating story that in fact encompasses childhood, children's literature and popular culture as well as films. Accessible yet thorough, this book is the first comprehensive study of Britain's contribution to the children's film industry.'

– Kimberley Reynolds, Professor of Children's Literature, Newcastle University

Cinema and Society series

General Editor: Jeffrey Richards

Acting for the Silent Screen: Film Actors and Aspiration between the Wars
Chris O'Rourke

The Age of the Dream Palace: Cinema and Society in 1930s Britain
Jeffrey Richards

Banned in the USA: British Films in the United States and their Censorship, 1933–1960
Anthony Slide

Best of British: Cinema and Society from 1930 to the Present
Anthony Aldgate & Jeffrey Richards

Beyond a Joke: Parody in English Film and Television Comedy
Neil Archer

Brigadoon, Braveheart and the Scots: Distortions of Scotland in Hollywood Cinema
Colin McArthur

Britain Can Take It: British Cinema in the Second World War
Tony Aldgate & Jeffrey Richards

The British at War: Cinema, State and Propaganda, 1939–1945
James Chapman

British Children's Cinema: From the Thief of Bagdad to Wallace and Gromit
Noel Brown

British Cinema and the Cold War: The State, Propaganda and Consensus
Tony Shaw

British Film Design: A History
Laurie N. Ede

Children, Cinema and Censorship: From Dracula to the Dead End Kids
Sarah J. Smith

China and the Chinese in Popular Film: From Fu Manchu to Charlie Chan
Jeffrey Richards

Christmas at the Movies: Images of Christmas in American, British and European Cinema
Edited by Mark Connelly

The Classic French Cinema 1930–1960
Colin Crisp

The Crowded Prairie: American National Identity in the Hollywood Western
Michael Coyne

The Death Penalty in American Cinema: Criminality and Retribution in Hollywood Film
Yvonne Kozlovsky-Golan

Distorted Images: British National Identity and Film in the 1920s
Kenton Bamford

The Euro-Western: Reframing Gender, Race and the 'Other' in Film
Lee Broughton

An Everyday Magic: Cinema and Cultural Memory
Annette Kuhn

Family Films in Global Cinema: The World Beyond Disney
Edited by Noel Brown and Bruce Babington

Femininity in the Frame: Women and 1950s British Popular Cinema
Melanie Bell

Film and Community in Britain and France: From La Règle du jeu to Room at the Top
Margaret Butler

Film Propaganda: Soviet Russia and Nazi Germany
Richard Taylor

The Finest Years: British Cinema of the 1940s
Charles Drazin

Frank Capra's Eastern Horizons: American Identity and the Cinema of International Relations
Elizabeth Rawitsch

From Moscow to Madrid: European Cities, Postmodern Cinema
Ewa Mazierska & Laura Rascaroli

Hollywood and the Americanization of Britain: From the 1920s to the Present
Mark Glancy

The Hollywood Family Film: A History, from Shirley Temple to Harry Potter
Noel Brown

Hollywood Genres and Postwar America: Masculinity, Family and Nation in Popular Movies and Film Noir
Mike Chopra-Gant

Hollywood Riots: Violent Crowds and Progressive Politics in American Film
Doug Dibbern

Hollywood's History Films
David Eldridge

Hollywood's New Radicalism: War, Globalisation and the Movies from Reagan to George W. Bush
Ben Dickenson

Licence to Thrill: A Cultural History of the James Bond Films
James Chapman

The New Scottish Cinema
Jonathan Murray

Past and Present: National Identity and the British Historical Film
James Chapman

Powell and Pressburger: A Cinema of Magic Spaces
Andrew Moor

Projecting Tomorrow: Science Fiction and Popular Cinema
James Chapman & Nicholas J. Cull

Propaganda and the German Cinema, 1933–1945
David Welch

Shooting the Civil War: Cinema, History and American National Identity
Jenny Barrett

Spaghetti Westerns: Cowboys and Europeans from Karl May to Sergio Leone
Christopher Frayling

Spectacular Narratives: Hollywood in the Age of the Blockbuster
Geoff King

Typical Men: The Representation of Masculinity in Popular British Cinema
Andrew Spicer

The Unknown 1930s: An Alternative History of the British Cinema, 1929–1939
Edited by Jeffrey Richards

Withnail and Us: Cult Films and Film Cults in British Cinema
Justin Smith

BRITISH CHILDREN'S CINEMA

FROM THE THIEF OF BAGDAD TO WALLACE AND GROMIT

NOEL BROWN

BLOOMSBURY ACADEMIC
LONDON • NEW YORK • OXFORD • NEW DELHI • SYDNEY

BLOOMSBURY ACADEMIC
Bloomsbury Publishing Plc
50 Bedford Square, London, WC1B 3DP, UK
1385 Broadway, New York, NY 10018, USA
29 Earlsfort Terrace, Dublin 2, Ireland

BLOOMSBURY, BLOOMSBURY ACADEMIC and the Diana logo
are trademarks of Bloomsbury Publishing Plc

First published by I. B. Tauris
This paperback edition published in 2021

Copyright © Noel Brown, 2017

Noel Brown has asserted their right under the Copyright,
Designs and Patents Act, 1988, to be identified as Author of this work.

For legal purposes the Acknowledgements on p. xi constitute
an extension of this copyright page.

All rights reserved. No part of this publication may be reproduced or
transmitted in any form or by any means, electronic or mechanical,
including photocopying, recording, or any information storage or retrieval
system, without prior permission in writing from the publishers.

Bloomsbury Publishing Plc does not have any control over, or responsibility for,
any third-party websites referred to or in this book. All internet addresses given
in this book were correct at the time of going to press. The author and publisher
regret any inconvenience caused if addresses have changed or sites have
ceased to exist, but can accept no responsibility for any such changes.

A catalogue record for this book is available from the British Library.

A catalog record for this book is available from the Library of Congress.

ISBN: HB: 978 1 78453 400 4
PB: 978 1 3502 4287 6
ePDF: 978 1 78673 101 2
eBook: 978 1 78672 101 3

Series: Cinema and Society

To find out more about our authors and books visit
www.bloomsbury.com and sign up for our newsletters.

Contents

Illustrations	ix
Acknowledgements	xi
General Editor's Introduction	xiii
Introduction	1
1 In the Beginning: Children and British Cinema in the Silent Era	10
2 The Children's Adventure Movie, 1930–60	32
3 Family Entertainers: Formby, Hay, Lucan, Wisdom	57
4 J. Arthur Rank, Saturday Morning Cinema and the Children's Film Foundation	80
5 Happiest Days: British Cinema and the Family Audience in the Fifties	106
6 Disney in Britain	137
7 Summers of Love and Winters of Discontent: The Sixties and Seventies	164
8 From Thatcher to Blair: The Eighties and Nineties	204
9 Exporting Englishness	230
Conclusion	257
Notes	268
Select Filmography	290
Select Bibliography	293
Index	296

Illustrations

1.1 Hepworth's own child and family dog starred in his seminal
production, *Rescued by Rover* (Hepworth Studios, 1905)   13

2.1 The criminal Pinker (George Hayes), pursued by hordes of
children at the climax of *Emil and the Detectives*
(Richard Wainwright Productions, 1935)   37

2.2 An example of the spectacular visual effects in Korda's *The
Thief of Bagdad* (London Films, 1940)   41

2.3 The young, streetwise gang at the centre of *Hue and Cry*
(Ealing Studios, 1947)   44

3.1 Will Hay, in his most famous guise as the comically
disreputable schoolmaster   65

3.2 Mother Riley (Arthur Lucan) holds court in *Old Mother Riley
MP* (Butcher's Film Service, 1939)   71

3.3 Norman Wisdom in his 'Gimp' persona   75

4.1 Simple animation is overlaid on the car's fender in *The
Adventures of Hal 5* (Children's Film Foundation, 1958)   93

4.2 Matt Busby meets the young footballers of *Cup Fever*
(Children's Film Foundation, 1965)   97

4.3 John (Mark Dightam) explores a fantasy world with Nick
(Robert Eddison) in *The Boy Who Turned Yellow*
(Children's Film Foundation, 1972)   101

5.1 Margaret Rutherford and Alastair Sim frame Joyce Grenfell in
The Happiest Days of Your Life (Individual Pictures, 1950)   112

5.2 Hayley Mills's ingénue Kathy and Alan Bates's runaway
murderer Blakey, in *Whistle Down the Wind*
(Allied Films, 1961)   135

6.1 Peter McEnery as *The Fighting Prince of Donegal*
(Walt Disney Productions, 1966)   149

6.2 The 'practically perfect' magical nanny, Mary Poppins
(Julie Andrews), with her surrogate family
(Walt Disney Productions, 1964)   155

Illustrations

6.3 Lady St. Edmund (Helen Hayes) nurses Casey (Jodie Foster) back to health in *Candleshoe* (Walt Disney Productions, 1977) 161

7.1 The Blue Meanie chief is effeminised by 'Nowhere Man' Jeremy in *Yellow Submarine* (Apple Corps Ltd., 1968) 171

7.2 The central family and the magical car: *Chitty Chitty Bang Bang* (Warfield Productions, 1968) 176

7.3 An early foreshadowing of the young protagonists' connection with the train in *The Railway Children* (EMI Films, 1970) 183

7.4 The fearsome General Woundwort dominates the frame in *Watership Down* (Cinema International, 1978) 199

8.1 The titular *Time Bandits*, accompanied by their unwilling companion, Kevin (Craig Warnock) (HandMade Films, 1982) 208

8.2 The plangent final scene of *The Snowman* (TVC, 1982) 213

8.3 The cheese-obsessed inventor Wallace, and his anthropomorphised dog, Gromit (Aardman Animations, 1993) 224

9.1 The protagonists as they appear at the start of their journey in *Harry Potter and the Philosopher's Stone* (Heyday Films, 2001) 232

9.2 The child protagonists, advanced to adulthood at the climax of *Harry Potter and the Deathly Hallows – Part 2* (Heyday Films, 2011) 242

9.3 Swashbuckling action comically realised in plasticine in Aardman's *The Pirates!* (Aardman Animations, 2012) 250

Acknowledgements

A book of this type owes its existence to a great many people. The first, and most obvious, debt is to those who made the films under discussion in the first place. I'm grateful to everyone at I.B.Tauris who has contributed to this book's development and completion, especially Anna Coatman for commissioning it, Maddy Hamey-Thomas for seeing it through to publication, and Jeffrey Richards for his initial enthusiasm, helpful suggestions and eagle-eyed corrections. I owe an intellectual debt to Terry Staples, author of a major historical account of children's cinema-going in Britain. Special thanks to Bruce Babington, who commented at length on the entire manuscript and with whom I discussed many of the ideas put forward in this book. The generous comments of the anonymous reviewers, and of Peter Krämer, were very helpful in refining certain important points. Thanks, for one reason or another, are also due to Robin Brown, Peter Clark, Alex Denehy and Maria Teresa De Oliveira Corrêa. Finally, I dedicate this book, with love, to my parents, Alan and Kate, and to Mauricio.

General Editor's Introduction

Noel Brown is rapidly becoming a leading authority on the history of children's cinema and the family film. Having authored *The Hollywood Family Film* (I.B.Tauris, 2012) and co-edited *Family Films in Global Cinema* (I.B.Tauris, 2015), he has now turned his attention to British children's cinema in this ground-breaking and thought-provoking book.

Children were among the earliest and most enthusiastic patrons of the cinema and this prompted twin areas of concern. The commercial concern of the industry was to provide films with the widest child and family appeal. The social concern for watchdogs, pressure groups, censors and reformers of all kinds was to counteract the perceived moral and physical dangers of cinema-going. In investigating the negative view of cinema, Brown examines the plethora of enquiries, reports and committees it spawned. But he also looks at positive moves to direct children's cinema-going with the creation of Saturday matinees, children's cinema clubs and organisations to supply children's films for showing at them, notably the Children's Film Foundation (1951–85).

Initially, children saw the same films as adults, but they had particular favourites. Brown analyses the proven child appeal and childlike characters of such slapstick stars as George Formby, Arthur Lucan and Will Hay. It was not until 1934 that the commercial cinema began to produce films aimed specifically at children. The first was *Emil and the Detectives*, and this was followed in 1937 by *Elephant Boy*, which produced the British cinema's first authentic child star in Sabu.

Taking up the story chronologically, Brown examines depictions of school and family relationships in 1950s films. He analyses the 15 live-action films made in Britain by Walt Disney between 1950 and 1979, identifying a nostalgic image of Britain and the British based on fantasy, folklore and Victorian classic novels foregrounding the values of family, friendship and individualism. He identifies the 1960s and 1970s as the golden age of children's films, when American money poured in to the newly cool and fashionable 'Swinging England' and resulted in the appearance of many enduringly popular children's and family films, such as *The Railway Children, Bugsy Malone, Watership Down, Born Free* and *Chitty Chitty Bang Bang*.

At the end of the seventies the money dried up, and with it the volume of children's films. Big money came back in the twenty-first century with the success of the *Harry Potter* franchise and a series of animated features from Aardman featuring the eccentrically English adventures of Wallace and Gromit. Brown assesses the tensions between British and American tastes and expectations as these franchises developed.

For each decade, Noel Brown establishes the social and cultural context of film production, and within the decades provides acute and insightful analyses of key films. The whole adds up to a major addition to the literature on children's cinema.

Jeffrey Richards

Introduction

Alan Lovell once called British cinema 'the unknown cinema'.[1] In the 1960s, when Lovell was writing, film scholarship was in its infancy. By the late 1990s Britain had become, in Lovell's revised estimation, 'the known cinema', but he still identified lacunae in the areas of film audiences, actors and the contribution of technicians.[2] Notably absent from Lovell's list of 'priorities for further investigation' was children's cinema, which to this day has remained largely 'unknown'. Britain's tradition of non-commercial children's films, represented by J. Arthur Rank's Children's Entertainment Films (CEF) and its state-backed successor, the Children's Film Foundation (CFF), has, at least, received its due, most particularly in Terry Staples's excellent book, *All Pals Together: The Story of Children's Cinema* (1997).[3] However, the wider field of British films for children and 'family audiences' from the 1900s to the present has largely been neglected.

This field is substantially larger than might be imagined. It has featured contributions by major British filmmakers such as Cecil Hepworth, Michael Powell, John Baxter, Val Guest, Philip Leacock, Pat Jackson, Bryan Forbes, Carol Reed, Alan Parker, Ken Loach, Terry Gilliam, Nicholas Roeg and Mike Newell. It includes iconic films, many of which are acknowledged classics of the British screen, including *The Thief of Bagdad* (Michael Powell et al., 1940), *Hue and Cry* (Charles Crichton, 1947), *The Kidnappers*

1

(Philip Leacock, 1953), *Whistle Down the Wind* (Bryan Forbes, 1961), *Born Free* (James Hill, 1966), *Yellow Submarine* (George Dunning, 1968), *Oliver!* (Carol Reed, 1968), *Chitty Chitty Bang Bang* (Ken Hughes, 1968), *The Railway Children* (Lionel Jeffries, 1970), *The Boy Who Turned Yellow* (Michael Powell, 1972), *Bugsy Malone* (Alan Parker, 1976), *Watership Down* (Martin Rosen, 1978), *Time Bandits* (Terry Gilliam, 1982), *The Snowman* (Dianne Jackson, 1982), *The Witches* (Nicholas Roeg, 1990), *Chicken Run* (Nick Park and Peter Lord, 2000), *Wallace & Gromit: The Curse of the Were-Rabbit* (Nick Park and Steve Box, 2005), the *Harry Potter* series (2001–11) and *Paddington* (Paul King, 2014).[4] Most of these productions were made for a mass market, and several rank alongside the most commercially successful Hollywood family films. However, between the 1940s and 1980s Britain was also a world leader in the production of specialised, non-commercial children's films. At one point, the Children's Film Foundation – which made shorts and features for children's matinees throughout the country from 1951 to 1985 – was Britain's second most prolific film producer. In short, children's cinema is one of the few filmic traditions in which Britain is, or was, internationally pre-eminent. Furthermore, British children's films have performed a central formative role in the lives of generations of people, and provide unique insights into the socio-political concerns of their time, reflecting, as all films must, prevailing values customs and belief systems.

This book, above all, is a cultural history: it explores the complex, ever-changing relationship between children's cinema and British culture and society. In so doing, it presents an implicit challenge to the lowly status of child-orientated films in critical discourses. Thomas Elsaesser argues that British cinema 'always functions around [a] polarisation – what one might call an "official" cinema and an "unofficial" cinema, a respectable cinema and a disreputable one'.[5] The former category includes historical epics, adaptations of literary 'classics', heritage films, documentaries and art-house films; in the latter, horror, 'lowbrow' comedies, erotica, teen films and other 'exploitation' genres. While epic poetry, opera, classical music, ballet and art films have traditionally found favour among the cognoscenti, children's cinema, alongside those other 'lowbrow' film genres listed above, has widely been disparaged or ignored by scholars. Journalistic accounts have long denigrated the form for its supposed eschewal of narrative complexity, ambiguity and

Introduction

complex stylistic mechanisms. Ironically, the avowed 'wholesomeness' of children's cinema underpins its lowly stature among cinephiles, for whom the need to remain 'suitable' for young people is seen to constrain artistic expression.

One of this book's main contentions is that children's film is not some other realm, separated from (or forever relegated beneath) legitimate, 'mainstream' cinema. As we know, films never exist in a social or cultural vacuum. To study children's cinema is to study popular culture; even the most apparently 'juvenile' films cannot be divorced from the wider tapestries of cinema and society. Indeed, the title of this book is slightly (though necessarily) misleading, because the majority of films discussed herein were produced for, and consumed by, mixed audiences of children and adults. 'Family films', as these productions are commonly known, are designed to appeal to a broad audience cross-section, maximising revenues for producers, distributors and exhibitors. All such films are open to a sometimes conflicting multiplicity of interpretations that allow audiences to bring their own values into play, colonising and democratising them.

This is the third in a trilogy of works that examine critically the overlapping children's film and family film genres, following my monograph, *The Hollywood Family Film: A History, from Shirley Temple to Harry Potter* (2012), and collection of essays (co-edited with Bruce Babington), *Family Films in Global Cinema: The World Beyond Disney* (2015). As with those earlier books, *British Children's Cinema* synthesises close readings of films, exploring their social and cultural meanings and techniques of composition, with discussion of their placement within the industrial and commercial logic of popular cinema. All three books also share a conviction that children's films and family films deal with serious meanings and constitute an important and unique form of cultural expression. However, whereas the history of the Hollywood family film mirrors that of Hollywood itself in pursuing mass audiences both nationally and internationally, the internal structures of British children's cinema are far more unpredictable. British-made children's films and family films entered the mainstream only intermittently prior to the turn of the millennium. While Britain has produced many more child-orientated films than is generally supposed – several hundred, at a conservative estimate – the form has never coalesced

3

into a consistent, industry-wide production avenue. As a result, this book articulates the fundamental duality of the children's film in Britain: its antithetical nature within the British film industry while embodying the intimacy and universalism associated with children's cinema in its broader iterations.

I should emphasise this is not an audience study. It is a genre study; or, rather, a study of one of the dominant national traditions within the larger geographic and historical dimensions of children's cinema. At times, it makes observations on the imagined 'spectator' implicitly constructed by all films, but this implied audience should not to be confused with 'real' spectators. Children's culture is a slippery entity in terms of the audiences it mobilises: children may reject cultural texts manufactured for (or even by) them, and they have always watched films, read literature and engaged in activities supposedly restricted to adults. Furthermore, many apparent 'children's films' are actually 'family movies', with the term 'children's films' more fittingly applied to the non-commercial CEF and CFF productions than to all-age films such as *The Railway Children*. I am largely unconcerned as to whether these films represent a 'pure', 'authentic' children's culture separated from adult interests if there is sufficient evidence (as with, say, George Formby's vehicles) that children responded enthusiastically to them. Historically, children and adults have often watched films together: many films that appeal strongly to young people are exhibited in movie theatres to a mixed clientele. In analysing the meanings, values, ideologies and social and cultural norms inscribed in such films, and the discourses that surround them, this book further complicates binary definitions of 'children's culture' and mainstream ('adult') popular culture. It also complements and provides a necessary counterpoint to Staples's oral history of children's cinema-going in Britain, which largely overlooks the child-adult 'doubleness' that, I believe, is central to the study of children's film.

Defining Children's Films and Family Films

For reasons already stated, defining 'children's film' is a deceptively simple proposition. It might be assumed that a children's film is simply one produced for, and primarily consumed by, children.[6] While this preliminary

Introduction

definition is useful, there are several problems with it. Firstly, how do we define 'children'? Childhood is a social construct as well as a biological category, and therefore subject to shifting sensibilities. The current legal definition of childhood in the United Kingdom as extending up to the age of 18 is too broad for our purposes. In this book, following the example of scholars such as Cary Bazalgette and Terry Staples, I adopt the admittedly imperfect understanding of the 'child audience' as encompassing children up to and including the age of 12.[7] Beyond that age, other overlapping categories used in commercial and everyday discourses, such as 'tween', 'adolescent', 'teen', or 'youth', come into play. The 'teen film' is seen as a distinct entity from 'children's film' both in popular and scholarly discourses. Secondly, how do we know which films are consumed primarily by children? Even during the CFF's heyday, productions intended *solely* for children were rarities, largely confined to the children's matinee and children's film festival circuit. Walt Disney, supposedly the quintessential purveyor of children's cinema, repeatedly insisted that his films were intended for audiences of all ages.[8]

My approach here is to treat children's cinema as a generic category: a body of films with their own internal structures and externally-imposed significations. Historically, children's films and family films have shared several broad, recurring textual characteristics. These include the reaffirmation of nation, kinship and community; the foregrounding of children (real or symbolic);[9] the exclusion and/or defeat of disruptive social elements; the minimisation of 'adult' themes and representational elements (e.g. sex, nudity, violence, criminality, sustained pessimism, profanity, drug abuse, poverty, and gore); and a story that, while acknowledging the possibility of an unpleasant or undesirable outcome, is finally upbeat, morally and emotionally straightforward, and supportive of the social status quo. In popular usage, the terms 'children's film' and 'family film' are often used more or less interchangeably, but there are subtle distinctions. Non-commercial children's films are more likely to be explicitly moralistic or educational, and commercial family films may include jokes, allusions, sub-plots, themes or adult stars calculated to broaden the appeal for older audiences. But genre is never a simple matter of what is presented on screen. Rather, it is manufactured through a complex interaction of textual and non-textual mechanisms. I suggest five non-textual manufacturing processes that, in conjunction with the textual characteristics outlined above, shape popular conceptions of generic identity:

1) *Marketing strategies.* Most films for children are actively marketed as such, both explicitly and implicitly, through promotional materials such as trailers, movie posters, print advertisements and press books. Unsurprisingly, marketing strategies for commercial films often position them to a broad 'family' audience rather than exclusively for children. These promotional strategies are largely confined to commercial cinema, and are less visible in relation to non-commercial traditions, such as CEF and the CFF.

2) *Rating/classification.* Since the formation of the British Board of Film Censors (BBFC) in 1913, films released in Britain have been allocated a suitability rating, denoting believed acceptability or otherwise for juvenile audiences and acting on the perceived need to protect children. Some publications, such as the BFI's *Monthly Film Bulletin* (1932–91) operated interpretive classification systems, communicating important information regarding suitability and appeal to parents, exhibitors and children themselves.

3) *Critical response.* Reviews, like ratings, play an important interpretive role in the formative process of generic classification. As well as offering judgements on a film's quality, reviews communicate important information such as plot, setting, tone and character. There is historical evidence that children have used reviews when deciding whether films are worth watching, and that parents have consulted them in determining which films are suitable for the consumption of their children.[10]

4) *Merchandising.* The majority of child-orientated films above a certain budgetary level are accompanied by extensive merchandising campaigns, encompassing a wide array of consumer products, such as toys, clothes, games and tie-ins with fast food or drinks manufacturers. The practice can be traced to Disney's partnership with merchandising executive Kay Kamen in the 1930s, and, in relation to children's cinema, was relatively unknown in Britain prior to the 1960s, since when it has become inextricably associated with multimedia family-orientated film franchises, including *Harry Potter* and *Wallace and Gromit*. Such

synergies are a quintessential component of family-orientated multi-media franchises, but less usually pertain to adult-orientated cinema.

5) *Exhibition strategies.* These include theatrical release (i.e. whether for standard movie programmes, children's matinees, or children's and family film festivals) and television broadcast strategies. (The time of day a film is scheduled typically reflects its perceived suitability for 'child', 'family' or 'adult' audiences.)

Individually, or more often collectively, these five manufacturing processes play a major part in creating and sustaining generic identity. However, it must be acknowledged that none of them, in isolation, gives the whole picture. Marketing and distribution strategies are used self-servingly by producers; film ratings are notoriously imprecise, as many 'U'-rated films, particularly those released between 1930 and 1960, are notably 'adult', articulating complex issues, containing sophisticated dialogue, and focusing exclusively on adult characters, while, equally, some films deemed unsuitable for children (such as the *James Bond* series) appeal strongly to them; reviews are highly subjective and inevitably circumscribed by contemporary attitudes; and merchandising and exhibition strategies depend on too many variables to be completely indicative. Nevertheless, these processes do inform popular consensus. Furthermore, when used diagnostically, they are invaluable to scholars as a means of identifying a corpus of texts that can be subjected to sustained analysis. Contextual indicators also afford necessary clarity on occasions where generic identity is not immediately clear: there are very few *textual* distinctions between a child-orientated 'family film', such as *Emil and the Detectives* (Milton Rosmer, 1935), and many of the non-commercial 'children's films' the CFF films produced for child matinee audiences. They also reveal how the boundaries between 'children's film' and 'family film' can be fluid. A handful of CFF films which began life in children's matinee programmes were later seen by general audiences, either in theatres or on television. In these instances, what began as 'children's films' were reconstituted as 'family films'.

Throughout this book, the word *genre* is applied both to children's films and family films. However, as I have argued elsewhere, both forms are more properly termed *master-genres*.[11] The various recurrent textual features noted above provide a generic template against which more specific, and historically variable, aspects such as story, narrative, tone and aesthetics are measured. Within this master-genre, a broad, formally diverse array of sub-genres operate, while still satisfying structural, ideological and emotive expectations associated with children's and family entertainment. For example, *Oliver!* might be termed a musical, a literary adaptation, or a period drama, but its primary generic identity – judging from contextual discourses, particularly reviews – is that of a 'family film'. Similarly, the *Harry Potter* series intersperses comedy, horror and teen film tropes within its fantastic mode, but the fact that its episodes are referred to, almost universally, as 'family films' testifies to broad recognition of the elements that place them within this framework: their child protagonists, emphasis on friendship and family, foregrounding of magic and fantasy, central good vs. evil thematic, broad suitability for children, and (admittedly long-deferred) happy ending. As Andrew Tudor once observed, genre is 'what we collectively believe it to be'.[12] This book advances a similarly contextualised (or democratic) view, taking due notice of how films are promoted and received.

Organisation

The book adopts a partly thematic, partly chronological structure. Chapter 1 introduces the key debates surrounding children and the cinema during the silent era (c. 1895–1929), and some of the early productions aimed at child and family audiences. Chapter 2 examines a sub-genre of films, termed 'children's adventure movies', which predominated in British commercial cinema between the 1930s and 1950s. Chapter 3 explores the textual strategies by which the films of comedians Will Hay, Arthur Lucan (as Old Mother Riley), George Formby and Norman Wisdom appealed to child and family audiences. Chapter 4 surveys the activities of Rank's Children's Entertainment Films during the 1940s and the Children's Film Foundation between the 1950s and 1980s, investigates the broader phenomenon of children's matinees and cinema clubs and situates them within the context of British commercial cinema. Chapter 5 analyses the relationship between mainstream British film and the 'family audience' in the 1950s, when the political and social primary of the family was at its height. Chapter 6 focuses on a group of films produced in Britain by

Disney between the 1950s and 1970s, and the means by which they negotiate a mid-Atlantic path between British and North American norms and values. Chapter 7 traces the periods of 'boom' for family films in the 1960s and the subsequent 'bust' of the 1970s, when US finance was withdrawn and British children's cinema entered a commercial nadir but creative resurgence. Chapter 8 examines the role of television and of Hollywood co-production in sustaining British children's films of the 1980s and 1990s. Chapter 9 looks closely at the *Harry Potter* series and Aardman's animated features, arguing that they attempt to reflect contemporary British values while exporting positive associations of twenty-first century Britain and Britishness for international consumption. Finally, the Conclusion discusses aspects of change and continuity within Britain's children's films, while evaluating their position in British cinema, culture and society.

1

In the Beginning: Children and British Cinema in the Silent Era

Commercial cinema began in late December 1895, when the Lumière brothers, Auguste and Louis, held their first public screening of projected motion pictures for a paying public at the Grand Café, Paris. Among the ten shorts on display was *L'Arroseur arrosé* (*The Sprinkler Sprinkled*, 1895), a 49-second film in which a young boy turns a garden hose on a grown-up gardener, and is rewarded for his impertinence with a smacked bottom. This modest offering has since been identified as the first 'children's film', and it dates to the very beginnings of cinema as a commercial proposition. However, French illusionist and filmmaker Georges Méliès was a more abiding influence on his British counterparts. Méliès produced possibly the first children's narrative fiction film, a six-minute adaptation of *Cinderella* (Fr. *Cendrillon*), in 1899. He was an early pioneer of the fantasy film, and his wonderful shorts *A Trip to the Moon* (*Le Voyage dans la Lune*, 1902) and *The Impossible Voyage* (*Voyage à travers l'impossible*, 1904) remain cherished instances of early narrative cinema.

Until around 1906, commercial cinema in Britain was still in its infancy, with little industrial infrastructure. As Rachael Low notes, 'anyone with the ingenuity to devise or adapt the elementary apparatus needed, and film a few hundred feet of "phantom ride", comic scene or news event, could claim to be a film producer.'[1] During this period, thousands of films were produced,

In the Beginning: Children and British Cinema in the Silent Era

many of them comprising only a couple of hundred feet of film (equating to less than a minute running time). There was little pretension to art, much less to originality, and several of the early British film pioneers – including Cecil Hepworth, G. A. Smith, James Williamson and R. W. Paul – borrowed or appropriated from Méliès (as well as each other) with impunity. Smith remade the Lumière brothers' *The Sprinkler Sprinkled* as *Gardener with Hose, or the Mischievous Boy* (date unknown), and Low suggests that Smith was also the first British filmmaker to produce 'trick films' in this vein with *Cinderella and the Fairy Godmother* (1898), which used double exposure as a visual effect. Paul's *The Magic Sword* (1902) similarly drew on fairy tale mythology, concerned 'a knight, a lady, a ghost, a witch, an ogre of large proportions, a battlement, a cave, an abduction of the lady by the witch, a magic cauldron, and a Good Fairy', and was described by the filmmaker as 'a sumptuously produced extravaganza.[2] The exchange was not entirely one-sided: in 1912 Méliès remade Paul's *Voyage of the 'Arctic', or How Captain Kettle Discovered the North Pole* (1903) as *À la conquête du pole* (*Conquest of the Pole*).

The inherited codes and conventions of children's literature and the British theatrical tradition ultimately played a greater role in the development of British children's cinema than the trick photography film. But many of these early 'trick films' were concerned with showcasing and advancing the technical potentialities of the new medium. Their child-friendly subject matter, which routinely drew on the fantasy, fairy tale and science-fiction literary forms, was a vehicle for spectacle, and a means by which the technical specificities of cinema could be promoted in ways not possible in the Lumière brothers' more realist mode. Furthermore, as Low observes, 'many of the pioneer producers came to cinematography through photography or the optical lantern', and this is another reason for their particular interest in trick photography films.[3] One of the most notable productions is Cecil Hepworth's lavish, ten-minute adaptation of *Alice in Wonderland* (1903). Based on Sir John Tenniel's illustrations, it was sold on the basis of its 'remarkable fidelity' to Lewis Carroll's book (1865), and that: 'No pantomime or stage effect is introduced in this film; the whole of the various scenes having been produced in pretty natural surroundings.[4] The description is notable in its attempt to distance itself from the theatrical tradition and instead assert its cinematic credentials, and in its refusal to assign itself to any specific audience demographic. Rather, like most early films, it was intended for 'everybody'.

At this point, most films were exhibited in family-orientated exhibition spaces such as music halls, village concerts and, later, fairgrounds. As Low recalls:

> It is to the fairground showman that the cinema owes its ultimate success. The new toy, a passing fancy in the music-halls, became a firmly established feature of the fairgrounds. It was they who bridged the gap between the music hall days and the later, more respectable picture palaces, and they disappeared only with the First World War – long after the coming of the regular cinema.[5]

There was a natural affinity between the cinema and the fairground. Both were quintessential family recreational activities, particularly amongst the working-classes. Music halls, too, despite the frequent incursion of more 'adult' material (especially by comedians), were venues in which families pursued an evening's entertainment. Specialised children's matinees, at this early point, were relatively rare. Low suggests that, after an 'early fad', exhibitors found them unprofitable 'without adequate co-operation from school authorities'.[6] There was little reason to suppose that cinema was more than an ephemeral and basically harmless curiosity, so the pressures that civic, religious and educational organisations later brought to bear on exhibitors to remove children from increasingly adult-orientated movie programmes had yet to be felt. One early instance of an explicit children's film performance is a tour by the Great American Bioscope in 1900, which showed in Mickleover, Derbyshire, in February 1900. The screening was promoted as 'free from vulgarity throughout' and the admission fee for children was 1d. as opposed to 3d. for adult patrons.[7] The practice of charging children reduced admission (typically half-price) was later adopted by theatrical exhibitors throughout the country.

Early British Films and Children

By the mid-1900s, British producers were developing more sophisticated narrative types. Cecil Hepworth was a key figure, both in the relative sophistication and popularity of his productions and in his films' particular appeal to the family audience. In 1905, Hepworth produced *Rescued by Rover*, which became 'the most famous story film of the period'.[8] This seven-minute short was, as Hepworth later recalled, 'a particularly family affair': 'My wife wrote the story, my baby – eight months old – was the heroine, my dog the hero, my wife the bereaved mother and myself the harassed father'.[9] It follows the dog Rover's attempts to rescue the baby after she is snatched from her pram by a beggar woman. Having located the baby, Rover alerts his master, who, with the dog's help, recovers her. Made for just over £7, *Rescued by Rover* proved phenomenally popular, to the extent that Hepworth twice had to remake the film after wearing out the original negatives. Moreover, it was a watermark in British cinema's maturation from amateurish experimentation to increasing formalisation. Low felt that it revealed 'an advanced form of film technique such as [D. W.] Griffith was to work out in his films', and on account of its success, Hepworth 'began to contemplate building an indoor studio for film-making'.[10]

Image 1.1 Hepworth's own child and family dog starred in his seminal production, *Rescued by Rover* (1905)

Hepworth made Rover – arguably British cinema's first bona fide star – the centre of a long-running series of films spanning 1905–13. Starting with *Black Beauty* in 1907, Hepworth also embarked on a series of horse films, which alternated (and sometimes combined) with Rover. Hepworth thus created the animal film, one of the key sub-genres of British children's cinema. He was also a leading populariser of the child-star film, with his *Tilly the Tomboy* series (1910–15), starring teenaged Alma Taylor and Chrissie White. 'The great aim and object of these Tilly girls', Hepworth recalled, 'was to paint the town extremely red, and the joyfully disarming way in which they thoroughly did it was the great charm of these delightful little comedies. Mischief without any sting in it is the one unfailing recipe for child-story pictures'.[11] Clarendon also produced a shorter lived series of shorts based on the misadventures of Did'ums, 'the truly awful eponymous curly-haired boy-child' whose storylines centre on 'baby-stealing, tormenting policemen, swapping hotel room numbers and so on'.[12] As with James Williamson's earlier short *Our New Errand Boy* (1905), in which the child 'plays cruel, unmotivated tricks on customers', all of these naughty child figures, as Laraine Porter argues, subvert 'the Edwardian era of childhood innocence'.[13]

There were several shorter-lived production cycles during the early-1910s that may have held particular interest for younger audiences. Some of these films – most of which are now, sadly, lost – are detailed in Rachael Low's compendious volumes on early British cinema. For instance, Low observes that 'novelties' like 'odd silhouette and puppet films [were] produced from time to time'; these included the puppet films *The Doll's Revenge* (Clarendon, 1911, 410 ft) and *Cinderella* (Butcher's, 1912, 997ft).[14] Another interesting movement was the 'boys' film', a screen counterpart to the 'penny dreadful or the later Gem and Magnet form of schoolboy serial literature'.[15] One rare instance is the Samuelson Film Manufacturing Company's serialised, two-reel western, *The Adventures of Deadwood Dick* (L. C. MacBean and Fred Paul, 1915). Another, more notable enterprise was the *Lieutenant Rose* films, a series of action-adventure two-reelers produced between 1910 and 1915 by Clarendon, directed by Percy Stow, and centring on a dashing naval lieutenant (played by P. G. Norgate). As Staples suggests, these films are very much in the *Boys' Own* tradition, their hero displaying the appropriate virtues of patriotism, loyalty and service to King and Country. Staples also speculates that 'children, perhaps mainly boys' would have found Rose 'a fairly attractive hero, one with whom they could identify'.[16]

These exceptions notwithstanding, the vast majority of British films from the silent period were intended for general audiences. This is true of many films that might now appear to be primarily child-orientated. Alma Taylor, star of the *Tilly* films (which Staples identifies as ideal fare for young girls), was massively popular amongst adults: a 1915 poll conducted by *Pictures and the Picturegoer* found her to be the country's most popular British-born film star, ahead of Charlie Chaplin.[17] This cross-demographic appeal mirrors that of the Hollywood star Mary Pickford (to whom Taylor has often been compared), and prefigures that of Shirley Temple in the 1930s. In family-orientated literary adaptations, such as Hepworth's productions of *Oliver Twist* (Thomas Bentley, 1912) and *David Copperfield* (Bentley, 1913), contemporary critical judgement emphasised their universal appeal. They were *suitable* for children, but not designed specifically for them. Of this period, Low observes that there 'seems to have been no particular effort to make special films for children'.[18] In fact, the idea of the 'children's film' was largely alien to producers and exhibitors, who were concerned with attracting as broad an audience base as possible. I have found almost no references to 'children's film' (or to related terms) in popular publications of the period.

The only definitive exception is the most overtly family-orientated British genre of the silent era: the Christmas pantomime film. This genre followed the post-1840s Victorian pantomime tradition as 'a Christmas family holiday, particularly aimed at children',[19] and was a yuletide perennial of British cinema from at least the mid-1900s to the mid-to-late 1910s. As Low recalls, such films 'were adapted anew year after year and sometimes accompanied by special films such as the Clarendon pair for Christmas, 1907, *The Water Babies* and *The Pied Piper of Hamelin*'.[20] Originally, they were probably shown at fairgrounds, in penny gaffs or as part of music hall programmes. They were heavily promoted in the trade press: Lion's Head Film placed a full-page advertisement in the *Cinema News and Property Gazette* for their 1,200 ft. Christmas 1912 production, *Nan in Fairyland* – 'A Treat for both the Children and their Parents'.[21] The paper also featured full-page advertisements for Hepworth's Christmas programme, which comprised three distinct but interwoven film pantomimes: *The Sleeping*

Beauty, *A New Aladdin* and *A Harlequinade Let Loose* (1912). Collectively these productions were promoted as 'The best children's picture that has been issued this year'.[22] The same issue also featured a special, 20-page section on 'The Yuletide Pictures', which provided 'no lack of material for the exhibitor's Christmas program'.[23] The section was explicitly written for exhibitors seeking to establish special children's shows, and insisted that: 'The succeeding pages should convince even the most sceptical that it would be possible to arrange a programme for children's matinees without including anything but pictorial versions of once-upon-a-time stories'.[24]

Christmas clearly signalled a suspension of normative entertainment standards; it was a time at which the particular perceived requirements of children were indulged, and desires on the part of mature adults to satisfy their 'inner child' were given free rein. However, this implicit distinction between child and adult needs was far from universal. Mass audiences, dominated by working-class patrons, were commonly constructed by films, and by surrounding discourses, as children. This is to use the word 'children' in its most symbolic and derisory meanings, in the sense of being passive, impressionable, uneducated, essentially homogenous and predominantly imbecilic. In his memoirs, Cecil Hepworth recalled that: 'It was said at one time, and it is still largely true, that cinema audiences were of an average mental age of eleven to thirteen years'.[25] By 1920, Hepworth felt that 'taste was on the whole improving', though he lamented that 'old-fashioned showmen continued to pander to the worst public'.[26] Similar sentiments were expressed by North American producer Maurice Tourneur who, while visiting Britain, remarked that: 'Film spectators are like children. They demand different and unexpected toys all the time'.[27] And addressing the fact that British producers consistently failed to produce children's films, Low avers that:

> There can hardly have seemed any need, since [children] flocked to see the Westerns, the slapstick comics and crime stories, and took even the social dramas and sentimental moralising in their stride. The stories were immature enough in any case.[28]

The overriding impression is that many – though not all – producers perceived little distinction between children and adults, at least in terms of their requirements. Filmmakers deliberately catered to the lowest common denominator. 'Childish' films, it will be noted, are not synonymous with 'children's films'.

The 'Child' Audience

Even if children were rarely afforded their own cinematic space, the commercial importance of the 'child audience' was widely acknowledged. This is particularly true before 1910, at which point more sophisticated exhibition venues such as the 'picture palaces' and neighbourhood theatres began to supersede the more child-orientated fairgrounds and penny gaffs. Low recalls that:

> It was realised early that a large (perhaps the largest) proportion of film audiences were children, for whom moving pictures had an immediate and irresistible appeal. The half-price admission was within their range. Theatres were open in the daytime, easy to slip into, and to sit in the dark and capture cattle rustlers, leap from a burning train or even watch a remorseful drunkard go mad – this made playing truant worthwhile.[29]

Exhibitors enticed children with reduced admission rates and afternoon performances, even when their movie programmes were not expressly tailored to the young spectator. Luke McKernan postulates that 'up to fifty per cent of cinema audiences were made up of children and adolescents, at least for the period to 1910', although such figures are impossible to verify.[30] A 1917 publication, *The Cinema: Its Present Position and Future Possibilities* – a report commissioned by the National Council of Public Morals (NCPM) – suggested that fully 90 per cent of all children between the ages of 8 and 14 'in thickly populated areas' went to the movies.[31]

Much of our knowledge of silent-era British film history is derived from 'adult' centres of discourse, such as reviews, articles and correspondences in the press and trade papers. However, there are two important sources which provide first-hand accounts of children's cinema-going during this period: the NCPM report, which draws on testimony from approximately 6,700 London children of elementary school age, and the 444 interviews conducted in the 1970s by Paul Thompson for a study of Edwardian Britain, many of which centre on respondents' memories of cinema as children prior to the Great War (forming the basis of McKernan's article). Both sources reveal the dominance of imported Hollywood films; this dominance continues to this day, and insofar as it has affected British production, it is a background theme throughout the remainder of this book. Allegedly more than 90 per cent of films shown in British cinemas were North American, but where Hollywood held a decisive advantage in the children's film market was in the production of serials, westerns and, by the early 1920s, cartoon shorts.[32] It was estimated that the serial *The Adventures of Elaine* (Louis J. Gasnier et al., 1914) – also known as 'The Clutching Hand' – was seen by 10,000,000 people and played in 40 per cent of British theatres.[33] Hollywood films served to plug the shortfall in British production during the First World War. One girl ('Ada') from Glasgow wrote to 'The Young Picturegoer' column of *Pictures and the Picturegoer* in March 1916 to voice her fears that the constant supply of US fare would cease: 'The thought of no more Mary Pickford, or Charlie [Chaplin], or Pearl White, or Tom Mix is too horrible to contemplate.'[34]

Evidence of children's film tastes during the mid-1910s roughly ascribe with the results of the various later studies on the subject. Dr C. W. Kimmins's London study for the NCPM found that 'girls are much more interested in domestic and fairy stories than the boys, and are far less interested in cowboy stories and adventures'; that 'Comics [i.e. comedies] are much more popular with the boys than with the girls'; that boys 'are much keener on serial films than girls'; that 'love films are far more popular with the girls than with the boys' and that the 'interest in purely love stories starts in most girls schools at about eleven years of age'.[35] A broader interest in comedies, war films and westerns was also noted, as was a slight disparity between children's tastes in middle-class and working-class districts. War films were more popular 'in well-to-do districts' than in the 'poor districts', a pattern reversed with regard to serials. Nonetheless, children preferred to see any film rather than no film. Even the most child-friendly productions of the period were rarely shown in isolation, but rather formed part of a larger package of shorts and feature films that typically lasted 2–3 hours in length. Exhibitors presented a 'balanced programme' of attractions to appeal to a varied audience. As Low observes, 'even after the advent of the long feature film, many exhibitors clung firmly to the idea that what the public

In the Beginning: Children and British Cinema in the Silent Era

wanted above all was variety'.[36] While some exhibitors altered their matinee programmes to accommodate children, the NCPM report ruefully noted that 'as a rule, the [afternoon] programme does not differ materially from that of the evening performance' and that, in any case, 'if a child prefers an evening performance to that of the afternoon, he will probably go to the former'.[37]

As McKernan emphasises, cinema-going for children was also a social experience. Many movie theatres were far from the plush 'picture palaces' of repute, but rather were insalubrious 'flea-pits', where attendants would spray perfumed disinfectants in an attempt to reduce the risk of disease spreading due to the cramped and poorly ventilated surroundings. Such theatres were cheap and easily accessible, which were important considerations, as most children attending without parents or guardians would have paid for their tickets with pocket money. McKernan adds that:

> Although some children visited the cinema as part of a London shopping trip, having travelled in with their families for the day, the majority chose from cinemas within walking distance. By 1911, there were between two and three cinemas per square mile within inner London.[38]

Respondents in Thompson's survey, like those in Staples's many years later, recall children's matinees as riotous events in which a cacophony of sounds – the crackling of the projector, the piano accompaniment, the rustling of sweets, incessant chatter, singing, and employees reading title cards aloud – more than compensated for the silence of the screen. McKernan stresses the inherent liminality of the movie theatre, arguing that children's matinee attendees 'gained not only entertainment, but the camaraderie of their friends, excitement, the glamour of the surroundings, and freedom from parental control'.[39]

Children and Reformers

This perception of children partaking of a culture beyond adult control was a matter of the gravest concern to civic, religious and educational bodies. Low suggests that most objections to children's cinema-going, apart from querulous fears for their eyesight, the juvenile delinquency extremists and sheer prejudice, were based on the reasonable view that although there might be nothing harmful in films as such, the majority of subjects treated were not suitable for young people.[40]

By the time the NCPM report – commissioned by a body composed of prominent religious, scientific and educational figures – was published, the matter had been festering for several years, particularly since the accidental deaths of 16 children in a Barnsley cinema in January 1908. This was a special afternoon performance hosted in the Harvey Institute by the World's Animated Picture Company, and prices, especially in the gallery, were as low as 1d. to guarantee high children's attendance. After around 550 children had been admitted, it was clear that the venue was far beyond capacity, and the management ordered the attendees to cease admitting further children. A fatal crush ensued as children leaving the gallery collided with those ascending the stairs. The inquest accused the management of negligence, having failed to engage sufficient staff.[41] An editorial in the *Manchester Guardian* presciently argued that: 'Children's entertainments are a business that ought to be run under very strict rules of discipline or none at all'.[42]

The Barnsley tragedy led to the first piece of government legislation that pertained to children's cinema attendance: a clause in the 1908 Children's Act that vaguely stipulated that 'a significant number of adult attendants' be present at performances seen largely by children. The following year, further concerns about fire hazards in the cinema led to the passing of the Cinematograph Act, which required local authorities to regulate on this matter. However, while the Act was intended only to address safety concerns, it was co-opted by various local authorities across England and Wales to censor film content. The London County Council (LCC) was the first local authority to act in this way, banning a film of the black American boxer, Jack Johnson, defeating a white man in the ring. Other councils followed suit, and a period of 'anti-censor agitation' ensued.[43] One indignant reader wrote to the *Sunday Times* in December 1912, insisting that 'the general public require vim! fizz! sparkle! and go! in their amusements', and proposing:

Why not special children's cinema shows in the afternoons, and the evening shows for adults only. But to regulate all our

> amusements from the children's point of view is sheer puritanical cant. We are not all children, and are quite capable of looking after our own morals. Soon, very soon, the enlightened hard-pressed public will rise up in all their wrath against these self-righteous kill-joys.[44]

The problem, as Low recounts, is that many reformers objected to the very concept of weekday matinees, believing that they encouraged children to play truant from school. Sections of the trade supported calls to ban children from evening cinema shows, in the hope that it would forestall the censorious fever gripping local authorities. But when 'the temptation to "play wag" in the daytime was essayed as a reason for banning children from the afternoon performances as well, exhibitors felt that things had gone far enough'.[45]

The film industry was naturally alarmed by local authorities unilaterally acting as censors, and by the ever-increasing threat of state censorship. Pre-emptively, it established the British Board of Film Censors (BBFC) in 1912. The Board was financed by the industry, and was charged with viewing all films and awarding a classification: either 'U' (suitable for universal viewing) or 'A' (adults, i.e. those over the age of 16). According to a BBFC document addressed to the Home Office, these two classifications were introduced in order to meet 'the complaints that have been made by licensing authorities in respect of the non-suitability of certain films for children's entertainments'.[46] The initial intention was that *any* film that received either a 'U' or an 'A' rating would be suitable for children ('clean and wholesome and absolutely above suspicion'), but that 'U' films were 'especially recommended for Children's Matinees'.[47]

Over time, the 'A' rating came to be regarded as denoting a film suitable *only* for adults. George A. Redford, a retired play reader at the Lord Chamberlain's office, was made the Board's first president, but the more significant appointment was that of Joseph Brooke Wilkinson – 'a man of Victorian principle and stern moral rectitude' – as secretary, a post he held until his death in 1948.[48] To begin with, the Board had only two prohibitions: nudity and representations of Christ. These were expanded significantly under the auspices of T. P. O'Connor, who succeeded Redford as president in 1916. Outlawed subjects included depictions of 'prostitution, premarital and extramarital sex, sexual perversion, incest, seduction, nudity, venereal disease, orgies, swearing, abortion, brothels [and] white slavery', as well as criticisms of 'the monarchy, government, church, police, judiciary or friendly foreign countries', and depiction of 'controversial' current issues.[49] The Board was putatively independent of the state, but as Richards and Robertson point out, its presidents 'were always appointed after consultation with the Home Secretary'.[50]

Critically, though, the BBFC's classifications were not legally binding. Initially, fewer than 50 out of 688 local authorities agreed to abide by its prescripts, and the remainder continued to use their own discretionary powers, exploiting the vagaries of the Cinematograph Act to ban and cut films as they saw fit.[51] Clearly, from this industry's perspective this situation was dissatisfactory; nor did the formation of the BBFC mollify reformers. In fact, the mid-1910s saw the first of several 'moral panics' concerning the relationship between children and screen media. Educationalists were the loudest voice in the debate, with separate 'investigations' into cinema's influence upon children conducted by the Liverpool Inspector of Education, the Birmingham Educational Committee, the Lancashire Committee and various other bodies. The tone of their reports was often hysterical. The *Times* summarised the Lancashire Committee's alarming discoveries:

> Over fifty per cent of the children of the poorest families go regularly to 'the pictures' in the evening. Many go every evening in the week. Some steal the money for admission. Their moral sense is lowered; they think less of cruelty, lying, theft; they are less thrifty; they derive a thirst of pleasure and amusement. They become fond of noise, 'ostentatious display', self-advertisement, and change. They are disinclined for steady work and effort. They display a lack of interest in school work; they are encouraged in superficial cleverness. 'Definite general fatigue', say the doctors, is caused; if the children's eyesight is not permanently injured, they are usually pale and tired.[52]

Several English towns – including Liverpool, Manchester and Blackburn – introduced restrictions to the hours during which children unaccompanied by adults could visit movie theatres.[53] Liverpool, for instance, passed regulation to prevent children under the age of 14 from entering cinemas after 6.30pm unless accompanied by a parent or guardian.[54]

Many watchdogs and pressure groups that were formed during this period agitated for reform. A conglomeration called the Educational Kinematograph Association was formed in May 1914 with the intention of 'improving the general character of the films'. It comprised several educational committees, the Nature Study Society, the Historical Association, the Workers' Educational Association and the Boy Scouts. The Headmasters of Eton, Rugby and Winchester, George Bernard Shaw, Sir Robert Baden-Powell and Dr Kimmins of the LCC were notable supporters.[55] In March of that year, Mrs Foard of the Southport branch of the National Union of Women Workers suggested forming a small committee of 'leading ladies of the town' to inspect films shown to children, suggesting that Saturday afternoons ought to be reserved for children's film performances.[56] Scout Master Stephen Lloyd wrote to the *Manchester Guardian* in June 1914 to attack films which portray 'jealousy, and unbridled passions of the lowest type, which one would only look to meet in the very scum of humanity', suggesting that: 'The effect that the sordid domestic tragedy type of film may have one the mind of young who flock to these places perhaps three or four times a week can be imagined'.[57] A final representative example (from countless others) is an interview in the *Observer* from November 1918 with the renowned critic and biographer Sir Sidney Lee, who averred that 'the evil is a very serious one for the rising generation' and that 'it might be necessary for the education authorities to seek some legal powers to prohibit the admission of children to picture palaces that abound in the poor districts through the kingdom'. 'It would seem desirable', Lee continued, 'that young people under sixteen should be excluded from picture palaces which do not take into reasonable account their educational requirements'.[58]

The number and volume of such attacks were highly damaging to the film industry. The trade called on the National Council of Public Morals to institute an 'independent inquiry into the physical, social, moral, and educational influence of the cinema, with special reference to young people', the result of which was the aforementioned, near 500-page report, *The Cinema: Its Present Position and Future Possibilities*.[59] The NCPM was a credible and influential lobby, headed by the Bishop of Birmingham. In sponsoring a study from an organisation known to be wary of the screen's influence on the young, the industry was hoping for a balanced and temperate set of recommendations that would discredit the most fiercely anti-film propagandists. After some consideration, the NCPM accepted the industry's invitation, subject to the understanding that it would not affect its long-held proposal for state censorship. On this matter, the NCPM ultimately stood firm, arguing that: 'For its own protection as well as for the ensuring of its continued suitability to the nation, it should have the support and the official countenance of the State'.[60]

However, the report was also a useful platform for the industry – ably represented by BBFC president T. P. O'Connor and secretary J. Brooke Wilkinson, and A. E. Newbould, chairman of the Cinematograph Exhibitors' Association of Great Britain and Ireland (CEA). Brooke Wilkinson insisted that marking a film explicitly as 'Suitable for Children' would meet opposition in the trade, as adult audiences 'would think it was a children's performance'.[61] He countered that: 'There are no films passed for universal exhibition, to my mind, that I dare not show in a Sunday school'.[62] Newbould added that: 'On the question of special children's performances I wish to say that a specially selected programme is not at present a commercial proposition', particularly as children 'who do attend are nearly always accompanied by their parents, and are seldom seen in the theatres after 8pm'.[63] To any attempt to restrict children's attendance, he maintained, 'The probable result would be that children would simply roam the streets, with their attendant evils and temptations'.[64] The NCPM committee was also frustrated in industry responses to its pleas for more 'educational' films. The report notes that: 'We were [...] told by representatives of the trade that the public would not tolerate a greater admixture of educational films than 10 per cent, in a mixed programme'.[65] On this issue, the NCPM could hardly object, as its own investigation showed that: 'The total number [of children] who preferred educational films was almost negligible'.[66] It was forced to concede, reluctantly, that the film industry was business, not public service, and would not accede to any proposal lacking a plausible commercial underpinning.

Little of consequence changed as a result of the NCPM report. Home Secretary Sir Herbert Samuel, who came to office in late 1915, was a firm supporter of state censorship, but after he was succeeded by Sir George Cave, and the well-connected O'Connor succeeded Redford as BBFC president, the plan to institute it was shelved.[67] The Home Office itself resisted state censorship, and its links with the BBFC actually strengthened during the 1920s. The situation remained largely unchanged until, in 1921, the LCC elected to exclude under-16s from the cinema altogether. Given that children were conservatively reckoned to make up 25 per cent of all audiences, this was disastrous for the industry. Talks were hastily arranged between members of the LCC, BBFC, CEA and the Home Office, and a compromise was reached: under-16s would be barred from films with an 'A' rating – which constituted around 25 per cent of films under release – *unless* accompanied by a parent or guardian. Exhibitors had lobbied hard against a complete ban on under-16s attending 'A' films, and the industry's position was clear: the movie theatre was 'the resort of the family', as T. P. O'Connor had it, and control over children's movie habits must remain the jurisdiction of parents, not the state.[68] Under pressure, in December 1922 the LCC conceded this point, to the approval of the *Times*, which observed that: 'Fathers and mothers and their deputies must surely be trusted not to take children to see films which are likely to do them harm'.[69] In 1923, on the recommendation of the Home Office, the new system was rolled out nationwide.

A regulatory framework was now in place in England and Wales (though not, for legal reasons, in Scotland) that gave the outward appearance of satisfactory compromise. But exhibitors were displeased, not just at the potential loss of custom but that programmes would have to be rearranged to ensure that 'U' and 'A' films were not mixed. One exhibitor, it was reported in the *Times*, publicly announced that they would flout the new regulations as a 'test case' to gauge whether offenders would be prosecuted.[70] Many reformers were also dissatisfied, and some were unmoved in their initial distrust of the film medium. In January 1927, the president of the Head Masters' Association, R. F. Cholmeley, expressed his conviction that films are 'suited only to the silliest people in their silliest moments'; that 'the flicker of the film has a tendency to injure the growing eye'; that 'few films have educational value'; and that:

> Frequent spectacles of savage crimes (often successful), sexual depravity, unbridled passions, loose morals, personal extravagance, and luxurious living [...] cannot fail to have a detrimental and degrading effect upon the juvenile mind'.[71]

Sydney W. Carroll of the *Sunday Times* staunchly defended the cinema from these accusations, insisting that: 'We cannot close our eyes to the immense improvements being made on every side every week by producers of genius with the aid of inexhaustible capital.'[72]

Others were less convinced. In December 1925, the National Union of Women Teachers passed a resolution condemning 'dreadful' films for children, claiming that: 'The worst pictures were shown in the slum quarters of our cities'.[73] Two months earlier, a writer for the *Manchester Guardian* documented his/her experience of accompanying a 4-year-old child to Saturday afternoon children's matinee. In such a performance, the writer claims, 'you will find ninety children to ten adults'.[74] The programme was described in the least complimentary terms:

> We saw some topical films, not of particular interest to children – troops marching, generals saluting, some bathing girls whose charms were sharply defined, and that sort of thing [...] The rest of the show was beyond belief. There was a film which was supposed to be humorous. The humour consisted chiefly in a nigger seeing all sorts of horrible things come at him out of the dark [...] If a man had been specially commissioned to produce something calculated to give a child fear of the dark – perhaps for life – he could hardly have done better than this film. It seemed to me to be playing on all the most sensitive spots of a child's mind with a fool's fingers.
>
> We had also a boxing film – two well-made savages pounding each other like mad [...] Then began the 'big picture'. It opened with a charming episode. An old man was standing by his wife's grave when someone exploded a charge of dynamite under him. We were treated to a 'close-up' of his contorted face as he lay with his clothes in ribbons, his body covered with earth, bleating out some dying charge to his son.[75]

The writer concluded by insinuating that these disturbing images elicited hallucinations in the young companion, and maintained that the cinema offers 'claptrap and balderdash, even when it isn't harmfulness'.[76] Such alarmist discourses testify to the level of opposition still faced by popular cinema in 1920s Britain. But this article also illustrates how children's

In the Beginning: Children and British Cinema in the Silent Era

matinee performances were patchwork affairs, assembled from a multitude of sources.

One correspondent for the *Times*, writing in May 1920, represented the matinee experience in more positive terms:

> intruding grown-up must put on the simple faith of a child [...]
> If he fails to enjoy the experience he must either be very clever
> or very foolish. He will almost certainly regret that the cinemat-
> ograph was not invented when he, too, was young enough to
> live in Arcadia.[77]

Children's matinees, as Carroll noted in 1927, were 'usually non-paying ventures'.[78] Those explicitly constituted on moral or educative grounds were doomed to failure, both through a lack of suitable films and, one assumes, by children's resentment at being deprived of the films that most interested them. The most profitable matinees were ones which, as above, were cheaply assembled and whose films were purely escapist, eschewing all traces of the patented wholesomeness that reformers wished to impose. In 1928, Sidney Bernstein, owner of the Manchester-based Granada thea-tre chain, initiated a programme of more respectable and upmarket chil-dren's matinees, but after a promising beginning, attendances declined to the point that the venture was abandoned in 1929. Bernstein blamed the local education authorities for a lack of co-operation, but Sarah Smith argues that: 'The real problem was that children preferred the exciting programmes on offer at other cinemas, rather than sitting through films chosen with children in mind [...] young patrons wanted gangsters and monsters, not literary adaptations and educational films'.[79]

Children and the Talkies

As in the United States, the arrival of sound on the British screen reignited the debate surrounding cinema's influence on the young. There were sev-eral new avenues of attack for critics. 'Talkies' availed the opportunity for salacious or otherwise 'adult' dialogue. Consequently, the emphasis shifted from a primarily visual to primarily verbal aesthetic. Additionally, the coming of sound revealed the extent to which foreign, and specifically

Hollywood, films dominated British screens, again raising fears of North American cultural hegemony. Legislation that required that British cinemas show a certain proportion of British-made films was introduced in 1927. But it also seems to have been generally believed, without much foundation, that British films were 'better' for British children than those imported from overseas. In 1926, the Board of Trade received a deputation from the National Union of Teachers advocating 'a bigger proportion of British films' on the grounds that they 'were on the whole superior to the American, the American being often very unsuitable for children'.[80] As Staples notes, post-sound Hollywood films were characterised by 'horror films and stories of high society, sex, crime and alcohol', and offered illicit thrills, whereas 'what few British films existed were mainly about the Great War'.[81]

The 1930–34 period of Hollywood cinema, known as the pre-Code era (i.e. prior to the self-regulatory Production Code, established in 1930, being made mandatory), saw many explicitly 'adult' films reach British screens. The proportion of 'A' films rose from approximately 20 per cent during the 1920s to around 50 per cent by the early-to-mid 1930s.[82] An even more alarming reality for reformers clamouring for 'better films' was that many of the 'quality' films being imported from Hollywood were deemed unsuitable for children. A 1932 article by Walter Ashley in *Sight and Sound*, the newly-established British trade magazine, examined approximately 600 films shown in London theatres during 1931–32, of which 120 were found (however arbitrarily) to be of 'a sufficiently high standard of merit to be worthy of detailed examination'.[83] Two-thirds – 80/120 were classified 'A' by the BBFC. As many as 77 per cent felt to be 'first class' were in the 'A' category.[84] 'In other words', the author concludes, '*the better the film, the less likely it is to be passed as suitable for children* – a conclusion that cannot be regarded as anything but disquieting'.[85] Ashley added that:

> The main responsibility for the excessive number of 'A' films […] does not rest with the censors but with the production companies […] It should not be beyond the wit of every company […] to produce at any rate a certain number of films which are both good of their kind *and* suitable for all ages.[86]

By 1933, under pressure from Will Hays, the head of their representative trade organisation, the Hollywood studios were slowly re-orienting towards the 'family audience', with prestigious, broadly-suitable films like *Little Women* (George Cukor, 1933). However, the fruits of this endeavour were hardly visible until the following year, when the Production Code was formalised. By this point, many British observers felt that the situation had gone on long enough.

The arrival of the talkies brought a widespread conviction that children required additional layers of protection, beyond those currently offered by the BBFC's established 'U' and 'A' classifications. The Home Office responded in two ways. Firstly, in 1929 it distributed a circular entitled 'The Kinema and the Children' urging (the c. 35 per cent) of local authorities in England and Wales that had not implemented the 1923 recommendation to ban unaccompanied under-16s from 'A' films to do so immediately.[87] Secondly, in the same year it contacted the BBFC suggesting the creation of a new 'C' (children's) classification. The BBFC rejected the proposal on the basis that such films would be undesirable to exhibitors.[88] The following year, the Theatres and Music Halls Committee of the LCC made a similar approach to the BBFC, which again resisted the move.[89] However, in October 1930 the Liverpool licensing authority elected to exclude under-16s from 'A' films altogether, and several other local authorities followed suit.[90] In some areas, this legislation was actively enforced. In January 1931, the Burlington Cinema Company of Vauxhall Road, Liverpool, was fined £10 for allowing children under the age of 16 to view an 'A'-rated British crime film, *Red Pearls* (Walter Forde, 1930).[91] However, such tough action was very much the exception rather than the norm. In 1931, it was suggested that only around 40 per cent of all local authorities in England and Wales actively policed this regulation.[92] BBFC president Edward Shortt promised change, pledging that 'prolonged and gross brutality and sordid themes' would no longer be tolerated.[93]

Various organisations began conducting their own in-depth studies into the relationship between children and the cinema, intent on uncovering firm evidence of pernicious influence. Five major investigations took place between 1931 and 1933, undertaken, respectively, by the Birmingham Cinema Enquiry Committee (1931), the Birkenhead Vigilance Committee (1931), the London County Council Education Committee (1932), the Sheffield Juvenile Organisations Committee (1932), and the Edinburgh Cinema Enquiry Committee (1933). Each of these studies sampled children's responses to a range of films, and their methods and conclusions are documented at length by Sarah Smith in her admirable study *Children, Cinema and Censorship* (2005), and by Staples in his indispensible *All Pals Together*. All except the LCC's were undertaken by what Staples refers to as 'self-appointed vigilance groups'.[94] All found evidence of children attending 'A' films, largely through the laxity of the theatres. The LCC study, Staples notes, was the only one to fall under the auspices of a statutory body, and with its especially large sample size of 21,280 children aged between 3 and 13 years, it is 'in many ways the most authoritative'.[95] Interestingly, it was also the only one to conclude that most films were 'free from what most people would regard as plainly unsuitable matter'.[96] But despite the propaganda that the average film was accessible to children as well as adults, the LCC report stressed that: 'What does emerge in a very striking manner is the fact that children would welcome more of the healthy adventure type of picture showing life in other lands; in short, that children ask for children's pictures'.[97]

These reports, with their often-conflicting messages, sustained rather than settled the larger debate. The 'flash point', as Smith has it, was the huge popularity among children of pre-Code Hollywood 'horror' films, beginning with *Dracula* (Todd Browning, 1931) and *Frankenstein* (James Whale, 1931).[98] The Home Office responded by forming the Film Censorship Consultative Committee (FCCC), which met for the first time in November 1931. On the advice of the FCCC, the CEA contacted its members to recommend 'in very strong terms that all exhibitors showing this film should make an announcement [that] *Frankenstein* is [...] not suitable for children'.[99] The CEA acted similarly with the release of *Dr. Jekyll and Mr Hyde* (Rouben Mamoulian, 1931) and *Murders in the Rue Morgue* (Robert Florey, 1932). In May 1933, a new category was finally introduced by the BBFC: 'H' (horrific), explicitly denoting unsuitability for children. Initially, this was not an official certificate, but merely an advisory label that may, as Smith postulates, have simply attracted children to the 'forbidden fruit of "unsuitable" films'.[100] In May 1937, the BBFC formalised the 'H' certificate, though the effect of the label was more symbolic than actual: only 55 films were classified as such between 1932 and 1950 (after which it was replaced by the 'X' certificate).[101] It is likely, as Smith and Staples suggest, that many children continued to evade such moves to restrict their access to illicit films.

Much of this chapter has been concerned with the discourses surrounding children and cinema in Britain during this formative period. This is largely because, until 1935, Britain had no tradition of children's films, and it is necessary to look at the social and industrial contexts to understand why this is so. What might be called 'family films' had been produced since the early days of British production, but they were aimed primarily at adults, with child audiences a secondary concern. British children, as this chapter has shown, were avid cinema-goers, but most films they saw – including the overtly child-orientated serials – were produced in the United States. In Britain, the 'children's film', as we understand the term today, was seen as alienating to adult audiences, and thus viewed by producers as box office poison. The few overtly children's films that reached the screen, such as the German *Emil and the Detectives* (Gerhard Lamprecht, 1931), and the Hollywood productions *Tom Sawyer* (John Cromwell, 1930), *Alice in Wonderland* (Norman Z. McLeod, 1933) and the Shirley Temple vehicles, were imports. By the mid-1930s, the tide was beginning to turn. Films addressing only the 'adult' and ignoring the 'family' were under attack from all quarters. Furthermore, the 'loss' of juvenile audiences – which was attributed to 'too many films with adult certificates' – was noted with considerable alarm in trade publications such as the 1934 edition of the *Kinematograph Year Book*.[102] British studios turned increasingly to productions suitable for all audience sections. In this context, as the following chapter will show, the first feature-length British children's films finally emerged.

2

The Children's Adventure Movie, 1930–60

Emil and the Detectives (Milton Rosmer, 1935) holds a uniquely equivocal position in the wider history of British children's cinema. It is the first post-sound British feature film explicitly made for children, and the first with a predominantly child cast. In these terms, it is an important artefact of 1930s British popular culture; but it is also a low-budget B movie largely ignored upon initial release, which soon fell into obscurity, was long believed lost, and received little attention when it was finally recovered by the British Film Institute in 2010. What is more, it is a shot-for-shot remake of the far more celebrated 1931 German adaptation of Erich Kästner's 1929 novel, directed by Gerhard Lamprecht, and scripted by Billy Wilder and Emeric Pressburger. It is curiously appropriate, in a country where children's screen culture was founded on imported entertainment, that Britain's first major children's film was basically a carbon copy of a foreign movie.

The British remake of *Emil and the Detectives* was produced on a small budget by the American-born Richard Wainwright, who made a succession of second features and 'quota quickies' during the 1930s. Such films usually failed to attain bookings in the larger and more prestigious theatres, so substantial 'general audiences' were out of reach. Furthermore, Britain had no tradition of child-centred feature films. The silent-era shorts starring Alma Taylor and Chrissie White were comic vignettes, forming only a tiny part of the movie programme. A feature-length British production sustained by juvenile actors remained an unknown quantity.[1] Juvenility was still widely disparaged by the British middlebrow orthodoxy, which owed much to Victorian principles of decorum. Implicit in such constructions was a leaving behind of 'childish things' with the onset of responsible maturity. The Victorian pantomime, and its film counterparts of the 1900s and 1910s, was an exception. Pantomime offered a licensed suspension of adult behavioural norms, where childlike desires could again be indulged. But this suspension was short-lived, and confined to the Christmas period.

By the same token, the British adaptation of *Emil and the Detectives* was not a vain stab in the dark. Hollywood child-star Shirley Temple was phenomenally popular amongst adult as well as child audiences. Her success – and that of other child-stars – suggested increasing receptiveness to explicitly family-orientated fare.[2] Moreover, Lamprecht's 1931 German adaptation of Kästner's novel had been enthusiastically received. The *Daily Express* thought it a tonic for those 'tired of gangsters', 'bored of bedrooms' and 'sick of sirens', feeling that its 'irresistible appeal' derives from its capturing 'the true psychology of the modern schoolboy'.[3] The *Manchester Guardian* approved that: 'The story is neither propagandist nor pretty-pretty, and the children are not lisping "kiddies" but children as children are meant to be, seeing things from their own point of view and going about them in their own way'.[4] And the *Observer* lauded it as 'a film for children of all ages', intelligible to 'everyone who has ever stalked adventure with a scooter, a penny pistol, and a furtive countersign'.[5] It concluded that it was 'the complete child's picture'; 'this is an accomplishment, in an industry that paradoxically caters for immaturity, that is at once refreshing and all too rare'.[6] These responses imply a distinction between 'childish' (immature, simplistic, regressive and undesirable) and 'childlike' (innocent, wholesome, unaffected and desirable) that will inform much of this chapter.

Wainwright's *Emil and the Detectives* was, as Bryony Dixon suggests, 'made as a result of long-term, proven popularity of the Emil story in Britain'.[7] The popularity of the book and German film were sufficient incentives in their own right, but there had also been a radio adaptation, broadcast by the BBC in February 1934, and a well-received stage version at the Vaudeville Theatre in London, also in 1934, produced by Henry Cass and scripted by Cyrus Brooks. Brooks, a prolific English-language translator of Kästner's novels, also received the screenwriter's credit for the British film. This screenplay drew on Brooks's own stage adaptation, as well as Kästner's novel *and* the German film. As Dixon notes:

> The script is identical, the music is the same, the dialogue is more or less translated word-for-word; even the movements of the actors are precisely translated [...] This can only mean that the British team were working from the same shooting script or had the film to refer to.[8]

Wainwright presumably felt that these links would serve to minimise risk, but upon release the film was largely overshadowed by the novel's earlier, more successful, adaptations. It was ignored by the press, save for a few lines in the British pages of *Variety*, which deemed it 'a happy idea to make an English version' of the German film, and that it would 'have an appeal wherever this tongue is spoken', in the *Yorkshire Post*, which averred that 'it should appeal to children', and in the *Daily Mail*, which thought it 'fairly successful but [it] does not quite realise the dramatic suspense or the character drawing of the original'.[9] Distributor Gaumont British's awkward marketing of the production as 'unusual entertainment' called attention to its incongruity within the larger patterns of 1930s British cinema. Indeed, the film was more a reflection of the still-moribund state of children's cinema in Britain than a sign of its belated flowering.

Emil and the Detectives and the Children's Adventure Movie Cycle

Emil and the Detectives forms part of a larger sub-genre of British children's adventure movies between 1935 and c. 1960. Although children watched films of all types, those examined in this chapter form a nucleus of *explicitly* child-orientated British productions. Broadly speaking, this cycle includes *Elephant Boy* (Robert Flaherty and Zoltan Korda, 1937); *Chips* (Edward Godal, 1938); *Just William* (Graham Cutts, 1940); *The Thief of Bagdad* (William Powell et al., 1940); *Front-Line Kids* (Maclean Rogers, 1942); *Those Kids From Town* (Lance Comfort, 1942); *The Grand Escapade* (John Baxter, 1946); *Hue and Cry* (Charles Crichton, 1947); *Just William's Luck*

(Val Guest, 1948); *Nothing Venture* (John Baxter, 1948); *William Comes to Town* (Val Guest, 1949); *The Kidnappers* (Philip Leacock, 1953); *Smiley* (Anthony Kimmins, 1956); *Innocent Sinners* (Philip Leacock, 1958); *The Child and the Killer* (Max Varnel, 1959); *The Boy and the Bridge* (Kevin McLory, 1959); *Snowball* (Pat Jackson, 1960); and *The Boy Who Stole a Million* (Charles Crichton, 1961). The word 'cycle' implies a unifying thread tying these films together. In industrial terms, there is no such connection. British producers and distributors remained distrustful of obviously child-orientated features, and this handful of child-orientated films is indicative less of broader production strategies than of the diffuse and experimental nature of feature film production in this country.

Before the formation of the state-backed Children's Film Foundation (CFF) in 1951, children's cinema in Britain depended for its existence on free-thinking and ambitious producers like Alexander Korda (whose films targeted 'family' audiences), socially-conscious moguls like J. Arthur Rank, directors such as John Baxter, Val Guest and Philip Leacock who were willing to work with children and were unafraid to target younger audiences, and peripheral industry figures content to pursue marginal profits by catering for the child-dominated neighbourhood and inner-city theatres and matinees. But despite the random nature of production, most of these films draw on common themes and conventions: their protagonists are single children or groups of children; they are intended substantially, though rarely exclusively, for child audiences; serious themes are rarely foregrounded, distinguishing the sub-genre from adult-orientated films with child protagonists, such as *The Fallen Idol* (Carol Reed, 1948) and *Mandy* (Alexander Mackendrick, 1952); children's agency and autonomy are emphasised, with adults typically relegated to the background; however, moral subtexts and overtones are always present. Finally, each attempts to explore or recuperate the quintessence of childhood, invoking childhood adventure and misadventure. Although several films in the above list operate within a fantastic (*The Thief of Bagdad*) or whimsical (*Hue and Cry*) framework, the central children retain their projections of naturalness.

Wainwright's *Emil and the Detectives* was neither successful nor influential, but nonetheless embodies many of the essential characteristics of the subsequent children's adventure movie cycle. It centres on a young boy, Emil Blake (John Williams), who is sent by his mother (Mary Glynne) from their rural home to stay with his grandmother in London during the school holidays. Travelling alone on the train, Emil encounters the sinister Man in the Bowler Hat, Pinker (George Hayes), who gives him drugged sweets, then steals the money entrusted to him by his mother. When Emil regains consciousness, the train has arrived at its destination and Pinker has departed. Emil gives chase, encountering a band of local children, the Detectives, led by Gussy (Donald Pittman) and the Professor (Bobby Rietti), who agree to help him recover his money. In the novel's most iconic moment, faithfully recreated, an increasingly anxious Pinker, on his way to the bank to deposit the money, finds himself pursued through the city streets by hordes of children. A chase, which begins slowly and quietly, builds to a frenzied extreme as both parties quicken their pace. Pinker takes refuge at the bank, but Emil proves to the clerk that the stolen money is his. Pinker flees, but is restrained by the huge gang of children waiting outside, and is led away by the police. It transpires that Pinker is a fugitive bank robber, with a £100 reward on his head. In the film's final scene, Emil and his friends are fêted at a civic ceremony held in their honour in Emil's home town.

The cross-generational appeal of the story, as Gillian Lathey observes, lies in its 'underlying faith in childhood that the otherwise cynical Kästner maintained throughout his life'.[10] It is true, as Dixon argues, that the British remake – transposing the action from postwar Berlin to 1930s London – lacks the socio-political resonances of the original, but that: 'The themes of the film, its characters, child focus and naturalism were all sufficiently translatable to British audiences to transcend its Germanic roots'.[11] Indeed, the children's adventure movie is antithetically related to the manicured, sentimentalised and ingratiating precocity of the Hollywood child-star film, epitomised by Shirley Temple but mirrored in the late-1930s vehicles of her less-celebrated British counterparts, Hazel Ascot and Binkie Stuart. *Emil and the Detectives'* children may aspire towards adulthood, but their adult impersonations are a form of child's play, rather than, as in the child-star film, calculated mimicry of adults conceived for the delight of grown-ups. Adulthood brings with it certain behaviours that must be imitated in order to sustain the fantasy. But when we see the Detectives light a cigar and take turns smoking it, each of them screw up their faces with distaste. For all their skills, they are still children, with all the attendant virtues and

The Children's Adventure Movie, 1930–60

Image 2.1 The criminal Pinker (George Hayes), pursued by hordes of children at the climax of *Emil and the Detectives* (1935)

vices: vigour, creativity, freshness and optimism, leavened by natural conflict and vulnerabilities that are best mitigated by unity of purpose.

The Detectives are portrayed sympathetically, with humour but sincerity. Their *de facto* leader, Gussy, is brave, decent and tough-talking, instantly agreeing to help Emil, but hot-headed enough to fight him over the affections of Cousin Polly (Marion Foster); their strategist, the Professor, is intelligent, rational and clear-headed; the Flying Stag (Ricky Hyland) insists on talking solely in caricatured Red Indian dialect. Emil himself is an intermediary between two extreme but enduring child archetypes. The first is the sweetly 'innocent' Enlightenment-influenced figure of Victorian- and Edwardian-era children's literature; the second is epitomised by Twain's Huck Finn, who lives partially outside the social system, and certainly beyond the confines of institutions such as family, church and school. Emil shares some of the latter's self-reliance, tendency to misadventure and sense of justice (as do the Detectives), but remains strongly embedded within the institutions Huck rejects as conformist and constraining. An early exchange between Emil and his mother illustrates both the closeness of their relationship, and her largely-successful attempts to instil correct moral and behavioural practice:

Mrs Blake: Emil, now pay attention. Here are five £1 notes and two ten shilling ones. You're to give them to grandmama. One's for you, and the other's for your keep. Where are you going to put them?

[He takes the money and puts it inside the breast pocket of his jacket.]

Emil: They won't get lost there, mum!

Mrs Blake: […] What else must you remember?

Emil: To see that my case isn't stolen; to keep my hair brushed; to wash behind my ears every day; to brush my teeth twice a week-

Mrs Blake: A day!

Emil: …Not to fall down and dirty my knees; not to begin eating at table before grandma; not to make too much noise eating my soup… I think that's all. Oh, and to say my prayers.

Mrs Blake: Anything else?

Emil: Oh yes! Not to forget you! I shan't do that, because you come in my prayers!

This didacticism reasserts itself in the scene at the police station after the children succeed in apprehending Pinker. Here, the boys are congratulated for their enterprise, and praised as being 'Just like real detectives'. But through their common goals, allied to their natural attributes, by catching Pinker the children succeed where the adult establishment failed. Perhaps, in the final analysis, this is what made the film such 'unusual entertainment'.

Sabu: The Child as Star

As Jeffrey Richards has argued, in 1930s Britain 'there was only one indisputable child star' – the Indian boy Sabu (1924–63).[12] Hazel Ascot and Binkie Stuart were child-stars in the Shirley Temple mould, which is probably why their films never achieved enduring success; as Richards suggests, 'audiences preferred the real thing'.[13] The illiterate son of a Muslim *mahout*, Sabu had worked closely with elephants for most of his life when he was cast in the pivotal role of Toomai in Alexander Korda's production *Elephant Boy* (Robert Flaherty and Zoltan Korda, 1937). With location filming in Mysore, the film was originally conceived as a vehicle for the acclaimed documentary filmmaker Robert Flaherty, and it is tempting to speculate that Sabu's naturalness – though he needed to learn his lines phonetically, as he knew no English at this point – partly reflects Flaherty's documentary approach to filming, as opposed to the rigorous coaching of the child-star. However, when Flaherty went well over budget, Korda recalled production to his Denham Studios and shot new footage to complete the film. Korda's new scenes reconstituted what was basically an expensive ethnographic nature documentary into a children's adventure narrative more in keeping with the source material, Kipling's 'Toomai of the Elephants' from *The Jungle Book* (1894).

Elephant Boy was a critical and box office hit (though its costliness meant it lost money overall), and made Sabu an instant celebrity in Britain: Korda insured his life for £50,000, and as Richards notes, he was 'sculpted by Lady Kennet, painted by Egerton Cooper, broadcast on the BBC and televised at Alexandra Palace'.[14] He was also enrolled at a top private school, and rapidly learned English. In a June 1937 interview with the *Daily Mirror*, Sabu claimed: 'I want to learn the English fast... I want to learn all I can now, to swim, to play games, to ride a horse and to drive a car'.[15] In short, Sabu adapted quickly to life in England. But his screen persona, in a series of family-orientated Korda productions including *The Thief of Bagdad* and *The Jungle Book* (Zoltan Korda, 1942), actively *resists* the socialising apparatus. Instead, he represents pleasing antitheses of exoticism and familiarity; otherness and intimacy; innocence and experience; affinity with the natural world but not with civilisation. *Elephant Boy* is distinguished by its central child–animal thematic, as embodied by Sabu as Toomai, and the elephant Irawatha as Kala Nag. The film's ending, in which Toomai is rewarded for finding the huge herd of elephants the white hunter Peterson (Walter Hudd) seeks with the promise of being made a great hunter and given the title 'Toomai of the Elephants', simultaneously suggests present and future fortitude and self-reliance. Sabu's on-screen friendship with the elephant is seemingly a reflection of the genuine closeness between them forged over almost a year of shooting in Mysore conducted by Flaherty.

In Korda's films, Sabu is the star, and his films derive expressive meaning from his presence. But they are big-budget extravaganzas offering a range of pleasures *beyond* those offered by the central child figure. Nowhere is this clearer than in *The Thief of Bagdad*, Korda's big-budget Technicolor remake of the Douglas Fairbanks production (dir. Raoul Walsh, 1924), with Sabu as the young thief, Abu. Filming began at Korda's Denham Studios in Buckinghamshire, but due to the outbreak of war, production moved to the United States, where the remaining studio scenes were filmed at the General Service Studio in Santa Monica. Location filming was conducted in Cornwall, Pembrokeshire and in Arizona (including the Grand Canyon). The location filming and the size and detail of the studio sets afford an unusual sense of scale. Undoubtedly Britain's costliest and most significant family film to that point, *The Thief of Bagdad* was also the country's first child-orientated film that attained global popularity. Unlike *Emil and the Detectives*, it is consciously constructed for a dual audience. Indeed, the film was released for the Christmas market, and attempted to mobilise the family audiences traditionally drawn to pantomime. This pantomimic appeal was noted in several reviews, including the *Daily Mirror*'s, which suggested that the film's 'truly amazing spectacle' plugged the gap left by pantomime's perceived decline, the *Daily Mail*'s, which thought it 'ideal Christmas entertainment' for the 'young in heart', and the *Spectator*'s, which noted that this 'gigantic and extravagant Christmas pantomime [...] like all good pantomimes [...] has points of appeal for children as well as for grown-ups'.[16]

The film's various aesthetic attractions thus bolstered Sabu's established appeal, presenting a highly bankable family entertainment package. *The Thief of Bagdad* was the first major film to employ Chroma key (better-known as 'blue-screen' or 'green-screen'). The technique was developed for the film by Lawrence ('Larry') Butler, and constituted a variation on the 'travelling matte' process. *The Thief of Bagdad* won Oscars (1941) for Best Cinematography, Best Art Direction (Colour) and Best Special Effects, with a nomination for Best Music (Miklós Rózsa). These celebrations of its technical (but not narrative) accomplishments closely mirror the Academy Award performance of MGM's *The Wizard of Oz* (Victor Fleming, 1939), which garnered Oscars for Best Music (Original Song) and Best Music (Original Score), and nominations for Best Picture, Best Cinematography,

The Children's Adventure Movie, 1930–60

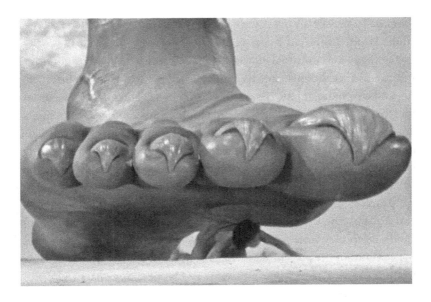

Image 2.2 An example of the spectacular visual effects in *The Thief of Bagdad* (1940)

Best Art Direction and Best Special Effects. After almost eight decades, *The Thief of Bagdad* remains one of the British cinema's most attractively presented entertainments. Most British films of the period offered up a mirror to everyday fears, pleasures and preoccupations. *The Thief of Bagdad*, with its deliberately cultivated dissociative 'timelessness', transported contemporary audiences to a fantastic and ethereal realm where such concerns could be left behind. Korda recognised the universalistic aspects of the narrative. As he later remarked, 'At heart we are all Abus, and we yearn to perform his kind of legerdemain – the kind that gives happiness to mankind. *The Thief of Bagdad* is the closest we may ever come to realising that ideal'.[17] Korda's statement may be self-serving, but it anticipates later appeals to the 'inner child' by producers such as Walt Disney.

However, the major point of departure from Disney's films – and, indeed, from the majority of children's fiction – is the ultimate trajectory of the child protagonist. Mickey Rooney's All-American boy Andy Hardy always had lessons to learn, each film representing another step towards an inexorable, but ultimately longed-for, adulthood. Abu, by contrast, remains immune to the socialising pressures exerted on him by his friend Prince Ahmad (John Justin), who dresses the usually bare-chested Sabu in restrictive clothes, plans to school him and bestow on him a position of authority. Instead, he escapes on a (stolen) magic carpet, promising to pursue 'some fun and adventure at last'. His youthful exuberance and adventure are not merely preserved but actively celebrated; the film ultimately presents a double 'happy ending'. Abu knows nothing of romantic love and cares little for Ahmad's affections for the princess (June Duprez), but ultimately he facilitates their union by reuniting the separated couple and killing the villainous Jaffar (Conrad Veidt) with an arrow. The marriage of Ahmad to the princess satisfies (chiefly adult) expectations for romantic fulfilment, and Abu's escape to a life of adventure satisfies the (literal and symbolic) child's desires for unfettered play without limitations, extending beyond the confines of the present narrative. For many audience members, satisfactions can be drawn from both these resolutions; from parallel desires for romantic fulfilment and for family, and for the seemingly contrary possibilities for independence and freedom. Korda may have intuited the film's ability to tap the 'child of all ages', but he was astute enough to provide for the adult spectator *unable* to regress to childhood; for the unregenerate grown-up.

The Child as Outsider

Sabu is an extreme example of the 'child as outsider' trope evident in several British children's movies of the 1930s–50s. *Hue and Cry* and *Innocent Sinners* also show the lone child or children existing outside the adult social system, operating with degrees of self-reliance, and engaging in their own cultivated forms of play. *Hue and Cry* draws heavily on *Emil and the Detectives*, with the basic storyline transposed from the (post-World War I) Berlin of Kästner's German novel/film to (a post-World War II) London. Both narratives centre on groups of apparently dispossessed children negotiating their way through devastated war-torn urban environments, and ultimately representing a hopeful belief in the potentialities of youth for building a better world. In both cases it is youth – streetwise, rough-hewn, sometimes fractious and opportunistic – that vanquishes adult corruption. But there are also marked points of departure. Whereas the British version of *Emil and the Detectives* merely palimpsests Berlin on to a broadly anonymous metropolis, *Hue and Cry* is centrally concerned with the relationship between postwar London and its young inhabitants, both damaged and disfigured by recent cataclysmic events, but yet enduring, defiant, and looking to the future.[18]

Hue and Cry centres on a working-class London street gang, the 'Blood and Thunder Boys', led by Joe Kirby (Harry Fowler), which stumbles on a smuggling operation orchestrated through code inserted into the pages of a children's comic. Dismissing Joe's discovery, police inspector Ford (Jack Lambert) nonetheless recommends him for a job with Covent Garden grocer Nightingale (Jack Warner). A visit to the comic's eccentric author, Felix H. Wilkinson (Alastair Sim), shows that he is unaware of criminals' activities, so the boys turn their attentions to the secretary of the publishers, who is revealed to have been intercepting Wilkinson's stories on arrival and inserting the code without the author's or publisher's knowledge. Ford is exposed as a member of the racket, and Nightingale its leader. Misdirecting the criminals by substituting their own code into the comic, Joe and the gang are able to bring them to justice. The film's ending again recalls *Emil and the Detectives*, with hordes of children descending on the criminals to apprehend them. But its climax is altogether more anarchic. Criminals are seen fighting off adolescent boys with punches and violent throws to the ground, while Nightingale is gruesomely – if comically – dispatched when Joe jumps from a great height on to his stomach, resulting in a macabre deflating sound.

A boys' own-style narrative which fondly evokes the comic book caper, *Hue and Cry* is a paean to childhood adventure and misadventure. The opening credits bill the all-male gang as the 'Blood and Thunder Boys', whose name seems consciously to evoke the (variously named) Dead End Kids, East Side Kids and Bowery Boys of late-1930s and 1940s Hollywood. Like their US equivalents, they are formidable, resourceful street toughs who, despite their rough edges, are unconventional heroes. Almost every single adult character in the movie – with the exception of Joe's barely glimpsed mother and father – is corrupt or remote. The criminals are shadowy and malign, the police bungling or crooked, and Sim's reclusive author totally withdrawn, selfishly refusing to help for fear of reprisal, and remarking, ironically, that he hates adventurous children. In the absence

43

Image 2.3 The young, streetwise gang at the centre of *Hue and Cry* (1947)

of the dependable social bedrocks of the family, school, church and state that would come to epitomise the Children's Film Foundation, children are forced to rely on their own abilities. Moreover, they are the film's moral centre, unmasking and defeating the wrongdoers single-handedly. The cynicism and corruption of the adult characters, and bravery, ethical integrity, and agency of the children, underpins the film's wider implication that youth, and not rapacious spivs like Nightingale and Ford, or weary, self-absorbed old-timers like Wilkinson and Joe's parents, embody what it means to be British in a postwar context in which many of the old certainties have been removed.

Hue and Cry owes more to the fictional tradition of sentimental nostalgic recollection of childhood than to the realism of *Emil and the Detectives*. The *Observer*'s C. A. Lejeune thought it 'a modern variant of the penny dreadful, the boys' novelette', and whilst acknowledging it as 'great stuff for young people', she predicted that it would 'set the older members of the audience wistfully recalling the days when we used to hurry to the newsagents for the latest adventures of Sexton Blake or Dixon Hawke'.[19] Similarly, the *Guardian* labelled it 'a boys' film', but moreover, 'a film for parents'.[20] The film envisions an embattled but ultimately victorious generation of British postwar youth who, despite surface non-conformism, epitomise celebrated British characteristics of fair play, decency and moral fortitude. They are not, as in *Emil and the Detectives*, merely innocently engaging in child's play. Shot almost entirely on location around London, this outdoor world, a relic of the terrible suffering and destruction of the war, is simultaneously the children's natural habitat, their playground. This normalising of the war-torn landscape, from the children's perspective, is ultimately optimistic; they are better equipped than the largely unseen representatives of adult authority to deal with the realities and challenges of postwar life.[21]

Several of these themes are revisited in *Innocent Sinners*, which centres on a semi-orphaned adolescent girl, Lovejoy (June Archer), and her efforts to build a garden amongst the rubble of the bombed slums of London. Again, the postwar city is constructed as a character in its own right, and serves as a playground for lost and orphaned children. The ravaged buildings and open spaces evoke a bleak idyll in their abundant potentiality for children's play. Shots of the skinny, haunted tomboy Lovejoy running around the rubble of Pimlico's devastated inner-city terraces, framed by Battersea Power Station billowing black fumes into the air, set to the jauntiest of musical accompaniment, are a reminder that the hardships and traumas of the wartime generation are not necessarily inherited by the baby boomers. The child's determination to make a garden on the site of a house destroyed in the blitz serves as a metaphor for growth and renewal. The unblunted but sympathetic child figures of Lovejoy and her friends Tip (Christopher Hey) and Sparkey (Brian Hammond) represent a hopeful reimagining of the war-torn setting. Not having lived through the war themselves, the children are able to view these locations as politically and emotionally neutral, and with a more utilitarian eye. The garden, like the children themselves, represents vitality in the unlikeliest setting.

These children are sympathetically but not sentimentally conceived. Needing to purchase gardening equipment from a pawn shop, Lovejoy initially tries hustling, but her begging by singing in the street is foiled by mean-spirited adults, so ultimately she resorts to stealing from a church collection tray. She finds a packet of flower seeds on the pavement, and pilfers a net (to keep cats off the freshly-sown earth) from a baby's push-chair. Nor does the film posit a Disneyesque affinity between child and nature; when a baleful-looking tomcat threatens to encroach on her territory, Lovejoy threatens to hurl a brick at it. The garden in its original location is destroyed by a gang of boys, leaving Lovejoy devastated. But one of the culprits, Tip, leads Lovejoy to a new site in the grounds of a derelict church destroyed in the blitz, and watched over by a figure of the Virgin Mary left behind in the church window. Initially, Tip resists helping Lovejoy to clear the scattered masonry, denying interest in a 'sissy garden', but, in a show of compassion, later helps her to prepare the ground. Moreover, in the spectacle of the lone girl, later assisted by initially hostile children, clearing rubble in an idealistic attempt to create something verdant and beautiful, youth is the arbiter of a new, possibly better, world order.

As with *Hue and Cry*, *Innocent Sinners* puts greater store in kinship ties forged by common actions and beliefs than in blood ties. Lovejoy's father is unseen, presumably dead. Her mother (Vanda Godsell) is an ageing prostitute. But the film is distinct from *Hue and Cry* in presenting a surrogate father in the benign, would-be *haute* restaurateur, Mr Vincent (David Kossoff), who runs the boarding house in which Lovejoy stays rent-free. Mr Vincent participates in the masquerade that her mother is a professional singer (though the streetwise Lovejoy surely knows the truth). In one scene, having discovered her lying slumped outside the room she shares with her mother, unable to enter because her mother is 'entertaining', he carries her downstairs and lets her sleep on an armchair, covering her with a blanket. Finally, he delivers motivating advice: 'most people want to drag you down, but don't let them'. In the context of this miserable home-life, Lovejoy's garden represents a variant on the time-worn children's literary conceit of the 'other world'. The garden, though, is more rooted to real-world forces; it is again destroyed at the end of the film when the ruined church is demolished to make way for a new one. By this point, the garden has served its purpose, facilitating Lovejoy's coming-of-age and engendering a sense of reciprocity between the film's previously antithetical child and adult figures.

The building of the garden is a rite-of-passage in other ways. Tip's willingness to help Lovejoy on the garden, and his inability to refuse her

The Children's Adventure Movie, 1930–60

requests for money, seedlings, tools, and a better supply of earth, hint at chaste adolescent infatuation. Tip also provides unlikely moral guidance, serving as father confessor to Lovejoy when it transpires that her original garden was funded by the church collection box, and handing out the penance that she will not be permitted to resume work on the new one until the money is repaid. This punishment she willingly accepts, having had her conscience pricked by the accusing glances of the Mother Mary statue from the church window. As might be inferred from the title, Christian themes of sin and redemption undergird *Innocent Sinners*, but Lovejoy also becomes accustomed to modern adult methods of trade and negotiation. Audaciously, she purchases some flowers on hire purchase – an early manifestation of the burgeoning credit culture that allowed the working-classes to escape austerity. In this sense, at least, *Innocent Sinners* divagates from the unregenerate otherness of *Hue and Cry*'s children, with Lovejoy undergoing a process of coming to terms with adult norms. Although she does not recognise it as such, her *raison d'être* is an exercise in healing and consensus-building; the boys and girls of *Hue and Cry*, though atypically driven by strong ethical codes, seek no such reconciliation with an adult society that is beyond redemption.

Representatives of such a society are many: most prominent are Lovejoy's neglectful, prostitute mother who eventually moves to Canada, abandoning her daughter to the charity of others, and the overbearing, affluent do-gooder Angela Chesney (Catherine Lacey), who owns a school for destitute children, but whose ostentatious benevolence obscures a desire to repress, not liberate, young people. She accuses Lovejoy of being too 'cocky and independent', words the child later uses with pride as qualities she wishes to retain. Tip's termagant mother (Pauline Delaney) is similarly harsh, observing of Lovejoy that 'she was born in the gutter and it's there she'll end', as is the Vincents' wretched tenant, who constantly exhorts them to evict Lovejoy because of her mother's failure to pay her rent. On the other side of the equation lay Mr Vincent, whose childlike dreams of opening a top West End restaurant are fulfilled at the end of the movie; Angela's sister, the ailing, wealthy spinster, Olivia (Flora Robson), who leaves her money to Vincent on the condition that he opens his restaurant and adopt Lovejoy; the young couple Charles (Lyndon Brook) and Liz (Susan Beaumont), who give

Lovejoy a young, potted rose bush for her to nurture; and the kindly stranger who guarantees Lovejoy's unorthodox hire purchase of a box of pansies. These are the representatives of the old order who have a part to play in Britain's rebuilding, alongside the new generation Lovejoy represents. Although full identification is denied to the remote, aloof Angela, she is nonetheless humanised at the end at the film, when she endorses her deceased sister's non-binding will, having been touched by Lovejoy's gift to Olivia of the rose bush.

Innocent Sinners takes another step away from the documentary-style realism of *Emil and the Detectives*, and from the comic-book whimsy of *Hue and Cry*. But it retains their sincerity and earnest desire to evoke the realities of childhood, in spirit if not in literal application. *The Times* observed the antithesis between 'the precocious little prodigies destined for stardom' and 'the ordinary, untidy, and boisterous variety who are genuine and real', embodied by June Archer, 'a sad-faced, impulsive little creature, all arms and legs, in a dress that is too short and shoes that pinch, and the ability to speak with her eyes, saying much by saying nothing'.[22] The *Manchester Guardian* thought the central children 'quite authentic and well-observed', although the *Financial Times* found it lacking 'that piercing quality of insight which in the past, as in *Poil de Carotte* [1925], *The River* [1951] and *Les Jeux Interdits* [1952], has created small masterpieces out of childish hope and disillusionment'.[23] The film also veers towards the poetic realism of *The Red Balloon* (*Le Ballon Rouge*, Albert Lamorisse, 1956), with the *Sunday Times* describing it as 'fairy tale stuff' and the *Financial Times* as 'halfway between fairy tale and neo-realism', suggesting a more adult mode of storytelling largely disavowed by its happy ending, and sustained interest in the intricacies – not merely the symbolic potentiality – of childhood.[24]

The Child and the Family

The ending of *Innocent Sinners*, in which the orphaned child is adopted to form a 'conventional' family, gestures towards a parallel cycle of films in which the central children are seen in relation to the needs and socialising role of the surrounding family. Prominent entries include *Just William*, *Just William's Luck*, *William Comes to Town*, and *The Kidnappers*. The child is still the narrative centre, and so these films are distinct from literal family movies such as *The Briggs Family* (Herbert Mason, 1940) and Huggetts series (1948–49), which explore the quotidian realities of domestic life and address a primarily adult audience, as well as from the domestic films of the 1950s discussed in Chapter 5. Rather, the family setting here operates as a microcosm of society-at-large, as a locus of the transmission of values and behavioural codes from one generation to the next. More prosaically, the contextual presence of the wider family unit fulfils the commercial imperative of widening appeal to adults.

Just William, the first big-screen adaptation of Crompton's immensely popular book series (1921–70), was produced in early 1939 but not released until July 1940. If *Emil and the Detectives*, with its German provenance, constituted a charming aberration within British children's fiction of the 1930s, *Just William* is perhaps its quintessence, with its middlebrow values, moralistic overtones, emphasis on the child as part of the family, and portrayal of the children as not-quite-competent. Young protagonist William Brown (Dickey Lupino) and his gang, the Outlaws, are middle-class children, and William is akin to the only-superficially-naughty youngest children of the respectable Hollywood families of *Ah, Wilderness!* (Clarence Brown, 1935), and *On Moonlight Bay* (Roy Del Ruth, 1951). *Just William* is an altogether more modest affair than those prestige productions, but remains notable as the last film directed by Gainsborough co-founder Graham Cutts, as well as for the casting of child-stars Dickey Lupino (Buster Keaton's cousin) and Roddy McDowall, and popular comic actors Fred Emney and Basil Radford.

In *Emil and the Detectives*, the children's ability to operate outside the bounds of the family unit is a marker of their agency, autonomy and individuality. Here, William's placement *within* the nuclear family structure is a reminder of the inevitability and the desirability of growing up. The family may be nurturing and protective, but it is also a socialising apparatus which inculcates moral, ethical and behavioural codes to live by. Both films court the fabled family audience, but while the former addresses the *child within the adult*, the latter addresses presumably reluctant parents accompanying their children to the theatre. *Just William* thus develops two parallel plotlines: the first concerns William's various misadventures, and the second revolves around his father's (Fred

Emney) standing for public office to oppose local political corruption. Although these plotlines intersect when William helps expose the nefarious businessmen planning on backing Mr Brown's rival in the local election, the perceived need for differentiated forms of address reflects an assumption that adult spectators require their own adult identification figures, engaging in the kind of serious business disavowed by William's adolescent antics.

William's parents and older siblings represent the socially- and culturally-prescribed trajectory of youth and innocence to maturity and experience. As in Crompton's stories, William's bluff father is portrayed as an older, more evolved version of his son. The mischievousness, rough edges and selfish tendencies of childhood have properly been tempered and rechanneled in adulthood by William's father into a profitable businessman's mentality and (responsible, restrained) desire for power, albeit on a small scale; a kind of benignly ratified social Darwinism. William is not the 'sweet little boy' his demurely indulgent mother (Iris Hoey) insists he is, but his mischievousness is hardly a prelude to teenage delinquency. Ultimately, what emerges from the dual (child-adult) narrative focus is a spirit of cultivated intergenerational co-operation, underpinned by the contrary but complementary skills possessed by the child and the adult. Children may be vulnerable and naïve, but embody virtues such as curiosity, vitality, unaffectedness, innate morality, and agency. As a corollary, they also possess an ability to sense and expose deceit in others (especially grown-ups). Adults, meanwhile, are usually separated into 'good' and 'bad' characters; 'good' adult figures include family members and the arms of the state, including policemen (but *not* local politicians, who, almost invariably, are corrupt). These are stolid, reliable characters that child spectators are encouraged to trust. They offer skills – strength, decency, intellect, and organisation – that represent a potent distillation of age and experience.

Just William's Luck, written and directed by Val Guest, is wholly unconnected with the Graham Cutts-directed adaptation of 1939; nor was it adapted from any of Richmal Crompton's stories. In fact, Crompton, eager to exploit the film's modest popularity, adapted the film into a novel of the same name, published in 1948. Guest was one of the stalwarts of British cinema for several decades from the 1930s to the 1970s, a prolific and versatile screenwriter and director whose films ranged from slapstick comedy and

The Children's Adventure Movie, 1930–60

children's films to horror and soft-core pornography. He claimed that: 'I have never in my life set out to make a picture for the lowest common denominator audience. Any picture I've made I've made because it was the sort of picture I would like to see'. But his two *Just William* films are also carefully positioned to exploit the pre-existing popularity of Crompton's book series, and, moreover, that of the BBC's radio adaptation of *Just William* (1946–48). This show was broadcast on the Light Programme station, typically in an early evening slot, but also repeated, variously, in early and late afternoon. The evening broadcast is especially pertinent, addressing 'family audiences' well positioned to listen during their evening meal. Like Hammer's film adaptations (1948–50) of the BBC's radio series *Dick Barton – Special Agent* (1946–51), Guest's *Just William* films could reasonably expect to mobilise a cross-demographic audience.

Just William's Luck is pitched somewhere between the evocations of unfettered children's play of *Emil and the Detectives* and *Hue and Cry*, and the structuring adult milieu of Cutts's *Just William*. Like *Meet Me in St. Louis* and the Hollywood domestic comedy cycle of the 1940s–50s, there are minor, episodic and only vaguely inter-related subplots involving each member of the household. These include William's (William Graham) obsession with obtaining a bicycle, which leads to his attempts to arrange marriage between his brother (Hugh Cross) and a neighbouring film star in the hope that his married brother will no longer require his bike; the frustration of the elderly family housemaid, Emily (Muriel Aked) at being underappreciated; Mrs Brown's (Jane Welsh) fleeting belief that her husband (Garry Marsh) is having an affair with the aforementioned film star; and William and the Outlaws' uncovering and ultimately foiling the attempts of a criminal gang to smuggle stolen fur out the country. Such storylines involve a complex double address, in which the perceived needs of child and adult spectators are held in balance. The film's final section, though, is overtly regressive, harking back to the children's comic two-reelers of the silent era. Totally without dialogue, this section relies on visuals and music to relate a series of events: the children's uncovering the gang of smugglers; their evading capture long enough to alert the police; their being discovered and kidnapped by the smugglers; their leaving a trail from the getaway van that the police can follow; and the criminals' eventual capture. This child-friendly mechanism is partly a corollary of Guest realising that

51

he could save money by filming without sound and later overlaying a music track.[25] Yet it also serves to shift the emphasis away from the adult world and towards the play space of the literal and symbolic child.

Another example is the dialogue given to the apparently sweetly innocent Violet Elizabeth (Audrey Manning), who successfully campaigns to join the nominally all-male Outlaws when she threatens to 'Scream until I make myself sick – I *can* do it, as well!'. Later, when the gang spot their nemesis, Hubert Lane (Ivan Hyde), spying on them and tie him up, Violet Elizabeth exhorts William to 'torture' him, in mimicry of the stories she has read; to 'pull his teeth out', 'stick pins in him' and 'pull his hair out'. Humour is derived from juxtaposing an image of childhood 'innocence' with demands for brutality, subverting the innocent child archetype. For children, especially young girls, Violet Elizabeth may be an emancipatory character, seeming to conform to social expectations regarding young femininity, yet secretly resisting them with unrepentant viciousness. For many adult spectators, at first sight doubtless she epitomises the child/daughter they wish they had, and then are glad they haven't got.

In other regards, the film asserts the innocence – or at least ignorance – of children in relation to adult codes of acceptability. In one sequence presented entirely without dialogue, the sign to William's hideout, 'The Bloody Tower', provokes consternation among a group of local parents, whose angry exchange of telephone calls ultimately compels William to strike a line of paint through the unintentionally profane 'bloody'. William later complains that the word is 'in all the history books – our form master even wrote it on the blackboard. But when I write it, it's wrong. Everything I do is wrong'. The scene is interestingly composed. A montage sequence relates the parents' telephone exchanges, but although their outrage is clear from their facial expressions, we hear nothing. In most family films, incidents of children's transgression and parental correction are presented from both sides, but here, punishments are perceived by spectators, as they are by children, as unjust and unfathomable. The film thus retains its focalisation on the child and disallows – even among adult spectators who understand the need for discipline – identification with the authoritarian grown-ups.

Despite its insistence on unsentimentally naturalistic portrayals of childhood, the film still employs nostalgic tropes of childhood reminiscence from the adult's perspective. The Outlaws anticipate a utopian

The Children's Adventure Movie, 1930–60

adulthood characterised by limitless freedom and additional physical prowess, but the adults recall a time when play was unfettered by responsibilities and constraint. This dichotomy is most interestingly conveyed in two sequences. In the first, the Outlaws encounter a tramp and become enamoured of his idyllic depiction of a life of simple wish-fulfilment beyond the boundaries of modern civilisation. The irony is that William's parents want him to become a doctor, a lucrative but highly pressured and regimented occupation that symbolises the conformism the Outlaws repudiate. But the undesirability of the tramp's lifestyle is later revealed when he turns up at the police station, and wryly tells the boys – in reference to the earlier encounter – that 'this is a place you *can* eat and sleep for nothing'. The second sequence is a rare private exchange between William's parents where mother attempts to defuse father's anger at his mischief-making by invoking his own mischievous boyhood. This reminder elicits indulgent smiles from Mr Brown, who recognises William as a less evolved version of himself. This dynamic is repeated in the closing scenes, where an initially stern Mr Brown, angered that William sneaked out of the house at night without permission, is again placated by his wife, and indulgently allows William to have the family dog sleep in his bedroom.

Importantly, these realisations underpin the more enlightened assumption that William is on the correct path. His naughtiness is excusable as a 'natural' (if not desirable) transient phase prior to an inevitable acquisition of proper codes of behaviour. His good deeds are rewarded in the closing scene, where he is visited in bed by each member of the family with gifts: cake from his mother and father, a bike from his brother, and a 'two bob' coin from his sister. This scene bears interesting comparison with a major plotline in the later film *William Comes to Town*, where William voices a desire to become a circus performer. As in the previous film, William's anarchism is permissible only within a firmly structured, stratified developmental trajectory in which, ultimately, 'childish things' (i.e. indulging base desires) are left behind, and properly middle-class British virtues of restraint, responsibility, decency and acquisitiveness are finally embraced. Like the vagabond's life endorsed by the tramp in *Just William's Luck*, and initially coveted by the Outlaws, the vocation of circus performer is instantly rejected, without explanation, by William's parents. Presumably this rejection extends beyond economic non-viability, and encompasses dearly-held – and necessarily classist – values of taste and decency emblematic of bourgeois living.

Whereas the *Just William* films were moderately profitable at best, *The Kidnappers*, like *Hue and Cry*, was exceptional in its cross-demographic popularity: it was the eighth most profitable film at the 1954 British box office.[26] It also received BAFTA nominations for Best Film and Best Actor (Duncan Macrae), and won Honorary Juvenile Oscars for Jon Whiteley and Vincent Winter. Marketed to a general audience with the tagline 'The frankly sentimental story of love, hate and adventure in a primitive land!', *The Kidnappers* is the first of several child-orientated productions directed by the talented Philip Leacock, who went on to oversee *Escapade* (1955), *The Spanish Gardener* (1956) and *Innocent Sinners*, all of which explore complex social and ethical concerns, in much the same way that the contemporary Iranian art cinema has used children and childhood for purposes of social comment. *The Kidnappers* is a subtle and occasionally provocative family drama. Unlike the majority of child-centred British films, it was widely reviewed, mostly positively, in the popular press. The *Spectator* described it as 'a touching, funny, sad, delightful film [which] should not be missed'; the *Daily Mirror* thought it featured 'some of the most moving and natural child acting seen on the screen since Jackie Coogan'; and the *Times* and the *Monthly Film Bulletin* (*MFB*) welcomed its sincerity and authenticity, though the latter qualified its praise by summing it up as a 'noteworthy, if not entirely successful, British production'.[27]

The Kidnappers bears some comparison with the films later produced by the US independent filmmaker Robert B. Radnitz in its intelligent storyline, deceptive simplicity of composition, projection of authenticity, refusal to juvenilise, narrative focalisation on children, and attempt to reflect childhood realities, rather than simply reproducing or fulfilling adult fantasies. The film centres on two pre-teen Scottish boys, Harry (Whiteley) and Davy (Winter), who go to live in Nova Scotia with their grandfather, Jim MacKenzie (Macrae) after their father's death in the Boer War. Unable to forge an emotional connection with their stern grandfather, who will not allow them a pet dog, the children discover what appears to be an abandoned baby. They decide to adopt it themselves, and to keep its existence secret. Eventually, it transpires that the baby belongs to a local Dutch family with whom the Boer-hating Jim has been feuding. Suspected of having kidnapped the Dutch baby in provocative escalation of the community's internecine antagonism, the older brother, Harry, is tried in court. The magistrate initially threatens to send the boy to a correctional school, but the Dutch father (Francis de Wolff) speaks out in support of the boy, who is released. Jim eventually sells his prized walking boots in order to buy a dog for the children.

The two boys, Harry and Davy, are excellently played by Whiteley and Winter. They present a blatant counterpoint to the conventionally sweet, 'goody-goody' children featured in contemporaneous CFF product. Nor are they seen to possess an innate, seemingly God-given ethical code, in the Shirley Temple vein. Rather, they are impressionable and occasionally amoral, and yet to learn civilised codes of behaviour. Temple would intuitively know that kidnapping – even with the best of intentions – is unacceptable, transgressing firm boundaries between right and wrong that have their roots in a transcendent connection between child and God. Harry and Davy learn their lessons the hard way. It is ironic that the film's most devoutly religious figure, the Calvinist Jim MacKenzie, is not only its most misguided, but is responsible for leading the good-natured but artless boys to misdeeds that almost destroy the family. His xenophobia towards the Dutch, borne through his son's death in the recent Boer War, is transmitted to Harry, who fights at school with a young Dutch-Canadian boy. Additionally, his starving the boys of affection by refusing them a pet dog ('you can't eat a dog') indirectly leads to the boys' unwitting kidnap of the baby. Finally, Jim refers contemptuously to the sympathetic Dutch doctor Willem Bloem (Theodore Bikel) as 'a Boer', an expression of racial hatred later adopted by Harry, and spoken with enough venom to raise eyebrows, considering the film's child orientation.

Yet the film possesses a strong moral centre. Jim, a harsh, unyielding figure, ultimately sees the error of his ways and apologises to a Dutch family when they speak in support of Harry in court, and comes to understand that there is more to being a 'good Christian' than knowledge of scripture. As played by the tall, gaunt, craggy-faced Glaswegian Macrae, Jim, in many regards, is the film's pivotal character. The narrative gradually develops audience sympathy for him through processes of familiarisation and revelation, and finally reformation. Although considerably rougher-hewn than the seemingly stern, subsequently lovable grandfather in Johanna Spyri's

Heidi (1880), Jim ultimately accepts his mistakes in his taciturn but meaningful apology to the local Dutch family, and demonstrates affection and fatherly responsibility for the boys. This is expressed, first, outrageously, by his serious threat to shoot the local magistrate in court if he sends Harry to a 'correctional school', and second, by selling his valuable boots (and walking home barefoot) in order to buy a dog for the children. Harry's inherited racial hatred of 'Boers' serves as reminder of this paternal obligation, and Jim's rehabilitation is necessary not only for his own social reintegration, but for that of Harry and Davy as well.

Contemporary responses to these films position them outside the dominant, mainstream tradition of British cinema. Most were unpretentious second features, and few received much attention. As we have seen, the exceptions to this rule were slicker and more prestigious offerings such as *The Thief of Bagdad* and *Hue and Cry*, which were seen as universally appealing, and thus family films in the truest sense. But lower-budget, more child-orientated films were often dismissed as curios or of marginal interest, or ignored altogether. While designed, to varying degrees, for family audiences, some were perceived as short-changing adults. Virginia Graham's *Spectator* review of *Just William's Luck* caustically observes that '[it is] what is known as good family entertainment, which means that it is enjoyable if shared with children but pretty dreary without them', and that it 'may prove, alas, a little daunting to the unaccompanied adult'.[28] Assessing the same film, the *Manchester Guardian* was scarcely more positive: 'Even the most prejudiced and reluctant escort of a juvenile addict will find it inoffensive'.[29] Both reviews imply that adult attendees were there by duress, fulfilling their parental responsibilities to accompany their children to the theatre. However, the wheel was turning, and by the 1950s there was a definite trend toward family films privileging adult requirements at least as much as children's. In this context, the provision of explicitly child-orientated films became almost solely the province of the state-backed Children's Film Foundation, as Chapter 4 will reveal.

3

Family Entertainers: Formby, Hay, Lucan, Wisdom

Legitimately child-orientated films in 1930s and 1940s Britain were scarce commodities. Most films that children saw were for 'the whole family', and many of these were comedy vehicles whose popularity was predicated on the magnetic central presence of a single star performer. George Formby (1904–61), Will Hay (1888–1949) and Arthur Lucan (1885–1954) were the pre-eminent 'family' entertainers of the period, whose films were equally popular with children as with adults. Unlike Norman Wisdom (1915–2010), who came to prominence in the 1950s, Formby, Hay and Lucan emerged from the more adult-orientated music hall tradition. Other early British film comedians, such as Max Miller and the Crazy Gang, retained an edge of ribaldry, but these four stars tailored their vehicles specifically to family audiences. While having to compete with comedies imported from Hollywood starring the likes of Laurel and Hardy and the Three Stooges (who also gained a sizable following among children), they consistently ranked amongst the biggest box office draws in Britain.

Formby, Hay and Lucan were already established stars prior to the advent of the 'talkies', making their living touring music halls through-out the country. Formby's father, James Booth, was a popular music hall comedian who also used the pseudonym 'George Formby'. After his father's death, Formby began touring music halls with his late father's material, accompanied by his trademark banjolele and characterised by his distinctive Lancashire accent. Will Hay made his professional debut in 1909 as a juggler, later developing the comic sketch for which he would become best known, centring on his crooked schoolmaster persona. Over the next 25 years, he established himself as one of the country's headline performers. Arthur Lucan was the creator of Old Mother Riley, the remarkably resilient elderly Irish washerwoman. Born and raised in Lincolnshire, Lucan played old women on the stage from an early age. Aged 26, he met and fell in love with his future co-star, the 13-year-old Kitty McShane. The pair later married, going on to create the enduring double act, 'Old Mother Riley and her daughter Kitty', which they performed to great popularity in variety theatre, radio and film over the next 40 years, as well as a Royal Variety Performance in 1934. Norman Wisdom, in many regards, is the odd one out, rising to prominence as he did in the postwar years. Demobilised from the army in 1946, Wisdom embarked on a career as a comic entertainer on the stage, creating his trademark character, the Gump (taking his cue from Chaplin's Tramp), a childlike buffoon in ill-fitting clothes and cap.

Each of these performers operated within the mode of comedian comedy. Narrative, in such a tradition, is subordinated to personality, and stories function merely as vehicles for these performers' magnetic on-screen presences. An important corollary is that there is no complex or intricate plot to distract, confuse or bore young audiences. These films trade heavily in established formulae and pleasurable repetitions, as with Formby's stock catchphrases ('turned out nice again!'). Furthermore, their modes of comedy are heavily reliant on slapstick, pratfalls, sight gags, and visual incongruities. As Richard Ford observed in 1939, slapstick was 'the type of comedy which children like' most.[1] Many of these films' core attributes can be found in later entertainment forms designed *specifically* for children: i) fast-paced narratives; ii) simple storylines; iii) relatively simple film syntax, with few, if any, techniques of distanciation; iv) a primarily visual aesthetic, with action privileged above complex dialogue; v) an absurd, Saturnalian fictional universal in which (adult) socio-behavioural norms are subverted; and vi) an emphasis on adults as symbolic children, thus playing against children's tendency to associate adults with authority. These recurrent elements will be recognisable to anyone familiar with children's film and television, but the main targets of these comedies, at least initially, were not children but working-class audiences more broadly. The supposed 'childishness' of such films reflected a common, if patronising, assumption that mass audiences were motivated by juvenile, unsophisticated desires. Thus, the distinction between the 'child audiences' and the 'adult audience' – so apparent at other points in this book – is less relevant here.

Child Appeal

Nevertheless, this cycle of films was central to contemporary British children's cinema experiences. The popularity of film and star are inextricably linked. Ford presented two contemporary surveys of British children's favourite film stars, both of which confirm the pre-eminence of imported Hollywood fare. The first sampled 136 theatre managers overseeing children's matinee performances, and was dominated by Hollywood western stars (e.g. Buck Jones, Ken Maynard) and child-stars (e.g. Shirley Temple, Jane Withers). Will Hay was the highest-placed British actor at #6, with Formby at #11 (ahead of Laurel and Hardy at #13), and the British child-star Binkie Stuart down at #20.[2] The second survey, conducted by Ford himself, sampled about 600 members of a London children's cinema club, and showed similar results, with Shirley Temple and Buck Jones placed highest, Gracie Fields the highest-placed British actor at #5 (reflecting her popularity amongst girls), and Hay next at #6.[3] Hay's high ranking is a testament to his virtues as a performer and to children's ability to relate to his filmic persona. But it also reflects the fact that, as with the Mother Riley vehicles, his low-budget films were perennials in children's matinees. As Staples observes, Hay 'provided most of the very few occasions when matinee children saw British films'.[4] Formby's films, like those of Gracie Fields, were higher-end products generally reserved for general audience programmes; only in later years did Formby make his way into the specialised children's film show. It is important to remember that children's preferences – as they are manifested in such surveys – often mirror the films and performers to which they had the most access. Alongside cheap, imported Hollywood productions, Formby's, Hay's and Lucan's films became the bedrock of generations of children's film shows, continuing to appear prominently in matinee programmes as late as the 1960s.[5]

Contemporary reviews also provide insights into how these films were understood in terms of their audiences. Mostly, reviews – when they were not wholly dismissive – highlighted their universal appeal. For instance, C. A. Lejeune's *Sight and Sound* review of *Jack's the Boy* (Walter Forde, 1932) – 'the first really indigenous British screen comedy since the days of the old Betty Balfour films' – approvingly noted that: 'You can take the whole family to see it'.[6] On other occasions, their particular interest to children was acknowledged. Hay's *Good Morning, Boys* (Marcel Varnel, 1937) was seen by the *Observer* as 'as eventful as a boys' twopenny weekly', and by the *Manchester Guardian* as having 'an engaging air of having been written out of school hours'.[7] Of Hay's *Oh, Mr Porter!* (Varnel, 1937), the *Manchester Guardian* wrote: 'Trains still appeal to the child in most of us, and the story is one which might be invented whilst playing at trains'.[8] The *MFB* thought that 'children will enjoy the circus acts' in *Old Mother Riley's Circus* (Thomas Bentley, 1941).[9] The same publication also endorsed Tommy Handley's *Tom Tom Topia* (Frank Chisnell, 1946), as 'the sort of film to introduce youngsters, who will love it, to the slick subtleties of ITMA [the BBC radio show, *It's That Man Again*]'.[10] Of course, such judgements were arbitrary. The *MFB* also warned readers that in Formby's *Turned out Nice Again* (Marcel Varnel, 1941) 'some of the gags have double meanings and may be thought unsuitable for children by careful parents'.[11]

Suitability ratings, too, were highly variable. Although the vast majority of these films were assigned the family-friendly 'U' classification, several were restricted to older audiences. *Boys will be Boys* and Formby's *Off the Dole* (Arthur Mertz, 1935) were both rated 'A' by the BBFC, as was *Old Mother Riley Meets the Vampire* (John Gilling, 1952). Even Disney's *Snow White and the Seven Dwarfs* (David Hand et al., 1937) was awarded the 'A' rating upon initial release (though the BBFC's judgement was widely disregarded by local authorities, many of which reclassified it as a 'U' production). We may look back on such judgements as capricious and unwarranted, yet they reflected contemporary sensitivities that bad behaviour on the big screen may translate to children's real-life conduct. However, contemporary studies of children's attendance habits bear out a long-standing suspicion that underage children and young people routinely flouted such restrictions, and often gained illicit access to supposedly 'adult'-orientated movies.[12] In any event, a consensus grew that Formby's, Hay's and Lucan's films were ideal for children. During the late 1930s and 1940s, Formby and Old Mother Riley both had their own full-page strip cartoons cataloguing their comic misadventures in the long-running British children's weekly, *Film Fun* (1920–62). Accordingly, as their popularity among adults declined, the final few entries in the Mother Riley series were pitched primarily at child audiences.[13]

Symbolic Childhood

From the start of his film career, Formby was well established as an entertainer for child as well as adult audiences. He was a regular performer in pantomime: in December 1934, shortly after the release of his feature debut, *Boots! Boots!* (Bert Tracy, 1934), Formby starred in the Manchester Hippodrome's Christmas performance of 'The Babes in the Wood', playing the part of Simple Simon, and producer George Loman called the staging 'a genuine children's entertainment of the old sort'.[14] The following year, he starred in a performance of 'Mother Goose' at the Liverpool Empire theatre that was broadcast by the BBC, alongside renditions of 'Jack and the Beanstalk', 'Red Riding Hood' and 'Cinderella'.[15] Of Formby's childlike persona, Jeffrey Richards observes:

> The cry 'Ohh, Mother' which he emitted whenever in danger and the gleeful 'Aha, never touched me' when he escaped his pursuers were the reactions of a child. He even put his tongue out at his pursuers on occasions. He had the trusting nature, the sunny optimism and survival instinct of the child [...] combin[ing] the appeal of the proletarian little man and the lost child at large in the grown-up world.[16]

This facade largely protected Formby from criticisms of his act's more 'adult' elements. His song lyrics were brazenly vulgar, often containing double entendres almost too blatant to merit the term. In January 1935, Formby indignantly withdrew from a charity concert at the Manchester Theatre Royal when magistrates demanded that he publish the words to his songs in advance before granting him a licence to perform.[17] Famously, his song 'With my Little Stick of Blackpool Rock' (i.e., penis) was banned by the BBC of the 1930s, and the ban remained in place for many years thereafter. Yet his primary, child-friendly persona so successfully occluded his secondary, more adult modes that their power to offend was largely obviated. Sexual suggestiveness remained central to Formby's appeal in the incongruity it established within his larger comic framework. But it was at least nullified, rendered safe, inoffensive, and endearing. Even for children who do not understand the comic suggestiveness of Formby's lyrics – and doubtless many *did* understand them – there remains the basic attraction of the melodic, innocently nursery rhyme-ish tunes as well as his idiosyncratic singing and playing style.

Nonetheless, the ribaldry of *Off the Dole* (Arthur Mertz, 1935) owes much to the inherited conventions of music hall, where innuendo played a larger role than was permissible in the heavily-policed film medium. It sees Formby's unemployed layabout, John Willie (whose name sources a handful of genitalia-related puns), put in charge of a detective agency. He is embroiled in various salacious activities, including being induced by a married woman to visit a naturist club to discover whether her husband is committing adultery, and hiding in the wardrobe of another woman's bedroom so he can witness her husband abusing her. Formby's later films move away from this preoccupation with sex, but retain his most widely commented-upon characteristic: the innuendo-laden songs. But as Richards persuasively argues, their lewdness is 'contained in and by stories whose attitudes to life and work were irreproachable', and they handle 'sex as escape valve rather than prescribed lifestyle'.[18] The films thus celebrate the absurdity of juxtaposing the most 'adult' of activities with the most childlike of individuals.

In the musical number 'I'm Going to Stick to my Mother', Formby sings of the special bond between mother and son, and of the wisdom of eschewing sexual temptation in the form of 'bits of skirt who bite your ear'. Later, Formby professes to be tempted with a young woman (played by his real-life wife, Beryl) at a naturist club, and plaintively announces: 'Mother, I'm slipping'. In the film's finale, where Beryl proposes marriage, he withdraws symbolically into awkward adolescence, refusing via the song 'With My Little Ukulele in My Hand':

> Some like to mix it with a crowd, some like to be alone
> It's no-one else's business, as far as I can see

> But every time that I go out the people stare at me
> With my little ukulele in my hand.

The song is a blatant, doubly-coded paean to male masturbation (which is comically exulted in preference to the dubious pleasures of married life) taken to farcical extremes when Formby sings of being a public spectacle while clutching his phallic ukulele. For grown-ups, the outrageous suggestiveness of the lyrics is inescapable, while for older children, songs such as this and 'With My Little Stick of Blackpool Rock' tap a prevalent mode of knowing schoolboy humour, in which almost any joke derived from 'secret' bodily functions, however banal, is a source of indulgent snickering.

In *No Limit*, the aimless farce and fruity antics of *Off the Dole* are displaced by a more wholesome storyline concerning George's attempts to win the Isle of Man TT motorcycle race. George's unblunted enthusiasm for speed and visceral excitement play up his boundlessly enthusiastic, overgrown schoolboy persona, as would Hay's ode to the boyish pleasures of steam trains in *Oh, Mr Porter!* The initial impetus for George entering the prestigious race is provided by a gang of children in his native Wigan, who mercilessly tease him about his unrealised ambition to be a racer. George is far more 'childlike' than these knowing, cynical children. Still living at home with his mother and grandfather, his naïve, inarticulate reactions are those of a young person leaving the nest for the first time. George later engages in an inept fistfight reminiscent of a clumsy playground skirmish with the caddish Tyldesley (Jack Hobbs). Socking Tyldesley on the jaw, with a hitherto unseen assertiveness, imbues him with the confidence to win the race. This act represents George's individuation; he is no longer an overgrown boy, but rather a grown man – albeit one preternaturally in touch with his 'inner child'.

The presence of children in *No Limit*, and of young Jimmy Clitheroe in Formby's *Much too Shy* (Marcel Varnel, 1942), is aberrant within the broader tradition of British comedian comedies. Children are destabilising forces within narratives predicated on symbolic child figures, in which childhood is manifested as comic disruption. Biological definitions of childhood assume less importance than its symbolic potentiality as the quintessence of anarchic freedom. Hay's films are the major exception. In his most familiar guise as a nefarious schoolmaster, and in his non-school films partnering Graham Moffatt, Hay walks the line between aged child desperately maintaining the pretence of responsible adult, and blustering, incompetent grown-up persistently outmanoeuvred by young people cleverer than himself. Although not devoid of slapstick, Hay's films rely more on wordplay, and his protagonists get by less on their wits than through a form of obfuscating waffle that disorientates potential adversaries. A singular point of attraction for child audiences is Hay's frequent descent into nonsense wordplay. In *Boys will be Boys* (William Beaudine, 1935), his schoolmaster leads the chair of the school's board of governors into his office, where they encounter the words 'Smart Alec is a gump' written in chalk on the door. Unfamiliar with the word, the governor asks Smart for an explanation; he replies: 'Gump is er... Let me see now. It's from the Latin. No, the Greek. It's, er, gump, gumpus, gumpi, gumpolium, gumpolio, gumpiffle. Erm, first person singular. It means a friend in need'. Hay's films routinely present the spectacle of adult authority undermined and satirised by young people. It is not simply the *presence* of children that is most notable, but also their agency, competence and propensity to win the day despite inhabiting a subordinate social position.

Boys will be Boys is a composite of Hay's 'Scholars' variety act, centring on an inept schoolmaster, and the 'Narkover' sketches by J. B. Morton (aka 'Beachcomber') in the *Daily Express*'s humorous 'By the Way' column. As the genteel but thoroughly disreputable Dr Alec Smart, Hay gains employment as headmaster at prestigious boys' school, Narkover, by forging his credentials, and then embarks on a seemingly endless series of blunders. Yet Smart is as much a victim as perpetrator. Upon arrival at the school, his welcome mat is tied to the tow-ring of his taxi, which then pulls away. He is then hoisted above the heads of a group of boys, who sing a cheerfully open declaration of war as they lead him away:

> We are the boys who soon will be
> Known to the dear old CID
> Up the old Narkovians, timple timple pah.

This is ironically counterpointed by the official school anthem, which runs:

> We're so refined and gentle, you can see that by our looks
> We learn a lot of things in school we never read in books

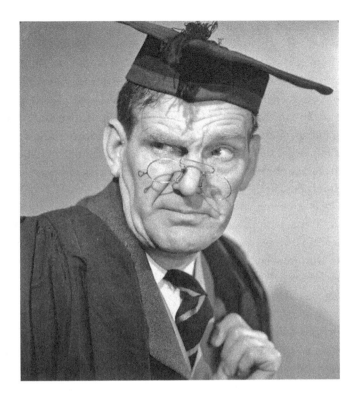

Image 3.1 Will Hay, in his most famous guise as a comically corrupt schoolmaster

We love our masters, every one, in fact for them we'll die
So every time we get the cane we all begin to cry.

Comparisons between Hay's school films and the later, better-remembered *St. Trinian's* cycle are inevitable, but misplaced. The feral, unblunted girls of St. Trinian's represent a symbolic atavism more than deliberate repudiation of civilised behavioural codes. Smart's boys are consciously and self-avowedly unprincipled. Their desires are shaped by knowledge of adult vices – gambling, drinking, and forms of career criminality, such as forgery. Furthermore, their actions are licensed by sure knowledge of their exalted social standing, with future university study furthering those credentials, before finally taking their place in some high office of society. An important corollary of these distinctions is that the St. Trinian's girls clearly belong to a Saturnalian world where codes, ethics and roles are turned upside-down for comic effect – a variation on Bakhtin's medieval carnival. The boys of Hay's films, though exaggerated, are more plausibly young men on the make. Sensing weakness (as young people tend to do) in their ultimate authority figure, they take advantage. In one scene, Smart is hit on the back of the head by a projectile from a sling-shot. He demands that the culprit stand up, intent on giving him a thrashing, but when the boy proves considerably larger than himself, Smart instead cuffs a much smaller boy! Ironic treatment of real-world power structures is a constant presence in Hay's school comedies.

In *Good Morning, Boys*, Dr Alec Smart is substituted with Dr Benjamin Twist, though audiences would be hard-pressed to see much difference in Hay's persona. The pupils here are more blatantly the off-spring of working-class spivs, ruffians and jailbirds. There is far greater collusion between Dr Twist and his boys; a sense of interdependency stemming from their mutually precarious positions. Twist is under threat of dismissal after the new chairman of the board of governors finds him and his pupils to be incompetent. Twist's pupils bail him out of trouble on several occasions, although they are hardly motivated by loyalty; rather, they enjoy unmitigated freedom under the present regime. They rig an inter-school exam in his favour, safeguarding his job, wade into a bar-room brawl to defend him, and finally help him expose the criminals responsible for stealing the Mona Lisa. But self-interest finally wins out: Twist ensures that the 50,000 Francs reward for returning the painting to the French government goes to himself, rather than to his boys. Unaware of his subterfuge, they hoist him up over their shoulders and lead him out, in celebration.

Hay's seemingly rigid sense of morality and decorum is always easily compromised. In *The Ghost of St. Michael's* (Varnel, 1941), he finds a group of boys eating lobsters and drinking whiskey in their dormitory late at night, and threatens to report them, before being persuaded to join them in the feast. Before long, a drunken Hay is holding court, singing and dancing to the delight of the assembled party. On such occasions, he and his boys affect a good-natured camaraderie. Charles Hawtrey's oleaginous schoolboy, Thorne, actually takes his place in a triumvirate as one of Hay's two comic foils (the other being Claude Hulbert's plummy,

Family Entertainers: Formby, Hay, Lucan, Wisdom

dim-witted Tisdaile), replacing his Gainsborough co-stars Marriott and Moffatt. Thorne and his fellows in the upper-fifth form actively defend Hay in court when he is under suspicion of murder, having realised that he is too buffoonish to have committed the offence; when he is dismissed from his post (due to rank incompetence) they have a whip-round and present him with £5; and later they save his life when he is nearly killed by a booby trap. By this point, the boys have become more like the brave, resourceful, faintly rebellious but essentially good-natured young protagonists of the *Just William* films (1940–49). This sense of children engaging, however precariously, on level terms with adults is a rarity in family films of the period. More conventional representations of the child prevailed, whether as innocent archetype, as in Hazel Ascott's and Binkie Stuart's vehicles, as a defenceless victim, as in Hitchcock's *Sabotage* (1936), or as attractive exotic, as with Sabu.

The genius of Hay's schoolmaster persona lies in the disjuncture between his surface persona of an upstanding member of society, a competent educator and a strict disciplinarian, and his real identity as a disreputable, cowardly charlatan. In every film, he manages barely to safeguard his ever-tenuous hold on his job with an endless litany of obfuscating verbiage. With echoes of Groucho Marx and Margaret Dumont, Hay manages in *Good Morning, Boys* to pull the wool over the eyes of an influential dowager impressed by his fraudulent air of knowledgeability, but who misses the tell-tale darting eyes and worried asides that reveal to the audience his precarious position. His schoolboys instantly see through such facade, revealing a truth, wilfully hidden to most children (taught to respect adult authority), that such power relations are often based on tenuous projections of hierarchy. This realisation is empowering to Twist's schoolboys, and doubtless vicariously for many child audiences. Yet ultimately the objection is less to the buffoonish schoolmaster than to the strict authoritarianism he appears to represent. In reality, Hay is nothing more than a child in a man's body. His blustering attempts to extricate himself from trouble, his transparent chicanery to obscure his ignorance, and his apparent asexuality (he squirms in discomfort when sung to suggestively in a nocturnal Parisian dance hall, and then misunderstands when the singer asks whether he has had any women in his life) all suggest a man who has never grown up.

Like many relics of music hall theatre, Old Mother Riley was built on broad farce, slapstick, wordplay and a range of comedic incongruities, such as the risibility of Lucan's masquerade and the deliberate tensions between the elderly persona and the bawdy happenings. But the main point of attraction for contemporary audiences was the sight of a man in drag. As with several other variety acts who graduated to the big screen, Lucan actively courted the 'family audience'. He and McShane continued to perform their act on stage, in pantomime around the Christmas period, and to national audiences on BBC radio. The series' central character dynamic is between Lucan's Mother Riley and McShane's Kitty, first seen on screen in a version of the duo's acclaimed theatrical sketch, 'Bridget's Night Out', featured in the revue film *Stars on Parade* (Oswald Mitchell and Challis Sanderson, 1936). Lucan here produces a bravura performance of verbal dexterity and loose-limbed clowning. It sees Mother Riley at home awaiting the return of her daughter from a night out. Her alternately concerned, self-pitying and contemptuous musings as to what her daughter is doing are accompanied by Lucan's trademark slapstick clowning, as he jumps manically around the small set like an acrobat.

The second half of the sketch follows Bridget's/McShane's return, and reveals their paradoxical fractious intimacy. Mother Riley angrily turns on her daughter for staying out late (until 3am) insisting that she knows 'from experience' that young women who remain out so late are 'up to no good'. The finale, in which Mother Riley outrageously manipulates Bridget into submission by intentionally arousing pity, is also typical of the subsequent series, invoking the primacy of family ties and the supreme authority of the parent, while evoking sympathy for McShane's daughter. As with Galton and Simpson's father–son dynamic in *Steptoe and Son* (1962–74), elderly parent and grown child are inextricably bound together by a corrosive interdependency. The mother–daughter relationship is softened in later films, but the possibility of antagonism is forever present. The relationship remains stultifying, necessitating the exclusion of all outsiders, an arrangement imposed and maintained largely by the parent. As with Wilfrid Brambell's Albert Steptoe, Mother Riley's trump card is a crippling emotional blackmail deployed when the relationship is felt to be in jeopardy, as it is on several occasions by the attentions of a possible husband for McShane.

Roughly contemporary studies of children's film preferences showed that children tended to feel protective towards elderly characters, associating them with kindly solicitude. Surely this cannot be the case with Mother Riley; patronising overtures of protectiveness would most likely be met with a threatening bony fist in the face. The child appeal rests largely on the comic subversions inherent in the character. Mother Riley is clearly a man in disguise; men dressed as women are grotesquely funny; old women dancing like a marionette and threatening to thump grown men are outrageous. But she is also an aspirational figure in two key regards. Firstly, like children, Mother Riley appears vulnerable and infirm, but always, like the boy heroes of *Emil and the Detectives* (Milton Rosmer, 1935) and *Hue and Cry* (Charles Crichton, 1947), overcomes her obvious physical disadvantages. Secondly, her crudeness, demotic speech, brazenness, lack of refinement and contempt for authority are essentially childlike. They suggest a rejection of adult codes of conduct rather than a complete ignorance of them – more a symbolic regression to childhood (recalling the senility of the last of Shakespeare's Seven Ages of Man) than a 'kidult' refusal to grow up. But such attributes nonetheless appeal to the child's latent/repressed predilection for the anarchism that the socialisation process – the moral and behavioural instruction provided at home, church and school – seeks to eradicate. For Freud, such repression is essential for an ordered society. Comic non-conformities like Old Mother Riley appeal to whatever part of the child and the successfully socialised adult that rebels against such enforced repression.

Populism and National Identity

Formby's and Lucan's vehicles, in particular, were perhaps the prototypical embodiment of an indigenous family entertainment that drew almost exclusively on British customs, idioms and social structures. Their films were intended solely for the home market, and – like those of Hay, Askey and later Wisdom – failed to translate to North America. In 1941, Formby moved to Hollywood studio Columbia on a lucrative contract, but still could not obtain a North American release for his films. Indeed, Formby never performed in the United States (though he did tour other English-speaking nations, such as Australia, New Zealand, Canada and

South Africa). Richard Gordon later recalled a disastrous showing of *Old Mother Riley's New Venture* (John Harlow, 1949) at New York's 55th Street Playhouse, and apparently US distributor Eliot Hyman allowed his option on *Old Mother Riley Meets the Vampire* (John Gilling, 1952) to lapse without any bookings stateside.[19] This is emblematic of what would become a familiarly non-reciprocal pattern of cultural exchange, in which the purposely less culturally-specific Hollywood family film – encompassing prestige literary adaptations, child-star films, series and serials – crossed freely to the British market, but British family films remained almost completely unknown in the United States.

Like music hall prior to its late-period gentrification, 1930s British cinema was a quintessentially working-class amusement. In Lucan's hands, Mother Riley becomes, as Richards notes, 'the inextinguishable life force of the slums, a veritable Brünnhilde of the backstreets', her combativeness 'an outward and visible sign of her refusal to be cowed or to conform'.[20] As the series developed, she was constituted increasingly as a sort of folk hero. In *Old Mother Riley in Paris* (Oswald Mitchell, 1938), she unwittingly brings a spy to the attention of the French authorities and is decorated for the deed. In *Old Mother Riley, MP* (Oswald Mitchell, 1939), she stands for Parliament in opposition to the plans of a corrupt local politician intending to demolish her house, is elected to the House of Commons and eventually rises to Cabinet level (as Minister for Strange Affairs). In *Old Mother Riley Joins Up* (Maclean Rogers, 1940), she enlists, albeit initially reluctantly, in the Territorial Army, and foils the plans of a gang of Nazi spies. And in *Old Mother Riley in Business* (John Baxter, 1940), she takes on an aggressive national chain, defending local small business owners (the 'little people') in the process.

Many of these films evince a strong localism, in opposition to the homogenised, London-centred image of the nation often represented in 'British' films. Formby, Lucan, Askey and Fields, in particular, were unashamedly Northern personalities, and their following in the provinces was especially large. In a 1944 report, 'The Film and Family Life', a Mass Observation researcher suggested that: 'Old Mother Riley is the biggest money-maker of all British films. In some parts of England cinemas that nothing else can fill are packed to the doors by Old Mother Riley'.[21] During World War II, though, these comedians' vehicles erected a united front of

Image 3.2 Mother Riley (Arthur Lucan) holds court in *Old Mother Riley MP* (1939)

a Britain pulling together in adversity, with regional differences temporarily put aside. In Hay's *The Ghost of St. Michael's* and Askey's *The Ghost Train* (Walter Forde, 1941), perfunctory anti-Nazi plots are tacked on to the end. In other cases, such as Hay's *The Goose Steps Out* (Will Hay and Basil Dearden, 1942), the propaganda element is more central and conveyed with greater seriousness. Discovering that he is the spitting image of a German spy, Hay does his bit by infiltrating Nazi Germany to recover the blueprints for a secret weapon. Formby, however, was the film comedian most fitted to the British cinema's war effort. His facile optimism, courage, indefatigability and spirit of consensus were perfect attributes to galvanise the beleaguered movie-going public, and to enlist a new generation of British citizens to the war effort.

Formby and his films matured a little during the war, a fact recognised by the *Manchester Guardian* in 1944 when they described him as 'our first authentic and strictly indigenous film comedian'.[22] In *Bell-Bottom George*

(Varnel, 1944), the main thrust of the narrative is Formby's obsessive desire to enlist in the Royal Navy. He remains predictably befuddled by a world populated by rules, codes and conventions of which he has little understanding, but a strong, newfound sense of patriotic duty asserts itself. In the musical number 'Swim Little Fish', Formby sings to his goldfish:

> Everything worthwhile in life is hard to get, my friend
> So don't give up and don't give in, it's worthwhile in the end...
> Always remember mother's good advice
> Steer clear of fishes who are not quite nice
> Do nothing fishy, fishy, swim, swim, swim.

The song addresses an imagined young listener with simple homilies on the virtues of perseverance, the correctness of self-advancement (particularly in the service of the nation), and, crucially, deference to authority, localised here in the mother figure, but which may be extended to the symbolic parent that is the state.

Formby is more symbolic teenager than symbolic child in *Bell-Bottom George*. He actively pursues the attractive Wren Pat (Anne Firth), coyly informing her – via the song 'If I Had a Girl Like You' – of his romantic ardour. Through this union, the film posits a future of marriage and children, imagining a victorious postwar Britain repopulating itself, with the concomitant transmission of British values to the next generation. Formby, and the audience, are still allowed many individual moments of frivolous indulgence, but they occur within a script that reminds spectators that the stakes are higher, with its story of two German spies attempting to send confidential information back to Nazi Germany. In the postwar years, British comedy reverted to the mild pre-war anti-authoritarianism, with the *St. Trinian's* films, in particular, portraying the establishment as populated by buffoons, stuffed shirts and bureaucrats. In contrast, the Royal Navy in *Bell-Bottom George* is crewed by salty but honest rank-and-file, governed by unimpeachable old boys. Moreover, Formby's eagerness to join the British forces and stand against the common enemy undoubtedly serves didactic functions. Just as youth organisations such as the Scout Movement and the Boys' Brigade prepared new generations of boys and young men for future service in the Armed Forces, so these wartime

Self-Parody and the Child Audience

The early-to-mid 1940s was nonetheless a period of artistic and commercial decline for these comedians. As their box office value waned, Hay and Formby drifted out of the industry altogether, while Lucan's Mother Riley laboured into the 1950s in a seemingly endless series of self-parodies, relying ever-increasingly on the indulgence of children's matinee attendees. *Old Mother Riley's Ghosts* (John Baxter, 1941) attempts to hold the series' two dominant tendencies – mild political commentary and farce – in balance, with its parallel plot of an unscrupulous executive of an engineering firm, Warrender (A. Bromley Davenport), attempting to con its owner out of a valuable patent, and the spooky shenanigans that ensue when Mother Riley inherits and takes possession of a supposedly haunted Scottish castle. These separate storylines intersect in the final act, when it transpires that the castle inheritance was a ruse to isolate Mother Riley and John Cartwright (John Stuart), son of the engineering firm's owner and inventor of the patent, in order to gain possession of it. When Mother Riley single-handedly overcomes their assailants, they are able to discredit the nefarious Warrender.

The castle section gives free rein to the series' more juvenile aspects, with its ghost sequences reminiscent of the spook house at the fairground, and a surfeit of comic violence as Mother Riley overcomes the baddies through various slapstick mechanisms. The film also foreshadows the series' subsequent tendency to self-parody, as one of the bad guys – played by Lucan himself – is asked to impersonate Mother Riley by donning a wig and women's clothes! Ironically, the disguise is a failure. The last Mother Riley film directed by the talented John Baxter, it marks a point of transition in the series. The issues of class and power that inflect the early films give way to a more farcical, child-orientated mode marked by increasingly outrageous storylines, lack of internal logic, less focus on the initially central mother–daughter relationship, and greater action and horseplay.

These inflections reach their fullest extension in the final instalment in the series, the notorious *Old Mother Riley Meets the Vampire*. The film is best remembered for Bela Lugosi's starring role as a mad scientist, in a piece of stunt casting intended, belatedly, to launch the series in the US, where it bombed. As in *Abbott and Costello Meet Frankenstein* (Charles Barton, 1948), Lugosi's presence strengthens the film's appeal to children, for whom Universal's 1930s horror films were highly popular. It is one of the best-remembered Mother Riley productions, though old age and alcoholism have visibly sapped Lucan's physical and verbal dexterity. Furthermore, the plot of a mad scientist who believes himself to be a vampire, and plans to take over the world with an army of uranium-powered robots is pure B movie schlock, closer in spirit to teen sci-fi exploitation than to music hall class commentary. The emphasis has decisively shifted from character to situation-based humour. The mad scientist/haunted house tropes, the mildly spooky high-jinks of the *Scooby-Doo* variety, and the speeded-up action sequences accompanied by parping comedy music, reaffirm what theatre managers up and down the land had known for several years: that the series was now primarily for children.

Norman Wisdom's emergence as Britain's leading film comedian of the 1950s and 1960s can be viewed either as a continuation of the form's descent into formulaic self-parody or as proof of its commercial reinvigoration. His screen debut, *Trouble in Store* (John Paddy Carstairs, 1953), was the second highest-grossing film at the 1954 British box office, behind *Doctor in the House* (Ralph Thomas, 1954) and ahead of *The Belles of St. Trinian's* (Frank Launder, 1954).[24] The success of all three films confirmed that comedy was again in the ascendancy, but Wisdom's vehicle is more child-friendly than the others which, in their adolescent innuendo, anticipate the more sexually-explicit British screen comedies of the 1970s. Wisdom stars as Norman, an incompetent department store stock clerk. His comic bungling and his chaste infatuation with colleague Sally (Lana Morris) are primary story elements, but Margaret Rutherford, who shares top billing, takes emphasis away from the nominal star with a scene-stealing cameo as a genteel, elderly kleptomaniac. The ending sees Norman foil an audacious robbery and, having been sacked, be reinstated by the manager, Freeman (Jerry Desmonde). However, he unwittingly sends Freeman plummeting down an empty lift shaft. Freeman, desperately holding on to the lift rope, tells Norman that he is once more dismissed. Norman turns diffidently to Sally and exclaims, 'You know what, Sally? I've got the sack again!' Both erupt into hysterical laughter and turn to camera as the credits roll, in characteristic British determination to accept defeat with good humour. The reaction embodies ironic delight in the slings and arrows of outrageous fortune, and an exhortation to austerity Britain to 'keep your pecker up'.

Discussing Wisdom's films in terms of their contemporary appeal to children is more troublesome than with Hay, Lucan or Formby, all of whom figured prominently in children's comics and rated highly in surveys of children's film tastes. Nevertheless, anecdotal recollection, contemporary ratings and reviews, programming for children's matinees, and the frequency and scheduling of television broadcasts, all reflect his substantial popularity among children. This appeal derives from a combination of Wisdom's filmic persona (innocent; kindly; childlike; vulnerable; working-class everyman) and his films' simple aesthetic, heavily reliant on slapstick and visual puns. His films merrily recycle old gags and comic set-pieces, most blatantly in Wisdom's inferior rehearsal in *The Square Peg* (John Paddy Carstairs, 1959) of the Marx Brothers' mirror gag from *Duck Soup* (Leo

Image 3.3 Norman Wisdom in his 'Gimp' persona

McCarey, 1933). For many viewers, such borrowings may evoke pleasing recollections of the original, although their presence also reflects the fact that few children would be familiar with them in their original form. These slapstick mechanisms are juxtaposed with Chaplinesque pathos. In *Trouble in Store*, Norman sings:

> I'm not good looking, I'm not too smart
> I may be foolish, but I've got a heart
> I love the flowers, I love the sun
> But when I try to love the girls, they laugh at me and run
> Don't laugh at me 'cause I'm a fool
> I know it's true that I'm a fool
> No-one seems to care
> I'd give the world to share my life with someone who really loves me.

Wisdom, like Formby, is an underdog, and his persecution at the hands of social superiors (often portrayed by the patrician Jerry Desmonde) serves to deepen identification in children, for whom, we might surmise, his misfortunes and natural disadvantages can be related to their own lowly social standing.

However, the prominence of the romantic plot in *Trouble in Store* suggests that the needs of adult spectators assume greater importance than in Formby's, Handley's and Lucan's later films. Studies revealed that preadolescent children had little interest in screen romance. Unlike Mickey Rooney's Andy Hardy, another randy, under-sized man-child who somehow gets the girl, Norman overtly appeals to the sympathies and maternal instincts of his objects of affection. His rapid oscillations between uninhibited laughter and tomfoolery, and sad, puppy-dog-eyed plaintiveness, are calculated to evoke protectiveness. This sympathetic mothering instinct turns to romantic attachment, albeit subject to comic treatment. In one scene, Norman begins eating a bowl of ice cream with an oversized soup spoon. Sally frowns and shakes her head, unobtrusively. Norman responds, circumspectly picking up a more appropriate desert spoon, looks to Sally for approval, and she nods her head with a smile. Norman then greedily digs into his ice cream, but unwittingly projects it on to the exposed chest of an elderly woman sitting beside him. Ignoring Sally's shocked exclamation, he proceeds to spoon the ice cream out of her bosom crevice and back into his bowl. The joke is that of licentious transgression of social norms, but the secondary implication is that of socialising a child yet to learn (adult) codes of decorum. The fact that, despite all social convention, Sally accepts Norman as a romantic partner represents an extension of the victory of the underdog metanarrative that recurs throughout the wider tradition of British film comedy.

While Wisdom's films constitute a resumption of the British comedian comedy after the decline of the late 1940s, they also break from it in two key regards. Firstly, story, setting, and character all assume greater importance. As Margaret Rutherford's appearances in *Trouble in Store* suggests, these films are not *just* vehicles for Wisdom to express his comedic talents. Indeed, the *MFB* observed that the 'major weakness' of Wisdom 'gump' stage act is 'its dependence on a first-rate script, which he lacks in this film'.[25] Story was often perfunctory in Hay's, Formby's and Lucan's vehicles, but their magnetic screen personae were the vital element in their appeal. In contrast, in Wisdom's vehicles, his basic presence alone is insufficient. Indeed, the *Times* remarked that: 'Mr Wisdom relies more on grotesque appearance and manufactured situation than inner inspiration'.[26] This reliance on non-performative elements might reflect Wisdom's limitations as a screen actor, but is also framed by a progressive shift away from the Formby style of comedian comedy to the more situation-comedy and ensemble mode of the *Doctor in the House* (1954–70) and *Carry On* (1958–72) series.

Secondly, Wisdom's films often position him outside the quintessentially British/English milieu inhabited by Hay and Formby. The *Manchester Guardian* observed that Wisdom's debut 'owes little to "Punch", Dickens, Ealing, or the village green [and] is far more reminiscent of the early Chaplin and perhaps of the Marx Brothers'.[27] This Hollywood slapstick mode largely eschews the culturally-English and working-class humour and demotic speech patterns of Formby and Askey. Admittedly, Wisdom strongly embodies the 'little man' coming out on top, but the adversarial dimension of Lucan's films is largely absent. He is psychologically rooted in permanent childhood (or premature senescence), a victim of a cruel world populated by unscrupulous grown-ups. But unlike Mother Riley, he does not possess the skills to fight back. Insofar as his films contain political commentary (which is largely confined to the David vs. Goliath metanarrative), Wisdom has little interest in it. He is, perhaps, a clown in the purest sense, with neither the comedian nor his characters driven by much beyond an overriding impulse towards clean, honest fun. This image had its strong admirers. In 1955, the *Catholic Herald*'s Grace Conway ventured that: 'Norman Wisdom in three films has become Britain's greatest film treasure. There may be a few folk whom his particular type of clowning leaves cold, but he has the common denominator of appeal which is acceptable to the majority'.[28] Whereas Formby, Lucan, Gracie Fields and Arthur Askey were largely defined by their regionalism, Wisdom lacks strong socio-geographic specificity, his cockney accent notwithstanding. He was, perhaps, the supreme embodiment of postwar consensus culture.

By the time *The Early Bird* (Robert Asher, 1965) was released, British cinema and society had changed (and was continuing to change) in profound ways. The film reveals the tensions between the need to innovate and to reflect new socio-cultural norms while remaining true to the essential innocence of the Wisdom persona. It dispenses with the preposterous romantic subplot, perhaps acknowledging that films in which Wisdom did *not* get the girl – as in *The Square Peg*, where Honor Blackman repels his advances – were emotionally unrewarding, and the alternative, given Sally's maternal obligations in *Trouble in Store*, were downright anachronistic. Why would intelligent, sophisticated women keep falling for Wisdom, unless they secretly yearned for a life of domesticity mothering a buffoonish man-child? *The Early Bird* articulates changing attitudes to sex and gender norms in other ways. Norman's boss, Mr Grimsdale (Edward Chapman), is having a supposedly covert (actually blatant) affair with his frumpish landlady, Mrs Hopkins (Paddie O'Neil), to his underling's obvious disapproval, until Grimsdale redeems himself in Norman's eyes by proposing marriage. In another scene, their business rival, Mr Hunter (Jerry Desmonde), is seen taking his secretary into a vault in his office to engage in surreptitious liaisons. And when Norman rings the family doctor to seek advice on how to treat the firm's sick horse, the doctor is seen living it large at a party, two girls waiting on his arm.

These sequences represent concessions to the incursion of a new, more permissive set of attitudes into a society that still adhered, outwardly, to 'family values'. Codes of decency still exist – hence the taboo attached to their violation – even as they are broken in this film with increasing regularity. Cynicism, hypocrisy, indecency and cruelty operate here under a thin veil of order and respectability, with Wisdom a lone representative of an imagined lost era of moral and sexual purity. As the only childlike figure in a world of adults pursuing the pleasure principle, Wisdom, more than ever, is a symbolic child. Yet he is also an agent for stability and conservatism rather than anarchism, fighting against the abandonment by stealth of highly-prized values of restraint (from sexual or narcotic excess). By the 1960s, the 'family audience' in Britain remained a potent symbolic presence, but how cinema could successfully address (or reconstruct) such an audience was far from clear.

For the most part, Wisdom's protagonists appear ignorant of such age-restricted 'adult' behaviours as sexual promiscuity and drug abuse (as appear to be taking place at the doctor's party in *The Early Bird*). When he becomes aware of Grimsdale's extra-marital affair with his landlady, he is incensed. Perhaps it is a reflection of the decline of the comedian comedy, and its impending obsolescence, that the licensed disorder of the music hall is supplanted by reactionary appeals to decency and decorum. By the same token, 'carnival' – a suspension of normative rules of social engagement – becomes redundant when it is no longer distinguishable from everyday life. Wisdom remained popular into the late 1960s, but his films were increasingly ghettoised to the Christmas period, meeting expectations for festive frivolity and wholesomely regulated comic anarchism. The moviegoing public surely would not have countenanced a further mutation of Wisdom's formula to accommodate sex and skin, as the *Carry On* films adopted to survive the 1960s; nor would Wisdom, who remained unfashionably committed to family entertainment. The early British comedian comedies were made when British film comedy was assuredly for 'the whole family'; when the phenomenally popular Max Miller failed to equal the big-screen success of his music hall contemporaries because his material was too 'blue'; and when the BBC, acting on its paternalistic responsibilities as an arbiter of national morality and family values, banned 'With My Little Stick of Blackpool Rock'. Children are a rarely mentioned but undeniable presence in relation to these films. Moreover, their interests are vital to the wider questions of taste and decency, consensus, and national unity that lay at the heart of the comedian comedy.

4

J. Arthur Rank, Saturday Morning Cinema and the Children's Film Foundation

This chapter explores the evolution of Britain's tradition of films produced for children's matinee audiences between the 1940s and 1980s. The importance of this cycle of films, in relation to those examined in Chapters 2 and 3, is twofold. Firstly, the productions of J. Arthur Rank's Children's Entertainment Films (CEF) between 1944 and 1950, and its state-backed successor, the Children's Film Foundation (CFF), from 1951 to 1985, were entirely non-commercial. Secondly, CEF and CFF releases were produced *exclusively* for children's matinee audiences. As such, they are children's films in the truest sense, rather than the family films intended for mixed audiences of children and adults that comprise the majority of films discussed in this book.

1930s Children's Film Culture

These films must be interpreted within a wider context where, as Sarah J. Smith observes, 'children's cinema-going experiences overlapped with those of adults'.[1] Admittedly, the proportion of explicitly 'adult' films had declined from their post-sound peak of 1930–34, when the *Daily Mail* remarked that 'family filmgoers' were being kept 'out in the cold'.[2] 'A'-rated features had risen from 43 per cent in 1930 to 63 per cent in 1933, but

80

declined to around 50 per cent by 1936 and 1937.[3] In his 1935 report, BBFC president Lord Tyrrell claimed that 'horrific' films were a thing of a past, and the following year he ventured that: 'The cinema is undoubtedly the cleanest form of entertainment in this country to-day'.[4] However, as William Farr pointed out, 'the best that can be said of most "U" films is that they are not unsuitable for children'; 'what are wanted are films positively suitable'.[5] 'There is ample evidence', wrote Home Office Under Secretary S. W. Harris in 1935, 'that the average cinema does not provide adequately for the needs of children, and that the best solution of what is really an urgent question lies in the production of special films for children'.[6] However, as exhibitor Richard Ford observed, such films 'at present and for many years to come can only be a theoretical objective'.[7] Ford believed that the alternative of the 'special cinema for children' was similarly 'impossible to establish' due to its economic non-viability.[8] This left only one solution: the provision of children's matinees in standard movie theatres.

As Ford explains, these were 'held on Saturday – nearly always on Saturday morning – because the Elementary Schools are not open, and because the cinema is not usually open for normal performances until after midday'.[9] Saturday morning cinema was a British cultural institution between the 1930s and 1970s. Children's matinees were held as early as the 1910s, but most were either non-commercial or unprofitable, like Sidney Bernstein's much-vaunted 1928–29 Granada programme. During the early 1930s, H. B. Woolfe's British Instructional Films, in conjunction with the ABC chain, ran a series of matinees, initially in four London theatres and subsequently in Birmingham, Norwich and Yarmouth.[10] The programme comprised a mixture of documentary and fiction films (silent movies as well as talkies), with M. Locket, British Instructional's Education Manager, claiming that British children generally disliked sound films but appreciated the commentary in instructional and documentary productions.[11] By early 1932, approximately 10,000 children were attending these programmes, and in 1934, the Children's Film Society began a long-running programme of matinees at the Everyman Cinema in Hampstead.[12]

However, matinees were not yet a way of life for British youth. The British Instructional and Children's Film Society programmes were characteristic of a specific trend in early-1930s British matinees. They were partly commercial, but relied on the support of voluntary local organisations, and as William Farr observed in *Sight and Sound*, tended to contain 'a large proportion of general interest and even instructional films, and apart from cartoons, very few fictional films, an unbalanced diet on which survival is doubtful'.[13] Purely commercial programmes, as were undertaken by independent theatres during the 1910s and 1920s, declined after the coming of sound.[14] Furthermore, as a *Sight and Sound* editorial lamented, not only was the quantity of children's matinees 'negligible in comparison with the number of children to be catered for', but there was consensus that programming – drawing heavily on Hollywood westerns, serials and slapstick comedy two-reelers – was unsatisfactory.[15] At the 1936 meeting of the Child Welfare Commission of the League of Nations in Geneva, it was claimed that 'Nothing but the best is good enough' for child audiences.[16] Yet it was estimated that out of 4,500 movie theatres nationally, only about 500 ran children's matinees.[17]

The fledgling British Film Institute (BFI), founded in 1933, took an active role in the development of children's film shows. Its publication, the *Monthly Film Bulletin*, offered information on the suitability of almost every theatrically-released film. Films were issued with one of four classifications: 'A' (suitable for adults only); 'B' (suitable for young people over the age of 16); 'C' (suitable for 'family audiences'); and 'D' (particularly suitable for children's matinees). As Ford observes, these categories offered cinema managers 'concrete advice, which the negative British Film Censorship [sic] fails to offer'.[18] Secondly, in November 1936 the BFI held a highly-publicised conference on Films for Children. Organised by William Farr, the conference was attended by prominent trade figures such as Sidney Bernstein, Simon Rowson and K. A. Nyman, child psychologist Emanuel Miller, Home Office official S. W. Harris, and representatives from over 100 educational, civic and religious bodies.[19] The most significant outcome was the BFI's publication of a list of short and feature films specifically recommended for children's matinees. Around 80 features were grouped into four categories: 'Adventure', 'Comedy', 'Western' and 'Story' films; these included Harold Lloyd, Jack Hulbert, Joe E. Brown, Buck Jones and Rin Tin Tin vehicles, as well as the British productions *Scrooge* (Henry Edwards, 1935), *Midshipman Easy* (Carol Reed, 1935) and *Tudor Rose* (Robert Stevenson, 1936).[20] 6,000 copies of this list, published in mid-1937, were distributed to licensing authorities, teachers, churches and exhibitors nationally.[21] Ford attributed the subsequent surge in the number of children's matinees to the success of the BFI's conference and its list of suitable films.[22]

The most significant change during the late 1930s was the 'matinee' evolving into the 'cinema club'. Oscar Deutsch's Odeon chain introduced cinema clubs to Britain with its Mickey Mouse Club, which began in Worthing in 1934 before rolling out nationwide in 1937. The films remained largely the same – a cocktail of westerns, comedy shorts, cartoons and serials. However, the Mickey Mouse Clubs pioneered an overtly didactic framework. Membership (as a 'Mickey' or 'Minnie') was free, but joining the club was mandatory, ostensibly to engender comradeship, but also to build brand loyalty. Secondly, as Deutsch proudly admitted: 'We don't only give them entertainment. We make a point of teaching them road safety and charity' and 'how to be good and independent citizens'.[23] Rival cinema chains established their own versions, including Granada with the Granadiers, ABC with the ABC Minors Clubs, and Gaumont with Shirley Temple or Popeye clubs. After Deutsch's death in 1941, the Odeon chain was acquired by J. Arthur Rank, a millionaire Yorkshireman whose family owned a chain of flour mills, and who recently had become a major industry figure with the purchase of Pinewood and Denham studios. In 1942, Rank also acquired the Gaumont chain, bringing the number of cinemas under his control to over 600. Having established the nation's largest cinema chain, Rank was to become the key figure in the development of specialised children's films.

J. Arthur Rank and Children's Entertainment Films

When the BFI's Oliver Bell pragmatically observed in 1938 that the production of purpose-made children's films in Britain was impossible, barring the intervention of the state or a 'multi-millionaire philanthropist', he could hardly have imagined that both scenarios would come to pass within a few short years.[24] J. Arthur Rank, according to Geoffrey Macnab, was 'driven in business by an unshakeable religious faith'; he was 'a scrupulous, paternal man', a staunch conservative who, prior to his entry to the industry in 1933, was largely uninterested in cinema.[25] In his paternalism, geniality and lack of ostentation, he was not a 'typical' film mogul, but by 1942, he was head of a film empire that comprised five studios, numerous production companies and almost 650 theatres. While Rank was sincerely motivated by the possibility of instilling 'good Christian values' in children, his entry to the world of children's cinema resulted from a chance exchange with the head of his Odeon cinema club, who had suggested incorporating a short film into the matinee programme to convey the idea that stealing was wrong.[26] When Rank was told that pictures that would 'do [children] good' currently did not exist, he replied: 'We must make some'.[27]

Rank's initial plan was to produce one ten-minute fiction film per week that would clearly articulate some moral principle. *Tom's Ride* (Darrell Catling, 1944), the first such film, centres on a schoolboy who finds a wallet full of money. Rather than use the money to buy the bike he desperately wants, he tracks down the rightful owner and returns the wallet. Production commenced in October 1943, and despite being hampered by the lack of suitable child actors – a consequence both of the wartime evacuation and legal restrictions of the employment of children under the age of 14 – the film was completed within three weeks, and released to Odeon and Gaumont cinema clubs.[28] Press and industry reaction was largely negative: it was felt that the story was too didactic, and the ending – in which Tom declines a cash gift from the wallet's owner, thus communicating the idea that virtue is its own reward – was unpopular among children.[29] Nonetheless, as Staples notes, it offered characters with whom children 'could identify on a social and urban context that was indisputably contemporary Britain'.[30]

Rank, not wholly satisfied with the initial film but convinced of the importance of the larger initiative, approached Mary Field – an employee of British Instructional Films – to head the newly-created Children's Film Department (CFD). Field determined that Rank's initial plan for a ten-minute fable per week was impracticable, and that a more diverse range of films was required, including documentary shorts, cartoons, serials and feature-length productions. As Field explained, 'all our films would have a documentary background, while the moral was to be implied rather than underlined, though it was by no means to be abandoned', and the CFD programme for 1945 included 'short stories showing farming conditions, fruit picking, the English canals and Niagara Falls'.[31] Field established the National Advisory Council, an independent body headed by Lady Allen of Hurtwood, a known supporter of children's cinema, and representatives from the Ministry of Education, the Home Office, the Scottish Office, the BFI, the BBC, and numerous other interested lobbies and organisations of a moral, educational or religious bent.[32] Although Macnab alleges that the Advisory Council served to 'constipate' the creativity of the independent filmmakers who produced these films on the CFD's behalf, it afforded the veneer of legitimacy required to forestall those who mistrusted Rank's motivations. Indeed, critics routinely assumed that Rank's interest in children was purely mercenary, but in reality, the enterprise was a significant loss-maker for his organisation.[33]

Adults were generally absent from Saturday morning cinema, but the CFD arranged a special press showing of its films at Leicester Square Theatre in June 1945. The *Church Times* noted the slow place and narrative simplicity, but admitted that 'children need a much slower tempo on the screen than the adult', as they 'miss allusions, and prefer all details to be thoroughly explained'.[34] The *Manchester Guardian* and the *Scotsman* endorsed the principle of special films for children, even if they felt that the films themselves left much to be desired, but a writer for the *Documentary News Letter* attacked the 'snob morality' and questioned 'whether [the films] are not positively harmful'.[35] Michael Gareth Llewellyn averred that the films were reminiscent

> of the stories I used to get as Sunday School prizes when I was a boy. These books were too unctuous and self-conscious even then for my youthful stomach. I always sensed the moral pill in the sickly jam.[36]

Llewellyn added that: 'I am almost driven to the conclusion that entertainment films made only for children ought never to be made'.[37] The organisation continued to diversify. In early 1947, the CFD changed its name to Children's Entertainment Films (CEF). The previous year, it had released its first three-reel production, *Jean's Plan* (A. C. Hammond, 1946). CEF's first serial, *The Voyage of Peter Joe* (Harry Hughes, 1946), which comprised six two-reel episodes, followed soon after, but the *Manchester Guardian* echoed prior criticisms in noting that it 'stirs in a somewhat heavy moral'.[38] Conversely, as Arthur Vesselo pointed out in late 1947, underlining the impossibility of satisfying all parties, the CEF three-reeler, *The Little*

Ballerina (Lewis Gilbert, 1947), was 'criticised in some quarters for not being sufficiently adult in treatment, and in others for not being sufficiently instructional'.[39]

In July 1947, CEF released its first feature-length production, the 80-minute *Bush Christmas* (Ralph Smart, 1947). Filmed and set in Australia to circumvent Britain's restrictive child labour laws, it proved highly popular there, and was adapted into a novel and radio play, and serialised in children's magazines. As with the later Australian-set British children's film, *Smiley* (Anthony Kimmins, 1956), *Bush Christmas* draws on the pastoral tradition while emphasising the parallel associations of adventure promised by the Australian outback. For British children, it offers a slice of exoticism, but like all CEF films, is strongly moralistic. The four child protagonists encounter two horse thieves who give them money in return for promising not to reveal their presence in town. Later that night, another horse is stolen, and the children belatedly relate their encounter with the thieves to the family head, and local policeman, Mr Thompson (Pat Penny). Furious that the children were playing rather than at school, that they accepted money from strangers, and that their belated honesty has come too late to prevent another theft, he announces himself to be 'ashamed' of them. In Twain's *Tom Sawyer* (1876), the central children try to evade adult morality, but here, they are its representatives, working throughout to redress their initial misdemeanours by bringing the horse thieves to justice. The film functions as an extended endorsement of Rank's cinema club motto, with the policeman's final speech delivered straight to camera: 'It's not only the police you're up against when you break the law; it's the community. These kids have proved themselves to be good citizens'.

Sight and Sound thought *Bush Christmas* 'far better' than Ealing's *Hue and Cry* (Charles Crichton, 1947), adding that: 'If CEF films to follow are as good, they will be good enough'.[40] The *Times* called it 'an experiment in juvenile entertainment which is a complete success', and the *Sunday Times'* Dilys Powell included it in her 'films of the week'.[41] Mary Field and Edward Forsythe, inspector of the Odeon and Gaumont Clubs, also regarded it as one of their finest achievements, and it even received a wide release in Rank theatres' standard movie programmes nationwide.[42] But criticisms of CEF never really subsided. Arthur Vesselo believed that: 'There is something of a negative atmosphere about certain of these films; they are just a little colourless, a little lacking in imagination, in true creative force'.[43] The films were also under scrutiny for their political content, the *Daily Worker*'s Ella Jones cautioning that children's matinees 'should be watched very carefully [...] for propaganda against socialism'.[44] Such reservations paled into insignificance when compared to the fallout generated by J. P. Mayer's *Sociology of Film* (1946). Mayer, intent on conducting a serious sociological study of children's film experiences, spent approximately 20 Saturday mornings amongst children in Rank's Odeon and Gaumont theatres. His subsequent book took great issue with the programme's over-reliance on serials ('pernicious in their psychological effects'), violent films ('some of the children at such performances have been really frightened and horrified'), and the lyrics of the Odeon club song ('obtrusive moralising').[45] His emphatic conclusion was that: 'It is *impossible* to provide entertainment divorced from moral and psychological norms'.[46]

Perhaps even more damaging was Mayer's incendiary article in the *Times* in January 1946, where he argued that 'children under the age of seven should not go to the cinema at all', that 'the supply of films suitable for children is far from sufficient', that 'the new films so far produced are [...] unsatisfactory and insignificant', and that 'obtrusive moralising is abhorred by children'.[47] The Rank Organisation's John Davis swiftly responded to Mayer's criticisms, insisting that the CEF was not perpetrating an 'attempt at mass education in the Nazi manner', but simply offering 'healthy cinema entertainment for the young' intended to 'inculcate a spirit of good citizenship and help build character'.[48] Davis added that the Odeon Club Song was scarcely different from Scouts law or religious instruction in schools.[49] Nevertheless, Mayer generated sufficient alarm that, in November 1946, the House of Commons debated the desirability of children's cinema clubs.[50] In July 1947, after sustained pressure from local authorities and educative bodies, the Attlee government appointed the Wheare Committee, headed by K. C. Wheare, a professor at Oxford University, to investigate and report on the vexed question of film censorship and children's cinema-going.[51]

The Wheare Report was published in May 1950, and drew various conclusions on the matter of children's matinees and the work of CEF. Several serious criticisms were levelled: it was observed that 'There were many examples of deplorable films being shown to children', and 'we rarely found the whole of the programme satisfactory'.[52] The Report echoed Mayer's criticisms of the Odeon Club promise, and of the deleterious effects of North American serials on young minds. However, Wheare reserved high praise for the general running of children's cinema clubs, and for the efforts of CEF specifically. He believed that clubs were generally 'inspired by a desire that children should enjoy happy and wholesome recreation', and that 'enjoyable, and often beautiful and interesting films are being increasingly made available to children' through CEF's efforts. The Report paid 'high tribute to the work of the Advisory Council and the CEF for the variety and quality of the films for which they have been jointly responsible', and concluded: 'We attach the greatest importance to the continuance and development of these projects'.[53]

In June 1950, however, less than a month after the publication of the Wheare Report, Rank dissolved CEF. The Rank Organisation had been plunged into financial chaos during the late 1940s, resulting both from the company's over-extension and punitive taxes levied by the government. Rank saw little alternative but to close his loss-making operations, which included CEF and G-B Animation (his ambitious attempt to establish an animation studio able to compete with Hollywood). Over the course of their six years in operation, the CFD and CEF produced 29 features, 164 shorts and several serials.[54] Rank had made a major contribution to children's cinema in Britain. However, these films were accessible only to members of Rank's Odeon and Gaumont chains. Theoretically, other cinemas were free to hire CFD/CEF productions for their own matinees, but seldom did.[55] Furthermore, even in Rank's own theatres, the proportion of CFD and CEF films remained very low. There were also valid criticisms of the films themselves, which were constrained by Rank's insistence that his films should impart ethical instruction. In his 1950 report on children's cinema for Unesco, Henri Storck – while broadly sympathetic to CEF – appealed for films 'whose scope is less narrow, less limited', lest children's films 'become an undesirable means of moulding children's minds uniformly'.[56] Nevertheless, many principles established by the CFD and CEF were carried forward into the next phase of specialised children's cinema in Britain, with the formation of the Children's Film Foundation.

The Children's Film Foundation and Mary Field

The Children's Film Foundation was formally established as a non-profit-making, independent organisation in June 1951, almost exactly one year after the abolition of CEF, by four trade organisations: the Association of Specialised Film Producers (ASFP), the British Film Producers Association (BFPA), the Cinematograph Exhibitors' Association (CEA) and the Kinematograph Renters' Society (KRS). The CFF was granted an initial £50,000 sum, and subsequently received an annual levy via the British Film Production Fund, which in turn was financed through a tax (the 'Eady Levy') on theatre admissions in Britain. As such, the CFF was financially autonomous and relatively secure. Mary Field was appointed Executive Officer, a post she held until 1959. Importantly, films produced by the CFF were made accessible to all theatres that wanted them for matinee performances. Initially, many exhibitors were reluctant to book CFF films.[57] In response, a rotational system was agreed in which four groups of exhibitors – Odeon, Gaumont, ABC, and a conglomeration of independents – would take it in turns to premiere new films.[58] It was also established that CFF productions should not be exhibited to non-matinee/adult audiences, nor could they be expected to show an overall profit. Any financial surplus would be ploughed back into the production fund.

The CFF and Saturday morning cinema served two primary ends. Firstly, and most obviously, CFF was geared towards 'the production, promotion, organisation, distribution and exhibition of cinematograph films specially suitable for showing at children's matinees and other performances given specially for children'.[59] This explicitly established that its films were *solely* for children. As Mary Field wrote, 'films aimed at family audiences with their direct appeal to adults as well as children are ruled out'.[60] Secondly, CFF and matinees were intended to limit children's attendance at 'adult' programmes, for reasons of paternalism (fears that 'mature' films might harm children), artistry (the belief that catering for children was inhibiting the artistic growth of the medium) and convenience to adults (many of whom disliked children's presence at evening programmes). In Sidney Bernstein's 1947 audience questionnaire, banning children from cinemas was the second most frequently-made suggestion among adult respondents.[61] In 1949, Roger Manvell, director of the

British Film Academy, and noted film panjandrum, averred that: 'From the point of view of the manufacturers the children are not really wanted'.[62] He added that: 'If the children went to cinemas of their own [...] then the film-makers could deal with their subjects in a different and more adult manner'.[63] In practice, most children attended *both* matinee performances and evening programmes.[64] The utility of the CFF, from the industry's perspective, was that – despite the progressively 'adult' trajectory of popular cinema in the 1950s, 1960s and 1970s – children's films could publicly be seen to be made, catering to the needs of children and protecting them from the excesses of the mainstream.

The CFF hit the ground running. In October 1952, the Foundation claimed already to have produced six features, six two-reelers, and six nonfiction 'interest' pictures.[65] Initially, the emphasis was on shorts and magazine programmes, but feature production was greatly stepped up in the late 1950s. During this early period, the programme was only approximately 90 minutes in length, far shorter than the post-1960s standard of two hours.[66] CFF shorts were highly regarded internationally, with several winning prizes; by this point, Britain was the world leader in children's film production, a fact Mary Field attributed to the extensive research CEF and later the CFF conducted into children's responses to films.[67] According to Field, its productions were widely exported to the continent, the dominions and the Far East.[68] At the 1953 Venice Festival of Films for Children, Britain's entry of three features and four shorts won the award for the best national selection, with *The Dog and the Diamond*s (Ralph Thomas, 1953) recognised as best long-form film.[69] *Johnny on the Run* (Lewis Gilbert, 1953), the first CFF production to be exhibited in the US, garnered the Best Children's Film award at the Stamford Film Council festival in Connecticut.[70]

Under Mary Field's direction, the CFF remained strongly moralistic and implacably middlebrow. Its films are characterised by abiding wholesomeness, representations of adventurous, but unfailingly polite, children, affirmations of benign authority, and strongly maintained boundaries between good and evil. According to Field, 'To achieve that sense of security for which they crave, young children like to think of a world divided into the good, who in the long run win, and the bad, who eventually lose'.[71] Furthermore, 'Children find security in the unquestioned skill and knowledge of parents, teachers, police and other friendly grown-ups. It is disturbing to them to find these Olympians can nod'.[72] Field was convinced that the physical appearance of adult characters should relate to their narrative function:

> In children's films, all fathers should be tall, slim and handsome in a thin-featured way. Mothers should be young, slender, pretty and well-dressed, but not too glamorous or fashionable, while teachers, policemen and all other adult characters that are on the side of right should be cast in the same mould. Only bad men in this dream-world may be fat, middle-aged or bald.[73]

1950s CFF productions are also notable for their relatively simple syntax, which eschews complex *mise-en-scène* or editing. Field argued that: 'The editing of a children's film requires [...] controlled simplicity and clarity. A child audience likes to be able to look at a scene longer than adults in order to be able to take it all in and, therefore, care must be taken not to cut too quickly from one scene to another'.[74] Storck echoed this view, observing that 'artistic direction' was regarded as 'a crucial problem' in the opinion 'of all who make children's films'.[75]

Five on a Treasure Island (Gerald Landau, 1957), a six-part serial adapted from Enid Blyton's 1942 novel, encapsulates many of the above aspects. Shown in weekly instalments of approximately 15 minutes, the serialised nature of the production necessitates a quicker-paced narrative that opens *in medias res*, and a structure that allows for regular dramatic incident building towards the weekly cliff-hanger. Nonetheless, its adherence to continuity editing principles places emphasis on character, rather than technique. As with Blyton's source text, the serial centres on a group of five children who uncover and foil a plot by two criminals to swindle Uncle Quentin (Peter Burton) out of a bounty of buried treasure. Like many CFF antagonists, the villains – an antiques shop owner and a small-time businessman – are dull, frustrated, greedy men. The children's ability to overcome their foes partially rests with their knowledge of survival skills taught in organisations like the Scouts, the Boys Brigade and the Guides. They find themselves stranded on an island during a storm, and cheerfully make themselves a fire, taking refuge in a ruined castle keep. They dive into the sea to search for lost treasure, and later fearlessly take on the criminals. George (Rel Grainer) – Georgina – escapes her femininity by embracing a tomboyish persona, commenting to her cousin, Ann (Gillian Harrison), how 'awful' it is to be a girl. Ann denies it, but subsequently proves to be something of a liability, while George's role in overcoming the criminals leads Uncle Quentin to exclaim, proudly, 'You couldn't have done better if you were a boy!'

The Adventures of Hal 5 (Don Sharp, 1958) is one of the better-remembered CFF productions, largely on account of its eponymous anthropomorphised car, a 1920s Austin 7. The story follows Hal 5 as it is sold by the affable Dicey (David Morrell) to a villainous car mechanic, Goorlie (John Glyn-Jones). When the car seemingly deliberately bumps into him, Goorlie arranges for it to be stolen as an insurance swindle. Hal 5 ultimately saves the day by driving a helpless Goorlie to Dicey's farm, exposing his villainy, then pushing him into a pond. Goorlie is sacked and replaced as garage manager by Dicey, whose first act is to restore Hal to its former glory. While Hal 5 has no dialogue, a face appears periodically on its fender (animation added in post-production), communicating emotions like happiness, dismay, and relief. When Goorlie kicks Hal 5 and gets his foot caught in the wheel spokes, Hal 5 glances gleefully in his direction, and audiences are invited to share in this *schadenfreude*. Other cathartic moments include Goorlie tripping on a hose and getting soaked with water. These ritual humiliations – akin to the pie in the face trope – are harmless but meaningful tokens of cosmic rebalancing. Goorlie is marked out as villain by his appearance (middle-aged, balding) as well as swindling upstanding men like the Vicar (William Russell) and former RAF Squadron Leader Dicey. Various lessons in conduct are also imparted: when one of the children answers the phone on behalf of an adult, he asks who is calling, offering to take a message; and when a group of local boys pull away a ladder while two children are on the roof of a house, the Vicar delivers a sermonising rebuke, and the boys apologise for the prank, admitting that it was 'very silly' and replacing the ladder in its original position.

There are degrees of stylistic progression in 1950s CFF output. *Toto and the Poachers* (Brian Salt, 1957) was the first Foundation feature film to be filmed in colour, while animation was used to notable effect in *The Monster of Highgate Ponds* (Alberto Cavalcanti, 1961). Nevertheless, these technological innovations occur within a larger framework that establishes and maintains tight narrative, representational and ideological constraints.

Image 4.1 Simple animation is overlaid on the car's fender in *The Adventures of Hal 5* (1958)

There is little intimation of socio-cultural tension, nor of the formal experimentalism of late-1950s British cinema. In politics and in composition, CFF remained staid. In other respects, the 1950s was a golden age. Attendances were at their peak. Chocolate and sweets had come off the ration in 1949, and their consumption was a perennial of the matinee experience.[76] The cost of admission remained low. Talent contests and other supplementary attractions reflected Saturday morning cinema's status as a social activity. However, despite its many accomplishments, CFF products, Staples estimates, constituted as little as 5 per cent of children's overall matinee viewing.[77] The bulk of the performance – much of which was made up of Hollywood westerns and serials – had barely changed since the 1930s. Furthermore, during the late 1950s, with competition from television and changing living habits, attendances began to decline. Some chains and many independent cinemas ceased running matinees altogether, and by 1963 the number of children's film clubs nationwide had fallen from approximately 2,000 to around 900.[78]

Branching out in the 1960s

Despite (or perhaps because of) ongoing decline in attendances, the CFF diversified into new genres, such as the sports film, and assumed more discernibly liberal attitudes to class and race. There was a shift away from employing stage school-trained child actors towards 'urban children who went to ordinary schools and were encouraged to develop their acting talents while retaining their own accents, pronunciation and diction'.[79] After 1965, it was decided that all CFF films would be made in colour. Equally important was the appropriation of new cinematic techniques imported from contemporary mainstream cinema. CFF producer Henry Geddes explained:

> Audiences have grown younger, but more sophisticated. They have learned the idiom of moving pictures by watching television. Quick cuts, close-ups, and slow dissolves – but not flashbacks – are as accepted a part of the children's world as spacemen and comprehensive schools.[80]

In 1969, a CFF publication, *Saturday Morning Cinema*, elaborated on this new ethos:

> Today the children's film audience is totally accustomed to the visual medium of the television screen [...] Films made for this audience must be as sophisticated technically as the best television material. Children can be distinctly unforgiving to film sequences that fall below this standard.[81]

It added that 'no film for children should be unacceptable to adults', and thus the Foundation 'no longer thinks of its productions as "children's films" but as "Junior Features"'.[82]

This document acknowledged that certain fundamentals, such as children's innate taste in entertainment, 'have really changed very little over the years': 'Stories about animals, pirates, secret hiding-places, treasure, mystery, and sport train constant appeal'.[83] It was still believed that: 'The major roles should be taken by characters with whom the children can identify themselves, or that the children would like to know and be with in real life'.[84] Additionally, 'many of the older films made for general distribution' – e.g. Laurel and Hardy, Chaplin, and Abbott and Costello shorts – were still widely being shown in matinees to great popularity.[85] Nevertheless, the 'realisation that children were demanding a new approach' led to the Foundation implementing a so-called 'New-Look' programme in 1963.[86] Previously, the CFF had itself conceived of stories, presenting filmmakers with an already partially-developed narrative, a policy that contributed to the standardisation of CFF products during the 1950s. Henceforth, independent filmmakers (such as Pat Jackson) were free to pitch projects, and it was noted that: 'Many more top technicians usually associated with adult features have found a new and enjoyable outlet for their talents by working in association with the Foundation'.[87]

Go Kart Go (Jan Darnley-Smith, 1964) is one such production. Like several prominent 1960s CFF features, it is built around sporting pursuits, a source of familiarity and pleasure for many children. Sport operates as a metaphor for the broader spheres of human interaction, representing (playful rehearsals of) the struggle for supremacy and the need for teamwork, persistence and determination. The film opens with Jimpy's (Dennis Waterman) gang trialling a homemade soapbox by riding down the slope on a busy road. In the process, Jimpy narrowly avoids colliding with several pedestrians, before a policeman arrives to chastise him. Jimpy is warned not to ride in densely-populated public areas. The policeman does, however, point them towards a nearby go-kart track. Various scenes follow of children building a go-kart from scrap metal and spare parts. The kart's trial run results in near-mishap when the steering column comes off in Jimpy's hands. Undeterred, the gang rebuild the kart's engine from scratch. Their victory is all the sweeter – and more laudable – because it is achieved through hard work, skill and fair play. Unlike his rival Harry (Frazer Hines), who runs him off the track and damages his kart, Jimpy does not resort to cheating. This ethical integrity is rewarded when the parents of the participants fund its repair. The rivals resort to even dirtier tactics when they hijack the kart, but are outmanoeuvred by Jimpy's gang, who have cunningly built a decoy kart for the rivals to steal while perfecting their own model. Undeterred, Harry's gang sabotages it by cutting halfway through its front axle. Jimpy's gang hurriedly manage to source a replacement from a nearby junk yard, and, inevitably, he defeats his competitor. The film thus celebrates and promotes the agency, skill and ingenuity of the children.

Shot on location in Manchester and Salford, the year before England's victorious World Cup campaign, *Cup Fever* (David Bracknell, 1965) follows a group of young footballers in their efforts to win a junior league competition. Much of the filming was undertaken in underprivileged urban landscapes, and the greyness of the location footage accentuates the black-and-white photography. The film opens with the piece of waste ground used by the Barton street junior footballers in lieu of a pitch being closed by the corrupt Counsellor Bates (David Lodge) to make way for a car park. Bates is revealed as the father of the captain of the Bartons' main rivals. The Bartons are aided by a sympathetic policeman (Bernard Cribbins) who arranges a training session with Matt Busby's Manchester United. Their visit to Old Trafford is the highlight of the film; any young football enthusiast would derive vicarious pleasure from Busby's personal introduction to each Barton member, and the team's subsequent training session with players such as Bobby Charlton, Nobby Stiles and George Best. On the day of the Junior Final, Bates's team plays dirty, but buoyed by the skills instilled by Busby's players, Barton is victorious. Busby's willingness to assist Barton's development further promotes the ideologies of community and consensus developed in CFF films. The idea of football as a unifying force recurs throughout, being adopted across class, regional and racial borders. For child audiences, Busby's United are inspirational figures that uphold the dominant meritocratic doctrine that there are ample material rewards to play for. These rewards are not for the indolent, but yet are accessible to anyone willing to work for them.

Adult authority usually has a benign face. Bernard Cribbins's policeman in *Cup Fever*, and members of the Armed Forces and clergy in other CFF films, are strongly paternalistic, reflecting a period in which the state assumed a more active role in the lives of individual citizens. However, post-1960s CFF films do not refrain from portraying corruption and pettiness among seemingly responsible adults. *Cup Fever's* Counsellor Bates is happy to accept backhanders from local business, and willing to sabotage the prospects of his son's rivals in the junior football league. The plummy, buffoonish government-appointed 'disposals man' played by Hugh Lloyd in *Runaway Railway* (Jan Darnley-Smith, 1965) repeatedly tries to condemn a well-maintained steam train servicing a small community to the breaker's yard. These are not easily-spotted moustache-twirling villains, though the

Image 4.2 Matt Busby meets the young footballers in *Cup Fever* (1965)

films' central children – who are repeatedly celebrated for their shrewdness and perceptiveness – usually have no problem unmasking them. Despite this more relativistic attitude towards authority, in a late-1960s CFF sample of 75 London school children aged between 7 and 12, policemen, schoolteachers and farmers ranked as the film characters felt most likely to be upstanding, reflecting the teachings of a socialisation process in which CFF films actively partook.[88]

Runaway Railway, which topically alludes to the Great Train Robbery of August 1963, opens with the last journey of steam train Matilda, a victim of Dr Beeching's railway closures. Local children Charlie (John Moulder-Brown), Arthur (Kevin Bennett), John (Leonard Brockwell) and Carole (Roberta Tovey), who have helped maintain Matilda, are dismayed to hear that it will be taken to the breaker's yard when it is, as they eventually prove, 'as good as new'. The children's idyllic closeness with the steam train reflects its status as an object of fascination for generations of British (especially male) children, and this is strongly reflected in the opening scene, where Charlie drives it unassisted. But like *Cup Fever*, the film endorses hard work and productivity. Scenes of children of both sexes repairing the engine, exchanging technical dialogue and compiling a list of required mechanical parts convey the message that only through industriousness and determination are important battles won. When the children succeed in foiling the train robbery and delivering the criminals into the hands of the police, Lord Chalk, a local landowner, suggests using their reward money to fund Matilda's purchase, and he accedes to take over the railway line on the condition that the children will 'help' him.

Where post-1960s CFF productions depart from their predecessors is in their clear, if not always successful, gestures toward sexual and racial egalitarianism. In *Go Kart Go*, the tomboyish girl, Squirt (Melanie Garland), is met by her mother's incredulous response 'But you're a little girl!' when she asks for a go-kart, and instead her father offers to buy her a doll. Her rebellious response is to use her toy car to run over her stuffed animal toy. *Cup Fever*'s football team is multiethnic, with a black and Asian player in the Barton squad. Concessions to equality only go so far; Squirt never does get her own kart. *On the Run* (Pat Jackson, 1968) is notable for one of the three child protagonists being black. The film opens with young Ben Mallory (Dennis Conoley) arriving in London to live with his father (Gordon Jackson). He meets Thomas Okapi (Robert Kennedy), the son of a usurped African tribal chief (Dan Jackson). Ben and his friend Lil (Tracey Collins) discover that chief Okapi's treacherous brother, Uncle Joseph (Bari Jonson), plans to kidnap Thomas. Ben and Lil are able to protect Thomas from Uncle Joseph until the police arrive to apprehend the villain. The friendship between the children is relatively free from racial hierarchy, but agency and ingenuity are nonetheless primarily invested in the white, British characters of Lil and Ben, who continually have to rescue Thomas. Furthermore, Thomas has little exotic affiliation beyond his skin colour, save for one unfortunate exchange when his stated unfamiliarity with the sea is countered by Lil admitting her unfamiliarity with the jungle (!). Uncle Joseph, a variation on the savage tribal fictional archetype (with a deep scar on his cheek signifying his malignancy), is an even more unfortunate victim of racial stereotyping.

Geddes and the Later Years

By the late 1960s, the CFF was Britain's second biggest producer of films. However, as Staples notes, 'plenty of matinee Saturdays [...] contained no CFF component at all, and many more [...] contained nothing but a serial episode'.[89] Matinee organisers still scratched around for suitable programming. Cinema-going in general was in steep decline, and consequently so were the number of theatres programming children's matinees. Young attendees now represented 'a self-selected minority', although those who did go reported high degrees of satisfaction.[90] This coterie appeal facilitated greater experimentalism in form, narrative and subject-matter, and many of CFF's 1970s films are among its most creative. Perhaps the most famous is *The Boy Who Turned Yellow* (Michael Powell, 1972), which marked the final collaboration of director Michael Powell and writer Emeric Pressburger. Powell, whose directorial career had never recovered from the critical and commercial failure of the 'X'-rated *Peeping Tom* (1960), remained a member of the CFF advisory board, representing the Producers' Association. Powell suggested to an 'appalled' CFF board that he and Pressburger reunite for a CFF film, an idea which he managed to push through despite chairman John Davis's and executive producer Henry Geddes's reservations.[91]

Despite limitations in form and resources, there is a palpable sense of artistic freedom in *The Boy Who Turned Yellow*. No longer bound by normative conventions of (adult) popular cinema, the whims of distributors and the capriciousness of censors, Powell and Pressburger have almost free rein to indulge their imaginative desires. Interestingly, the film's first image is one of constraint: a sign at the school entrance reading 'Parents – please do NOT bring your cars into the school. Thank you'. The camera cuts to children playing on the grass, establishing a thematic relation between adult constraint and children's freedom (in thought and act). A school visit to the Tower of London is then subverted when young John's (Mark Dightam) pet mouse escapes and immediately appropriates the scarf worn by Lady Jane Gray at her execution. The next scene takes place at John's school, where the teacher is conducting a tedious lecture on the properties of electricity. John falls asleep, revives enough drowsily to write 'Electricity's good for you', before again passing out. On his journey home, he and the entire train and its contents turn yellow. John's concerned mother asks him whether he is ill, to which he replies: 'No, Mum; just yellow'. That night, he is awoken by a voice which directs him to turn on the television set, whereupon a yellow man appears, and introduces himself as Nick (Robert Eddison) – short for 'electronic'. Nick, who explains that John is his friend because he is yellow, takes him on a series of adventures (almost causing a nuclear meltdown), before John narrowly evades execution at a bizarre, medieval-style ceremony at the Tower. Finding himself back in school, John is now able to provide his teacher with a detailed account of how electricity works.

Distinctly lacking the moralistic overtones of most CFF productions, *The Boy Who Turned Yellow* is nonetheless one of its most explicitly educational. The audience is told a great deal about electricity, including its wave pattern, speed of travel, the voltage of UK houses, and the function of transformers and conductors. The meaning of words such as 'extraterrestrial' and 'perimeter', and a little of the history of the Tower (such as the function of the Tower Ravens) are also explained. It may be that Pressburger, unaccustomed to CFF conventions, felt that this pedagogic angle was a necessary element. Powell's contribution is primarily aesthetic, providing striking imagery (such as the yellow tube train arriving into the station) and ethereal sounds which render it unlike anything else on television or movie screens. The temptation is to search for hidden meanings within the dialogue and imagery. Nick tells us that everyone else affected by the yellow 'plague' were just ordinary people that had been 'turned yellow', but that John was yellow all along – as evidenced by his yellow scarf and top hat. Does yellowness thus symbolise youth, receptiveness, or curiosity? Is it a signifier of optimism and happiness – as in the Beatles' song 'Yellow Submarine'? What is the significance of the mice, which feature prominently in both opening and closing credits, while a whistled rendition of 'Three Blind Mice' is played over? Is it a disservice to Powell's and Pressburger's craft, and to children's cinema, to limit our interpretation to known quantities?

Like most CFF features, *The Boy Who Turned Yellow* received scant critical notice. The *MFB* felt that the prescripts of the 'children's film' served to inhibit Powell and Pressburger, while predicting that children would be confused and dissatisfied by its abstruseness.[92] In the event, the film won the 'Chiffy' award for best CFF film (as voted for by matinee attendees)

J. Arthur Rank, Saturday Morning Cinema

Image 4.3 John (Mark Dightam) explores a fantasy world with Nick (Robert Eddison) in *The Boy Who Turned Yellow* (1972)

several times, and was the Foundation's first film to be shown on national television. The CFF evidently still had trouble predicting audience reaction to its films. Henry Geddes reiterated in a 1972 interview that the Foundation existed 'primarily [...] to entertain', and that 'children will not [...] be preached at'.[93] Nevertheless, several late-1970s productions were explicitly political. Previously, CFF productions had maintained an apolitical facade, while endorsing the sanctity of family, the value of community, and the strength and virtue of the nation. 1960s films bespoke a healthy mistrust of politicians, particularly at the local level (manifested in innumerable crooked councillors in films such as *Cup Fever* and *A Ghost of a Chance* [Jan Darnley-Smith, 1968]), while the arms of the state – especially the police and armed forces – invariably remained stolid, trustworthy and dependable.

The anti-pollution, anti-big business film, *The Battle for Billy's Pond* (Harley Cokliss, 1976), would have been impossible to conceive in the more middlebrow CFF of yesteryear. When young Billy (Ben Buckton) discovers that the fish in his pond have been poisoned, he and his friend Gobby (Andrew Ashby) investigate, and find that the pond is being polluted by waste pumped from a disused quarry by a local firm, Con-Chem. The police remain sceptical, remarking: 'With their reputation, they'd be down with a ton of hot bricks on anyone accusing them of pollution without some good, hard evidence'. The boys are able to secure the vital evidence against the firm, and although they are apprehended by two rough-neck Con-Chem employees, the police arrive in time to catch the offenders. Although clearly driven by environmentalist concerns, the film's negative portrayal of Big Business remains abstract, and its young hero is motivated by simple and laudable awareness of his environment, acting on learned values of justice and compassion in a way the more ethically compromised grown-ups do not. Childhood, as personified by Billy, is sentimentally equated with nature, positioning his protest as an articulation of Mother Earth's unspoken rage against its defilement at the hands of human greed and irresponsibility. The familiar CFF bumbling villains of yesteryear are replaced, hardly reassuringly, by unscrupulous advanced capitalism. While Billy successfully forces the representatives of the establishment to intervene, there are other battles still to be fought. On one level, the film serves as a recruitment campaign for a new generation of eco-aware public citizens.

Not all 1970s CFF films are so portentous. The appealingly oddball *Sammy's Super T-Shirt* (Jeremy Summers, 1978) is a classically British underdog tale centring on 12-year-old weakling Sammy Smith (Reggie Winch), who spends his free time fanatically attempting to build his muscles under direction from Professor Hercules' body-building tapes. When his favourite t-shirt accidentally becomes irradiated in a nearby research lab, Sammy discovers that it confers upon its wearer super-strength and speed. Most of the film is a wish-fulfilment fantasy, as Sammy turns the tables on his bullies with his new-found powers. The standard child-as-victim dynamic is reversed by Sammy's ability to repel his adult pursuers – who wish to retrieve the t-shirt to sell it – with feats of strength and gymnastics, which include stopping the pursuers' van with his hands, running at incredible speeds and propelling a rowboat with unfeasibly quick paddling movements with his arms. Inevitably, the final moral, as Sammy's t-shirt fails him and he is forced to rely on his natural attributes to win a race, is a celebration of perseverance. Few CFF films manage to present (or disguise) their message with such panache. *Sammy's Super T-Shirt* again demonstrates that the CFF's still ultimately earnest agenda was increasingly leavened by comedy, whimsy and symbolism.

As Jonathan Rosenbaum observed of *The Battle for Billy's Pond*, 'The Children's Film Foundation maintains a level of workaday efficiency exceeding that of the rest of British commercial filmmaking'.[94] The point was echoed by the *Daily Mail's* Margaret Hinxman, who remarked that the CFF 'commands the respect of the world', for 'there is no comparable organisation anywhere'.[95] But increasingly, the CFF was forced to position itself in relation to television and Hollywood cinema. Like *Star Wars* (George Lucas, 1977), *The Glitterball* (Harley Cokliss, 1977) was a sci-fi film released in May 1977. There the comparisons end; *Star Wars* was mounted on a budget over 200 times that of *The Glitterball*, recouped several hundred million dollars in gross receipts worldwide, and generated a multi-billion dollar franchise. Family films were now re-emerging into the cultural mainstream, and with unprecedented force. The primacy of the Hollywood family blockbuster was at least as significant as the popularisation of television in signalling the death knell for British children's cinema. *The Glitterball*, in contrast, was more modestly budgeted at around £50,000. The film opens with the arrival of an alien visitor, similar in size and shape to a billiard ball. It finds its way into the home of Max (Ben Buckton). A closer point of comparison than *Star Wars* might be *E.T.* (Steven Spielberg, 1982). The Glitterball is a symbolic child, requiring shelter, food and protection from outside interference, and like E.T., it has a seemingly insatiable appetite for food, as conveyed in several stop-motion sequences where it devours the contents of the kitchen cupboard. And as with child and alien in Spielberg's film, Max and the Glitterball develop methods of non-verbal communication. The Glitterball is rescued by its comrades, while Max's father (Barry Jackson) refuses to believe in the UFO's existence, again hinting at an adult narrow-mindedness not shared – or yet to be developed – by the more curious, receptive and imaginative children.

Change within the CFF was inevitable. Faced with the virtual obsolescence of the matinee, in June 1982 it was renamed the Children's Film and Television Foundation (CFTF). It brokered a £1.2 million deal with the BBC to produce nine films for television, while both the BBC and ITV broadcast numerous older (but not black-and-white) films from the CFF back catalogue during the mid-to-late 1980s. However, in 1985, the

Conservative government abolished the Eady Levy, which had sustained the Foundation since its inception. The CFTF was left with no outlet for its productions, and its lack of funding forced it to discontinue distribution to the dozen or so remaining matinees nationwide.[96] In its final batch of films, the CFF/CFTF tried hard to remain relevant. The *MFB* felt that *Friend or Foe* (John Krish, 1981) represented a 'creative recharging' in which 'long-lived adult stereotypes have finally died off', and noted its strong anti-war theme.[97] *Haunters of the Deep* (Andrew Bogle, 1984) is notable as an early entry in the children's horror film sub-genre. Like *Terry on the Fence* (Frank Godwin, 1985), it acknowledges changing family structures by positioning one of its child protagonists within a fractious single-parent family, while the latter film explores juvenile delinquency and child abuse, both paralleling and responding to the more realist imperatives of contemporary British children's television programmes, such as the BBC's hugely popular school-set drama, *Grange Hill* (1978–2008).

The CFTF slowly faded out of the limelight. It was one of several investors in two innovative family films during the late 1980s: the children's *film noir* production *Just Ask for Diamond* (Stephen Bayly, 1988) and the Roald Dahl adaptation *Danny, the Champion of the World* (Gavin Millar, 1989). Thereafter, its ambitions to serve as a springboard for worthwhile British children's films were frustrated by lack of government support. Since the 1980s, successive British governments have clearly perceived little or no public interest in supporting home-grown children's cinema. Private enterprise is considered more desirable. In the 1990s and beyond, Hollywood distribution deals with British firms have allowed several British family films traction in the global market. The relative freedom from the overt didacticism of CEF and CFF productions in, say, the *Harry Potter* series (2001–11), may be celebrated by those who argue that the state has no business inculcating moral and behavioural values in young children. Indeed, the existence of the CFF, as with the Soviet-era Russian studio Soiuzmultfilm (1935-) and the Children's Film Society, India (CFSI, 1955-), reflected a more interventionist phase of socialist government anathema to free market economics and laissez-faire social policy. The CFF remains notable in two other regards. Firstly, and unlike Hollywood co-productions, which are forced to reflect international cultural norms in pursuing global audiences, its films unambiguously reflected and recapitulated British norms and values. Secondly, and again in contrast to the more broadly-encompassing 'family film', CFF productions – for good or for ill – were manufactured specifically to meet the psychological and cultural needs of young children.

5

Happiest Days: British Cinema and the Family Audience in the Fifties

With the formation of the Children's Film Foundation (CFF), the 'child audience' no longer existed as a category in mainstream British cinema in its own right, independent from the larger, and implicitly more adult-orientated, 'family audience'. The specific needs and desires of young children, it was supposed, were now being met by CFF product; there was no commercial demand for films like *Emil and the Detectives* (Milton Rosmer, 1935) and the *Just William* series (1940–48). But there was still a sizable market for films produced specifically for parents and children enjoying an afternoon or night out at the pictures, and it is these films with which this chapter is concerned. The British film industry prided itself, at least publicly, as a purveyor of family entertainment. 'Adult' films, according to propaganda dating back to the beginnings of cinema, had no place on movie screens. Over the course of the 1950s, this position became insupportable. Explicit European art films appeared in Britain for the first time, and indigenous producers and directors began pushing accepted boundaries of screen violence, sexuality, and otherwise adult themes. Furthermore, cracks started appearing within the family viewing habit, and within the institution of the family unit itself. *Mandy* (Alexander Mackendrick, 1952) and *The Divided Heart* (Charles Crichton, 1954) saw the modern British nuclear family as a site of social tension and fragmentation. The

Happiest Days: British Cinema and the Family Audience in the Fifties

surge in films addressing only 'adults' and neglecting 'families' was paralleled by the advent of the 'youth' or 'teen' film. Both developments seemed to portend the end of 'family viewing'.

David Kynaston characterises the period 1951–57 as 'Family Britain';[1] Arthur Marwick describes the years between 1945 and 1958 as marked by 'social consensus'.[2] Britain had 'won the war'; the Welfare State was founded in 1948; the 1951 Festival of Britain and the Queen's Coronation the following year galvanised the nation (and the Coronation, broadcast by the BBC, is widely credited with popularising television); postwar austerity gradually gave way to consumerism and relative affluence; rationing ended in 1954 and 'credit culture' was broadly embraced in the form of hire purchase; divorce rates were still low and 'family' was still at the centre of most people's daily lives. But 'consensus' was hardly absolute. Attlee's postwar Labour government, wilting under its impossible welfare reforms, was the quintessential bureaucratic behemoth; there were deep class divisions; crime rates rose steadily during the late 1940s and early 1950s, then alarmingly so after 1955; the 1956 Suez Crisis confirmed that the days of Empire were over and that Britain was no longer a major global power; the Teddy Boy publicly symbolised rebellious youth; 'permissiveness', in the form of illicit drug taking and pre-marital sex, were on the rise. Analysis of British cinema of the 1950s, mirroring contemporary society as a whole, invite interpretation through a series of binaries: child and adult, individual and family, youth and the establishment, liberal and conservative, consensus and discontent, religion and secularisation, and cohesion and fragmentation.

Many of these oppositions, crude though they are, play out in British children's films and family films of the period. School-set films such as *Vice Versa* (Peter Ustinov, 1948), *The Happiest Days of Your Life* (Frank Launder, 1950), *Tom Brown's Schooldays* (Gordon Parry, 1951) and *The Belles of St. Trinian's* (Frank Launder, 1954) identify or imply a shift in social definitions of childhood and adulthood. Conversely, domestic comedies like *Mr Drake's Duck* (Val Guest, 1951), *Father's Doing Fine* (Henry Cass, 1952), *Twice Upon a Time* (Emeric Pressburger, 1953), *Life with the Lyons* (Val Guest, 1954), *Raising a Riot* (Wendy Toye, 1955), *An Alligator Named Daisy* (J. Lee Thompson, 1955), and *No Kidding* (Gerald Thomas, 1961) are exercises in consensus-building. They present functional and uplifting images of family life; but they also construct an implicit family audience comprising parents and children happily partaking of the same screen entertainment. Such family films were instrumental, upholding and promoting unity and reciprocity among its supposed consumers. The rise of explicitly 'adult' films, and of youth cinema more broadly, represented a disruption to this consensus and, by 1960, was making major inroads on the middle-brow mainstream cinema. The 'child audience' was increasingly marginalised. The films discussed in this chapter, then, represent a national cinema, and a society, in transition.

The School Film

What I loosely refer to as the 'school film' has its basis in structures of power and authority governing child-adult interrelations. *Vice Versa*, *Tom Brown's School Days*, *The Happiest Days of Your Life* and the *St. Trinian's* series (1954–66) are all centrally concerned with exploring these themes: *Vice Versa* via Victorian burlesque; *The Happiest Days of Your Life* and *St. Trinian's* via comic farce; and *Tom Brown's School Days* via serious-minded exposition on maturation and civic responsibility. As Cary Bazalgette and David Buckingham observe, 'Childhood and adulthood is, inevitably, the key opposition that has to be explored in any study of children's culture'.[3] This opposition, of course, is a central and overriding concern in the majority of family films, and is implicit in the very representational presence of the family unit. However, these school-set films explicitly seek to explore *what it means to be a child and an adult*, not as biological categories but in terms of the definitions and meanings that society affixes to them.

In its lack of faith in older generations, *Vice Versa* recalls, to some degree, *Hue and Cry* (Charles Crichton, 1947). Both films expose adult hypocrisy and corruption, and posit a perhaps unbridgeable gap (in ethics, outlook and behavioural conduct) between the generations. However, *Vice Versa* shifts the narrative emphasis from the child to the adult. Rather than effacing the older generation, as in *Hue and Cry*, this mechanism allows adults to rediscover the pleasures and unaffectedness of childhood. Adapted by Peter Ustinov from F. Anstey's 1882 original 'body swap' novel, *Vice Versa* centres on the relationship between pompous Victorian businessman, Paul Bultitude (Roger Livesey), and his schoolboy son, Dick (Anthony Newley).

Happiest Days: British Cinema and the Family Audience in the Fifties

The film opens with Dick expressing his dread about returning to his boarding school, run by the tyrannical schoolmaster Dr Grimstone (James Robertson Justice). Bultitude dismisses Dick's fears, insists that his own schooldays were the happiest of his life, and expresses his wish that he and Dick could exchange places. The film allows this through a fantastic *deus ex machina* (a magic stone brought from India) which transports Paul's consciousness into Dick's body, and vice versa.

Amongst the proliferation of self-referential gags, silly names and voices, and protracted scenes of late-Victorian burlesque, there are pertinent observations on the central child/parent dynamic. Dick is receptive, unaffected, imaginative, honest, lives for the moment, has little conception of deferred gratification or decorum, is chastely infatuated with young Dulcie Grimstone (Petula Clark), despises affectation and is happiest eating sweets and drinking pop. His father is the model of the gentlemanly patriarch: stern, humourless, vain, intransigent, and preoccupied with public image. However, as Dick discovers, the outwardly respectable, widowed Bultitude is having a covert affair with the gold-digging Fanny (Kay Walsh). Unusually, what is at stake is not Dick's maturation, but rather his father's recovering his 'inner child'. It is Dick who effects this required transformation. He exposes Fanny's scheme to fleece his father; he unwittingly engineers his father's marriage with the kindly family maid by demanding kisses from her while inhabiting his father's body; and he wisely invests the family fortune in developing an early motor car. With father and son restored to their proper places, a grateful Bultitude promises Dick a placement at the exclusive public school, Harrow, and increased pocket money. The film presents a coda, in which an elderly Bultitude addresses the viewer to confirm his and Dick's future happiness and plenitude.

The film, following the novel, laments that the socialisation process necessitates repudiation of childhood's greatest virtues. The fault lies within adult society, not within the (separate) sphere of the child, as Ustinov illustrates by emphasising the ridiculousness and hypocrisy of adult codes governing matters such as intersex relations and honourable 'gentlemanly' combat. All of these films interrogate the extent to which child and adult are psychologically separated by education, employment, marriage and parenthood. *Hue and Cry*, *Vice Versa*, *The Happiest Days of Your Life* and the *St. Trinian's* films all posit a renegotiation of social terms of engagement between adults and children; or, at least, question their validity, thus prefiguring – though not formally – the rise of youth culture. In Will Hay's schoolmaster comedies, power reversals were essentially saturnalian; the spectacle of children bettering adults remained incongruous. Here, the mode of comedy, though farcical, is no longer absurdist. It exploits for comic potential genuine tension points that threaten to overturn these hierarchies.

Tom Brown's School Days follows Thomas Hughes's 1857 novel, centring on 11-year-old Tom Brown (John Thomas Davies), who is sent to famous British boys' school Rugby, and learns how to conduct himself with the English gentlemanly virtues of honour, decency, compassion and fair play. In the process, he is inducted into the ways of the school by classmate East (John Charlesworth), endures the vicious bullying of older boy Flashman (John Forrest), whom he finally vanquishes, takes vulnerable new boy Arthur (Glyn Dearman) under his wing, and indirectly participates in the modernising reforms of venerable headmaster, Dr Arnold (Robert Newton). The film follows its source in conceiving of the British public school as a microcosm of British virtue, and – somewhat anachronistically – reaffirms its proper socialising potential. In this sense, *Tom Brown's School Days* divagates from contemporary British films such as the Boulting brothers' *The Guinea Pig* (1948), which attacks the institution, and Launder and Gilliat's *The Happiest Days of Your Life* and subsequent *St. Trinian's* series, which satirically turns it on its head. These films are not without nostalgic inflections (happiest days, indeed), but they recognise the hypocrisy of a system that the Victorian-era *Tom Brown's School Days* upholds.

The Happiest Days of Your Life wilfully abandons gentlemanly self-restraint. Due to an administrative error, Nutbourne, a lowly English boys' school governed by the benignly oddball Wetherby Pond (Alastair Sim), is invaded by the intake of a girls' school, St. Swithin's, and its uncompromising headmistress, Miss Whitchurch (Margaret Rutherford). Initially antagonistic, Mr Pond and Miss Whitchurch are forced to co-operate to deal with the logistics of running the temporarily mixed school. Events are complicated by two visiting parties whose presence threatens to expose the impropriety of the situation: the parents of some of the girls, and the board of governors from another boys' school where Pond hopes to be appointed headmaster. Pond and Whitchurch desperately try to manage events so

Happiest Days: British Cinema and the Family Audience in the Fifties

that neither party suspects that anything is amiss, but in the final act of the film, the masquerade is exposed spectacularly when boys and girls are seen fighting *en masse* on the school's playing field.

What is at stake here is not just Pond's and Whitchurch's increasingly fragile composure, but also the control and propriety demanded by their professions. In the final scene, his hopes of appointment as headmaster of an exclusive boys' school dashed, Pond is reduced to vacant imbecility. His stupefied acceptance of Miss Whitchurch's suggestion that he go to educate the natives in Tanganyika underlines the futility of the British public school's *raison d'être* of instilling order and discipline on feral youth. Human nature – chaotic, impulsive, and pleasure-orientated – will win out in the end. While Miss Whitchurch, an elderly spinster who, one suspects, never had much of a childhood to regress to, remains comparatively unflappable, there is something of the childlike in St. Swithin's' Miss Gossage (Joyce Grenfell), whose first act upon arriving at Nutbourne is to write her surname in the dust on the stairwell, and who later asks lugubrious mathematics master Billings (Richard Wattis) to 'Call me "Sausage"'.

This topsy-turvy world satirically pressurises, though not entirely deconstructs, concepts of rational self-control, civility, and stoicism – all central to British national identity. In *Hue and Cry*, the child-adult reversals are framed primarily in moral terms; the children inherit their Britishness from a decimated older generation whose survivors have grown corrupt. In *The Happiest Days of Your Life*, children represent a vague force of nature capable of regressing adults to a conceptual state of pre-socialised childhood, and are refigured as knowing, cynical, and resourceful. The climactic coming together of the normatively segregated male and female pupils in the final scenes threatens the bursting forth of incipient sexuality that Pond and Whitchurch are unable to contain. It also satirically comments on the traditional practice of segregation (built on Victorian sexual repression) and the current trend towards co-education, specifically fears that mixed groups of boys and girls would be unable to restrain their potent adolescent sexual drives. The children's comic revolt is no doubt cathartic for large portions of the mature audience, for whom the autocracies subverted are daily workplace realities. The failure of Sim and Rutherford in the film's final scenes allows adults to recall their own childhoods, and derive vicarious satisfaction from such longed-for reversals. References to adults

Image 5.1 Margaret Rutherford and Alastair Sim frame Joyce Grenfell in *The Happiest Days of Your Life* (1950)

partaking in illicit behaviours such as sex, drinking, gambling and philandering further expose the thinness of the veneer of order and respectability, and the boundaries between child and adult. This is especially pertinent in relation to the English upper-middle-classes, for whom stoicism and self-control are so intrinsic to conceptions of self.

The Belles of St. Trinian's is based on cartoonist Ronald Searle's *St. Trinian's* strips (1941–52), depicting the riotous goings-on at a fictional girls' school, an even less salubrious establishment than Nutbourne College. The financially-struggling St. Trinian's is run by eccentric, unorthodox Miss Fritton (Alastair Sim), whose pedagogic ethos is to allow the girls in her charge to indulge their desires unimpeded. She proudly explains that: 'In other schools, girls are sent out quite unprepared into a merciless world. But, when our girls leave here, it is the merciless world which has to be prepared!' These girls perpetrate 'arson, faked fivers and poison pen letters' with impunity. The wealthy Sultan of Makyad (Eric Pohlmann) decides to send his young daughter to St. Trinian's, unaware of its dire reputation. With the school under threat of impending closure, Miss Fritton invests her remaining money in backing the Sultan's prize racehorse, Arab Boy, in a forthcoming race. However, her unscrupulous brother, Clarence (Sim), plans on backing a rival horse and sabotages Arab Boy's prospects by 'kidnapping' it. The children, many of whom have invested their own money in Arab Boy, collude with Miss Fritton in recovering the horse, which succeeds in winning the race, securing St. Trinian's future.

In *Happiest Days*, the children's urges for unrestrained play are kept largely in check. Here, their disorderly instincts provide the substance of the film. In the opening image, the school's sign is blasted by machine gun fire, and the first appearance of the fourth formers is of them descending on the outwardly peaceful school like a plague of locusts, climbing out of the school bus' windows – after surreptitiously removing the driver's trousers – amidst hysterical cries of gleeful mayhem. They spend their time fighting, creating homemade gin in chemistry class and gambling on horses. The older girls of the sixth form are overtly sexualised and lazily decadent. In one scene, a group of them absconds from a hockey class to join former ministry inspectors Rowbottom-Smith (Guy Middleton) and Woodley (Arthur Howard) for a languid liquid lunch in the afternoon sun. The film's climax descends into an orgy of violence, with children openly assaulting adults. The attack is perhaps justified, at least within the film's ethical schema. Sim's Clarence and his associate Benny (Sid James), and the likeable spiv Flash Harry (George Cole), are not entirely dissimilar to the unscrupulous racketeers of *Hue and Cry*: jaded, immoral figures who have turned their backs on the postwar consensus. But rather than pointing the way to a brighter future, as in *Hue and Cry*, these children appear likely to supplant the old order with an even less desirable nihilism.

The Belles of St. Trinian's depicts childhood as characterised by vices and fallibilities anathema to the Romantic image. The children's riotous antics suggest carnival (inversion of social norms), rather than mimesis (reflecting them). Alternatively, their aberrant activities might be an extreme affirmation of the *realities* of childhood. Certainly, the film is closer to Freudian conceptualisations of childhood as governed by base impulse rather than innate goodness and innocence. A third possibility – one that

I would favour for all of the films in the cycle – is that the film addresses the symbolic child, constructing a playspace where inversions of child–adult power relations may pleasurably, and safely, be (re)experienced.

The Domestic Comedy

Children, as Christine Geraghty puts it, are 'everywhere in postwar British cinema', but so too are families.[4] David Kynaston observes that 'to an unprecedented, almost cultish extent, children were seen as the future, and it was to them, more than any other section of society, that the new welfare state was devoted'; but, crucially, 'almost all activators were agreed that it was the family that provided the indispensable framework for a child's development'.[5] Visions of family and community dominate the 1950s mainstream British cinema. Within a prevailing interest in the composition and collective activities of the family unit are dominant attitudes towards childhood, particularly, as Geraghty observes, 'issues of education, discipline and children's psychological needs'.[6] Family relations had been at the centre of the recent Huggetts film series (1948–50), and would be again in *Life with the Lyons*. But in those films, for all their various misadventures and conflicts, the long-term survival of the family unit is never in doubt. In the films discussed in this section, family is always precariously maintained, forever at the mercy of damaging external disruptions and internal tensions.

Mr Drake's Duck, an early entry in the 1950s domestic comedy cycle, concerns a newly married American couple, Mr and Mrs Drake (Douglas Fairbanks, Jr. and Yolande Donlan), who move to England and take over a Sussex farm. One of their Aylesbury ducks is found to possess the remarkable ability to lay uranium-enriched eggs. The British authorities quarantine the farm, and a consortium of War Office bureaucrats and forces personnel wreak havoc in their search for the animal. The film is devoid of child characters, and it is central to its comedy that the serious business of marriage – the procreative aspects of marital relations – is constantly postponed. Its repeated images of disturbed utopia articulate degrees of discomfort regarding intrusions into an increasingly self-contained domestic environment, mirroring similar tendencies towards suburban living in the United States. In the Disney film, *The Million Dollar Duck* (Vincent McEveety, 1971), the bird's ability to lay solid gold eggs operates as wish-fulfilment

Happiest Days: British Cinema and the Family Audience in the Fifties

fantasy. Here, magical intervention operates as comic disruption, a barely-endurable strain on the fledgling marriage.

Vice Versa, The Happiest Days of Your Life and the *St. Trinian's* films present children and youth as a reforming or revolutionary force that will soon overthrow the old order. They satirically articulate a prevailing ano-mie within British institutions (school representing society in microcosm). While the appallingly feral St. Trinian's girls represent insurgent youth in its least appealing guises, the children are a symptom, not the cause, of wider social processes of fragmentation. In *Mr Drake's Duck*, similar anxi-eties are localised in the portrayal of the adults. The smooth exterior of the husband/prospective father – embodied by the urbane Douglas Fairbanks, Jr. – is only slightly frayed by the seemingly endless list of bureaucratic frustrations, which elicit short bursts of macho rage. However, Mrs Drake's attempts to remain the 'good wife' and maintain domestic order are repeat-edly foiled. She is reduced to the verge of a nervous breakdown, worrying about her inability to prepare sufficient meals to keep the invading troops happy, and even begins to lose her powers over language itself, mangling sentences and stuttering incoherently. *Mr Drake's Duck* asserts the primacy of the self-contained family unit, and then works comically to disrupt it. The ending, in which the duck is found and taken away, teases the pos-sibility of the newly married couple commencing with the long-delayed business of making children. But their plans are again disrupted with a final twist (the wrong duck had been taken) that heralds the return of the government inspectors.

In *Father's Doing Fine*, children again represent a longed-for future of domestic fulfilment. Its structure borrows from Hollywood's parallel cycle of domestic comedies, with the dual focus on the aristocratic wid-owed matriarch, and her four daughters and their respective romantic entanglements. Each family member (and generation) is thus afforded its own narrative space. For all the bohemian decadence of Lady Buckering's (Heather Thatcher) household, the film ends happily with an unambigu-ous affirmation of family and marriage, with her engaged to the family doctor (George Thorpe), two of her daughters similarly betrothed, one daughter freed from an engagement with an odious leftwing intellectual, and the eldest daughter having given birth to twins. The pointed elabo-ration of an upper-class domestic environment initially characterised by unorthodoxy, if not outright dysfunction, serves to cast doubt on the narrative inevitability of its final affirmation of family and kinship, and to reinforce the message that (secret) desire for such domestic harmony is a human universal, transcending borders of class and culture. As Richard Hoggart observed in 1957, for many Britons 'the real business of life is getting married and having a family'.[7] While *Meet Me in St. Louis* (Vincente Minnelli, 1944) privileges the role of the maturing child within the domestic environment, *Father's Doing Fine* withholds the arrival of children to the end of the film. In this sense, marriage and giving birth become symbolic ends in themselves, signalling the passing of individualist desires and the onset of responsible and settled maturity, in which childlike pleasures and indulgences are to be eschewed.

The more serious-minded *The Spanish Gardener* (Philip Leacock, 1956) expounds on the possibilities of family breakdown ensuing from such a disconnect between parent and child. The film centres on the relationship between Michael Hordern's Brande, a British diplomat posted in Spain, and his young son, Nicholas (Jon Whiteley). Brande, a pompous, middle-aged divorcee, resents his lack of promotion and attributes it to the minor scandal caused by his wife leaving him. A humourless and emotionally repressed man, Brande prizes his ostensibly intimate relationship with his son, but fails to see that his domineering approach – insisting on home-schooling Nicholas and preventing him from associating with other children – are having an invidious effect. Much of *The Spanish Gardener* revolves around Brande's fears that his Spanish gardener, Jose (Dirk Bogarde) – younger, handsome, 'strong as a donkey' and emotionally available – is usurping him. Brande's paternal pride is piqued by Nicholas choosing to spend his free time working alongside Jose in the garden. His envious gaze is later seen in a public pelota match in which Jose's impressive athletic feats are punctuated by Nicholas's enthusiastic, repetitive cries of 'Jose!' and cross-cutting to Brande's mounting dismay. As the gathered observers mob the victorious Jose, Brande storms off in the opposite direction, as Nicholas runs after him and asks, 'is there anything wrong, father?' Brande petulantly responds: 'Nothing, except that I have a splitting headache'.

The following scene expounds on Brande's anger and tacit jealousy towards Nicholas's new, and in many ways superior, father-figure, Jose:

Nicholas: You *were* angry, father.

Brande: Not angry, Nicholas. Disappointed.

Nicholas: Is it because you didn't like the game?

Brande: It wasn't the game you took me to see, was it? That was a pretence. It was deceitful.

Nicholas: I wanted it to be a surprise for you. I thought you'd be proud of him.

Brande: Whatever you thought, Nicholas, doesn't alter the fact that you were deceitful.

Nicholas: I'm sorry, father. I didn't mean to be.

Brande: Nicholas… [Takes him by the arm.] You and I are alone now. Since your mother left us. There are times when it isn't easy. But I've never wavered in my devotion to your care. I ask little in return, Nicholas, but the knowledge of your love.

Nicholas: But I *do* love you! I do!

Brande: Do you? This afternoon I wondered. It hurt me deeply that my son could be so thoughtless of my feelings.

Nicholas: I never want to hurt you!

Brande: I know you don't. [Embraces him.] In future we must be more careful not to hurt each other.

Nicholas: Yes, father. I will.

The scene re-establishes Brande's emotional and physical dominance over his son. But his relationship with Nicholas deteriorates further when his villainous adjutant, Garcia (Cyril Cusack), frames Jose for stealing from the household. Brande – ignoring Nicholas's protestations of Jose's innocence – has the gardener arrested and imprisoned. In an excellent scene, which sees Brande and Jose travelling via train to Jose's trial in Barcelona, Brande hears echoes of his son's voice, advanced to adulthood, recalling Garcia's guilt, Jose's innocence and goodness, and his own jealousy and rage reflected back at him. Jose escapes from the train before Brande can exonerate him, but Brande later locates Jose and Nicholas in a remote cave in the hills. Brande overcomes Nicholas's antipathy – his assertions that he now hates his father, and that his overtures of friendship are a deception – to tend Jose's injuries, winning Jose's and Nicholas's forgiveness in the process. The ending sees father and son moving to Stockholm, with the promise of renewed contact between Nicholas and his absent mother. In this way, the film divagates markedly from A. J. Cronin's far less child-friendly novel (1950), in which Jose is killed when Brande sabotages his escape attempt; Nicholas thus refuses to forgive his father, and moves to America to live with his mother.

In the British domestic comedy, such visions of irreparable family breakdown are wholly unrealised, whatever tensions may exist. The hugely successful *Raising a Riot*, directed by Wendy Toye, brings the nuclear family to the forefront. The film's central figure is stolid, diffident Tony Kent (Kenneth More), a naval officer on leave, who is forced to run the household – and look after his three children – single-handedly in the temporary absence of his wife, Mary (Shelagh Fraser). As sociologist Elizabeth Bott discovered, sharing of roles between husband and wife in the 1950s was increasingly common in the nuclear family setting.[8] However, Kent lacks both the practical skills to run the household and the emotional intelligence to manage his children. His willingness to assume his wife's domestic duties does not derive from belief in sexual egalitarianism, or even a solicitous desire to lighten his wife's load. Rather, having rejected offers of help from matronly Aunt Maud (Olga Lindo), he arrogantly supposes that he will be able to master the alien environs of the family home. Initially, he attempts bribery as a means of retaining control over children Anne (Mandy Miller), Peter (Gary Billings) and Fusty (Fusty Bentine), buying them a dog to keep them on side. His cookery skills are so hopeless that he resorts to garden secateurs to break a string of sausages when his own teeth prove insufficient. Kent finds himself caught between two models of child-rearing. His initial inclination is a no-nonsense, distancing, masculine-coded disciplinarianism. This creates an embarrassing situation when the children launch a pseudo-military 'commando raid' on a neighbour's house, and steers Kent towards the more feminine-coded approach of intimacy and moral guidance.

As in many 1950s family comedies, children are reduced largely to a symbolic presence, unwittingly dealing reverses that initially undermine, ultimately reaffirm the dual father-mother role of the patriarch. Even Mandy Miller, Britain's leading child actress, fulfils the stock role of the sensible eldest child, an artless confidant for Kent in his hour of uncertainty. In her ability to take care of her younger siblings and provide sage emotional support for her father (in her mother's absence), she is figured, unmistakably, as a wife-and-mother-in-waiting. The title invokes the spectre of orgiastic chaos, but these children are mainly level-headed, restrained and well socialised. A brief exception is a children's party which descends into pandemonium, the children delightedly hurling food at each other, while two starchy adults are forced to retreat after cream pies are thrown in their faces. This staple scene of child-orientated cinema comes to a sober conclusion, though, as Kent quickly re-enforces order with a furious, cane-wielding entrance. The party scene articulates, on one level, embrace of childish impulse and a temporary repudiation of the restraint that the socialisation process teaches us is vital to an ordered and functioning society. In the *St. Trinian*'s films, and the later ironic Dionysian fantasy of *Bugsy Malone* (Alan Parker, 1976), this impulse is uncurbed; an invitation is extended to child and adult spectators to engage vicariously, and thus (re)experience the quintessence of childhood without censure.

In *Raising a Riot*, the chaotic impulse emanates from a weakness in the socialising process, caused by Kent's temporary absence and, indirectly, by Mary's longer-term absence. The children's party scene functions ultimately to test Kent's paternal authority. Have his experiences as a lone parent rendered him toothless or effeminised? His ability to re-establish control suggests, rather, that he has added new strings to his bow – the ability to empathise and educate his children, as Mary would ordinarily do – without losing his basic masculine potency. Yet the film ends with Kent's epiphany that the distinct role of the wife and mother cannot be dispensed with:

Mrs Kent: Darling, Aunt Maud says you've been wonderful with the children.

Mr Kent: Does she? Well, I wouldn't like to claim too much. But if she cares to say so.

Mrs Kent: In fact, you've been such a success I think you should take over more often. Then I can go out and get myself a job.

Mr Kent: Not on your life. If you leave me alone again with that dreadful brood for five minutes I'll… As a matter of fact, darling, I made an awful hash of it. I wouldn't be a woman if the entire United Nations went down on their bended knees and begged me to be. Do you know what a woman has to be? A cross between a saint and a dray horse, a diplomat and an automatic washing machine, a psychiatrist and a bulldozer, a sanitary engineer and a mannequin.

Mrs Kent: Darling, I do *know* what a woman has to be.

Although Kent is happy to acknowledge the manifold difficulties of his wife's domestic role, he pointedly refuses to participate further in the daily running of house and home, or to support her in pursuing a career beyond the confines of the family home. It seems that women, as with children, must know their place.

No Kidding, a relatively late entry in the domestic comedy cycle, centres on a young married couple, Mr and Mrs Robinson (Leslie Phillips and Geraldine McEwan), who inherit a dilapidated house in the country and turn it into a summer camp for wealthy children. Mr Robinson reluctantly plays along with his wife's insistence that the children are afforded complete freedom. After a series of near-disasters, in which the children, naturally, abuse the privilege, Robinson pulls rank and imposes tighter discipline. In the final scene, the children refuse to leave with their parents until they receive a promise never to be abandoned again. A satire on fashionably laissez-faire approaches to child development, *No Kidding* pragmatically reasserts the importance of discipline. Mrs Robinson's utopian platitudes that children require absolute freedom to express themselves crudely caricatures Dr Benjamin Spock's *The Common Sense Book of Baby and Child Care* (1946; published in Britain in 1955). As in the seemingly liberated, actually conservative *St. Trinian's* films, anarchy prevails as a result of these philosophies being put into practice. Likeable Mr Robinson has some sympathies with his wife's approaches, but eventually hardens to the conviction that limitations are necessary, first when the children vandalise the house and estate, and then when a group of them, led by the sexually liberated teenager, Vanilla (Julia Lockwood), drives the Robinsons' car to an all-night cafe. Pushed to his limit, Robinson returns the children home safely, and when his wife exclaims happily, 'They're all right!', he furiously replies, 'No they're not, they're all *wrong*! Wrong as it's possible for children to be, do you hear? Selfish, spoiled, thoughtless, uncontrolled… *Wrong*!' Realising her fault, Mrs Robinson penitently admits: 'It's all my fault'.

Through its farcical extremes, *No Kidding* puts the old adage, 'Give them an inch and they'll take a mile', into action. This is true of Mrs Robinson as much as the children. Her response to the almost equal footing her husband affords her is to err with 'typical' feminine lack of pragmatism and wrongheadedness. The film is a conservative rebuttal of modernity on two fronts; given too much freedom, women and children disastrously get out of control. It behoves the decent, fair-minded but resolute patriarch to reassert his (benign) control over his family. When the children help to fend off an interfering local busybody attempting to close down the school by being on their best behaviour, but immediately afterwards begin fighting again, Mrs Robinson asks her husband to stop them, but his response signifies his temperance and fair-mindedness: 'There are times for freedom, and this is one of them'. Having offloaded their surrogate children, but having gleaned valuable childrearing experience, the Robinsons agree to have a baby of their own. *No Kidding*, like the other films in this cycle, thus tempers its support for the nuclear family with acknowledgement that change – but not too much change – in parent-child relations is needed.

No Kidding is part of a larger cycle of family comedies of the late 1950s and early 1960s in which child appeal is fused with more overtly adult subtexts, situations and verbal comedy. As with *Carry on Teacher* (1959) – also directed by Gerald Thomas and produced by Peter Rogers – a large cast of children, who revel in subversion and disorder, provide identification for younger viewers. Like the *Carry On* series, as well as the later *St. Trinian's* entries and *A French Mistress* (Roy Boulting, 1960), *No Kidding* reflects a transition in the family comedy towards a bawdier mode, while stopping short of the inescapable innuendo of the *Carry Ons*. The continuities as well as the progressions are evident from *The Happiest Days of Your Life* to *St. Trinian's* and *Carry On* to the Robin Askwith-starred *Confessions* sex films (1974–77). All trade on characteristically British qualities of self-restraint and/or repression in the face of temptation. In the early films, it is the contrary impulse to act as reason and decorum demand, and retain full possession of oneself, against the desire to run wild, to let loose the pleasure principle. In the later films, the temptations are almost invariably sexual in nature. Yet in both, discomfort and embarrassment regarding sex finds an outlet through coy innuendo.

As the 1960s progressed, there was progressively less need for suggestion. When Barbara Windsor's ample breasts finally break free from their constraints (of the brassiere and the censor) in *Carry on Camping* (Gerald Thomas, 1969), it is no more than the logical development of the 'sex sells' philosophy adopted by Launder and Gilliat in *Blue Murder at St. Trinian's* when busty glamour model Sabrina was cast in a background role. Increasingly, the presence of children is incongruous in relation to these films' dominant emphases. It became apparent that the general public was more interested in childish adults running wild than *actual* children doing so. Ironically, the *Carry On* raunchiness and verbal lewdness is now considered part of its antique charm, with its sexual suggestiveness reinterpreted as a marker of chastity or restraint rather than randiness, in an age where attention has refocused on more extreme forms of sexual expression.

Adaptation and Halas and Batchelor's *Animal Farm*

Britain's production of prestige, family-orientated literary adaptations was at a low ebb for the duration of World War II. Resources and creative talent were needed elsewhere, and energies were instead channelled into more topical genres, such as the war film. David Lean's postwar Dickens adaptations, *Great Expectations* (1946) and *Oliver Twist* (1948), were widely regarded as masterpieces, epitomising the kind of wholesome but lush and cinematic films felt to be the bedrock of the indigenous cinematic tradition. The *MFB* thought that *Great Expectations* fully utilised 'the visual power of the cinema' and that it was 'a unique and reassuring British film', but, interestingly, did not deem it suitable for children, classifying it 'AB' (adults and adolescents only).[9] Conversely, several prestige films that followed – including *Oliver Twist, Treasure Island* (Byron Haskin, 1950), *Scrooge* (Brian Desmond Hurst, 1951), *Ivanhoe* (Richard Thorpe, 1952), *The Prisoner of Zenda* (Richard Thorpe and John Cromwell, 1952) and *The Pickwick Papers* (Noel Langley, 1952) – were adaptations of long-established favourites among generations of British youth.[10] The South African-born Hollywood screenwriter, Noel Langley, was a key figure in this cycle of adaptations. Having made an important contribution to the

Happiest Days: British Cinema and the Family Audience in the Fifties

development of Hollywood child-orientated cinema by scripting MGM's *The Wizard of Oz* (Victor Fleming, 1939), Langley worked for several years in Britain, writing the screenplays for *Tom Brown's Schooldays, Scrooge, Ivanhoe, The Prisoner of Zenda*, and *Father's Doing Fine*, and directing Renown's adaptation of *The Pickwick Papers*.

Most of these productions were literary adaptations in the classical Hollywood mould: conspicuously expensive (utilising big stars and Technicolor), displaying ostentatious 'fidelity' to the source narrative, and assuredly 'for the whole family'. But Halas and Batchelor's adaptation of Orwell's *Animal Farm* – released in December 1954, and Britain's first feature-length animation – diverges markedly from the Hollywood model in its approach to animation and to family-orientated filmmaking more broadly. Halas and Batchelor had been Britain's leading animation studio since the 1940s, though in size and output it was dwarfed by the major Hollywood firms. Run by the husband-and-wife team of John Halas and Joy Batchelor, the studio made animated shorts for the Ministry of Information during the war. Its background in propaganda films was a major point of attraction for the American independent filmmaker Louis de Rochemont, who engaged Halas and Batchelor to produce the adaptation. Unbeknownst to Halas and Batchelor, de Rochemont had acquired the rights to *Animal Farm* with the covert financial support of the United States' Central Intelligence Agency (CIA). The CIA, which supplied the bulk of the film's projected budget of £90,000, saw in Orwell's novel an anti-communist allegory which could serve as effective Cold War propaganda.[11]

The storyline largely adheres to Orwell's allegorical narrative, centring on a group of oppressed farm animals who rise up to overthrow the tyrannical human farmer Jones, form a society of equals on communist principles, and then witness their utopia subverted by the dictatorial pig Napoleon, who seizes power, governs by force, and systematically abolishes the community's founding principles of natural egalitarianism. The major point of difference is the film's ending. Orwell's novella terminates with the remaining animals unable to differentiate the pig Napoleon from the representatives of human society; the film adds a brief but significant coda, as the donkey Benjamin marshals together the downtrodden inhabitants of the farm. The narration tells us that:

> To the animals it seemed that their world, which may or may not become a happy place to live in, was worse than ever for ordinary creatures. And another moment had come when they must do something about it.

The animals advance menacingly on Napoleon's house. As the music swells to a triumphant fever pitch, there is a close-up of Napoleon's terrified face as the animals break into his plush drawing room, and the camera pans to a portrait of him hanging on the wall, which is smashed and tumbles to the ground. The final image sees a procession of animals, seemingly victoriously, walking in unison from Napoleon's devastated home, as the screen fades to black.

As a concession to mass audiences, this coda goes as far as it reasonably could in positing a more hopeful future without negating Orwell's vision. Some sources claim that it was a CIA imposition, though it can scarcely be regarded as a 'happy ending' in the conventional sense. The success of this 'second revolution' is deliberately uncertain. Even its equivocal acknowledgement that this new world 'may or may not become a happy place to live in' offers nothing more comforting or definitive than the Old Testament accession that 'Thou mayest' triumph over evil, celebrated by Steinbeck for its empowering potential in *East of Eden* (1952). This refusal to disambiguate recurs in later British family films where a 'happy ending' would be anathema to their cultivated view of the world, including the animated features *Watership Down* (Martin Rosen, 1978) and *When the Wind Blows* (Jimmy Murakami, 1986), which tread a similar path between 'family' and 'adult' suitability.

Not only is *Animal Farm* the sole indigenous film of its type made purposely for propaganda purposes, but it also makes a clear break from North American animation. It eschews the more rounded character animation characteristic of Disney's work in favour of more impressionist portrayals; it uses darker tones; the themes are more adult-orientated; and the conventional happy ending is denied. Halas and Batchelor, as Daniel J. Leab reveals, consciously resisted former Disney animator John Reed's attempts to 'add Disneyesque touches to the animation', though there are points where child-orientated animation conventions reassert themselves.[12] 'Cute' touches include a duckling's endearing attempts to keep up with the other animals, climb stairs and to work in the field with an

Happiest Days: British Cinema and the Family Audience in the Fifties

outsized scythe, despite its physical disadvantages, and trying to evade maths lessons. In the best Disney tradition, these vignettes are accompanied by familiar tinkling flute music, emphasising the bird's adorableness. Generally, though, *Animal Farm* owes more to the visually darker, unsentimental allegories produced by the Soviet Union studio Soiuzmultfilm than with the likes of Disney and the Fleischer Brothers.

Watership Down and *When the Wind Blows* follow a similarly adult-orientated route. Increasingly, this refusal to juvenilise has bemused successive generations of British audiences accustomed to child-orientated Hollywood animation, and perhaps partly explains why a strong, self-sustaining tradition of feature animation has never emerged in Britain. Like those later films, *Animal Farm* intersperses quiet plaintiveness with moments of visceral brutality. The film was not a major commercial hit; as Leab drolly observes, the 'prophet Orwell' did not translate into the 'profit Orwell'.[13] Production took three years rather than the anticipated 18 months, and the costs ultimately crept to £150,000 (still extremely economical by Disney standards).[14] Much of the critical reception in the US focused on the film's suitability for children. The New York *Daily News* warned its readers that this was an 'adult film', and an 'uncomfortably realistic and vitriolic satire on dictatorship'.[15] Similarly, the *New York Times* called it 'vivid and biting' but cautioned that: 'The cruelties that occur from time to time are more realistic and shocking than any of the famous sadisms that have occurred in Disney films'.[16]

Similar expressions of surprise and notes of caution were largely absent from British critical responses, which instead concentrated on the degree of fidelity to Orwell's vision. *Sight and Sound* felt that the 'radically altered' ending was 'inevitable', but that 'the fundamental meaning of book and film is the same'.[17] The *Observer*'s C. A. Lejeune defended the new coda, which gives 'a gleam of hope, where Orwell left us with nothing but despair', arguing that: 'Despair is no programme, and the screen no place for nullity'.[18] *Kinematograph Weekly* went as far to assert its suitability for 'all classes and, except for tiny tots, all ages', a position echoed in *Daily Mail*, which, somewhat caustically, labelled it 'the child's guide to the Communist fallacy'.[19] *The Times* also thought it overly child-orientated, believing that it failed sufficiently to depart from the conventions of children's animation and occasionally strayed into 'irresponsible humour, as with the Disney-esque

125

baby chicken [sic]', but praised its faithful translation of the bitterness, satire and emotion of the novel.[20] Moreover, the film was seen to demonstrate that: 'The cartoon need not spend so much of its time among the frenzied fantasies of the comic "short" and is capable of the imaginative interpretation of a serious idea'.[21]

Clearly, the film's relation to a great and cherished work of British fiction is foremost in these critics' minds. Equally apparent, however, is a genuine conviction in the potentialities of animation – specifically its incipient indigenous tradition – as a medium for mature and serious artistic expression. Halas and Batchelor held similar aspirations, and voiced their desire to adapt Bunyan's *The Pilgrim's Progress* (1678). Unfortunately, *Animal Farm* proved to be a false dawn for Halas and Batchelor, and, indeed, for British animation. No further home-grown animated feature appeared until July 1967, with the release of Halas and Batchelor's similarly uncommercial adaptation of the Gilbert and Sullivan opera *Ruddigore*. By that point, Disney and Hollywood animation had further tightened its grip on the British market, reinforcing the medium's close association with child audiences that *Animal Farm* disavows.

Teen Films and 'Adult' Movies

Such films with clear 'adult' themes and situations were hardly a 1950s invention, but during this decade there was increasing mainstream acceptance of them, as signified by the 1951 introduction of the 'X' rating (replacing the seldom-used 'H' certificate) to permit the release of films regarded as 'wholly adult in theme or treatment'. Advocates of cinema as a free and independent art form had long since lobbied for an easing of censorship restrictions, arguing against the requirement to accommodate the 'family' trade. In 1938, Alfred Hitchcock wrote:

> The power of universal appeal has been the most retarding force of the motion picture as an art. In the efforts of the maker to appeal to everyone, they have had to come down to the common simple story with the happy ending [...] The cost of making a picture is so great, and there are so many aspects of the business – world markets, American markets, and so on – that we find it difficult to get our money back, even for a successful

Happiest Days: British Cinema and the Family Audience in the Fifties

> film with a universal appeal, let alone in films that have experi-
> mented with the story or the artist. That is the one thing that has
> kept the cinema back. I should say it has pretty well gone a long
> way to destroying it as an art.[22]

For the industry, though, respectability and prestige were more important
than 'artistic' credibility. Until the 1950s, Hitchcock's dream of 'specialised'
theatres showing 'serious' films was largely unrealised. Both supply and
demand were insufficient.

The introduction of adult-themed films was a gradual process.
Hollywood producer David O. Selznick's *Duel in the Sun* (King Vidor et al.,
1946) provoked shock and indignation among several British critics, who
felt that its violence and sexuality were beyond the pale. The *Daily Express'*
Leonard Mosley thought it 'a most shocking film'; the *Daily Mirror's* Reg
Whitley wondered why 'Selznick should make a picture which can only do
harm to the industry'; and the *Daily Herald's* P. L. Mannock felt that: 'To
show this film to children will be an outrage. Unhappily, short of an instruction to showmen from their governing body, nothing will stop millions
of youngsters from seeing its sordid violence'.[23] Not everyone was so hostile. The 'X' certificate reflected a change in personnel, and mindset, at the
BBFC. The new BBFC president, Sir Sidney Harris, and secretary, Arthur
Watkins, were more receptive to so-called 'art' films.[24] As Watkins remarked
in October 1950:

> Grown-up filmgoers are having their intelligence sacrificed for
> the sake of the youngsters, whom we cannot keep out [...] [The
> 'X' certificate] will enable us to pass unquestionably adult films,
> instead of having to refuse a certificate.[25]

'Quality' foreign films, such as the Japanese *Rashomon* (Akira Kurosawa,
1950) and the French *La Ronde* (Max Ophuls, 1950), and hard-hitting
Hollywood productions like *Quo Vadis* (Mervyn LeRoy, 1951) and *Death
of a Salesman* (László Benedek, 1951), were passed for distribution. The 'X'
rating did not pre-empt a change in attitudes; it responded to it. Initially,
the certificate was applied mainly to foreign films receiving only limited
release. As *Sight and Sound* observed in early 1954, the major British theatre chains were willing to book 'X' films only on rare occasions, on the
grounds that: 'The traditional "family audience" is considered too valuable

127

to be sacrificed'.[26] During the late 1950s and 1960s, this mindset gradually changed, and the 'X' film entered the mainstream.

Significantly, the 'X' rating was instituted in accordance with the recommendations of the Wheare Report – the very same document that had agitated for the formation of the Children's Film Foundation. The state-backed CFF was formed at precisely the point at which commercial cinema was shedding its public identity as a family entertainment. The British state, unlike the US government, was still staunchly paternalistic. It perceived a duty not just to protect 'vulnerable' parties from potentially damaging 'adult' material, but also to provide programming which would nurture and educate young minds. However, the long-held establishment view of the British people as insufficiently mature to handle challenging or censorious culture was slowly giving way to the conviction that adult minds are capable of choosing their own amusements (and, indeed, have the right to do so). Initially, fears were raised that the 'X' rating was being misinterpreted as signifying purely sensationalist or pornographic content.[27] In early 1952, the BBFC issued a statement clarifying that: 'The Board greatly hopes that the new category will provide an appropriate place for adult films of high quality [...] which, although unsuitable for children, make a legitimate appeal to their parents'.[28]

The advent of the 'X' rating, coupled with cinema's increasingly 'adult' trajectory, led to renewed calls to limit children's film-going. The December 1953 meeting of the Catholic Teachers' Federation called for greater production of children's films and 'stricter supervision' over their attendance, while also voicing a familiar nationalistic aversion to North American films on the grounds that: 'Our way of life [is] preferable'.[29] These were not minority views. The Wheare Report had recommended a complete prohibition on children under the age of five, a minimum age of seven for unaccompanied children, and a ban on unaccompanied children under the age of 12 after 8pm.[30] These recommendations were not carried out, but in January 1956, the Home Office introduced new regulations preventing unaccompanied under-12s from attending evening shows after 7pm.[31] The attempted ghettoisation of the child audience to the matinee programme will have been welcomed by those convinced that children had no business watching 'grown-up' films, and by those simply irritated by children's presence at evening shows. Yet children had always watched

Happiest Days: British Cinema and the Family Audience in the Fifties

'adult' movies. One of the most revealing findings of the Wheare Report was that *Gone with the Wind* (Victor Fleming, 1939) was equally popular among children as *Dick Barton: Special Agent* (Alfred J. Goulding, 1948).[32] The *Manchester Guardian* argued that this confirmed the need for 'more special children's films', but the data could easily be interpreted as signifying the exact opposite.[33]

The audience was fragmenting. Movie-goers had long been referred to with homogenising descriptors like the 'mass audience' or 'general audience', as if pluralistic audience sections divided by age, class and sex were a unified whole. This illusion had unravelled. The CFF, with its gold stamp of state approval, served young children; serious-minded adults were able, if they so desired, to frequent smaller art-house theatres; and, most significantly, the teen audience – previously not regarded as a discrete entity – had become a lucrative, independent market. In the middle was the traditional family audience, an increasingly beleaguered faction whose interests were publicly represented by a small number of prudes (educators, church leaders and civic organisations) who rarely attended theatres, but loudly expressed their disenchantment with cinema's salacious trajectory. The cultural landscape was certainly changing, but hardly consensually, or in a way that was fully comprehensible. Boundaries of acceptability in mainstream cinema were being pushed. The enormous popularity of *It's Great to be Young!* (Cyril Frankel, 1956), a musical comedy centring primarily on older teenagers, attested to the power of the hitherto unexploited teen audience, a financially solvent and increasingly autonomous market. A new generation of producers stepped into the breach.

British studio Hammer was at the forefront of the emergence of the teen film. An early instance was its Dick Barton films (1948–50), based on the popular BBC radio show (1946–51) centring on the adventures of the former commando. The first in the series, *Dick Barton: Special Agent*, distils into its 69-minute running time many of the most lamented characteristics of the 'children's film': a clichéd storyline, atrocious dialogue, crudely-drawn characters, poor acting, low production values, and a reliance on pratfalls. The radio series – broadcast on the BBC Light Programme – purportedly addressed a broader family audience in its early evening slot (where it played to millions of listeners each weeknight), but it was, in truth, most popular among young boys and adolescents. Its sequels, *Dick Barton Strikes Back* (Godfrey Grayson, 1949) and *Dick Barton at Bay* (Godfrey Grayson, 1950), are closer to the tone of the radio series, with less slapstick and cartoonish villains. The storylines are typical Boys' Own fare, but the higher production values in the sequels – including extensive location filming – suggests that Hammer envisaged a wider market beyond the children's cinema club. The Dick Barton films are British analogues of the Hollywood 'Poverty Row' children's and youth films of the 1930s and 1940s. Hammer produced a succession of youth films in a similar vein, including *The Saint's Return* (Seymour Friedman, 1953) and *Men of Sherwood Forest* (Val Guest, 1954). While targeting young and adolescent (and chiefly male) audiences, these productions were avowedly wholesome and unobjectionable, representing a genre of escapist family films that critics might dismiss from an artistic standpoint, but could scarcely object to on moral grounds.

By the mid-1950s, a new, edgier brand of youth exploitation film was emerging, aimed more squarely at older and more financially independent teenagers, and explicitly calculated to thrill, to horror and to titillate. In British Lion's *Devil Girl from Mars* (David MacDonald, 1954), England is invaded by Patricia Laffan's black leather-clad Martian dominatrix, who intends to procure Earthmen to help repopulate her planet. This, and other films such as *Stranger from Venus* (Burt Balaban, 1954), took their cue from the Hollywood sci-fi cycle of the early 1950s; but they also responded to increasing trade recognition of the need to address young cinemagoers to arrest the precipitous decline in cinema attendance. In early 1954, an editorial in *Sight and Sound* largely dismissed the threat from television (a 'passing charm'), but reiterated that 'it is the younger section of the population which forms traditionally the main body of regular film fans' and that 'the film industry must recognise [...] the need to encourage the cinema-going habit in the younger generation'.[34] Hammer's *The Quatermass Xperiment* (Val Guest, 1955) shifted the emphasis in British youth cinema from sci-fi towards horror. The title consciously plays the illicit connotations of the over-16s-only 'X' certificate, and in its grotesque, tragic narrative of a British astronaut slowly transformed into an alien monster, the film consciously abandons the child-friendly amiability of Hammer's earlier youth releases.

Happiest Days: British Cinema and the Family Audience in the Fifties

During the late 1950s, Hammer produced a succession of lavish and commercially successful adaptations of horror classics, including *The Curse of Frankenstein* (Terence Fisher, 1957), *Dracula* (Fisher, 1958) and *The Mummy* (Fisher, 1959). Their violence and sexuality may be tame by modern standards, but their mature content represented entry to an illicitly alluring adult world. As in the US, the teen film branched into new styles and genres. North American independent Sam Katzman produced the first major rock 'n' roll pic with *Rock around the Clock* (Fred F. Sears, 1956); Britain responded with the hugely successful biopic *The Tommy Steele Story* (Gerard Bryant, 1957), as well as the more modest *Rock You Sinners* (Denis Kavanagh, 1957). The West End musical adaptation *Expresso Bongo* (Val Guest, 1959) offers a rougher-hewn (fictionalised) retelling of the rise of teen rocker Tommy Steele, with its unscrupulous agents and evocatively seedy Soho settings of nocturnal coffee bars and strip clubs. Even with liberalising censorship restrictions, *Expresso Bongo* pushed the 'A' rating to the limits, but ensured that older children and adolescents could attend with 'adult' supervision (although the *MFB* warned parents taking children to 'expect some embarrassment').[35] Early 1960s teen musicals, such as the Cliff Richard vehicles *The Young Ones* (Sidney J. Furie, 1961) and *Summer Holiday* (Peter Yates, 1963), steered the genre back towards wholesomeness.

By then, a new cycle of youth-orientated, anti-establishment 'adult' films were reaching British screens. *Room at the Top* (Jack Clayton, 1959), *Look Back in Anger* (Tony Richardson, 1959), *Saturday Night and Sunday Morning* (Karel Reisz, 1960), *A Taste of Honey* (Tony Richardson, 1961) and *The Loneliness of the Long Distance Runner* (Tony Richardson, 1962) became known as 'kitchen sink dramas', a label that highlighted their realist credentials and preoccupation with working-class issues (though the movement's figureheads were chiefly middle-class and well-educated). Cynical, politically left-wing and often savage, they represented a major assault on the British middlebrow orthodoxy. The so-called 1950s consensus was broken, or rather exposed; the children's rebellion against the adult establishment in *The Happiest Days of Your Life* had proven prophetic. On the other side of the fence, independent Hollywood producers such as Ray Harryhausen and Milton Subotsky moved to England and spent much of the 1960s producing low-budget special effects movies for family and teen audiences, anticipating the 1970s mainstream popularity of all-age blockbusters such as George Lucas's *Star Wars* (1977). Children's and family movies, then, endured into the 1960s and beyond, as we shall see in the following chapter. But after the advent of the youth film and the parallel 'adultification' of British screens, no-one could plausibly argue that cinema was a 'child-friendly' medium.

Whistle Down the Wind and the End of Consensus

Despite the insurgent rise of the teen film, and the incendiary spirit of the kitchen sink drama, no British film conveys more clearly the end of the 1950s consensus, and the symbolic potentiality of youth, than the child-centred *Whistle Down the Wind* (Bryan Forbes, 1961). The film focuses on young Kathy Bostock (Hayley Mills), who becomes convinced that a dishevelled runaway murderer, Blakey (Alan Bates), who takes refuge from the police in a stable on her family's rural farm, is the reincarnation of Jesus Christ. The idealistic but naive Kathy recruits other local children to this belief, unaware of the vast manhunt underway in the local area. The climax of the film sees the children rise up to protect Blakey as the police descend on the farm and take him away. *Whistle Down the Wind* is a comparative rarity: a British family film that has attained critical as well as popular acclaim. The latter may be gauged by the fact that it was adapted into a Broadway/West End musical in 1996, with music by Andrew Lloyd Webber. The former partly reflects its vicarious association with the burgeoning British social realist film cycle via the casting of archetypal 'angry young man' Alan Bates, on the one hand, and its lyricism and allegorical dimensions, which invite comparisons with recent child-centred but adult-orientated films such as *Les Quatre cent coups* (Francois Truffaut, 1959), on the other. However, the movie poster's tagline – 'A Story About Kids… For Everyone!' – emphasises the film's family-friendly universalism. One of the top ten highest-grossing films of the year at the British box office, it was nominated for four BAFTAs, including Best British Film and Best British Actress.

The children's mistaking Blakey for Jesus may be interpreted as indicative of their youthful naivety, partially reflecting their sheltered rural upbringing. Equally, it accords with the film's symbolic representation of childhood as embodying innocence and virtue. Childhood, in this sense, enters into conflict with the film's view of adulthood as overburdened with worldly vices: pragmatism, cynicism, brutality, lack of imagination and disconnection with nature. These grown-ups are personifications of Marcuse's 'one-dimensional man'. Joylessly self-preoccupied, they merely pay lip service to Christian precepts of love and forgiveness, and have little understanding of transcendent concepts of beauty and lyricism, all of which are localised within Kathy. Religious faith is evidently in decline in the bustling, industrialised nearby town of Burnley. In one scene, the camera pans across a sign which reads, 'Something is missing from this CH–CH – UR', i.e. 'you are'.

Family relations are even more precarious. Kathy's mother is deceased and Mr Bostock (Bernard Lee) is rarely present, instead spending most of his time working or drinking in the pub. Auntie Dorothy (Elsie Wagstaff) – potentially a nurturing surrogate mother – is sour and distant, eager to remind her brother that his children are not her responsibility. Other adult figures are similarly unsympathetic. The coarse, malingering farm hand Eddie (Norman Bird), an unlikeable comical figure, attempts in the film's opening scene to drown a litter of newly-born kittens by trapping them in a sack and dumping them in a river. Representatives of the Christian church fare little better. While discussing the Blakey case with a policeman, the Vicar (Hamilton Dyce) harshly instructs a schoolboy not to clean his boots in a nearby puddle. The young Salvation Army worker (Patricia Heneghan) whom Kathy's brother Charles (Alan Barnes) approaches to adopt a rescued kitten airily replies that Jesus will look after it. Her euphemistic lack of concern unwittingly sets the subsequent events in motion, when her words are interpreted literally (in accordance with her own Biblical teachings).

None of these adults are contemptible, but they are far from the reassuring or solicitous presences of the CFF films. Blakey is the only adult character truly to make an emotional connection with the children. In his refusal to deny his assumed divine identity – even at the film's climax, when it can do him no good – he appears to intuit that the children must be protected from the truth, and from corrupting adult society in general. These children represent a potential better future world order. In this sense, *Whistle Down the Wind* anticipates the optimism and revolutionary spirit of the impending counter-cultural movement. A key moment in this regard occurs during the Sunday School sequence, where the young teacher (Diane Clare) nervously fends off questions from Kathy about what would happen to Jesus if he returned in person to the world as it is today:

Teacher: Well, I'm afraid the world hasn't changed *that* much, Kathy. There are still bad people, as well as good.

Kathy: But would they crucify him?

Teacher: I suppose some of the bad people might try... But this time, all the good people would have to try even harder to stop them. [Looks around the classroom.] We know what we'd do, don't we? What would we do? If Jesus came back on Earth. What would we do? Hmm? We'd praise him, wouldn't we? What would we do?

All the class: Praise him, miss. Praise him.

The ending may remind one (in keeping with the film's Biblical themes) of Matthew 5:5: 'Blessed are the meek: for they shall inherit the earth'. But this is no apocalyptically re-imagined Sodom and Gomorrah, evoking a civilisation corrupted beyond salvation. Rather, society has been twisted, almost imperceptibly, out of shape, whilst its individual members remain convinced of their own righteousness. Kathy uncritically accepts the high-sounding words espoused by her elders. Among the adults, Blakey alone perceives the need to keep the next generation free from knowledge of greed, corruption and brutality.

Kathy and many of her friends have spent their entire life on the farm, near a small village, with only occasional visits to the nearby Burnley, and Sunday school classes are their primary source of worldly knowledge. As such, they retain a slightly fantastical, anachronistically feudal worldview. Kathy literally believes that her farm will be visited by 'shepherds, wise men, lords, ladies, bishops and people, the mayor of Burnley!' when Jesus's return is revealed. Malcolm Arnold's score highlights the Biblical parallels, overlaying sections of 'We Three Kings' as the children visit Blakey in the lambing barn. Unquestionably, Blakey's allowing the children to continue believing in his divinity is manipulative and self-serving; it allows a failed, despicable man to re-imagine himself as adored, reformed messiah. Ironically, he is obviously irreligious: when Kathy first sees him, he blasphemously exclaims 'Jesus Christ!' – an expression the devout young girl has clearly never heard in a profane context. Later, when presented with

Image 5.2 Hayley Mills's ingénue Kathy and Alan Bates's runaway murderer Blakey, in *Whistle Down the Wind* (1961)

a copy of the New Testament ('your book') by one of the village children, Blakey reacts with bemusement, and when asked to tell a story, he puts the Bible to one side and begins reading from a modern magazine. Yet there are clearly redemptive aspects to the masquerade. Seemingly not without a conscience or sense of moral duty, despite his vilification, Blakey never harms any of the children, and appears genuinely affected by Kathy's distress shortly before his arrest.

The film valorises the child's moral purity, while attacking the hypocrisy of a society that imparts religious dogma while casually disregarding its most important tenets. The Vicar is unable to give Kathy a satisfactory answer when she asks him why God allows some people to live and some to die. Ultimately, his evasive and long-winded reply turns to expressions of dissatisfaction regarding children 'taking guttering and lead [...] from the church'. Kathy is a much better Christian than the pompous, authoritarian churchman. When, in the final scene, Blakey – having surrendered himself to the police – is handcuffed, his pose resembles Jesus on the cross. After he is driven away, the crowd of children who have gathered to see him quickly disperse, leaving a tearful Kathy alone, save for two young latecomers, to whom Kathy hopefully promises that Jesus will 'be coming again'.

It is one of the film's tragedies that society's corruption is visible only by those who live outside its many intricate complexities, which collectively deaden the innocent, virtuous spirit embodied by Kathy. Blakey, temporarily removed from society's vices, and through close contact with the not-yet-socialised children, perhaps undergoes such a spiritual revelation. The childlike qualities once presumably possessed by the likes of Eddie, Auntie Dorothy and the Vicar have been eroded by age and experience. Furthermore, not all of the film's child figures are naive, innocent and unspoiled. Charles is vocally sceptical of Blakey's identity after he neglectfully allows a kitten gifted to him to die of starvation. Later, Charles alerts his father to Blakey's presence, asserting: 'It *isn't* Jesus – it's just a feller'. Other children, such as Jackie (Roy Holder), the lazy, football- and television-obsessed Sunday School attendee, and the school bully, Raymond (Barry Dean), who twists Jackie's arm almost to breaking point and slaps Kathy's face when they announce that they have seen Jesus, are adults-in-waiting. They do not possess the Romantic child characteristics of Kathy and her followers. Each of the film's children will grow up, by and by; what the film is unable to forecast is whether they will develop the same flaws as their parents, or rather, alternatively, use their knowledge, wrought through experience, to avoid repeating the same behavioural patterns; whether, in fact, they will mirror the trajectory of the present generation of Western youth rebelling against adult authority.

6

Disney in Britain

Between 1950 and 1979, Disney made 15 live-action films in Britain: *Treasure Island* (Byron Haskin, 1950), *The Story of Robin Hood and His Merrie Men* (Ken Annakin, 1952), *The Sword and the Rose* (Annakin, 1953), *Rob Roy, The Highland Rogue* (Harold French, 1953), *Kidnapped* (Robert Stevenson, 1960), *Swiss Family Robinson* (Annakin, 1960), *Greyfriars Bobby* (Don Chaffey, 1961), *The Three Lives of Thomasina* (Chaffey, 1963), *The Fighting Prince of Donegal* (Michael O'Herlihy, 1966), *Bedknobs and Broomsticks* (Stevenson, 1971), *Diamonds on Wheels* (Jerome Courtland, 1973), *One of Our Dinosaurs is Missing* (Stevenson, 1975), *Escape From the Dark* (Charles Jarrott, 1976), *Candleshoe* (Norman Tokar, 1977) and *Unidentified Flying Oddball* (Russ Mayberry, 1979). Initially, Disney's filming in Britain was a means of circumventing trade restrictions implemented by the postwar Labour government, but the practice continued long afterwards. Given the voluminous quantity of Disney scholarship, it is perhaps surprising that these British-made films have not received more attention. Only the Anglicised, enduringly popular *Mary Poppins* (Robert Stevenson, 1964) – which, in fact, was filmed at Disney's Burbank Studios in California – has gained much critical recognition. What links most of the above films is that they are filtered through a similarly gauzy, nostalgic image of Britain and 'Britishness'; a sort of mid-Atlantic folk memory,

137

rooted in pleasurable associations and belief systems. Their immediate sources include British history, especially romance and adventure; legend and folk tale; and children's period fiction.

At a time when British children's films were made almost exclusively in black-and-white, and largely studio-bound, Disney's British films were notably exotic. They were lavish, colourful, filmed on location, and informed by Hollywood production standards and narrative conventions. Previously, only Korda's Sabu vehicles had provided such a package; everything else, from Disney's own *Snow White and the Seven Dwarfs* (David Hand et al., 1937) to the likes of MGM's *The Wizard of Oz* (Victor Fleming, 1939), had been imported from Hollywood. Unusually, the British Disney films do deal with a geographically and nationally differentiated Britain, with films set in Scotland and Ireland, thus moving beyond the parochial Englishness the majority of so-called 'British' films invoke. This chapter focuses on two partly distinct and partly overlapping cycles within Disney's British films. The first cycle, represented by *The Story of Robin Hood, The Sword and the Rose, Rob Roy, the Highland Rogue, Kidnapped* and *The Fighting Prince of Donegal,* embodies a dialectic between projections of escapism and a notably anti-imperialist agenda. The second cycle, typified by *Greyfriars Bobby, Mary Poppins, Bedknobs and Broomsticks* and *Candleshoe,* reconstruct Victorian/Edwardian-era fantasies of patriarchal family unity, reflecting contemporary Anglo-American anxieties concerning the perceived decline of the nuclear family. This chapter is concerned with how these ideologies are manifested in films that continually assert their escapist, apolitical functions, and how far these British Disney films, made for a transatlantic audience, successfully negotiate questions of national identity.

Disney's Gambit: *Treasure Island* and the British Cycle

Treasure Island, released in June 1950, was a significant departure from Disney's established style. Not only was it Disney's first fully live-action film, but it marked a new direction for the studio in several other regards: it is unashamedly escapist, free from the artistic pretensions of the studio's earlier animated films; it targets 'the child of all ages' rather than attempting to engage children and adults as *separate* entities; and it represents the beginning of a very profitable and long-standing preoccupation with Britishness. In many ways, these early British films establish a template for Disney's subsequent live-action tradition. When Walt Disney acquired the adaptation rights to Robert Louis Stevenson's 1883 novel from MGM, he intended to shoot the movie in Hollywood.[1] His decision to film in Britain – at Denham Studios, and on location in Cornwall, Devon and Bristol – was a matter of financial expediency. At this point, British trade restrictions designed to boost local industry prevented foreign companies from exporting 100 per cent of earned capital. The only viable recourse for Hollywood studios was to reinvest the frozen capital in locally-produced films.

Stylistically, though, *Treasure Island* is of a kind with Hollywood productions, with the sort of gaudy, storybook visualisation of the 'Old World' associated with big-screen historical romances. Stevenson himself, of course, played fast and loose with historical realism in his child's-eye evocation of a world of pirates and treasure, over-the-top villainy and resourceful boy heroes. Nonetheless, the film's evocation of an earlier era – with tokenistic historical trappings such as horse-drawn carriages, cobbled streets, white cliffs and pirates who shout 'Arrr!' – is little more than semantic texture. 'Britishness' as a concept, as well as an image bank, is very much in play, but the films' inherited motifs are hard to locate, at least with much specificity, in 1950s Britain. While lighter and less self-consciously arty than Disney's early animated features, *Treasure Island* was the studio's first feature film in *any* medium aimed squarely at boys. Its animated features were clearly designed to transcend class, racial, gender and demographic boundaries as fully as possible. But *Treasure Island* deviates from this model in its emphasis on (male-associated) action over (female-associated) sentiment, and its all-male casting, confirming the novel's established association with generations of male youth. The live-action medium is also a major factor in the film's mobilising of a slightly different audience-base. While animated features were still rare and prestigious cinematic 'events', a contrary tendency perceived them as mere 'cartoons', a chiefly child-orientated medium unfit for adult consumption. Live-action films were free of this stigma. Indeed, the US trade paper *Boxoffice* reported that *Treasure Island*'s commercial success was partly a result of its attracting a higher proportion of adults than was usual for a Disney feature.[2]

Another point of departure from the company's animated films was Walt Disney's level of involvement. 'Uncle Walt' famously oversaw almost all aspects of production on his animated features, leading Paul Wells to label him an 'extra-textual auteur'.[3] Disney saw his own role as 'a little bee' moving 'from one area of the studio to another' to 'gather pollen and sort of stimulate everybody'.[4] Based as he was in California, Disney was unable to devote as much attention to his British films, and accounts differ as to the extent of his involvement. *Treasure Island* director Byron Haskin recalled that Disney was 'almost wholly detached from the film, the writing and editing included', but set designer Gus Walaker remembered him showing keen interest in his work.[5] Michael Barrier observes that *Treasure Island*'s 'serious and often foreboding' tone and level of screen violence – one of the pirates is seen being shot in the face at point-blank range; others are stabbed and slashed with cutlasses – 'was new for a Disney feature', but counters that: 'There is no reason to believe that Disney was not fully aware of it or that it did not have his approval'.[6] And according to Ken Annakin, who directed *The Story of Robin Hood*, the storyboards for that film had already been completed – presumably by Disney himself – by the time he was assigned, so as to 'enable Walt to exercise control, and supply his creative input from six thousand miles away'.[7] On balance, it would seem that Walt Disney was firmly committed to his British films, even if his own direct involvement was necessarily abbreviated.

Treasure Island was a huge box office hit. With rentals of just under $5 million, it grossed around two-thirds that of the much costlier animated feature *Cinderella* (Clyde Geronimi et al., 1950). Critics were largely appreciative. The *Manchester Guardian*, while regretting that Carol Reed or David Lean ('both of them magnificent in directing children') had not beaten Disney to the source text, and deeming the film's blazing Technicolor 'a destroyer of mystery', conceded that it 'is an honest job, respectful of its text and likely to reappear annually in British cinemas at pantomime time'.[8] Critics were divided on the matter of the film's primary audience appeal. The *Sunday Times*' Dilys Powell enthused: 'You couldn't find a subject with more action, or action better suited to the cinema', hinting at the film's universalism.[9] The *Catholic Herald*'s Grace Conway felt that 'Grown-ups are merely gate-crashers', whereas the *Daily Mirror*'s Reg Whitley thought it 'The best children's picture yet made for grown-ups'.[10] Two prominent

Disney in Britain

dissenting voices were the *Observer's* C. A. Lejeune, who lamented Disney's juvenilisation of the source material, thinking the film 'Less of a buccaneer adventure than a thoroughly well-organised party game', and the *MFB*, which 'Recommended [it] with confidence only to children unacquainted with the book, and to uncritical uncles and aunties'.[11]

Disney and British National Identity

A follow-up, *The Story of Robin Hood*, emerged two years later. Filmed exclusively in Britain (with second-unit filming undertaken in Sherwood Forest itself), the film signals an important departure from *Treasure Island* in its emphasis on points of tension within British national identity, a recurrent focus in Disney's subsequent 1950s British films. Indeed, in *Robin Hood*, two antithetical forms of 'Englishness' are played against each other. The first, embodied by Robin Hood (Richard Todd), his murdered father (Reginald Tate), the 'merrie men', Maid Marian (Joan Rice), and King Richard the Lion Heart (Patrick Barr), represent idealised freedom of movement and expression (within legal and ethical parameters), bravery, physicality, affinity with natural surroundings, self-reliance, friendship and community, camaraderie, humour, honest simplicity in dress, manners and lifestyle, classlessness, and sexual egalitarianism (localised in Maid Marian's feistiness and capacity for self-reliance). In later films, many of these attributes are transferred to Scottish and Irish rebels struggling to overcome an invading England, which has come to represent the undesirable qualities here embodied in the villainous Prince John (Hubert Gregg) and Sheriff of Nottingham (Peter Finch): cruelty, perfidiousness, cowardliness, rule by fear and intimidation rather than by consensus, lack of affinity with nature, ostentation, and control through economic imperialist oppression.

Prior to *The Fighting Prince of Donegal*, the ultimate arbiter of power and authority in these films is always ultimately benevolent, with the disruptive force a scheming or usurping underling. In *Robin Hood*, the antagonists are the King's brother, Prince John and his right-hand man, the Sheriff of Nottingham; in *The Sword and the Rose*, it is a nobleman of the Royal Court, the Duke of Buckingham (Michael Gough); and in *Rob Roy*, it is the Scottish Royalist, the Duke of Montrose (again played by

141

Gough). Good King Richard, who departs for the Holy Land at the beginning of the film, explicitly states that: 'The strength of England stems from the well-being of her humblest peasant'. Furthermore, Robin Hood's personal crusade against the extortionate taxes levied by Prince John and the Sheriff of Nottingham is imbued with moral authority by the approval of the legitimate representatives of church (unorthodoxly personified by Friar Tuck) and crown (the Queen Mother, and the returned King Richard, who bestows on Robin an earldom). High taxes imposed on simple, poor folk by already-wealthy elites are always an unethical form of social control. In *Robin Hood* and *Rob Roy*, they are the catalyst for armed revolt.

It is important to expand upon the importance of time and place within these films. It is worth recounting a brief exchange in which Robin Hood and Will Scarlet (Anthony Forwood) attempt to enlist Little John (James Robertson Justice) to their cause:

Will: Would you be of a mind to join us, John Little? You would eat fresh meat every day, sleep soft, have money in your poke.

Robin: So be it, you shoot your own meat and make your own bed and collect your own wages to give to poor souls in greater need.

Authentically shot on location in Sherwood Forest, the film's settings are so attractive, so seductively evocative of Shakespeare's Arden at its brightest, most verdant and languorous, that Robin and Will's appeal seems less a necessary reminder of nature's potential severity than an invitation to partake in its manifold pleasures. The unspoken dialectic here is between the forest's unalloyed pastoralism and the corrupt civilisation the rebels have left behind, an antithesis at the heart of Raymond Williams's masterful study, *The Country and the City* (1973). As Williams reminds us in relation to the rural/urban opposition:

> The English experience is especially significant, in that one of the decisive transformations, in the relations between country and city, occurred there very early and with a thoroughness which is still in some ways unapproached.[12]

Pre-industrialisation is now a distant memory; the recurrence of such pastoral narratives in the twentieth century (and beyond) no longer bespeak anxiety for a feared future loss, as to some degree it was with Shakespeare,

Twain, Tocqueville and Thoreau, as much as nostalgia for an imagined past where man and nature were perfectly aligned. This is not quite the Eden-like, Golden Age pastoralism, but more akin to Williams's later, more mediated form; a rural agrarianism where 'man had to earn his bread in the sweat of his brow' but where, equally, the sun never sets and harvests are plentiful.[13]

The Arcadian resonances of the pastoral 'Green World' (as Northrop Frye called it) are definitively invoked in Disney's Sherwood Forest. Filmed on location, in high summer, its verdancy precludes the overt romanticism of *As You Like It* (1599) and *A Midsummer Night's Dream* (1605), both typically recreated on stage, as was the Sherwood Forest of the silent-era Douglas Fairbanks adaptation (Allan Dwan, 1922). But a rougher-hewn version of the pastoral landscape abides in the vast plains, craggy outcrops and rolling heather of *Rob Roy*'s, *Kidnapped*'s and *The Fighting Prince of Donegal*'s Scottish highlands and Irish moors – the last outposts (at least in the British Isles) of a seductive, emboldening natural world overtaken by human activity. The films all posit a central structuring opposition between the unspoiled landscapes at their heart and an invasive, creeping urbanisation marked by antithetical associations, which reveals a central, and justifiable, anxiety that the encroachment of civilisation, by entering the wilderness, must destroy it.

The Sword and the Rose, in many regards, is a continuation of *The Story of Robin Hood*'s treatise on the individual vs. the state. The film centres on the historical romance between Henry VIII's (James Robertson Justice) sister, Princess Mary (Glynis Johns), and a noble commoner, Charles Brandon (Richard Todd), the Duke of Suffolk. The love affair is interrupted by courtly *realpolitik*, as King Henry brokers Mary's marriage to the elderly King Louis XII (Jean Mercure) of France. After Louis's death, a desperate Charles and Mary secretly wed without royal permission, upon which Henry sentences Charles to death before Mary convinces him to bless the union. The needs of the nation, the royal line, and the feudal social structure, are balanced against those of the heart: a recurrent antithesis in the historical romance genre. Heavy on dialogue and intrigue, and lacking the young identification figures of *Treasure Island* and *Kidnapped*, *The Sword and the Rose* failed to draw audiences in similar numbers. Adult subtexts assume greater prominence. In one comic sequence, Mary plies the elderly King Louis with wine until he faints, a ploy to render him incapable of consummating the marriage; Mary's recoiling from his touch assumes a physical (i.e. sexual) revulsion. Throughout, she also has to repel the aggressively amorous attentions of the Dauphin (Gerard Oury), who eagerly awaits the king's death, gleefully anticipating inheriting Mary as Queen.

The trappings of historical authenticity – courtly dances, banquets, wrestling contests, duels between noblemen, lute music, and various kinds of period finery – are present, but there is little of substance. Despite the purported advisory presence of historian Charles R. Beard, who had also provided 'technical advice' on *Treasure Island* and *Robin Hood*, the *MFB* attacked the film's 'rompingly inaccurate and comic-strip' approach.[14] Beard's much-publicised presence suggests that at least the appearance of historical accuracy was important to Disney. However, projections of authenticity are largely expedient. *Robin Hood* and *Rob Roy*, the closest in spirit to the folk tale tradition, are predicated on a distillation of valorised national characteristics rooted in ideals of community and consensus, pleasurably embodied in a single heroic figure. Robin Hood and Rob Roy are heroic archetypes, synonymous with the projected ideals and aspirations of their respective countries. Charles Brandon, though, is not England's champion, but a conventional hero interested only in his marriage suit. *The Sword and the Rose* says little about England, aside from conveying the impression – also present in *Rob Roy* – that it is ruled by self-serving, Machiavellian politicians and scheming, treacherous noblemen.

Rob Roy moves decisively away from this English milieu in centring on the rebel Scot, Rob Roy MacGregor (1671–1734), and his series of highland uprisings against King George I's military forces. The film opens with the storybook-like conceit of a written prologue:

> The early eighteenth century. When England chose German George the First to be King, the Scottish Highlanders rose in revolt and fought bitterly to enthrone their own James Stuart. But the English armies marched into the Highlands crushing every uprising until only a small band of proud and stubborn Clansmen kept alive the flicker of rebellion.

Again, Disney worked hard to establish a convincing historical backdrop. According to contemporary publicity materials, it brought in no fewer than 500 Scots, newly returned from fighting in the Korean War (1950–53), to participate in the extensive highland battle sequences filmed on location in The Trossachs and Aberfoyle, near Stirling.[15] Another blatant public-relations exercise was engaging Mrs Euing Crawford 'to supervise the weaving of original Scottish tartans to be used in the film'.[16] By this point, British reviewers were largely forgiving of Disney's commodification of British history, the *Manchester Guardian* noting the film's placement in 'an international, supranational world', and the *Catholic Herald* acknowledging that Rob Roy, 'Like Robin Hood, exists partly in history, partly in legend'.[17]

This is 'legend' with distinct ideological overtones, though. Walt Disney regarded the swashbuckling *Rob Roy* as little more than a 'Scottish western'.[18] However, in contrast to Richard Todd's just, heroic protagonist, the English are gratuitously murderous and conspicuously lacking honour and nobility. In an early exchange between the sympathetic royalist highlander, the Duke of Argyll (James Robertson Justice), and a bloodthirsty British army general, Cadogan (Martin Boddey), the latter reports that he has 4,000 mercenaries 'from the continent' at his command, ready to 'sweep through the highlands with fire and sword'. Cadogan then threatens to report Argyll's refusal to wipe out the rebels to the British Prime Minister, Walpole. The fact that the English forces should need to recruit continental mercenaries to bolster their forces is an obvious indictment, and contrasts with the presentation of the highland rebels who, as Argyll claims, are the 'finest men in the world', fighting for what they believe is a righteous cause. Unlike the English, they are not motivated purely by power and the desire to subjugate. Argyll's proud Highland tones sharply contrasts with the practiced, genteel Englishness of his treacherous, scheming fellow Scot, the Duke of Montrose, who attempts to inveigle himself into Royal favour.

Ultimately, in allowing Argyll and Rob to bypass the perfidious British Prime Minister, Walpole (Michael Goodliffe), and deal directly with King George (Eric Pohlmann), the film posits a compromise. The largely-unseen Walpole is imbued with typical politician's vices: deviousness, ruthlessness, and cowardly anonymity in the name of good policy, but King George, like Rob, is a man of honest principle. Rob recognises this, and offers his

145

sword to the King, who returns it, explaining, with a contemptuous glance at Montrose: 'The king does not fear the bold enemy. The king fears only the self-seeking friend'. George playfully remarks that Rob is 'a great rogue'; Rob sincerely retorts, 'And you, sire, are a great king'. The exchange plays the king's primary intended meaning, of 'infernal nuisance', against the secondary interpretation of the word as 'illustrious', 'sublime', which Rob assumes in his laudatory reply. Thus the film allows Rob Roy a personal victory, with his honour intact, his clan afforded amnesty and the fighting temporarily suspended. But English imperialism is ultimately reaffirmed – at the expense of the Scots' right to self-governance – through the ludicrous conceit that a nation's invasive colonialist policies are excusable if the man putatively in ultimate charge is gentlemanly and honourable.

Rob Roy is the first of several British Disney films in which the despotic English attempt to seize political control of a foreign territory. While *Rob Roy* (as with the later *Kidnapped*) articulates basic affiliation with Scotland and the Scots people, ultimately, its broader worldview is as confused as that of its originator, Walt Disney himself. Its sympathies with the Jacobite cause are almost forgotten in the film's climactic restoration of the old order and subduing of the highlanders' rebellion. The only way this ending can plausibly be sustained in light of what has gone before is by transferring the animus from the German-born King to the contemptible Scottish agitator, Montrose. But if King George is ultimately benevolent, and the rebels' initial rejection of him is more a reflection of their racial prejudices than his ability to rule, then the film's investment in the Jacobite cause becomes suspect. In fact, the film relinquishes its support for the Jacobites in the name of restoring order, perhaps recognising its obligations, as a family film, to draw a firm moral lesson (and to reaffirm the ideological status quo). Alternatively, it may have more to do with not offending English sovereignty, and, moreover, potentially alienating a valuable market. These films remained popular in England. *Rob Roy* was selected for display at the 1953 Royal Film Show, attended by Queen Elizabeth II, a fact that bespeaks the film's ideological legitimacy in the eyes of the British establishment.

Disney's adaptation of Stevenson's *Kidnapped* (1886) articulates many of the same nationalistic concerns but posits a similar symbolic rapprochement between the conflicting nations. The film's central figure, young lowland Scottish loyalist David Balfour (James MacArthur), embodies qualities of intelligence, reason, compassion and bravery. But it is in the thoroughly Scottish rebel highlander Alan Breck Stewart (Peter Finch) where valorised heroic characteristics of nobility and righteousness are localised. These two figures, each holding enviable traits lacking in the other, work towards a mutual reciprocity. While both possess a strong moral compass, David represents values of order and restraint, Breck of instinct and impulse. Just as David successfully reproves Breck for the latter's tendency towards barbarous brutality, the worldly, cynical Breck instils in David a healthy and well-founded disregard for unregulated authority. It is tempting to see in David and Breck's friendship a microcosm for the united Scotland in which Stevenson grew up. Moreover, at the time of Stevenson's writing the Jacobite uprisings were viewed as sufficiently distant historical events as to facilitate this ultimately hopeful image of unification between loyalist and rebel Scots, and perhaps, by extension, between England and Scotland.

Disney's decision to retain one specific scene from the novel, which might easily have been excised, is worth considering. Here, Breck comes face to face with an old rival, Robin MacGregor (Peter O'Toole), the son of notorious highlander rebel, Rob Roy. MacGregor initially threatens to betray Breck for the £100 reward on his head. The two men proceed to exchange insults, seemingly preparing for a duel with cutlasses. At this point, their elderly host, Duncan (Abe Barker), suggests that the two men, both renowned pipers, resolve their differences by determining who possesses greater musical skill. Both perform creditably, gaining the other's respect. Breck charitably accedes to MacGregor's superiority, and they part amicably. Skill with the bagpipes is clearly figured as a quintessentially Scottish marker of masculine potency, on an equal footing with prowess with a sword or cutlass. The bagpipes connote kinship and shared frames of references. This scene – outwardly incongruous in what is primarily a fast-paced adventure narrative – seems designed to bolster the film's shaky credentials as 'national' cinema. But the bagpipes are less a quotidian reality of life in Scotland than an easy reference point for outsiders. They relate to what Colin McArthur has called the 'Scottish Discursive Unconscious', which, as it operates in Hollywood cinema, 'constructs Scotland as a timeless melange of bagpipes, kilts, castles, clansmen, heather, whisky and mist'.[19]

The *Fighting Prince of Donegal*, released shortly before Walt Disney's death in 1966, also draws on such familiar iconographies. It is also the most overtly political of Disney's British films. In its naïve, idealistic portrayal of armed rebellion against socio-political oppression, and its heavy investment in the figure of the lone rebel, it is as bound up as its predecessors with vague but complex ideologies of freedom and individualism. However, it is almost impossible not to view *The Fighting Prince of Donegal*, which focuses on the campaign of the Prince of Donegal, 'Red' Hugh O'Donnell (Peter McEnery), against the occupying military forces of Elizabeth I, as a deliberate allegory for the current political situation in Northern Ireland. The earlier films, admittedly, invested in righteous heroes battling a tyrannical English state. But even if England's rulers in those films had not been essentially benevolent, such representations have little contemporary political resonance, beyond, perhaps, faintly re-emerging feelings of nostalgia and patriotism. Their historical feuds have been consigned to the history books, or to folk tale narrative.

But *The Fighting Prince of Donegal*, produced just prior to the start of the modern Troubles in Northern Ireland, mirrors unresolved tensions and anxieties that, even in the relative stability of the 1960s, occasionally descended into sectarian violence. The presence of a permanent British military occupational force was considered as inflammatory by contemporary Irish republicans as by 'Red' Hugh O'Donnell. As in several of the earlier British Disney swashbucklers, *The Fighting Prince of Donegal* localises English villainy in a treacherous underling, Captain Leeds (Gordon Jackson), who is motivated by jealousy at his non-aristocratic background. Yet the unseen Queen Elizabeth remains a shadowy, unknowable presence, never humanised or rationalised. In one telling remark, it is explained that she 'does not bluff. She's a politician, yes, but she's a realist. She'd hang her grandmother if there was a threat to the crown'. This hard, unyielding ethical pragmatism is contrasted with the brash, ebullient and unashamedly passionate O'Donnell, who believes that 'Victory goes to him that takes the greatest risk'. As ever, Disney ensures that such political concerns do not overwhelm the child-friendly narrative. The treatment of these themes remains largely escapist; almost, but not quite, reducible to the American periodical *Boys' Life*'s seductive references, in its review, to 'leaping parapets, creeping through dungeons, swimming moats, [and] storming walls'.[20]

Image 6.1 Peter McEnery as *The Fighting Prince of Donegal* (1966)

Possible tension points that might disturb these films' child-friendly escapism are toned down, bowdlerised or removed altogether. This includes *Treasure Island*'s more graphically violent passages, *Kidnapped*'s occasional word of Gaelic, and the unattractive brutality of the historical figures whose exploits inspired the sanitised, domesticated heroes of *Rob Roy* and *The Fighting Prince of Donegal*. Do these films successfully negotiate a mid-Atlantic path between British and North American customs and ideologies? Certainly, aspects of them can be located in the United States of the 1950s. Kevin J. Harty argues that *The Story of Robin Hood* 'nods repeatedly in the direction of McCarthyism and its obsession with the "enemy within"' in Prince John and the Sheriff of Nottingham's crusade to uncover traitors amongst their own people.[21] Douglas Brode contends that the British Disney films articulate Walt Disney's preference for freedom and individualism in opposition to state governance, thus 'glorify[ing] social bandits involved in revolutionary activity against an existing power structure based on the rawest form of capitalism'.[22] Brode emphasises Walt's identification with the Scottish rebels, who represented to him, as he stated in his introduction to *Rob Roy*'s US TV screening in October 1956, 'a great love of *liberty* and *beauty*'.[23] Steven Watts also points out these films' expression of Walt Disney's 'antielitism and intense suspicion of governmental power and the oppressions of wealth', arguing that the British heroic outlaws Robin Hood and Rob Roy are prototypes for the studio's late-1950s versions of the American rebel heroes Davy Crockett and Johnny Tremain.[24] Like their British precursors, these figures constituted 'New World individuals who defended the people, battled privileged oppressors, and sought justice outside the parameters of government'.[25]

Walt Disney, Watts reveals, had actively been pursuing American individualist heroes cut from the same cloth as Robin Hood and Rob Roy.[26] Disney clearly saw the British films, on some level, as allegories for the US condition. But they also comment on the loss of freedom and individualism within Britain, where the battles won in this fictional universe have already been lost in the 'real world' (i.e. in the audience's present). The corrupt future Englands of *The Sword and the Rose*, *Rob Roy* and *Kidnapped* reveal that the Robin Hoods have been overcome by the Sheriffs of Nottingham; self-serving politicians, aristocrats and bureaucrats have spread far and wide; the lunatics have taken over the asylum. These films thus look, with hopeful symbolism, to those relatively few unconquered worlds where such battles still need to be fought. England – indeed Britain itself – may have fallen, but as Disney's later 1950s narratives of freedom reveal, there is still America: 'The land of the free'; the New Jerusalem. For Robin Hood and Rob Roy, substitute Davy Crockett and Johnny Tremain, both quintessential embodiments of American individualism. And for the few remaining pastoral outposts of the pre-industrial British Isles, read the similarly unspoiled, and far more accessible, plains of the American west.

Disney and the British Family

The British family is almost ubiquitous in Disney's 1960s and 1970s live-action films, from the Anglicised continentals of *Swiss Family Robinson*

(Ken Annakin, 1960) to the reconstituted Victorian and Edwardian families of the four films examined in this section: *Greyfriars Bobby*, *Mary Poppins*, *Bedknobs and Broomsticks* and *Candleshoe*. In both Britain and the US, as Neil Smelser has argued, 'The Victorian family persists as a kind of ghostly model' that continues, more than a century since its heyday, to represent 'Victorian stability, solidarity and serenity'.[27] Although, as Smelser observes, 'There were not one but many types of Victorian family', the prototype – what Ann Oakley later termed the 'conventional family' – comprises parents and children residing together in a single-family household.[28] This remained the preferred family type in 1960s North America, when the supposed solidarity of the 1950s nuclear family began to give way under the strain of serially rising divorce rates, career-orientated women, and, as several historians have observed, a creeping ethos of individualism that promoted individual happiness over that of the collective well-being of the family unit.[29]

These four films, then, far from being politically withdrawn or ideologically displaced, are intrinsically reflexive. Each identifies problems in society and in the family in microcosm that an enlightened or inspirational outsider must resolve; each reasserts the nurturing, protective qualities of the literal or symbolic family; and each places emphasis on young children and mature adults, marginalising or altogether dispensing with older teenagers and young adults. In *Greyfriars Bobby*, an animal film based on Eleanor Atkinson's supposedly true-life 1912 story of a Skye terrier reputed to have spent 14 years at the graveside of his deceased owner, the central animal succeeds in unifying a fractious community in which small decencies and kindnesses have given way to a selfish individualism. Vulnerable members of society, such as Bobby's elderly and penurious owner, Auld Jock (Alex Mackenzie), a homeless and otherwise-unloved man who dies of pneumonia, slip through society's net. In *Mary Poppins*, a similar lack of cohesion is localised in the family unit itself, which is reunified through the interventions of Julie Andrews's eponymous nanny. Both films identify a problem in the functioning of society (the family and the 'local community' being seen as vital socialising apparatuses), and over the courses of their narratives undertake to repair it. But as with Dickens's *A Christmas Carol* (1843), change comes not from within, but rather is imposed through magical intervention.

It cannot be coincidence that in both *Greyfriars Bobby* and *Mary Poppins*, the agent of change is a being of almost transcendent perfection – the legendary animal and the 'practically perfect' nanny – capable of gaining the trust of children and melting the hearts of adults. Bobby inspires goodness through unwitting example; Mary is more explicitly a didactic figure who provides moral guidance, but the end result is the same: in galvanising a new generation of young citizens, they point the way to an imagined better future. In both films, people need merely to be set back on the right path. Even very sympathetic characters, such as *Greyfriars Bobby*'s kindly restaurateur, Mr Traill (Laurence Naismith), who feeds groups of orphan children in his restaurant, maintain a facade of unfeelingness, as when he sternly rebukes Auld Jock for praising his hospitality after feeding and housing the sick old man. Individuals like the same film's dour cemetery warden, James Brown (Donald Crisp), and *Mary Poppins*' tyrannical bank owner, Mr Dawes Sr. (Dick Van Dyke), are not innately malign or callous, but have lost touch with the vital spark of life, deadened by years of grind. If the children in both films graduate to a more 'traditional' eschewal of self and embrace community spirit, hopefully positing an alternative manifesto for self-obsessed, individualistic 1960s youth, then the reform of their elders perhaps constitutes a reminder that the world is still theirs (though it will not be for much longer), and that there is time to change.

After Cecil Hepworth's early silent-era efforts, the animal film – a perennially popular sub-genre of the family film in Hollywood – had never caught on in mainstream British cinema, possibly because the genre's anthropomorphic tendencies run contrary to its strong realist lineage. Such films were apt to be seen as fanciful, overly sentimental and juvenile. Contemporaneous British animal films like *Ring of Bright Water* (Jack Couffer, 1969), *Run Wild, Run Free* (Richard Sarafian, 1969), *Call of the Wild* (Ken Annakin, 1973), *The Belstone Fox* (James Hill, 1973) and *Tarka the Otter* (David Cobham, 1979) all exhibit a contrary desire to convey the felt reality that nature is an unceasing battle of tooth and claw. *Greyfriars Bobby* is more overtly Hollywoodesque in approach, deriving from a filmic tradition that includes Lassie and Rin Tin Tin, and Disney's own *Old Yeller* (Robert Stevenson, 1957), where animals reflect and respond to human values of love, affection, kindness, unaffectedness and empathetic understanding. *Greyfriars Bobby* ends with such a gesture of friendship and inclusiveness, as the formerly taciturn Mr Brown invites Mr Traill into his house for a drink, and a chorus of benevolent child and adult voices, intoning 'Goodnight, Bobby', fade into the music as the dog takes its customary place on the mound above Auld Jock's grave.

Mary Poppins is such a landmark film that omitting it from the discussion on the basis that it was made entirely in the US would be dogged literal-mindedness. It is directed by a British man, adapted from a British novel, mostly populated by British actors, set in London, and infused with the distinct, patented 'Britishness' that is the core focus of this chapter. Before *Harry Potter*, the American-made *Mary Poppins* was comfortably the most popular 'British' children's film ever in terms of overall attendances. It drew around 14 million UK admissions, placing it at 25th in the BFI's 2004 list of the 100 top films at the British box office. The only other indigenous child-orientated films that made the list were *Harry Potter and the Philosopher's Stone* (#11, 17.5 million admissions), *Harry Potter and the Chamber of Secrets* (#24, 14.1 million), *Oliver!* (#74, 9 million), *Swiss Family Robinson* (#89, 8.3 million) and *Chicken Run* (#93, 8.1 million). *Mary Poppins* was also the sixth highest-grossing film of the decade in North America, won five Oscars, was selected for preservation by the US National Film Registry in 2013, and has generated a Disney live-action blockbuster based on the making of the film, *Saving Mr Banks* (John Lee Hancock, 2013).[30]

Famously, the film centres on the efforts of a magical nanny to repair a malfunctioning Edwardian British family in which the father, Mr Banks (David Tomlinson), is preoccupied with work, Mrs Banks (Glynis Johns) is equally focused on her efforts as a 'suffragette', and their children, Jane (Karen Dotrice) and Michael (Matthew Garber), are lonely and misbehaving. Revealingly, the central family unit is structurally nuclear (the 'typical' family household in 1960s North America) rather than extended (as was more usual in Britain until around 1950).[31] As I have argued elsewhere, *Mary Poppins* says less about the socio-historical conditions of early twentieth-century Britain than about the dominant national concerns of 1960s North America – principally, the perceived decline of the family, the transition from a middle-class, adult-orientated culture to a seemingly more liberal, youth-dominated one, the middlebrow establishment's response to the counter-cultural movement, and the inexorable rise of symbolic 'others': working women, racial minorities, blue-collar workers, and gays.[32] *Mary Poppins* reasserts the primacy of the white, middle-class, God-fearing nuclear family while, in the process, eradicating all traces of liberalising change, either through non-representation, or, as in proto-feminist Mrs Banks's case, deconstructive lampooning. Even the filmic form itself, which revives the 1940s Hollywood family musical, harks back to older, increasingly old-fashioned, narrative and stylistic patterns.

The linkages between Edwardian Britain and the United States of the 1960s are strengthened by the curious figure of Mary's friend, the chimney sweep Bert (Dick Van Dyke). Early in the film, Bert, in musical portent of Mary's arrival to heal the Banks family, sings:

> Wind's in the east, mist's coming in,
> Like something is brewin', about to begin,
> Can't put my finger on what lies in store,
> But I feel what's to happen… [He smiles] All happened before.

The verse adopts a fairy tale-like narrative framing mechanism, akin to 'once upon a time', but involves a complex temporality in which Bert apparently relates the events of the film (c. 1910) from the audience's present (1964–65). Do these words imply that family transcends changing historical circumstances and cultural norms? This is the first of several instances where Bert is privy to knowledge and insight denied to the film's other characters. Later, he impresses upon Mr Banks the evanescence of childhood, his sombre tone (and North American cadences) suggesting sentiments relayed back from an age of relative enlightenment.

In many ways, the stern, businesslike Mr Banks is heir to domineering, but ultimately sympathetic, classical-era Hollywood family comedy *patres familias* like Mr Smith (Leon Ames) from *Meet Me in St. Louis* (Vincente Minnelli, 1944) and Clarence Day (William Powell) from *Life With Father* (Michael Curtiz, 1947). But whereas those fathers only *appear* tyrannical and consumed by bureaucracy, Mr Banks really is. His newspaper advert for a nanny demands 'a general […] who can give commands', and he reproves the children for their own version of the notice, which requests a nanny with 'a cheery disposition', never 'cross or cruel', who will 'love us as a son or daughter'. While the classical-era Hollywood patriarchs were moderated by the presence of level-headed matriarchs who appeared to defer to

Image 6.2 The 'practically perfect' magical nanny, Mary Poppins (Julie Andrews), with her surrogate family (1964)

their husband's authority as putative head of the family, but actually ruled the roost, Mrs Banks is the polar opposite: seemingly independent and ambitious, but in reality weak-willed, becoming tearful when chastised by her husband, and displaying scant emotional affinity with her children or aptitude in the daily practicalities of mothering. Mrs Banks sings with certitude that 'our daughters' daughters will adore us' for her reformist efforts, yet she is almost as bad as her husband in neglecting the needs of her family by self-indulgently pursuing her own pet cause. The 1940s/50s films had presented audiences with nostalgic images of 'how we used to be', or, more aptly, 'how we *wish we were*'. *Mary Poppins* has a more active agenda: not merely showing images of the past for pleasure, but demonstrating how its true and authentic virtues – discipline, education, reciprocity, community spirit – remain relevant.

Throughout, Mary is a locus of precision and order, though of a different kind to the joyless regimen Mr Banks embodies. She disapproves of the undisciplined, contagious laughter and play of Bert's Uncle Albert (Ed Wynn), who spends his days in ceaseless levity literally floating helplessly about his house, consumed by bouts of convulsive hysterics. Although she reluctantly indulges Uncle Albert, she warns Jane and Michael against taking play to the nth degree in a way that impedes productivity. But she does recognise the importance of play within certain parameters: in the trippiest segment of the film, she treats the children, and Bert, to a tour around a magical animated landscape. Later the same evening, however, when the children excitedly recall the adventure, Mary denies all knowledge of it; such play must carefully be regulated, lest it get out of control to the exclusion of all else, as it does with Uncle Albert – the antithesis of the stern, humourless, Mr Banks. A more desirable state resides somewhere between these two extremes, maintaining Mr Banks's professionalism while borrowing something of Albert's carefree levity. In juxtaposing Mr Banks's climactic celebration of childish play with news of his instatement as an executive board member at the bank, the film's ending makes clear that the balance has correctly been struck, ensuring that his newfound facility to access such a condition does not overwhelm his ability to earn a wage and govern his family. Nor, by implication, does it overtake the necessary sobriety of society-at-large, as Plato and Aristotle cautioned against in condemning the unrestrained laughter of the buffoon.

The role of the gently-manipulative matriarch is assumed by Mary herself. Disturbed at frivolous talk of day-trips and subversive lingual tongue-twisters like 'Supercalifragilisticexpialidocious' – Mary's word for when you 'can't think of what to say' – Mr Banks attempts to dismiss her with commonsensical appeals to efficiency and sobriety. However, Mary outmanoeuvres him by voicing her intention to take the children to his bank the following day, so that they may appreciate the value of stocks and shares and learn the philosophy of acquisitiveness. Far too literal-minded to realise that his arguments have been turned against him, Mr Banks agrees to what he assumes was his idea in the first place.

Mary transforms the family through good example, with qualities Bruce Babington sees as embodied more generally by Andrews's filmic persona: 'teacherly, gentle, solicitous, candid, occasionally commanding'.[33] To these may be added her virtues of neatness and order, precision in action, gesture and enunciation, calmness, gentility and etiquette. What elevates Mary from mere pomposity and didacticism is her magical abilities. While her own persona never deviates from the immutable characteristics listed above, she nonetheless allows immersion into a magical 'other world' of manifold possibilities beyond the hermetic one inhabited by Mr Banks. Intrinsically, Mary represents conservative values of order and stability, but through her magical abilities, she assumes the broader associations of freedom and imagination her pristine, conservative facade apparently repudiates.

One might cynically suggest that *Bedknobs and Broomsticks* is little more than a thinly-veiled imitation of *Mary Poppins*. Roy Disney had intimated as much shortly after Walt's death in 1966, when he voiced his intention to release 'at least one *Mary Poppins* every year'.[34] Though that policy quickly stalled, the two films share their writer-producer (Bill Walsh), director (Robert Stevenson), composer (Irwin Kostal), songwriters (the Sherman Brothers), some of the cast (David Tomlinson; Reginald Owen) and many of the same technicians, and Julie Andrews was offered, but rejected, the central role. In fact, Disney had purchased the film rights to Mary Norton's *The Magic Bed-Knob* (1943) as early as 1945, and the film was due to enter production in 1966, less than two years after the release of *Mary Poppins*.[35] However, Walt Disney was wary of the films' possible over-similarity, and suspended the project. When production eventually recommenced in 1970, Hollywood's cycle of nostalgic family musicals had passed its box office sell-by-date. The direct resemblances to *Mary Poppins*, which Walt had resisted, were positively embraced under Roy's auspices – an early sign of the parody and pastiche that characterised the final films in Disney's British cycle.

The differences between *Mary Poppins* and *Bedknobs and Broomsticks* are largely cosmetic. The earlier film's evocation of Edwardian London is advanced to England's south coast at the onset of World War II. As with *Mary Poppins*, the central thematic is the (re)construction of a happy, functioning nuclear family. In the earlier film, this family is already complete, but in *Bedknobs and Broomsticks* an entirely new, surrogate family is composed from three separate sources: the eccentric spinster and white witch, Eglantine (Angela Lansbury); the individualistic conman, Emelius (David Tomlinson); and the orphaned children Charlie (Ian Weighill), Carrie (Cindy O'Callahan) and Paul (Roy Snart), evacuated from war-torn London. The joining together of these disparate factions appears unlikely, given Eglantine's stated aversion to children, Emelius's inability to live by established norms of conduct, and the children's clearly working-class origins. Ultimately, war, and the threat of the home invaded and possibly destroyed by a seemingly overwhelming enemy, forces the family together, just as Mary Poppins provides the impetus in the earlier film. Although Eglantine comes to regard the children as her adopted offspring, the family is shown to be complete only after Emelius returns to the fold in fulfilment of his masculine/paternal responsibilities, having previously refused the children's request to stay and 'be our dad'.

Child-orientated films in general, and *Mary Poppins* and *Bedknobs and Broomsticks* in particular, perennially seek to establish that warmth, happiness and optimism still have their place, in spite of the tiresome refrain – much alluded to in journalistic accounts of contemporary society – that we live in an age of cynicism and moral ambiguity. The musical number, 'The Age of Not Believing', sung by Lansbury, ostensibly addresses the modern, maturing child's inability to dream and imagine:

> When you rush around in hopeless circles,
> Searching everywhere for something true
> You're at the age of not believing
> When all the 'make believe' is through.
>
> When you set aside your childhood heroes
> And your dreams are lost up on a shelf
> You're at the age of not believing
> And worst of all, you doubt yourself.
>
> You're a castaway where no-one hears you, on a barren isle in a
> lonely sea
> Where did all the happy endings go? Where can all the good
> times be!

You must face the age of not believing
Doubting everything you ever knew
Until at last you start believing
There's something wonderful, truly wonderful in you!

The film extends these sentiments to contemporary society and culture as a whole. Lionel Jeffries's adaptation of E. Nesbit's *The Railway Children*, released a year earlier, articulates many of the same concerns, but aims for documentary-style realism. *Bedknobs and Broomsticks*, by contrast, self-reflexively draws attention to its ideological agenda, making obvious the allegorical function previously only implicit.

Candleshoe, released six months after George Lucas's *Star Wars* (1977), finally makes explicit the antithesis between modern, urban America and an ahistorical, semi-pastoral England at the heart of Disney's British film cycle. An opening, ten-minute prologue filmed on the streets of Los Angeles introduces us to the streetwise, cynical, self-confessed 'delinquent', Casey (Jodie Foster). With her gang of street urchin friends, she steals food, deliberately provokes a rival gang by pilfering their basketball, evades police patrols and generally causes minor mayhem for her own amusement. Foster's persona is only slightly softened from the teenage New York prostitute she had recently inhabited in *Taxi Driver* (Martin Scorsese, 1976). In both films, she possesses an innate affinity with the depraved city streets, and paralysing inability to understand the wider world beyond its confines. She is also an orphan; her foster parents, for whom she steals in order to pay her way, sell her to the mercenary Bundage (Leo McKern), who recruits her in his scheme to swindle a wealthy dowager, Lady St. Edmund (Helen Hayes), owner of the British manor house, Candleshoe, out of her presumed fortune. Casey, it transpires, bears a striking resemblance to Lady St. Edmund's missing granddaughter (and heiress), and she willingly agrees to inveigle her way into the household in return for a share of the proceeds. Foster displays the same appealing juxtaposition of knowingness and vulnerability as in the far more adult-orientated *Taxi Driver*. This combination allows her to perceive, and comment upon, the disparity between the bewildering and uncompromising world of the modern metropolis and the gentility and kinship and family ties characterising the timeless Englishness of Candleshoe.

In Casey, then, the film presents a powerful symbol of modernity, in its least desirable forms. The following exchange between her and Lady St. Edmund is revealing:

Lady St. Edmund: I don't suppose your experience of family life has been a happy one.

Casey: What family life? I'll tell you, the only thing I remember about family life is nothing. Zero. From one foster dump to another. I mean, who really cares about a kid you take in for the welfare money and food stamps? I mean, who really cares? It's a racket, just like everything else. The whole world's a racket. First thing I ever learned. Get up out of bed in the morning with your dukes up, you know? Got 'em up, first punch is yours.

Lady St. Edmund: I see...

Casey: Yeah, well... Maybe you do, and maybe you don't.

Lady St. Edmund: But you can't go through life alone.

Casey: I ain't alone. I got me. Listen, if you don't hand it out, you don't have to worry about not getting it back.

Prior to her inevitable transformation, Casey embodies individualism, aggression, cynicism, selfishness, and disregard for friendship, family and law and order. These undesirable aspects are incongruous because her outward appearance is one of childlike innocence, allowing the film to present the familiar image of youth corrupted by modern vices. Where *Candleshoe* obviously breaks from the cynical or nihilistic representations of childhood depicted in the likes of *Paper Moon* (Peter Bogdanovich, 1973) and *Taxi Driver* is that Casey is given an opportunity for redemption.

In shifting from Los Angeles to rural England, Casey crosses time zones in more ways than one. While the film is set in the present-day, Candleshoe and its estate appear devoid of the accessories of modern living. The vintage car is just about the only concession to industrialisation, and televisions and modern everyday appliances that may disrupt the antiquarian veneer are missing altogether. In the film's final scene, after Casey's duplicity has been exposed, but her allegiance confirmed when she helps her adopted family repel Bundage, Lady St. Edmund elects to accept her as her missing granddaughter after all. Like the borderline criminal Emelius in *Bedknobs and Broomsticks*, Casey brings certain skills that the rather staid, conventional British family lacks, as in the scene where her streetwise hustling allows the family butler, Priory (David Niven), and Lady St. Edmund's adopted orphaned children, to sell far more food at the local street market.

The film's other major concession to modernity is the acknowledgement that 'family' need not be supported by rigid class distinctions or lineage. For all his servitude, Priory is clearly the *paterfamilias*, and the local children Lady St. Edmund takes into the household are her surrogate grandchildren. The film acknowledges, if only implicitly, that the old certainties of family and community have been disrupted by changing priorities and belief-systems, specifically the normalising of divorce, loosening kinship ties (evident in Casey's and the British children's statuses as orphans) and the surging 1970s ethos of individualism.[36] But family may endure in different forms, with the mutual love and support offered by Candleshoe's residents superseding old definitions based on blood ties or class and racial distinctions. The working-class Priory, the oriental British adoptee Anna (Sarah Tamakuni) and the rough-edged American street urchin Casey are all happily and successfully integrated in a new kind of family structure. The film, in its rather artless and idealistic way, asserts

Image 6.3 Lady St. Edmund (Helen Hayes) nurses Casey (Jodie Foster) back to health in *Candleshoe* (1977)

modern Western society's need to adopt new family structures if the institution is to survive the uncertainties and divisiveness of the new age. This new, multiply-sourced family may not offer the same symmetry in form, continuity between the generations or nostalgia for old behavioural patterns, but it does provide much of the same longed-for stability.

Youth-dominated mass audiences, it seems, were not much interested in representations of family, British or otherwise. *Candleshoe* was only the 15th most profitable film of 1978 at the British box office.[37] Ironically, in fixating on the British family unit, Disney had alienated the commercial 'family' market. Spielberg's *Close Encounters of the Third Kind* (1977) ends with its protagonist leaving his family behind in the name of personal fulfilment, while *Star Wars* and *Superman* (Richard Donner, 1978) – the other dominant family blockbusters of the period – deal with family only tangentially. One might argue that such films, through their undeniable affirmations of friendship and fidelity, involve an even broader definition of family than the one advanced in *Candleshoe*. Besides, as *Close Encounters* reveals, by this point there was a growing acceptance that family could equally be stultifying and inhibiting to personal growth and expression (or even function as a locus of madness, as R. D. Laing posited).[38] The decade's most popular family-life films were cynical and adult-orientated, as witness the likes of *Paper Moon* and *The Godfather* (Francis Ford Coppola, 1972). The vulnerable elderliness of Helen Hayes and David Niven in *Candleshoe* might tacitly acknowledge that the older generation, who had provided a solid bedrock, and for whom the family was sacrosanct, has almost had its time. By the time of Spielberg's *E.T.* (1982) the family is broken, struggling on against the odds, bound together by mutual dependency but shattered by the absence of the adulterous father and by the still-present mother evidently on the verge of psychological breakdown. There is no happy reconciliation or lasting magical intervention. E.T. departs, and although Elliot promises to keep him in his heart, the same cannot surely be said for the other members of the beleaguered family – a group of individuals gathered under one roof more than a collective bound by common beliefs and unity of purpose.

'That corner of the Disney studios that is forever England plainly still flourishes', the *MFB* wryly observed in its review of *Bedknobs and*

Broomsticks.[39] Yet while Disney's preoccupation with representations of Britishness reveals a complex interplay of commerce and ideology, ultimately these films always carried a strong economic underpinning. The relative underperformance of Disney's 1970s British films signalled the end of the British cycle. Of course, Disney's fixation with Britishness (i.e. Englishness) was also strongly apparent in its animated features, especially *Alice in Wonderland* (Clyde Geronimi et al., 1951), *Peter Pan* (Geronimi et al., 1953), *101 Dalmatians* (Geronimi et al., 1961), *The Jungle Book* (Wolfgang Reitherman et al., 1967), and *Robin Hood* (Reitherman et al., 1973). As Paul Wells argues, ultimately the English milieu 'worked as a distanciation from the cultural destabilisation that escalated in the United States [...] Disney had become detached from its own artistic credo and aspiration, and the socio-cultural context in which it was produced'.[40] Such films had entered into too great a conflict with lived experience, and with the new Hollywood family entertainment paradigm. Spectacular action-adventure narratives were the order of the day. But then, as we have seen, the notion that Britishness – or Englishness – is coterminous with gentility and sophistication is a peculiarly alien one, impossible to reconcile with Britain's own cinematic tradition.

7

Summers of Love and Winters of Discontent: The Sixties and Seventies

Commercial British children's cinema of the 1960s and 1970s can squarely by divided into periods of 'boom' and 'bust'. The mid-to-late 1960s was definitely 'boom': family-orientated series such as *James Bond* (1962–), *Carry On* (1958–92) and the *Beatles* (1964–69) were internationally popular, riding a wave of transatlantic popularity for all things 'British'. Hollywood studios invested massively in British films, many of which were intended for family audiences. The 1970s, just as assuredly, was 'bust': a financial crisis in 1969 almost bankrupted several Hollywood studios, leading to a severe shortfall in investment;[1] several British studios were financially crippled; and, in 1971, the government withdrew financial support to the National Film Finance Corporation (NFFC).[2] The 1970s was a barren time for British cinema in general, with chronic lack of investment and precipitously declining admissions. Ironically, several British children's and family films of the 1970s are now regarded as classics, and the decade has come to be seen as a 'golden age' for British children's cinema. However, this perception is based largely on selective recollection of a handful of key productions. By the end of the 1970s, Britain's independent tradition of children's films was virtually dead.

164

The Missing Audience

Early-1960s discourses concerning children and cinema expressed familiar fears about society's descent into permissiveness, tempered by growing acceptance that things really had changed. As a study of school children's leisure activities observed, the 1944 Education Act's definition of a child as 'a person who is not over compulsory school age' was no longer appropriate:

> What distinguishes modern children at play from their predecessors is their urge to read adult periodicals, to dance, to listen to records, to talk with those of their own age in clubs and cafes and other places where they feel relatively free from the restrictive influence of adults.[3]

Cinema was once widely mistrusted as an unregulated space where children could escape adult supervision. During the silent era, children were believed to comprise up to 25 per cent of film-goers, but a 1961 study by the Screen Advertising Association (SAA) found that children between ages 8 to 15 comprised a mere 16 per cent of audiences.[4] The bulk of movie-goers – 60 per cent, according to the survey – were aged 16 to 34, a demographic described as 'young, vital and acquisitive'.[5] It is easy to see why producers embraced the youth market, particularly given that cinema attendances had fallen from a high of approximately 1,640 million attendances in 1946 to 515 million by 1961.[6]

News that Prince Charles and Princess Anne (aged 11 and 9 respectively) had seen the 'A'-rated *Ben-Hur* (William Wyler, 1959) made the front page of the *Daily Mirror* in August 1960.[7] Reviewer Donald Zec conceded that 'some children might be shocked, frightened and even suffer nightmares' watching its 'gruesome' and 'bloodthirsty' sequences, but argued that 'holiness, not horror, is the major theme of this massive, important film', so parents should not be dissuaded from permitting their children to see it.[8] Much of the controversy had now shifted from 'A' to 'X' films. In September 1962, the Moral Law Defence Association – a conservative lobby with the patronage of the Archbishop of Canterbury – urged the BBFC to abolish the 'X' rating.[9] The Association attacked cinemas showing 'X' films in tandem with 'U' and 'A' films, alleging that: 'In one week during the recent school holiday, 17 of 31 cinemas in London were showing "X" films'.[10] This was an acknowledged problem. In early 1963, the manager of the Essoldo cinema in Pendleton, Greater Manchester, was fined £20 for allowing four schoolboys (age unknown) entry to a double-feature 'X' evening programme.[11] Police, alerted by a local councillor who had noticed an inordinate number of young spectators, found 26 children under the age of 16 in the audience. The theatre manager claimed that 'every practical measure' had been taken to prevent children being admitted, but insisted that 'it was not easy'.[12] The perennial trouble is that children – particularly adolescents and teenagers – do not wish to be 'protected' from adult content. In late 1962, Hilary Halpin, former chair of the London County Council's Children's Committee, claimed that underage teenagers 'looked through their local newspaper film columns and rejected films which had not an "X" certificate as being not worth seeing'.[13]

The Boom: Family Films in the 1960s

Despite the drastic narrowing of the theatrical audience, and of 'child audiences' more particularly, Britain's production of high-budget family blockbusters was nearing its peak in the early-to-mid 1960s. Some genres, such as the rock 'n' roll film, carried over from the late-1950s explosion of youth culture. Others, such as low-budget fantasy, emerged from the British independent film sector, or from larger studios that still believed that a concrete and lucrative 'family audience' was waiting to be mobilised. The most important development, though, was the injection of North American finance. The nominally British films *Tom Jones* (Tony Richardson, 1963) and *Zulu* (Cy Endfield, 1964) were bankrolled by Hollywood.[14] According to the state-funded NFFC, between 1962 and 1965 North American firms financed 107 out of 200 British films, as compared to just 46 funded by the NFFC.[15] Because US companies tended to support higher-budget films, the proportion of US capital in the British production sector was disproportionately high, reaching 90 per cent by 1967.[16] Hollywood finance papered over deep cracks in the industry. Major British studios, such as Rank and British Lion, were in dire straits, and, as Sir Michael Balcon lamented in July 1966, the biggest loss was the British 'medium-budget film' which reflected the national 'outlook and character'.[17]

Summers of Love and Winters of Discontent

The major Hollywood studios were pre-eminently interested in big-budget family films. Blockbusters such as *My Fair Lady* (George Cukor, 1964), *Mary Poppins* (Robert Stevenson, 1964) and *The Sound of Music* (Robert Wise, 1965) provided the template for the prestige British family musicals *Oliver!* (Carol Reed, 1968) and *Chitty Chitty Bang Bang* (Ken Hughes, 1968). US finance and distribution facilitated other keynotes of 1960s British children's cinema, such as *Born Free* (James Hill, 1966) and *Yellow Submarine* (George Dunning, 1968). There was an unprecedented period of activity in the field of youth and family cinema, with producers eager to capitalise on the teen market. The following list of teen- and family-orientated cycles and sub-genres illustrates their diversification and proliferation as the decade unfolded:

1) The rock 'n' roll film, usually featuring real artists, e.g. Cliff Richard in *The Young Ones* (Sidney J. Furie, 1961), *Summer Holiday* (Peter Yates, 1963) and *Finders Keepers* (Sidney Hayers, 1967); the Beatles in *A Hard Day's Night* (Richard Lester, 1964), *Help!* (Lester, 1965), *Yellow Submarine*, and *Let it Be* (Michael Lindsay-Hogg, 1969); Gerry and the Pacemakers in *Ferry across the Mersey* (Jeremy Summers, 1965); various in *Pop Gear* (Frederic Goode, 1965).
2) The family comedy, e.g. *Inn for Trouble* (Pennington Richards, 1960); *No Kidding* (Gerald Thomas, 1961); *Call Me Bwana* (Henry Geddes, 1963); *One Way Pendulum* (Peter Yates, 1965).
3) The family adventure film, e.g. *The Scarlet Blade* (John Gilling, 1963); *Those Magnificent Men in Their Flying Machines* (Ken Annakin, 1965); *A Challenge for Robin Hood* (Pennington Richards, 1968); and, to some degree, the *James Bond* series.
4) The family musical, e.g. *Oliver!*; *Chitty Chitty Bang Bang*; *Goodbye, Mr Chips* (Herbert Ross, 1969).
5) The animated feature, e.g. *Ruddigore* (Joy Batchelor, 1967); *Thunderbirds are Go* (David Lane, 1967); *Thunderbird 6* (David Lane, 1968); *Yellow Submarine*.
6) Sci-fi and fantasy films, e.g. *Mysterious Island* (Cy Endfield, 1961), *Jason and the Argonauts* (Don Chaffey, 1963); *First Men in the Moon* (Nathan H. Juran, 1964); *Dr. Who and the Daleks* (Gordon Flemyng, 1965); *Daleks – Invasion Earth 2150 A.D.* (Flemyng, 1966); *One Million Years*

167

B.C. (Chaffey, 1966), *Jules Verne's Rocket to the Moon* (Don Sharp, 1967); *They Came from Beyond Space* (Freddie Francis, 1967); *Captain Nemo and the Underwater City* (James Hill, 1969).

7) The animal film, e.g. *Zoo Baby* (David Eady, 1960); *Old Mac* (Michael Bayley, 1961); *Born Free*; *An Elephant Called Slowly* (James Hill, 1969); *Ring of Bright Water* (Jack Couffer, 1969); *Run Wild, Run Free* (Richard Sarafian, 1969).

Only two of these cycles – sci-fi/fantasy and the animal film – were leading presences in 1970s British children's cinema.

The Beatles on Film

A Hard Day's Night, the first of four theatrically-released Beatles films, retains a family-friendly 'U' rating but captures the youth-driven edginess of early Beatles. Shot economically in black-and-white in cinéma vérité style, it is comic jamboree, loosely working its narrative around a profusion of slapstick and sight gags, interspersed with musical interludes and culminating in a 'live' concert performed by the band in front of hordes of rambunctious adolescent fans. Released at the height of Beatlemania, *A Hard Day's Night* was a box office smash that deftly engaged with general audiences while disavowing middlebrow values. Richard Lester recalls that:

> The general aim of the film was to present what was apparently becoming a social phenomenon in this country [...] Anarchy is too strong a word, but the quality of confidence that the boys exuded! Confidence that they could dress as they liked, speak as they liked, talk to the Queen as they liked, talk to the people on the train who 'fought the war for them' as they liked [...] [British society was] still based on privilege – privilege by schooling, privilege by birth, privilege by accent, privilege by speech. [The Beatles] were the first people to attack this [...] they said if you want something, do it. You can do it. Forget all this talk about talent or ability or money or speech. Just do it.[18]

These comments, oversimplified as they are, nevertheless capture a spirit of 'opposition', through which the Beatles are figured as arbiters of youthful vitality, benevolence, egalitarianism, irreverence and a vague anti-establishmentarianism, that is never sufficiently pointed as to constitute an open call-to-arms. Their 'universality' is not compromised – except in the minds of critics like the *New Statesman*'s Paul Johnson, who characterised their female fans as 'the least fortunate of their generation, the dull, the idle, the failures'.[19] Also worth noting is Geoffrey Nowell-Smith's suggestion that *A Hard Day's Night* is 'an unstable compound'.[20] But this 'instability' is primarily formal rather than ideological; in terms of overall message, the film equates identity with music and its universalism, thus celebrating collectivism rather than individualism.

Filmed in colour (in 'a haze of marijuana', as the band later admitted) with a substantially larger budget, *Help!* is a striking departure. The loose, maguffin-type plot features a murderous Eastern cult seeking a sacred ring, unknowingly worn by Ringo. Pursued by the cult, the Beatles flee to the Austrian Alps, then take refuge in Buckingham Palace, and finally fly to the Bahamas, where they engage in a final confrontation culminating with the ring falling off Ringo's finger. While the film's random comic absurdity owes much to *The Goons* (1951–60), its Eastern elements capture the group's burgeoning interest in mysticism. *Help!* sees the Beatles in transition, as the *MFB* highlighted:

> Even those who find the Beatles a singularly boring institution are likely to be interested in Dick Lester's way of selling them, for this is a visual virtuosity in such a lavish, and ultimately exhausting sort that for every point well taken one gets the feeling that five or six others have shot by at somewhere around the speed of light. It is pleasing, and tremendously unusual as applied to something as square and middlebrow and marketable in its own right as Beatlemania now is, to find a greater degree of alertness.[21]

The success of the Beatles, and their films, is attributable in large part to their ability to resist, at least on the surface, absolute absorption into the socio-cultural mainstream through continual reinvention and revitalisation.

Yellow Submarine strikes an appropriate balance between the band's counter-culture ideals and family-friendly accessibility. Animated over an 11-month period and employing around 200 artists under the direction of Canadian expat George Dunning, the film's art direction was by Heinz Edelmann. Edelmann's psychedelic artwork – which bore strong similarities to that of the famous German-born American artist Peter Max – was crucial to the film's visual aesthetic. *Yellow Submarine* is best experienced on the big screen: with its startling colours and avant-garde art direction, enriched by some of the Beatles most iconic songs, it is quintessential cinematic spectacle. Ironically, its repeated broadcasts on British television – especially over the Christmas holidays – have secured its position as a family classic. Its gently anti-establishment message has passed, like the 1960s counterculture itself, into accepted cultural history, as thoroughly 'British' and ideologically legitimate as the Queen's Speech.

Yet *Yellow Submarine* is assuredly transatlantic. It is a colourful, fun, psychedelic confection which, as Adrian Schober observes, 'incorporates surrealistic visuals, music, nonsense, wordplay and non sequiturs, along with a multitude of literary, art and pop references'.[22] The film opts for a loose good vs. evil fantasy narrative. The 'Fab Four' (impersonated here by voice actors) have to overcome the dastardly, music-hating Blue Meanies, who have invaded the idyllic Pepperland, turning its inhabitants to stone and draining the land of colour with their immobilising, catapult-projected giant green apples. The inhabitants of Pepperland might easily be participants in the infamous 1967 Summer of Love, though more wholesomely intoxicated by music, rather than drugs. The Meanies are representatives of the adult establishment. Their method of attack, making the land 'dingy, drag and quiet', surely symbolises the establishment militantly clamping down on the new generation of counter-cultural youth finding new means of expression through film, music, literature, fashion and narcotics.

Significantly, the Blue Meanie chief (Paul Angelis) is vanquished when Jeremy (Dick Emery) – a curious 'nowhere man' the Beatles encounter earlier in the film – reads romantic poetry to him. This causes pink flowers to bloom spontaneously on the former's body, signalling the effeminisation (or perhaps bohemianisation) of the establishment, and thus its ultimate defeat. The old order is recreated in the image of the new. Real-world Blue Meanies may always be with us, but the film envisions a rapprochement by allowing the reformed Meanies and the people of Pepperland to live together. John calls out to the Meanies: 'Hello, blue people. Won't you join us, hook up, and otherwise co-mingle?' The Meanie chief plaintively muses, 'It's no longer a blue world', and begins using the previously-outlawed word 'yes'. Jeremy delightedly exclaims: 'Yes! Ah, "yes" is a word with a glorious ring! A true, universal, utopious thing! Engenders embracing and chasing of blues, the very best word for the whole world to use!' This utopian vision of peaceful coexistence between the Pepperlanders and the transformed Meanies underpins the universalism of the Beatles themselves. The band's democratising presence is reasserted in the final scene, where they perform the song 'All Together Now', the title of which is repeated in subtitles in numerous languages.

It is curiously appropriate that Jeremy serves as the eventual harbinger of peaceful coexistence. He speaks what appears to be gibberish and is discovered in a strange, abstract 'nowhere land' where normative physical rules do not apply. Yet his short pink tail and blue face embodies the film's opposing forces, one faction dull, negative and bureaucratic, one insistently hedonic. A 'nowhere man' is everyman; 'a bit like you and me', as the Beatles' 1965 song famously asserts. Furthermore, Jeremy's 'nonsense' speech is deceptively simple, casting light on basic and elemental truths obscured by selfish human drives. As Lewis Carroll and Edward Lear demonstrated, literary nonsense breaks down semantic complexities that

Image 7.1 The Blue Meanie chief is effeminised by 'Nowhere Man' Jeremy in *Yellow Submarine* (1968)

uphold established structures of language and, thus, authority. Here, it is used democratically, as a way of subverting linguistic configurations while remaining meaningful. Its subversions appeal (or we suppose they do) to children still learning, under duress, the rules and codes of adult discourse. Simultaneously, nonsense speech withholds from adults the logical syntactic and semantic structures to which they are accustomed. This can prove either delightfully whimsical or irritatingly obtuse, depending on inclination and capacity to suspend expectations for interaction founded on logical, predictable premises.

Yellow Submarine was apparently conceived of as a primarily child-orientated animation, in the vein of the ABC show. But the whimsical, allusive script, Edelmann's psychedelic art direction, and the Beatles' timeless songs combine brilliantly to create a film equally accessible to child and adult audiences. Critical and popular reception was extremely strong, although some wondered what to make of it. The *Observer*'s Nigel Gosling thought that it 'packs more stimulation, sly art-references and pure joy into 90 minutes than a mile of exhibitions of op, pop and all the mod cons', but the *Daily Mail*'s Cecil Wilson 'sank back punch drunk from the dazzling imagery'.[23] In many regards, as the *MFB* observed, it is a product of its time:

> Derivative in its reference, not in its style (which is unique) – a fantasia of all the second-hand influences that have characterised so much of what has passed for art in the last decade [...] [It is] a memorial to an age in which hardly a week passes without a revival of some hitherto forgotten fad.[24]

In other respects, *Yellow Submarine* was ahead of its time, injecting a plethora of cultural references (both verbal and visual) into a seemingly straightforward children's adventure narrative, in the vein of contemporary Hollywood animation. Gavin Millar's *Sight and Sound* review praised the film's blend of 'the knowingness and the simplicity', but argued that, 'during its evolution through twenty-one scripts the children have been left behind'.[25] This view encapsulates a prevailing misconception that children's films must be pitched towards the lowest common denominator, eschewing narrative, verbal or aesthetic sophistication in the pursuit of the most simplistic pleasures.

172

Family Blockbusters: *Oliver!* and *Chitty Chitty Bang Bang*

Oliver! and *Chitty Chitty Bang Bang*, released in September and December 1968, are highly typical of this phase of Hollywood co-production. They also reflected an ongoing belief, articulated by British critic Penelope Houston in her 1963 book, *The Contemporary Cinema*, that the youth film 'engages the full-time attention of only a few', and that 'to be really successful, a film has still to cut across all the barriers of age and class and nationality'.[26] Both releases are characterised by conspicuous expense, fulsome orchestral musical numbers, lavish set design, large casts, and extreme length. *Oliver!* was adapted from Lionel Bart's 1960 stage musical, itself an adaptation of Dickens's *Oliver Twist* (1838). Bart's production had been a tremendous money-maker in both Britain and the US. The adaptation rights were acquired by the British studio, Romulus Films, whose founder, John Woolf, engaged Carol Reed to direct.[27] However, finance from Columbia Pictures was necessary; as Reed observed, 'only Americans can afford' musicals.[28] Retaining the storyline and most of the songs from Bart's production, the film was a substantial hit, earning over $10 million in US rentals alone. It also won Oscars for Best Picture, Best Director, Best Art Direction, Best Music, and Best Sound.

Oliver! presents a highly bowdlerised take on Dickens. Like *Oliver Twist*, it deals with serious issues of class and morality, and child labour (although modern interpretation focuses more on depictions of domestic abuse). It follows the adventures of young orphan Oliver Twist (Mark Lester) from his early life in a workhouse to being sold into effective slavery, falling in with a band of juvenile pickpockets led by Fagin (Ron Moody), his adoption by the benign, upper-class Brownlow (Joseph O'Connor), his kidnap by Fagin and the murderous blackguard Bill Sikes (Oliver Reed), and his eventual re-entry into high society. There are moments of sudden and shocking violence, as when Sikes bludgeons his girlfriend, Nancy (Shani Wallis), to death when she tries to protect Oliver. However, the presentation largely eschews seriousness, embracing the overt sentimentality that lurks in the background of Dickens's novel and overtakes it only periodically.

Dickens's Victorian reputation as one of the great 'family entertainers' was consolidated in the first half of the twentieth century with an endless series of stage and screen adaptations of his work. *Oliver Twist* is one of his most potentially child-orientated works. Its central magical intervention, Oliver's 'rags to riches' transformation, and its special emphasis on the child figure evoke children's literature such as Twain's *The Prince and the Pauper* (1881). But the text remains more complex and ambiguous. Adults are a potential source of kindness and refuge (Brownlow; Nancy; Fagin, whose relationship blurs the boundaries between paternalistic and mercenary). But they are also malign arbiters of conformity, as with Bumble (Harry Secombe), the owner of the workhouse, and the drunken magistrate eager to condemn Oliver on sight, as well as of chaotic violence, embodied in Sikes. For Dickens, authority on its own terms is neither to be trusted nor respected. However, in contradistinction to Victorian and Edwardian children's literary convention, there is no solace for Oliver in the company of other children, outwardly fellow victims of an iniquitous social system, but hardened in this instance into unfeeling cynicism. The other children in the workhouse encourage Oliver to request more food from Bumble, an act which gets him expelled. His fellow pickpockets display little loyalty towards him, despite the misleadingly solicitous number 'Consider Yourself', in which friendship and loyalty are fraudulently extolled as a means of enrolling him in Fagin's criminal outfit.

Points of tension arise from a fundamental disjuncture between the social realism of Dickens's novel and the characteristic sentimentality of the family musical genre. Mark Lester's angelic singing voice (actually that of Kathe Green) invokes the delicate perfection of Jackie Coogan, Shirley Temple and Freddie Bartholomew. For viewers familiar with the conventions of the Hollywood family film, Brownlow's 'rescue' of Oliver is almost structurally inevitable. This is true even for those viewers unacquainted with the basic storyline, whether handed down by Dickens or by Lionel Bart. By the same token, Sikes's murder of Nancy and murderous pursuit of Oliver are so out of keeping with the film's hitherto pervasive cheeriness (with only occasional, fleeting plaintive punctuations) that, for the uninitiated, they are wholly unexpected. As the *MFB* quipped, 'child labour, pimping, abduction, prostitution and murder combine to make *Oliver!* the most non-U subject so far to receive a "U" certificate.'[29] For this author, these points of dramatic tension are prominent in childhood memories of the film. Since they work by suggestion rather than brutal depiction,

Summers of Love and Winters of Discontent

aspects such as Sikes's bludgeoning Nancy to death have evaded censors, both on theatrical release and on television, where *Oliver!* is shown routinely in matinee slots. Like *Yellow Submarine*, the film has since become as dissociated from late-1960s cultural-industrial contexts as Bart's musical was from Dickens's social realist milieus.

Chitty Chitty Bang Bang's subject matter is more overtly juvenile. The film was made by many of the same creative personnel responsible for the *James Bond* series, but whereas the Bond films had at their core fantasies of masculine omnipotence free from the structures and restraints of the nuclear family, *Chitty Chitty Bang Bang* more conventionally reaffirms the pleasures and necessities of domesticity. The film centres on eccentric Edwardian inventor Caractacus Potts (Dick Van Dyke), who lives in a rural farmhouse with his elderly father, Grandpa Potts (Lionel Jeffries), and two children, Jemima (Heather Ripley) and Jeremy (Adrian Hall). While Caractacus tries and fails to sell one of his inventions, toot sweets, to confectioner Lord Scrumptious (James Robertson Justice), Jemima and Jeremy meet the confectioner's daughter, Truly Scrumptious (Sally Ann Howes). Initially antagonistic, Caractacus and Truly become mutually attracted, and Truly accompanies the family on a picnic to the beach in the family's vintage racing car, Chitty Chitty Bang Bang. Caractacus relates a story of the dastardly German Baron Bomburst (Gert Frobe) who wants to steal their car, having heard of its magical properties. The group then enter a fantasy world where Caractacus's stories come to life. Bomburst succeeds in kidnapping Grandpa Potts, taking him to the kingdom of Vulgaria. Caractacus, Truly and the children follow in their flying car, where eventually they depose the Baron, free Vulgaria's inhabitants and return to the 'real' world. Caractacus is visited by Lord Scrumptious, who informs him of his plans to sell the toot sweets as a dog treat, and that he can expect to be wealthy as a consequence. Caractacus then proposes to Truly, who accepts.

Popular anecdotal recollection of the film tends to focus on the Child Catcher (Robert Helpmann), the sinister, long-nosed villain who kidnaps children on behalf of the child-hating baroness with lures of ice cream and lollipops. The Child Catcher only appears in three scenes, but his incongruity in a film where sentiment is continually invoked and where most of the menace is comically unthreatening, allied to Helpmann's wonderfully

Image 7.2 The central family and the magical car: *Chitty Chitty Bang Bang* (1968)

discomforting performance, makes the character one of the film's most memorable aspects. But for all its whimsical and fantastical adventures, the film's central theme, and its final note of triumph, is the establishment of a 'traditional' nuclear family, with Caractacus and Truly coming together in marriage and finally providing the strong, stable parental structure for the children. While Caractacus expresses with misty-eyed idealism the joys and satisfactions he, as a single father, derives from his relationship with his children in the song 'You Two', the sentiment is not wholly reciprocated. Truly, whose firm kindliness delineates her as the quintessential Edwardian matriarch, immediately reproves Caractacus for allowing the children to play truant from school. Later, she changes her mind, admitting that: 'You're more than just a father to those two children'. Caractacus replies: 'Oh, yes. Nursemaid, private tutor, chief cook and bottle washer, everything... Except what they really need'. As Truly and Caractacus exchange awkward glances, the unspoken but inescapable suggestion is that the children need a mother; this takes precedence over his own manly desires.

Like many family films, *Chitty Chitty Bang Bang* asserts the incompleteness of the single-parent family structure. Moreover, by reiterating the necessity of separate gender roles, it is a conservative rebuke to women pursuing their own careers outside the family home. Caractacus, albeit shakily, fulfils his duty as provider, but is unable to offer the moral guidance and instil codes of good conduct that prospective wife-mother

Truly can. Perhaps to pre-empt inferences that the domestic arrangement benefits only Caractacus, in the following scene's musical number, 'Lovely Lonely Man', Truly reveals that:

> My life now has a plan
> To someday make him see
> That I need him as much as he needs me.

Yet Truly is introduced as sensible, well-balanced and financially independent, 'incomplete' only insofar that she is unmarried. In contrast, Caractacus is a man-boy who spends all his time and money inventing curios. His own father disapproves of his irresponsible fecklessness, advising him to find steady employment in keeping with his age and commitments. As Caractacus tells himself, shortly before proposing to Truly, 'You have to be practical... Face the facts... After all, a man with responsibilities can't walk around with his head in the clouds all the time. A man should keep his feet solidly on the ground'. Marriage thus represents Caractacus's graduation to a more 'proper' adult identity.

The film was heavily marketed towards children. Contemporary British newspapers featured children's colouring contests, with the prize a miniature replica of the film's iconic flying car.[30] There was a considerable merchandising push, with 'thirty-nine million food packages bearing the Chitty motif', 'balloons by the million', 'enough Chitty T-shirts to cover the entire Soviet armed forces', 'Chitty wallpaper', 'paper cups, plates, saucers, jigsaws, dolls, cars, paperbacks, and long-playing records'.[31] Much of the critical discourse centred on its 'family entertainment' potential. The *Daily Express* reported that the December premiere would be attended by the Queen, Prince Philip, Prince Charles and Princess Anne, and quipped that: 'If it's the whole family you're after, you might as well start at the top'.[32] But the *Times*' John Russell Taylor complained that:

> It is not really a children's film. It is too long: 152 minutes plus interval is quite a stretch to hold a child's attention, or even an adult's. It is too lacking in incident, its wonders are not wonderful enough [...] and all the ineffectual romantic interest will probably bore children stiff.
>
> On the other hand, if it is not a children's film, whose is it? Not, I would have thought, most grown-ups! [...] it will be the

sort of film that children are taken to see and don't really like by grown-ups who don't like it themselves but think the children will. If this is what is meant by an all-purpose family film, this is it, but surely there must be more to it than that?[33]

The *MFB*'s Jan Dawson concurred:

> While toffee in moderation may be an excellent thing, a universal coating of treacle is apt to prove more sickening than sweetening; and *Chitty Chitty Bang Bang* [...] is likely to upset the most settled of stomachs. Offering what passes these days for seasonal cheer, it follows in the declining tradition of English pantomime, attempting to produce 'family' entertainment by disguising its adult material [...] in the cutest of children's clothing and endowing its cherub-faced child characters with a sprightly sanctity that seems best calculated to appeal to dewy-eyed maiden aunts.[34]

Conversely, the *Guardian* ignored the film's adult aspects and channelled its opprobrium towards the veneer of juvenility:

> 'Chitty Chitty Bang Bang' can safely be recommended only for the most undemanding children in the under-5 bracket. Anyone older than that is apt to run wretching from the cinema. In fact, this film is so saccharine and silly that it makes any Disney feature look like the profoundest of sour gherkins.[35]

Such coruscating hyperbole may raise a weary smile, but these responses do raise salient points regarding the film's position between the overlapping but distinct parallel traditions of British and Hollywood children's cinema. While the cast and production crew remain primarily British – with Dick Van Dyke, thankfully not attempting a cockney accent, an obvious enticement for US spectators – *Chitty Chitty Bang Bang* constitutes a marked departure from the British norm. In retrospect, it is a precursor to post-1990s co-production, with all that entails: big budgets, starry casts, abundant action and special effects, strongly emotive cues, and the ubiquitous happy ending; and in terms of context, extensive marketing and merchandising campaigns, representing a synergistic attempt to position the film as multimedia phenomenon.

In other respects, *Oliver!* and *Chitty Chitty Bang Bang* were dead ends, both for home-grown children's films and for British cinema in general. They upheld largely bourgeois values, making them politically suspect to younger, more liberal audiences living through the feminist and civil rights movements of the 1960s. Furthermore, in terms of formal composition, they appeared blandly conformist. Their sentimentality (in an age where realism was highly prized), preference for old-fashioned, sweet orchestral musical numbers (in the age of rock and roll, and edgier musicals, like *Hair* [1967]), outmoded romanticised representations of childhood, and extreme length (necessitating an intermission, inviting comparisons with opera and other highbrow forms) all bespoke an undesirable antiquity. Moreover, these films were no longer for 'everyone' – the prototypical definition of the 'family audience' – but rather served the needs of a narrowing, perhaps even coterie, audience. *Easy Rider* (Dennis Hopper, 1969), *Midnight Cowboy* (John Schlesinger, 1969) and *Woodstock* (Michael Wadleigh, 1970), and the failure of the middlebrow musicals *Star!* (Robert Wise, 1968) and *Hello, Dolly!* (Gene Kelly, 1969), were totemic of a wider transformation of an adult-orientated cultural landscape into a youth-orientated one. Investment in British extravaganzas ground to a halt after Hollywood's financial crisis of 1969. British children's films in the 1970s thus reverted from populist transatlanticism to a more characteristically 'British' style: low-budget, unformulaic, naturalistic; and now entering new territory, sometimes quixotic, obscure, and confoundingly downbeat.

'Permissive' Films

As *Daily Mirror* columnist Donald Zec observed, by the late 1960s, British cinema had become 'the hot medium'.[36] 'The trend', Zec argued in October 1968, 'is towards the most explicit portrayals of sex, the most frank examination of perversion and human brutality'.[37] Censorship, inevitably, was in the spotlight, and BBFC secretary John Trevelyan admitted that while, in his view, 'the public is not ready' for 'the complete sex act on the screen', 'if they want it – they can have it'.[38] In July 1970, the BBFC updated its ratings system, introducing a new 'AA' classification that allowed entry to over-14s only; it made the 'A' rating merely advisory; and it increased the age threshold for 'X' films to 18. The practical effect was twofold: children no longer required adult supervision to attend 'A' films, and many productions previously rated 'X' would fall into the 'AA' category. Additionally, films that would otherwise have been banned could now be exhibited under the more liberal 'X' banner.[39]

The industry was still divided on the relative merits of 'family' and 'mature' pictures. John Davis, head of the Rank Organisation's theatre chain, told the *Daily Mirror* that 'The cinema built its great tradition by providing family entertainment', a tradition undermined by 'the increasing availability of X-certificate films, some with limited appeal'.[40] Not everyone shared this perspective. J. S. Stansby, proprietor of the Rex Theatre, Wilmslow, wrote to the *Guardian* in October 1968, arguing that:

> Considering the range of intellect, interests, maturity and experience in the average family, the 'family film', in the sense of film appealing to and enjoyed by each member of the family, must be a very rare bird, and impossible to define.[41]

Stansby emphasised that: 'Family type films do exist, and are shown, but [...] with few exceptions they are not wanted'.[42]

The tide seemed to be turning again towards family films with the news, in April 1969, of Bryan Forbes's appointment as production head for ABPC, recently acquired by US media giant EMI. Forbes vocally opposed 'the pornography of violence' overtaking British movie screens, and promptly announced a programme of family films, reiterating that: 'There is nothing wrong in wishing to reach the widest possible audience'.[43] One of the main beneficiaries of Forbes's tenure at ABPC was Lionel Jeffries. Jeffries abhorred the adult trajectory in contemporary cinema. Having long harboured ambitions to direct, and fresh from his role as Grandpa Potts in *Chitty Chitty Bang Bang*, he purchased the adaptation rights to E. Nesbit's *The Railway Children* (1906) for £2,000.[44] Various moguls, as Jeffries recalled, rejected the project, insisting that: 'This isn't the right time to make that kind of film'.[45] Jeffries claimed that one Hollywood studio agreed to produce it as a musical starring Julie Andrews, and set in the American mid-west.[46] Instead, he turned to ABPC, where his friendship with Forbes was pivotal in getting the film into production and securing the director's chair. The resulting film, released in December 1970, is one of the quintessential family films.

The Railway Children and Other Stories

Released in December 1970 for the Christmas family trade, with movie posters (ungrammatically) marketing it as 'A Film for Adults to Take Their Children, Too!', *The Railway Children* was promoted as a wholesome, nostalgic film for general audiences. Jeffries explained that:

> I found the climate of the E. Nesbit story just right for me, a way in which to start entertaining people and help, not destroy, our industry. There are hardly any films being made for children and for the middle-aged and older age groups.[47]

Forbes bluntly positioned it as a palliative for a conservative majority dismayed by 'the spate of violence and pornography on both the large and small screens [...] There is a crying need for films which all the family can go and see'.[48] Expectations for the film were not especially high. The *Guardian* predicted that: 'The public will go – but whether it's what they really want is another question'.[49] As co-star Sally Thomsett later conceded, 'we thought it was a little film for kids'.[50]

The film begins with a framing device in which the narrator, Bobbie (Jenny Agutter), looks back on its events from mature adulthood. Bobbie begins by introducing her family: her younger sister, Phyllis (Thomsett), brother, Peter (Gary Warren), and parents, Mother (Dinah Sheridan) and Father (Iain Cuthbertson). The domestic harmony of the family's affluent life in Edwardian London is disrupted when Father is arrested and imprisoned for as-yet-unexplained reasons. Now penurious, the rest of the family is forced into a simpler, pastoral life in Yorkshire. The children forge a symbolic connection with the local railway station, whose steam trains they imagine 'sending their love to Father'; and they befriend the station porter, Mr Perks (Bernard Cribbins) and an Old Gentleman (William Mervyn), to whom they wave as his train passes through the station every morning. The narrative is episodic, the children embarking on a series of minor adventures: they flag down a train after subsidence makes the track unsafe, bringing them commendations for public spirit; come to the assistance of a Russian dissident (Gordon Whiting) exiled from pre-Communist Russia; gather gifts from members of the local community to mark Mr Perks's birthday; and rescue an injured boy, Jim (Christopher Witty). Jim is revealed as the Grandson of the Old Gentleman, who helps secure the release of Father, wrongly imprisoned for selling state secrets. Each episode flows more or less sequentially from the last, as if reconstructing the imperfect recollections of an adult looking back on childhood.

The attempt to represent the world through the eyes of children was exceptional, having previously largely been confined to CFF productions, second-feature films and adult allegories, such as Carol Reed's *The Fallen Idol* (1948) and *A Kid for Two Farthings* (1955). The child's subjectivity is most effectively presented in two sequences. The first conveys the trauma of Father's disappearance, which is framed by distantly observed, unfathomably half-heard conversations. The second is in the memorable and powerfully affecting closing scenes, where the emotional catharsis surrounding Father's return, as he emerges from a cloud of steam on the station platform, is strengthened by the audience's vicarious sharing of the moment with Bobbie. Accordingly, the internal subjectivity of the adults – notably Father's plight and Mother's barely-glimpsed grief – are elided. Equally, *The Railway Children* is 'nostalgic' and 'charming' partly because it resurrects lapsed but enduringly comforting visions of childhood perfection and social conviviality, made all the more appealing by the occasional hints of disquiet (in the untold but presumably horrendous ordeal Father undergoes; in the Russian's exile and separation from his family). Jeffries attempts to delineate an authentically naturalistic fictional space; in interview, he claimed to have eschewed 'tricksy photography', embracing 'typical documentary techniques' as if simply, and without mediation, representing the world as it really was.[51]

However, a contrary sentimentalism can be localised in the representation of the unfailingly sweet, gentle, generous, brave and honest children. Even Peter's covert stealing of coal for the fire is motivated by a desire to aid Mother's recovery from illness, and he is instantly reproved by both sisters. Idealised depictions of childhood virtue and innocence were normative in children's literature of Nesbit's era, but the presence of such images of 'perfect' childhood inevitably projects different meanings in the 1970s. The children's cuteness is mirrored by their precision in language and enunciation, which contrasts with the bluff colloquialisms of the locals, the comparative unattractiveness of the comically dishevelled cab driver, and the remarked-upon ugliness of Perks's name. These upper-class registers

Image 7.3 An early foreshadowing of the young protagonists' connection with the train in *The Railway Children* (1970)

are subtly hierarchical – a fact already recognised by the CFF, which had largely abandoned 'goody-goody' child protagonists due to their unpopularity with children.[52]

We should not ignore the film's intrinsic virtues: Jeffries's skilful adaptation of Nesbit's source material; his simple and unfussy direction, so well attuned to the needs of the script; the fine period detail and beautiful locations; the understated, memorable performances; and the almost tangible warmth and sincerity. It was the fifth most profitable film at the British box office in 1971, and critics responded overwhelmingly positively.[53] It formed the basis for the first ever Royal Matinee Performance, as attended by Viscount Linley (aged 9), Lady Sarah Armstrong-Jones (6) and James Ogilvy (6).[54] Accordingly, the *Daily Mirror*'s Ian Christie, while positive, regarded it as a 'children's film'.[55] In contrast, the *Daily Express*'s Katherine Hadley emphasised its cross-demographic appeal, describing it as a 'Pied Piper affair': 'Teenagers queued alongside housewives. The Royal children went. And everybody had a lovely weep.'[56] The *Observer* deemed it 'a loving valentine to those good old Edwardian days' which is 'simple, sunny and sentimental in exactly the right "Meet Me in St. Louis" way', and the *Catholic Herald* appreciated the 'loving recreation of an age barely past when certainties were more secure, values and problems clearer, and neither children nor parents ashamed to love each other'.[57]

The latter review hints at a more socially-determined set of appeals, recognising that, for all its purported innocence, *The Railway Children* is also a reaction against modern society. Soberly and responsibly (though not without good humour), it promotes values of family unity, social cohesion and friendship, tolerance and sincerity. Ultimately, *The Railway Children* has transcended these specificities, to the extent that, in 1999, the British Film Institute deemed it one of the top 100 British films of the century. Its many showings on British television in the intervening years – often during symbolic periods of family unity, such as Easter and Christmas – only partially explain its purportedly 'timeless' appeal. To many older viewers it surely presents a double nostalgia, for their *own* lost days of innocence (as adults remembering their childhood, and their childhood experiences of the film) as to society's.

Jeffries went on to direct another four family films: *The Amazing Mr Blunden* (1972), *Baxter!* (1973), *Wombling Free* (1977) and *The Water Babies* (1978). None approached the critical and commercial success of *The Railway Children*, and several of Jeffries's planned projects, including a biopic about Salvation Army founder General Booth and a musical adaptation of Peter Pan, remained unrealised.[58] Meanwhile, Forbes's 'family' programme at EMI continued with *The Tales of Beatrix Potter* (Reginald Mills, 1971), an audacious adaptation of Beatrix Potter's illustrated stories as a ballet film completely devoid of dialogue, with classical music. The narrative comprises distinct episodes featuring prominent characters from Potter's original stories, including Peter Rabbit, Jemima Puddle-Duck, Squirrel Nutkin and Little Pig Robinson. Wisely, choreographer Sir Frederick Ashton attempts to capture the basic movements of the animals rather than impose on them human-like balletic grace. What emerges is primarily a spectacle – though, inevitably, a decidedly old-fashioned one. Even in 1971, ballet and classical music were comparatively highbrow. Moreover, the film is made for exhibition on the big screen, where its aesthetics can more fully be appreciated. For these reasons, *The Tales of Beatrix Potter* has not benefited from the same profitable afterlife through television and theatrical reissues as *The Railway Children*.

Summers of Love and Winters of Discontent

While *The Railway Children*'s middlebrow inclinations are largely offset by its charm, *The Tales of Beatrix Potter* withdraws further into an institutionalised view of family entertainment. The *Sunday Times*'s Alan Brien saw it firmly as an adult's conception of young people's entertainment:

> packing in the Whitsun holiday traffic of children accompanied by mystified au pairs, grannies who know every story by heart, and graduate mothers relieved to mix culture and a quiet snooze, [it] has eliminated most of the dark, dangerous underside of those creepy little fables. The costumes are superb, the dancing ingenious if static, the music derivative and tuneful. Beatrix Potter has become Art, a little disappointing perhaps to children who hope for narrative excitement, rather reassuring to parents who feared Disney in his most vulgar, hair-raising style.[59]

In its episodic structure, emphasis on music and visual appeal in preference to dialogue, the film bears certain similarities with early British children's television; specifically, programmes like *Muffin the Mule* (1946–55) and *Andy Pandy* (1950–57), where dialogue was kept to a minimum in order to engage pre-school audiences.

Many wholesome family films of the early 1970s were poorly received. The 'U'-rated historical epic, *Cromwell* (Ken Hughes, 1970), was a massive flop. The *MFB* concluded that: 'It will offend the purists and bore the kiddies'.[60] The same publication attacked *David Copperfield* (Delbert Mann, 1970) for sanitising Dickens's novel and for lacking 'the verve and visual exuberance of the equally sentimentalised *Oliver!*'.[61] In March 1971, Bryan Forbes resigned as production head of EMI Films. Although *The Railway Children* and *The Tales of Beatrix Potter* had made money, *Hoffman* (Alvin Rakoff, 1970) and *The Man Who Haunted Himself* (Basil Dearden, 1970) were less profitable, and Forbes's programme was apparently viewed as 'square' and outdated.[62] His resignation, adding to the continuing decline of the CFF, was a further blow to children's cinema. Other than animal films and low-budget fantasies, for the remainder of the decade the genre largely consisted of occasional big-budget extravaganzas (e.g. *Alice's Adventures in Wonderland* [William Sterling, 1972]), rare runaway hits (e.g. *Digby, the Biggest Dog in the World* [Joseph McGrath, 1973]), wholesome, low-budget children's literary adaptations (e.g. *Swallows and Amazons* [Claude

Whatham, 1974]), and quirky personal projects (e.g. Alan Parker's *Bugsy Malone* [1976]).

Alice's Adventures in Wonderland is a comparatively lavish staging of Lewis Carroll's 1865 novel, with a budget of around £400,000. It is also one of the best acted, with a cast including Ralph Richardson, Peter Sellers, Roy Kinnear, Dudley Moore, Spike Milligan, Michael Hordern and Flora Robson. During production, director William Sterling told the *Guardian* that:

> I don't underrate the vast potential of the family audience. In the musical version we are using Carroll as a springboard – we're very faithful to the spirit of the fun and the dialogue, but we're tending to take off in a 1972 fun and adventure and family way.[63]

In contrast, the *Times* saw a deeper purpose:

> A curious fixture of inanity and surrealism, sometimes working on different levels, sometimes not working at all [...] The film's images nevertheless serve to emphasise the darker themes of the Reverend Mr Dodgson's often remarkably sinister narrative. The long tunnels, the flood of tears, the ferocious storm, the abrupt changes in size, the squabbling, illogical and homicidal adults, make up a vivid catalogue of adolescent scorns and terrors. The song over the final credits, 'You Make Me See the Me I Never Knew', suggests that Sterling and his team indeed had something more in mind than a family musical, and there are times when they almost get it across (the pig, for instance, would surely please Bunuel).[64]

This was, indeed, a period in which formal experimentation in British children's cinema was permissible to a limited degree, facilitated by the relative absence of the structuring conventions that circumscribe Hollywood family films. One can adduce the influence of European art house cinematic techniques here, as in Jeffries's *The Railway Children* and *Baxter!*. These techniques are clearly associated with a more 'adult' cinematic mode, but with perhaps a lone exception – the extraordinary *The 5,000 Fingers of Dr T* (Roy Royland, 1953) – Hollywood live-action child and family films have leaned heavily towards a comparatively simple visual style.[65] Operating outside the rigid institutional framework of the Hollywood studio system,

Summers of Love and Winters of Discontent

British producers – if they were able to secure financial backing and distribution – had fewer constraints.

An obvious example is *Bugsy Malone,* an enigma in a decade of oddities and incongruities. A parody of Hollywood gangster films such as *Little Caesar* (Mervyn LeRoy, 1931) populated entirely by child actors, *Bugsy Malone* was not a sizeable box office hit on initial release. It has since become regarded as a classic, adapted for the stage and referenced in dozens of films, popular songs and television shows. For adults, its curiosity stems partly from the blatancy of its cultural borrowings. It plunders the cultural image bank of prohibition-era gangland Chicago, with speakeasies and mob violence against a backdrop of stylised, intentionally artificial-looking sets. One might hesitate to place *Bugsy Malone* within the 'family' category, because its child/adult appeal is so strongly demarcated that it almost contravenes the genre's putatively unifying principles. That is, its adult appeal rests largely on ironic detachment, recognition of its oddities and incongruities and – at least among more analytical viewers – decoding its intertextual references and the implications of its styles and strategies. For children (including this author in younger days), the film is merely delightfully anarchic. There are certainly ludic aspects to the 'splurgings', in which characters are shot with guns that fire custard, each shot followed by a rapid zoom and freeze-frame of the victims' faces.

The film inverts the genre's convention of adult as symbolic child, with adults masquerading as children (e.g. Mary Pickford) or determinedly regressing to childhood (e.g. George Formby). The roles inhabited by children here are obviously those of adults: they talk and act like grown-ups; some even have pencil moustaches drawn on their top lip. They fight and kill using adult machines, they run adult businesses (speakeasies, restaurants and barber shops), they live by adult socio-behavioural codes (even if crime film conventions allow their frequent transgression), and they are motivated by adult desires, such as the pursuance of money, romance and power. These are pygmy simulacra of adults, rather than children ruling the world by their own rules. Child spectators are invited to revel in the film's unprecedented opportunities for freedom from overbearing adult authority, while relishing its lampooning of those very adult preoccupations which appear simultaneously irresistible, imitable, unfathomable and absurd.

There are many examples of self-referential comedy that draw attention to the film's tongue-in-cheek artificiality. For instance, Bugsy, while explaining to Blousey (Florrie Dugger) about his past employment, mentions his time as a boxer and, mimicking Brando in *On the Waterfront* (Elia Kazan, 1954), tells her 'I could've been a contender'; later, when one of Fat Sam's (John Cassisi) goons is unable to understand a line in Italian, he is directed to read the on-screen subtitle; the same goon apologetically tells Fat Sam that he cannot drive (i.e. because he is too young); people are driven using pedal-driven cars and limousines; and Fat Sam attempts to construct a splurge gun with a barrel attached to the front of a hand-cranked 1920s film camera, a sight gag that requires some knowledge of cinematography. Some of these allusions are equally accessible by child and adult spectators; others, such as the Brando reference, exclude – though without disturbing the engagement of – young children. However, the climactic 'gunfight' at Fat Sam's between his forces and those of his rival, Dandy Dan (Martin Lev), tacitly signals the end of the 'serious' business of the film, and make-believe segues into childish play. Every single member of the cast gets coated in whipped cream and custard pies amidst anarchic scenes of battle that give way to revelry. Children, the scene reminds us, can only suppress their subversive instincts for so long. The final musical number, 'You Give a Little Love', signals the *deus ex machina* cessation of hostilities. Several actors break out of character (perhaps they are fictional characters stepping outside their fantasy?), including Foster, who self-referentially comments, rhetorically, 'So this is show business?' before being splattered with custard pie.

The Animal Film

Between the late 1960s and late 1970s, the most important British children's film cycle was the animal film, which encompassed *Born Free*, *Ring of Bright Water*, *Run Wild, Run Free*, *Sandy the Seal* (Robert Lynn, 1970), *Black Beauty* (James Hill, 1971), *Living Free* (Jack Couffer, 1972), *The Belstone Fox* (James Hill, 1973), *Call of the Wild* (Ken Annakin, 1973), *Digby, The Biggest Dog in the World*, *The Lion at World's End* (Bill Travers and James Hill, 1974), *Watership Down*, and *Tarka the Otter* (David Cobham, 1979). With the exception of the comedic *Digby*, the Hollywood-style

Summers of Love and Winters of Discontent

Black Beauty and the animated *Watership Down*, these films are linked by recurrent features: simpatico central relationships between humans and animals; emphasis on an ultimately ungovernable, untameable nature; mankind as intrusive or destructive force, diametrically opposed to the 'natural' order; a tendency simultaneously to embrace and to repudiate anthropomorphism and sentimentality; punctuating moments of brutal realism; and implicit or explicit criticisms of modernity, in which animal is equated with nature, thus representing an antithesis to human civilisation.

The enormous transatlantic success of *Born Free* reinvigorated the long-moribund animal film. The winner of two Oscars, the film is adapted from Joy Adamson's autobiographic 1960 novel of the same name, and centres on the relationship between Joy (Virginia McKenna), her husband, game warden George Adamson (Bill Travers), and a young lioness they name Elsa. It relates George's shooting and killing a lioness that charges him, and the Adamsons' subsequent adoption of its cubs. After several months, they send two of the cubs to a zoo, but keep Elsa in the family home until she grows to maturity, at which point they release her into the wild. As with Joy Adamson's source text, the film actively embraces anthropomorphism of the kind pointedly rejected by such later films as *The Belstone Fox*. When trying to get the lion cubs, which have been refusing food, to feed for the first time, Joy adopts a baby voice, dejectedly addressing them as 'My little sweety baby'. When one of the cubs licks milk from her hand, Joy decides to call it Elsa, because 'She reminds me of a little girl I knew at school. She was the smallest of us all and she wasn't very good at games, but she was very bright and brave and good, and I liked her very much. Her name was Elsa'. References to their cubs' playfulness, inquisitiveness, gentleness, innocence and intelligence explicitly equate them with children. The film goes further, attributing to the animal more cognitively developed human emotions like embarrassment, and moral qualities, such as goodness and compassion.

Interesting, the film differentiates between the domesticated, apparently 'naturally' gentle and humanistic Elsa and the various large, savage wild lions George shoots as game warden. Elsa operates as a surrogate daughter for the childless Joy. Is their relationship attributable to some ineffably 'childlike' quality Elsa possesses, as is implied by Joy's preference for her over the other cubs? There is little attempt elsewhere in the film to sanitise nature. In the first scene, a man-eating lion kills a young woman washing her clothes by a river. The camera cuts from a long-shot of the charging lion to an extreme close-up of the woman's screaming face, then to a wide shot of the river, as the woman's clothes, mixed with blood, flow downstream. George's killing of Elsa's mother, however, elicits genuine regret when he realises that the animal was instinctively protecting her cubs. The crucial difference is that, in the latter case, the lioness was behaving in a way empathetically comprehensible to humans. Conversely, the man-eating lions, although clearly driven by innate predatory impulses, transgress human ethical boundaries. Elsa, in contrast, is never threatening, and reinforces the animal-as-child archetype (or myth), representing a desirable reciprocity between human civilisation and the natural world.

Much of the final third of the movie is devoted to the Adamsons' attempts to retrain the domesticated Elsa for life in the wild. Ironically, this involves her shedding her human qualities, being taught to hunt and kill, to hold her own among the viciously territorial lions of the wild, and to find a mate. The latter is initially a source of comedy when Elsa is encouraged to approach a young male lion, and the two begin an elaborate courtship before Elsa inexplicably runs back to the Adamsons' car. George comments, drolly, 'There's a name for girls like her'. Joy's narration reveals that: 'We suffered all the agony of parents whose teenage daughter is out on her first date'. In many ways, this is a maturation narrative. Joy, symbolic mother, must relinquish her selfish desire to keep Elsa close, which, she realises, will keep her safe but simultaneously 'Fat, and lazy, and dull, and stupid'. She likens releasing Elsa into the wild to her own choice to live in the wilderness, which 'represents freedom'. Late in the film, Elsa makes her first kill, a warthog, after which 'She proved again and again that she could feed herself'. Shortly afterwards, Elsa successfully mates with a male lion and subsequently mothers her own cubs. Her trajectory in the latter part of the film – becoming 'Wild and free', as George puts it – is clearly bittersweet for the Adamsons, signalling the end of their parent-daughter fantasy.

Ring of Bright Water reunites *Born Free*'s stars, Bill Travers and Virginia McKenna, and is also based on an autobiographical source: author Gavin Maxwell's best-selling autobiography of 1960, centring on his domestication of an otter. The film also draws much of its pathos and authenticity from its rooting in real life. Again, the animal represents openness, truthful simplicity and freedom from dull, everyday life. Travers's Graham Merrill begins the film as a frustrated office-based administrator, appalled that he has become 'A code number that gets a pension, an expectancy of life calculated in years and days'. Graham later spots an otter through a pet shop window, and they exchange a lingering glance. His voiceover narration tells us that:

> From that first day, I imagined that the otter had somehow singled me out from all the thousands of people who passed the pet shop window every day... Every time I passed he seemed to be watching me, and me alone. At first I thought it was only my imagination, but whatever I did he seemed to sense that I was there, and fixed me with his beady eyes. Clearly, I was the chosen one.

Graham's impulsive purchase of the otter, which he names Mij, expresses itself as tacit rebellion against the joyless regimentation of his city life; Mij's predictable ransacking of his London apartment cathartically releases Graham from the materialism and consumerism embodied by the post-industrial city, allowing him – as with many dissatisfied city slickers during the individualist movement of the late 1960s – to retreat to the wilderness in search of spiritual fulfilment. The 'truth' Graham seeks is not to be found in some utopian pantisocracy or borne through free love and narcotics, but rather within the pastoral 'ring of bright water' to which the title lyrically alludes.

The otter is a peculiarly British animal to use as the centre of a family film. Savage, not adorable in the accepted sense, unsuitable for domestication, historically regarded as a pest and hunted mercilessly for sport, the otter bridges the divide between man and nature more so than conventionally domesticated animals, displaying adaptability to land and water, possessing intelligence and playfulness, but remaining thrillingly untameable. As in *Born Free*, audiences are denied an ingratiating happy ending. Unaware that Mij is a beloved pet, and driven by received ideas that otters are vermin, an amiable roadside digger beats him to death with his spade, believing him to be 'just an otter'. Despite such traumatic episodes, these films place greater emphasis on the cyclicality of nature, and the dialectic between its beauty and barbarism, than on the lives of individual animals.

Mij, like the mother goose whose goslings Graham adopts after she is shot by poachers, successfully procreates, thus ensuring natural continuity. This fact makes somewhat bearable the violent death of Mij, as with Tarka in the later film.

Run Wild, Run Free centres on an autistic adolescent boy, Philip (Mark Lester), who lives on a rural farm in Dartmoor with his parents (Gordon Jackson and Sylvia Syms). Philip has refused to speak since the age of three, but on the moors he encounters and is entranced by an albino colt, which he tames with the encouragement of a sympathetic neighbour, the Moorman (John Mills). Through his relationship with the white colt, and friendships with the Moorman and a young girl, Diana (Fiona Fullerton), Philip eventually comes to terms with his place in the world. Early in the film, the Moorman takes Philip to a bird's nest hidden in bracken, and they watch as a chick hatches. The Moorman explains:

> That's the wonderful thing about the moors. The whole thing heaving and bursting with new life in the spring, yet it's almost invisible. Now, look around. What can you see? You can't see anything, can you? But it's there, just the same... The moor's alive, Philip. Sleeps and breathes and eats and drinks. Sometimes it's serene and peaceful. Feels kindly towards us. Other times it's angry and dangerous. It can even kill us sometimes, if it takes a notion to it. And right now, in the centre of the moor, deep down in the black peat, there's a heart beating. You can feel it, sometimes.

In expressing the parallel wonders and dangers of a natural world that is tangible, wondrous yet unfathomable, this passage of dialogue might stand as a shorthand articulation of the larger philosophies of this filmic cycle. But *Run Wild, Run Free* is ultimately more hopeful in its vision of human-animal reciprocity than *Ring of Bright Water* or *The Belstone Fox*, whose protagonists are either further isolated or destroyed by their close relationship with a wild animal. In contrast, Philip is healed, strengthened by the experience, and by the end of the film is ready to reclaim his place within society, richer and wiser (like the Moorman) as a consequence.

Twice the spectre of human selfishness and brutality – in the form of a fox hunt – infiltrates the narrative, both times with disastrous consequences.

On the first occasion, the overwhelming sights and sounds of the hunt, punctuated by unearthly bugle noises, alarms Philip's tame kestrel, which, in blind terror, flies into a tree, gets its leash caught on a branch and is killed. On the second occasion, Philip's colt bolts, throwing both of them into a peat bog. The ending verges on *deus ex machina* as Philip, his parents and the Moorman try and fail to heave the colt from the bog. Philip wades into the bog to exhort the colt to free himself, speaking intelligibly for the first time. There is a close-up of the animal's eyes as it recognises Philip's depth of feeling, and, perhaps somehow appreciating the enormity of his breakthrough, pulls itself free. The ending subsumes naturalism to feel-good sentimentality in a hopeful play towards an unrealised box office success. *Run Wild, Run Free* bears some comparison with Ken Loach's more adult-orientated *Kes* (also released in 1969), which develops an urban working-class milieu. In both films, the animal represents escape from a miserable home life, and a counterpoint to an uncaring and remote adult society, but in *Kes*, the kestrel is killed in an act of human cruelty, condemning the boy, we suspect, to a life of miserable drudgery.

The Belstone Fox, described by the *Daily Mail*'s David Lewin as 'the most original film I have seen in years', opens with a brutal scene in which two men in search of foxes dig into the ground, uncover a burrow in which a vixen is guarding her cubs, and bludgeon the animals to death.[66] The voice-over narration intones: 'And so begins the strange and terrifying story of the Belstone fox'. A surviving cub is rescued by professional huntsman Asher (Eric Porter), who names it Tag. Asher's decision to spare the cub and wean it with a hound dog is viewed with scepticism by the squire, Kendrick (Jeremy Kemp), who permits it only on condition that he 'keep [the fact] quiet'. The film's opening sections develop a tripartite relationship between Asher, Tag, and the hound Merlin, with whom Tag is happily paired as a cub. The film's major reversal is Asher's decision, under pressure from Kendrick, to make Tag the quarry in a fox hunt. By this stage, Tag has attained degrees of notoriety in the fox hunting fraternity for his boldness and cunning. Asher's willingness to allow Tag to be hunted by the pack is not so much a withdrawal of paternal protection as a desire to test Tag's mettle, as signalled by his words, 'Let's see what you're really made of'.

This leads to the film's most gruesome sequence. Asher, fervently leading the hunt, is thrown from his horse and badly wounded. Tag, being pursued by the pack of hounds, leads them across a railway track. Tag and Merlin cross safely, but the rest of the pack is killed by an oncoming train. The camera quickly cuts between the carnage on the tracks, as limbs and bloodied bodies fly through the air, and Asher's face as he shields his eyes, then cries out in anguish. Subsequently, Asher hardens to the obsessive pursuit of vengeance; he rationalises this to Kendrick by claiming that, if left alive, Tag will reuse the same strategy to escape the pack again. He refuses Kendrick's suggestion of hunting Tag with guns, insisting it 'wouldn't be right' and that they must kill him 'traditionally' through the hunt. Increasingly ailing, Asher follows Merlin into the mountains, where he finally discovers Tag and Merlin peacefully side-by-side in a cave. Intending to kill Tag, he pulls out a knife, before suffering a fatal heart attack. Asher's body is later discovered with Tag and Merlin loyally having remained by his side, keeping vigil. The final shot sees Tag alone, indefatigable, on top of the barren mountain.

Ironically, it is the decent but compromised Asher, a master of the hunt with 40 years' experience, who imposes human qualities on the animal. Having saved Tag's life, paired him with Merlin, preserved him from the hunt, and enquired of his safety after his release into the wild, Asher feels personally betrayed when Tag leads his pack across the rail track. Ironically, the real culprit is Asher, who insists on hunting Tag, secretly hoping, as a point of personal pride, that the fox will escape. Asher casts Tag as symbolic child; his inability to resist attaching human morality to the animal reaffirms these films' recurring theme: that of nature's purity, hardness and endurance. In contrast, the changeability of human civilisation is persistently highlighted. Asher's daughter, Jenny (Heather Wright), proclaims herself anti-hunting. During Jenny's birthday party, two of her upper-crust college friends snub Asher, then condescendingly refer to his assistant Stephen's (Dennis Waterman) job as a 'doggie thing'. One of the film's most potent images is of a young child, having been taken on her first fox hunt, being 'blooded' – i.e. having the hunted animal's blood smeared on her face to initiate her to the practice. The camera slowly zooms on her blank face as the music becomes discordant, and she reaches her hand up to her bloodied cheek. The child's horrified incomprehension, coupled with the youthful and progressive Jenny's ethical objection to the hunt, and Asher's transformation from decent family man to bloodthirsty obsessive,

Summers of Love and Winters of Discontent

all suggest that traditional pursuits such as fox hunting have become outmoded. These allusions to modernity are contrasted with nature's eternality.

Most animal movies, from Rin Tin Tin to Lassie, straightforwardly equate animals with children, but this cycle of films generally rejects the association. Tag's ability to survive and to evade his pursuers rests on his own innate skills. Indeed, for the ageing and increasingly indulgent Asher, it is important that the animal is afforded the opportunity, but not the means, for survival. One is reminded of the sun god's double-voiced warning and empowerment of the rabbits in *Watership Down*: 'All the world will be your enemy... And when they catch you, they will kill you. But first they must catch you'. The sentiment is echoed here when the hunter, Tod (Bill Travers), remarks of Tag: 'You can hunt him as much as you like, but you'll never catch him... Never'. These films imbue their animal protagonists with natural defences (cunning, endurance) against a world of manifold dangers, where comfort, reassurance and safety are unknowable. Equally, their defences are often insufficient. In *Born Free*, the lioness Elsa is vulnerable to human poachers. In *Ring of Bright Water*, the otter Mij is beaten to death with a shovel. In *Tarka the Otter*, Tarka is unable to evade the pursuing hounds. And even in *The Belstone Fox*, Tag survives only because Asher keels over before he is able to deliver the death blow.

If *The Belstone Fox* reveals the savagery and injustice of fox hunting, *Tarka the Otter* does likewise for otter hunting. Based on Henry Williamson's 1927 novel, with a screenplay by naturalist and author Gerald Durrell, *Tarka the Otter* is a starkly brilliant riposte to the overtly sentimental, often sanitised Disney nature documentaries of the 1950s. It is also one of the bleakest and most brutal family films ever made. The film follows the dog otter Tarka, interspersing documentary-style footage of wild animals and staged sequences shot on location with a sparse narration by Peter Ustinov. It presents various episodes in the otter's life, including his birth, the violent deaths of his mother (shot by a hunter) and father (savaged in a hunt), the honing of his predatory instincts, his finding a mate, and his eventual apparent death at the hands of Deadlock, the leader of the pack of hounds, who possesses 'an insatiable lust for otters'. Although unstinting in its distressing details, the film shows many scenes of animals engaged in pleasurable activities. In an early scene, Tarka's mother and father are seen mating underwater. Later, we see Tarka delightedly taking a shower in a

195

stream, the narration reminding us that: 'Like all otters, Tarka revelled in falling water, going wild with joy, rolling in ecstasy as he tried to catch the twisting rope of water'.

Tarka's predatory inclinations are never denied. There are various scenes of him catching and eating fish, and the voiceover explains: 'The more he killed the more he wanted to kill, and he feasted on them till his jaws were tired'. There is no implied tension in the film's alternate representations of its animal protagonist as symbolic child and vicious predator. Tarka's child-like attributes are highlighted when he leaves his birthplace to discover a new home: 'The estuary was a new world to Tarka, where new sights and sounds, a new world in which every nook and cranny had to be explored to satisfy an otter's singular curiosity'. Tarka later encounters a female otter, White-Tip: 'Tarka's emotions were as intense as they were quick', we are told; 'He was in love with White-Tip'. While he is successfully repelled by a rival dog otter, several months later Tarka again scents White-Tip and they mate. The otters 'played and played, they frolicked together, and there was great joy in their having found each other again'. Humans throughout are a disruptive, malign force, intruding into a world that is not their own. In a portent of Tarka's ultimate fate, his father is killed in an otter hunt early in the film. We see and hear the hunters massing, shouting, the clamour of their footsteps in the river and their trumpets as they close in. The camera then cuts to Tarka and his mother, silently observing from their holt, and as the noise dies down, Ustinov's deadpan narration announces, simply: 'Tarka's father is dead'. The humans' appearances are invariably threatening: the salmon poachers, illegally stealing from the estate's streams under cover of night; the fishermen who trawl the sea and attempt to catch Tarka in their net, asserting that his skin will fetch 'a few bob'; the rabbit hunters who take a pot shot at Tarka; even the old woman who unwittingly throws a bucket of water over him from her window above.

Anthropomorphism occasionally asserts itself. Before Tarka's birth, his mother's 'world had been a wilderness'; now 'her world was in the eyes of her first-born. She was overjoyed when Tarka's lids unsealed and his eyes peeped upon her, blue and wondering'. Towards the end of the film, Tarka sleeps with White-Tip and their cubs, dreaming, we are told, of travelling 'to a strange sea, where otters were never hungry and never hunted'. It is characteristic of the film's weighing the joys and beauty of nature against its quotidian viscerality that this yearning fantasy is juxtaposed by the return of the otter hunters. For the hunters, 'the first meet of the otter-hunting season was a grand social occasion'. They toast their anticipated success with glasses of sherry, interspersed with polite, genteel conversation. Then the hounds, which 'Loved the huntsmen, who called each of them by name', arrive and the hunt finally commences.

The cruelty of the hunt is in the protracted chase as much as the kill itself. The huntsmen allow Tarka a four-minute head start, 'a sporting chance' that serves only to instil fear in the quarry and build pleasurable anticipation in the hunters as, inexorably, the exhausted otter is brought down. Neither the hunters nor the spectators, who observe with curiosity, are despicable people; the fault is with the arrogant assertion of 'natural dominion' (supported by scripture) over animalkind. Tantalisingly, during the climactic, 15-minute hunt, it seems at several points that Tarka may elude his pursuers, but there is no happy ending. In the final scene, Tarka is cornered by Deadlock, and they struggle underwater. Deadlock's dead body rises to the surface, but there is no sign of Tarka. Do the three bubbles that appear on the surface in the moments that follow suggest his escape upstream, or merely his final breaths? Perhaps they symbolise White-Tip's and the two cubs' escape? Is a hopeful interpretation of this scene permissible, given the film's harshly pragmatic interpretations of life in the wild, or merely an over-optimistic reading deriving from its 'children's film' modalities? Certainly, such questions invite reflection on the movie's generic identity, and on how definitions of the genre respond to accepted and inherited conventions.

The animated film *Watership Down* has come to be defined largely in terms of its incongruity with such conventions. Directed by American Martin Rosen, it allegorically centres on rabbit civilisation, delineating a society with its own laws, customs and language, though bound by earthly preoccupations and threats, such as surviving against natural and human predators. It follows a group of rabbits, led by Hazel (voiced by John Hurt), who leave their warren after Hazel's brother, Fiver (Richard Briers), receives a vision of the warren's imminent destruction at the hands of humans. The rabbits journey in search of Watership Down, a utopian plane where they can establish a new community, free from predation. In the process, they encounter various dangers, but finally reach their destination. However, the all-male community lacks any does, so Hazel decides to procure some from a rival warren, Efrafa, led by the fearsome and dictatorial General Woundwort (Harry Andrews). A pitched battle ensues between Woundwort's and Hazel's followers, which ends with Woundwort's defeat. The film presents a short coda: the passing of seasons is represented the falling leaves and renewed verdancy, with new generations of rabbits inhabiting the peaceful, pastoral warren. An elderly Hazel is invited by the ghostly Black Rabbit (Joss Ackland) to join his coterie in the afterlife; the film ends with their spirits flying through the air towards the sun.

Watership Down has attained widespread notoriety for its supposed unsuitability for children. There are several gory scenes in which animals are mutilated or killed by machinery or fighting. As with *Animal Farm* – and in obvious contrast with Disney – its colours are oppressively drab, and the muted colour palette is matched by the often doom-laden orchestral score and funereal tone. Comedy is marginalised, or rather localised to the figure of Kehaar, a black-headed gull portrayed by Zero Mostel. Kehaar remains anomalous for several reasons. Firstly, he is voiced by an American amongst an otherwise uniformly British voice cast. Secondly, he remains a comical figure with his outrageous European accent and his obsession with finding 'big water' (i.e. the ocean). Thirdly, he is freed (both by his wings and his demeanour) from the oppressive threat constantly hanging over almost every other character.

Watership Down, whose Royal World premiere was attended by Prince Charles, was a major commercial hit, becoming the sixth most popular film of 1979 in British theatres.[67] Significant factors in its popularity were the success of Richard Adams's Carnegie Medal-winning 1972 novel, and the single 'Bright Eyes', a plangent ballad performed in the film by Art Garfunkel, which became the best-selling track of the year. But the film also attracted controversy. The debate began when the BBFC awarded *Watership Down* a 'U' rating, reasoning that:

> Animation removes the realistic gory horror in the occasional scenes of violence and bloodshed, and we felt that, while the film may move children emotionally during the film's duration, it could not seriously trouble them once the spell of the story is broken, and that a 'U' certificate was therefore quite appropriate.[68]

Summers of Love and Winters of Discontent

This decision is still the most complained about in the history of the BBFC. It was instantly criticised by the film's director, Rosen, who personally requested that the BBFC assign it the 'A' rating.[69] Tellingly, Rosen believed that only in Britain was *Watership Down* considered a children's novel; in the US, it was viewed more as an adult allegory.[70] Contemporary British critics did not agree. The *Spectator*'s Ted Whitehead saw it as 'a straightforward children's adventure story', and while the *Guardian*'s Derek Malcolm asserted that it is 'as appealing to adults as children and, just possibly, to people who don't normally go to the cinema', he insisted that: 'It is not true [...] that the film is too violent and disturbing for children'.[71]

Conversely, anecdotal reminiscence by generations of grown-up British youth casts the film as a locus of childhood trauma. While undeniably selective and over-emphasised, such attitudes reveal historical changes in the ways that children's cinema and animation are perceived. It is not simply that *Watership Down* presents adult representational elements unappealing to children. Standards of acceptability in family films have progressively

Image 7.4 The fearsome General Woundwort dominates the frame in *Watership Down* (1978)

liberalised since its release, to the extent that mild swearing, sexual content and relatively strong violence are now considered suitable for children's consumption. Yet the film's various animated sequences of rabbits being savaged to death is apparently more disturbing than instances of violent mayhem in say, the *Indiana Jones* films (1981–2008). Presumably, this is largely because *Watership Down* presents psychologically disconcerting incongruities in the fictional realm of anthropomorphised animals, which runs contrary to the domineering, sentimentalised Disney image. Or, as Rosen explains, violent rabbits created problems 'because of the legacy of the Disney studio'.[72]

The manner of address is different to Disney, where the stated aim, as Walt Disney proudly conceded, was to access the child of all ages, 'that fine, clean, unspoiled spot down deep in every one of us'.[73] Such pleasures are essentially regressive. Whereas contemporary Hollywood animation (e.g. Pixar films) is often predicated on strategies of dual address – engaging child and adults are *separate* entities – much of the grown-up appeal is based on whimsy and intertextual allusion, within a framework which privileges narrative play and emotive uplift, rejecting the downbeat, elegiac tone that *Watership Down* embraces. Furthermore, the 'mature' interest in the latter partly derives from its mythological themes and allegorical dimensions, aspects which may fully be accessible only to older children. In any event, *Watership Down*, like *Animal Farm*, was a lone beacon of light for theatrically-released British animation of the period. Four years in the making, its meticulous construction precluded the kind of rapid industrial turnovers characteristic of North American animation. It remains a curiosity, largely, no doubt, because of its incongruity with the broader sphere of children's animation. If its incongruities elicited mild bemusement or consternation at the time of release, today they are more apt to provoke reactionary nostalgia, along the lines of 'they don't make them like they used to'.

The Fantastic Turn

Low-budget sci-fi and fantasy was a staple of British children's cinema in the 1960s and 1970s. Such films were typically low-budget releases,

Summers of Love and Winters of Discontent

resembling Hollywood exploitation quickies of the 1950s. Whereas Hollywood largely abandoned these genres during the 1960s, in Britain they were a mainstay of children's matinees. US producers such as Ray Harryhausen and Milton Subotsky moved to Britain to take advantage of lower production costs and greater receptiveness to fantasy. Stop-motion animator Harryhausen made a succession of profitable films (most of which were financed and distributed by Hollywood studios), including *Mysterious Island, Jason and the Argonauts, First Men in the Moon, One Million Years B.C., The Golden Voyage of Sinbad* (Gordon Hessler, 1973), *Sinbad and the Eye of the Tiger* (Sam Wanamaker, 1977), and *Clash of the Titans* (Desmond Davis, 1981).[74] Subotsky's company, Amicus, was more teen-orientated, but did produce two successful adaptations of *Doctor Who* (1963–) serials, *Dr. Who and the Daleks* and *Daleks – Invasion Earth 2150 A.D.*, which exploited the enormous mid-1960s wave of 'Dalekmania'. During the 1970s, producer-director team John Dark and Kevin Connor released a series of low-budget fantasy films. *The Land that Time Forgot* (1975), *At the Earth's Core* (1976) and *People that Time Forgot* (1977) were all produced by Amicus, but part-funded and distributed by the Hollywood indie studio AIP, which had been a major force in the emergence of the US teen film during the 1950s; Dark and Connor's later collaborations, *Warlords of Atlantis* (1978) and *Arabian Adventure* (1979), were produced by EMI. The Dark/Connor films mine much the same territory as Harryhausen's stop-motion fantasies, but rely on more primitive model and puppet effects often combined with live-action footage via rear projection. Other notable productions during this period included *Jules Verne's Rocket to the Moon, They Came from Beyond Space, Slave Girls* (Michael Carreras, 1967), *Captain Nemo and the Underwater City, When Dinosaurs Ruled the Earth* (Val Guest, 1970), *Creatures the World Forgot* (Don Chaffey, 1971), *The Terrornauts* (Montgomery Tully, 1971) and *The Thief of Baghdad* (Clive Donner, 1979).

Most of these divagate from the children's film prototype, eschewing the wholesome, middlebrow, educative and uplifting aspects of the master-genre. They have no aspirations towards social comment, pedagogic intent, or ethical instruction. Ideological aspects tend to be implicit or subtextual. Story and narrative are pretexts for spectacle, action, adventure, and special effects. Within such an aesthetic, dialogue is often perfunctory, or as in *When Dinosaurs Ruled the Earth*, non-existent. Although their putative target is the vaguely-defined 'youth' audience, these films – most of them rated 'U' or 'A' – sometimes evidence uncertainty over audience composition. There are erotically titillating aspects in *When Dinosaurs Ruled the Earth*, with shots of scantily-clad, bikini-wearing young women, and – in the uncut version of the film – a nude scene that was excised for British and US family audiences. The film's tagline – 'Enter an age of unknown horrors, pagan worship and virgin sacrifice…' – gestures toward the horror tropes later more fully embraced in the Dark/Connor productions. *The Land that Time Forgot*, like many teen films, is ultimately downbeat, with its protagonists stranded on a doomed island overtaken by a volcanic eruption. These films are thus partially defined by their alterity. The impression that they embody a parallel and subsidiary cinematic tradition is reflected in Harryhausen's recollection that his films were viewed as 'vaguely disreputable'.[75]

In many ways, these British sci-fi and fantasy films prefigure the Hollywood fantasy extravaganzas of the late 1970s, particularly in their blurring the previously intractable boundaries between 'child' and 'adult' popular culture. Children, of course, had always watched, and even enjoyed, films intended for adults; contrarily, the phenomenal global popularity of George Lucas's *Star Wars* (1977) and Steven Spielberg's *Close Encounters of the Third Kind* (1977) revealed a willingness among adults to pay to watch films apparently intended, primarily, for children. Intergenerational appeal was always the foundation of 'family' entertainment, but these Hollywood productions differed in two key regards: firstly, many adults viewed them independently of children, and secondly, they do not engage with children and adults as *separate* entities, but rather address an imagined 'kidult', who may be of any age.[76] *Star Wars* and its successors killed, rather than sustained, British sci-fi and fantasy films, rendering their inexpensive pleasures obsolete. In the process, the 'family film' was reinvented as a youth-driven, mass-market phenomenon in which pleasure took prominence over pedagogy. In a sense, the wheel had turned full circle since the early 1960s: youth had won the war against maturity. But whereas the youth-driven, British social realist films of the early 1960s

202

represented an anti-establishment zeitgeist, the late-1970s family block-busters were thrilling, ideologically conservative and emphatically main-stream. Moreover, they were all imported from the US. If British children's cinema was to remain commercially viable, henceforth it would require assistance from Hollywood.

8

From Thatcher to Blair: The Eighties and Nineties

The 1970s had represented virtually the last gasp for Britain's independent tradition of theatrically released children's films. In 1985, Thatcher's Conservative government abolished the Eady Levy, the tax on theatre admissions that had sustained the Children's Film Foundation (CFF) and the National Film Finance Corporation (NFFC). This rendered the CFF (renamed the Children's Film and Television Foundation) virtually redundant, and further weakened independent production. Theatre attendance slumped to an all-time low of 54 million in 1984, a year in which 74 per cent of the adult British population did not go to the cinema at all.[1] While much of the blame for this decline was apportioned to television, TV networks actually sustained British children's cinema during these dark days, investing in home-grown animation and, in the case of Channel 4, funding several Children's Film Unit (CFU) productions. Spearheaded by the Bristol animation studio Aardman, British children's cinema enjoyed something of a resurgence during the late 1990s, presenting marketable distillations of 'Britishness' for international consumption, and attracting renewed Hollywood interest in co-production ventures that has carried over to the new millennium.

Black Jack, Time Bandits and *The Witches*

During the late 1970s and early 1980s, the prospect of such recovery appeared remote. The three films discussed in this section – *Black Jack*

204

(Ken Loach, 1979), *Time Bandits* (Terry Gilliam, 1981) and *The Witches* (Nicholas Roeg, 1990) – were, like Alan Parker's *Bugsy Malone* (1976), produced by major figures in the British film industry as a personal reaction against the paucity of indigenous children's films, and the current state of the Hollywood-dominated genre. *Black Jack*, Loach's first theatrical feature for almost a decade, was produced in 6 weeks on a budget of £500,000, and received most of its funding from the soon-to-be defunct NFFC.[2] Based on Leon Garfield's 1968 novel, *Black Jack* was developed when producer Tony Garnett discovered that a children's film, with French production involvement, would be eligible for NFFC funding, as well as from Loach enjoying Garfield's novel while reading to his own children.[3]

The film is set in mid-eighteenth century Yorkshire. Black Jack (Jean Franval) himself is a violent, hulking Frenchman who survives his public hanging for murder, but the film's actual centre is Tolly (Stephen Hirst), a young draper's apprentice whom Black Jack forces to accompany him in life as a highwayman. Black Jack and Tolly encounter Dr Jones (Russell Waters), the owner of a private mental asylum, recently engaged by wealthy Mr Carter (William Moore) to institutionalise his violent adolescent daughter, Belle (Louise Cooper), in case she disrupts his other daughter's wedding to a nobleman. Belle escapes, and Jones bribes Tolly to recover her. Instead, he and Belle travel to a nearby fair, where they meet Dr Carmody (Packie Byrne), a seller of fraudulent medical restoratives, who offers to take them in to his band of travelling entertainers. Carmody's apprentice, Hatch (Andrew Bennett), alerts Jones to Belle's whereabouts, and blackmails him into giving him money in return for not disclosing to Carter that Belle has escaped. Hatch also blackmails Carter, but Carter is shot dead in a scuffle. To save face, Jones has it known that Carter killed himself, a fact Carmody and Tolly keep hidden from the recovering Belle, as suicide was considered a hereditary form of madness. However, Black Jack informs Belle of the truth, and she admits herself to Jones's asylum. Eventually, Black Jack helps Tolly rescue Belle from Jones's squalid asylum. Tolly takes her to the harbour, where they are met by his uncle, a ship's captain. The final scene sees the ship, with Tolly and Belle happily reunited, elegiacally floating downriver.

Black Jack won a critics' prize at the Cannes Film Festival, but was poorly received in Britain. The *MFB* thought it 'a considerable let down', lacking 'the vitality to impose itself on childhood imagination'.[4] The *Times*, while viewing it as 'a holding yarn' between more substantive Loach projects, saw it as possessing 'a charm that is hard to resist'.[5] *Sight and Sound*, though, registered a conflict between the film's 'political gloss' and its children's adventure story modalities.[6] 1979, the year *Black Jack* was produced, was also the year that Loach's ideological antithesis, Margaret Thatcher, was elected to power, and critics were perhaps confounded by its apparent retreat from socio-political activism. Garnett and Loach, who had not made a theatrically-released film since 1971, apparently saw *Black Jack* as an opportunity to restore his theatrical presence by exploiting (admittedly meagre) funding possibilities open to children's films, denied to more contentiously political and downbeat material.

Black Jack nonetheless allows Loach to express his ideologies via a more populist aesthetic. His class consciousness manifests itself in the presentation of the two 'doctors': the affluent Dr Jones and the impoverished Dr Carmody. Jones possesses the refinement and credentials to pass as a gentleman, but is a callous, corrupt figure, accepting money from the Carter family, who rid themselves of Belle so that she can no longer embarrass them. The fact that, under the loving care of Tolly and the travellers, Belle almost fully recovers implies that her repressive domestic situation is responsible for her years of psychosis. Dr Carmody's medical credentials are highly dubious, but he nonetheless exhibits paternalistic concern towards Tolly and Belle, accepting them into his band of fellow travelling performers. These characters are expressive in the folkloric sense, their playing and singing traditional folksongs functioning as a marker of authenticity. Loach does not attempt to re-establish order upon this topsy-turvy world, and the ending is lyrical and understated. Tolly and Belle are given a hopeful chance of romantic fulfilment, but existence will be hard in a world ruled by tyrants like Carter and administered by apparently civilised, actually barbarous men like Jones; a society that turns even good men like Carmody into deceitful charlatans. Jones and Hatch remain free, as does Black Jack, an agent of chaos throughout the film. As with many children's movies operating outside the genre's mainstream firmament, the superficial 'happy ending' scarcely effaces the ambivalences of the wider narrative. For a director who has built his career on realism and authenticity, a final image of pastoral stillness is the best that can be offered.

As an independent British fantasy film in the post-*Star Wars* (George Lucas, 1977) epoch, *Time Bandits* is exceptional. Scripted by former *Monty Python* members Terry Gilliam and Michael Palin, its £2.5 million production costs were raised by former Beatle George Harrison and his business manager, Denis O'Brien, directors of HandMade Films, in which the Pythons themselves held a stake.[7] As with *Black Jack, Time Bandits* entered production because its director was unable to raise finance for his preferred project – a satirical parody of Orwell's *1984* (1948), then entitled *The Ministry*, eventually made as *Brazil* (1985). Gilliam turned to *Time Bandits* 'with the sole intention of making a movie that at least had a chance of being financed, and one that the whole family could enjoy'.[8] However, both Gilliam and Palin were disenchanted with the state of children's cinema. Gilliam told the press that: 'I don't like most children's films, like a lot of late Disney, because they're wet and insipid. I really wanted to amaze, astound and transport; in fact, to make it look like my animations'.[9] Palin described it as 'a kind of *Wizard of Oz* affair […] the sort of film you could take your child to without feeling martyred yourself as a parent'.[10]

The film captures *Monty Python*'s characteristic mixture of eruditeness and undergraduate facetiousness, with the dramatic *non sequiturs* and parodic inclinations familiar holdovers from that series. It centres on 11-year-old Kevin (Craig Warnock), whose dull suburban life is interrupted one evening by the sudden arrival in his bedroom of a group of dwarves, the eponymous Time Bandits, who are using a map stolen from the Supreme Being (Ralph Richardson) to ransack history for treasures. Kevin is abducted, and together the group travels, with seeming randomness, to the Napoleonic Wars, the Sherwood Forest of Robin Hood, to Mycenaean Greece, and the RMS Titanic. They are pursued by the devilish Evil (David Warner), who desires the map for himself. When Evil finally acquires it, the Supreme Being spontaneously arrives and destroys him, explaining that he allowed the map to fall into the Bandits' hands to test the powers of Evil, his creation, who he claims 'turned out rather well'. Kevin is returned home, but his odious parents, refusing to heed his warning, touch a fragment of Evil and are blown to smithereens. As this short summary might suggest, the film is both a *bricolage* and a multiply sourced parody. Stereotypes are exaggerated (Napoleon is obsessed with his height to the exclusion of all else), expectations are subverted (Robin Hood is recast as an upper-class

Image 8.1 The titular *Time Bandits*, accompanied by their unwilling companion, Kevin (Craig Warnock)

twit), and inherited conventions are debunked (the happy ending is comically/cathartically inverted).

Concurrently, the film invests in the symbolic potentiality of the child as arbiter of inquisitiveness, imagination and ability to think and behave independently. Kevin's knowledgeableness (he is seen reading in his bedroom) allows him to recognise Napoleon, Robin Hood, and King Agamemnon, and understand their historical milieus. Modernity – particularly manifested in an encroaching Americanisation of British life – is repudiated, with Kevin's bookishness satirically commenting on the stereotype of the TV-obsessed modern child. Gilliam claimed that: 'British kids still read, and are still uncorrupted by a lot of the Americanisation that's going on'.[11] Sean Connery's Agamemnon is established as Kevin's ideal father. Masculine, imposing but kindly and solicitous, he harks back to a time prior to modern society's putative emasculation of the patriarch, a phenomenon explored more directly in *Back to the Future* (Robert Zemeckis, 1985) and *Hook* (Steven Spielberg, 1991). Kevin's own father is dull, unhandsome, self-absorbed, uncaring, ignorant, and unloving. He is obsessed with status, but only within his own, hermetic world, where achievement is measured against that of the neighbours, and dictated by marketing men. Dulled by television, Kevin's parents are symbolically dead already, so it is of little surprise, nor regret, when they are obliterated, along with their suburban home.

Playing against the perceived fraudulent cheeriness of happy endings, the deaths of the parents was a subject of disagreement during production. While Gilliam believed that 'The audience is kids and every kid has this fantasy about getting rid of his parents', O'Brien insisted that 'It'll alienate the audience'.[12] Gilliam recalls that there were two distinct objections to the scene. The first was purely commercial; the second was paternalistic: '[the idea] that children might be disturbed [...] did concern me'.[13] Gilliam won the argument when a test screening for children revealed that the ending was one of the film's most popular aspects.[14] Gilliam correctly intuited that this sequence would be humorous and liberating for child audiences, given the parents' association with unwelcome restriction. In subordinating the inherited formulae and norms of children's cinema – which derive from social standards of propriety and paternalism – to the child's own believed desires, the film engages children on their own terms, rather than conforming to accepted (adult) standards. In the event, the ending passed largely without comment, and the film was a transatlantic hit. The *Sunday Times*' Alan Brien contended that Gilliam and Palin – whose reputations were built on violating socio-behavioural codes – had not gone far enough in this instance, describing it as 'the most thoroughly satisfying, frightening, comical, even, I imagine, educational, children's film in years', but 'despite Gilliam's own unrivalled cartoonist's flair, it lacks the atmosphere of bursting, uncorkable imagination run riot'.[15] The *Observer*'s Philip French thought it a 'very British family movie' that 'never quite coheres. The rhythms aren't right, comic momentum builds only to disperse'.[16] The film, nevertheless, was Gilliam's first to receive wide US distribution, and paved the way for more experimental works, such as *Brazil*.

The Witches, adapted from Roald Dahl's 1983 book, was conceived by producer Jim Henson as a vehicle for the animatronic creations of his British-based company, Jim Henson's Creature Shop. It centres on 9-year-old Luke (Jasen Fisher) who goes to live with his grandmother (Mai Zetterling) in England after his parents are killed in an accident. When Luke's grandmother takes ill, they travel to the English seaside to allow her to convalesce. Their hotel is hosting the annual convention of English witches – under the cover of an NSPCC gathering – led by the malevolent

Grand High Witch (Anjelica Huston). Luke uncovers a scheme to wipe out every child in the country, but is himself caught and turned into a mouse. Luke, in mouse form, alerts his grandmother to the scheme and together they steal a phial of the poison and add it to the soup served to the witches for their evening meal. All of them are turned into mice, and the Grand High Witch is killed in the ensuing fracas. Luke is eventually returned to his old form by the benign witch, Miss Irvine (Jane Horrocks), and with his Grandmother determines to travel to America to eradicate that country's contingent of witches, too.

The Witches is a notable departure from Roeg's established oeuvre. The director of *Walkabout* (1971) and *Don't Look Now* (1973), his commercial stock had fallen somewhat after a succession of underwhelming Hollywood films. Roeg explained his interest in the assignment partly as a desire to produce a film for his young sons, and partly to explore how children deal with adult emotions of fear, hate and jealousy.[17] He also alluded to the blurring boundaries between 'child' and 'adult' culture, observing that: 'It's a story that's essentially written for children, though I'm not quite sure what that means because many stories that are made into films for adults are really very childish.'[18] Conversely, producer Mark Shivas observed that the film would put Roeg into the mainstream, 'and I think the mainstream is exactly where Nic wants to be'.[19] Perhaps this explains the tacked-on, unambiguously 'happy ending', in which the boy, unlike in the novel, is restored to humanity. This conscious, commercially determined reversal infuriated Dahl, who believed that such endings serve the needs of adults, not children.[20]

Refreshingly, for what is essentially a Hollywood production, *The Witches* is unafraid to embrace a mildly horrific mode. As such, it avoids slipping into the blandly anodyne null space inhabited by many family films. For some adults (though fewer in this age of the kidult), children's films are something to be endured for the sake of their offspring. Common prejudices construe the genre as defined by tiresomely repetitive ideological, narrative and emotive patterns, with little deviation from established tropes seen to be permissible. Dahl turns many of these conventions on their head: the nuclear family, far from being reaffirmed, is immediately torn apart, and replaced with an inherently unstable relationship between boy and ailing grandmother; the central child's best friend is selfish, fat and greedy; the villains are disturbingly close to 'normal' people. Dahl's skill for comic abjection retains its fascination for adults who have graduated from other 'childish' preoccupations. Pleasures, for child and adult alike, rest in the film's perverse incongruities in context of the wider genre.

Auteurs tend to profess to make 'children's films' for one of two reasons: a sense of social responsibility, or a desire to please their own (usually young) children. In both cases, the dalliance is seen to be fleeting; a curious foray into foreign territory where normative rules governing the auteur's mastery of tone and technique are temporarily suspended. Roeg, a gifted technician, largely eschews 'tricksy' techniques (e.g. jump-cuts, montage sequences), and, indeed, there is a general acceptance that such stylisation is inappropriate for child audiences. It is symptomatic of a broader, elitist dismissal of children's culture that Roeg, as with Loach in *Black Jack*, was criticised for investing himself in such inconsequential material. The *MFB*'s Tom Milne saw *The Witches* both as 'likeable' and 'a sad waste of time [...] for a director of Roeg's achievements and ambitions'.[21] This leads to a seldom-acknowledged third motivator: the lure of commercial success. *The Witches* is one of Roeg's most profitable assignments, while *Bugsy Malone* and *Time Bandits* helped establish Parker's and Gilliam's mainstream credentials. A broader hypocrisy frowns at the notion that 'children's culture' is governed by capitalistic imperatives, so one can easily perceive why most 'auteurs' would prefer to discourage this inference.

A New Outlet: Television and the Made-for-TV Children's Film

Television was to provide an important new outlet for children's films in the 1980s. British animation, supported by each of the national TV networks – the BBC, ITV and, from its formation in 1982, Channel 4 – reached new heights. Cosgrove Hall Productions, formed in 1976 under the wing of Thames Television, produced the acclaimed animated shorts *Cinderella* (Mark Hall, 1979) and *The Pied Piper of Hamelin* (Hall, 1981), and then the feature-length *The Wind in the Willows* (Hall and Chris Taylor, 1983), *The BFG* (Brian Cosgrove, 1989) and *The Fool of the World and the Flying Ship* (Francis Vose, 1990), all of which were shown on ITV. TVC, the country's leading animation studio since the days of Halas and Batchelor, produced *The Snowman* (Dianne Jackson, 1982), one of the most successful animated shorts ever made, and broadcast by Channel 4 on Boxing Day 1982. Channel 4 also financed early productions by the Quay Brothers, Alison De Vere and Aardman, in addition to the TVC shorts *Granpa* (Dianne Jackson, 1989) and *Father Christmas* (Dave Unwin, 1991).

The Snowman, based on Raymond Briggs's 1978 picture book, has become a national institution. Repeated every Christmas Day by Channel 4, its consumption is a Christmas ritual for many families. Although it is a peculiarly British creation, *The Snowman* was nominated for Best Short Film at the 1983 Oscars. Devoid of dialogue, it centres on a young boy who builds a snowman which comes to life. While displaying remarkable fidelity to the picture book, with its hand-drawn animation rendered with pastels, the film nonetheless departs suggestively from the source narrative in its more overt fantasy orientation. Whereas the book largely comprises scenes of exploration through the child's everyday world, the film's centrepiece is the snowman leading the boy on a magical flight over the metropolis en route to the North Pole, where they meet Father Christmas. The interlude provides a suitable vehicle for Howard Blake's wistful, now iconic choral number, 'Walking in the Air'. A notable departure from Briggs's more secular narrative, this excursion strengthens the film's association with Yuletide, and, consequently, positive associations such as warmth and conviviality (embodied by Father Christmas), communal celebration (in the scenes of the assorted snowmen, gathered together, dancing hand-in-hand with the boy), receptivity to magic and adventure, and a willingness to partake in transcendent fantasies beyond those offered by everyday situations.

The Snowman would almost certainly never have been produced without Channel 4's involvement. John Coates, co-founder of TVC with George Dunning in 1957, had read the government's White Paper (The Broadcasting Act, 1981) on the establishment of Channel 4 and its promise of support for independent production, and hastily acquired the book's adaptation rights.[22] Coates presented an eight-minute sample of the proposed film to Paul Madden, the channel's animation consultant.[23] Madden invested £100,000, publisher Hamish Hamilton £75,000, and Coates mortgaged his house in order to raise the remainder.[24] Coates stipulated that the book's visual aesthetic should faithfully be recreated on screen.[25] He also retained Briggs's poignant ending, in which the Snowman, left outside overnight, melts in the morning sun.

Image 8.2 The plangent final scene of *The Snowman* (1982)

The eventual 'death' of the snowman is the film's most memorable aspect, and it encapsulates the cruelty of loss. The film's absence of dialogue emphasises the boy's simpatico relationship with the snowman, conveyed through facial and bodily gestures that circumvent the need for verbal language (and mirror children's well-documented affinity with animals). However, in the closing sequences this lack of voice assumes different meanings. The boy's stillness and silence as he stands over his friend's remains, as the credits roll, put one in mind of grief's inarticulateness, its ability to strip language and agency. Director Dianne Jackson viewed the ending as conveying 'the vulnerability of a child's love', imparting the lesson 'that even love which loses also gains something in return'.[26] Briggs, famously unsentimental, explained that: 'I don't believe in happy endings. Children have got to face death sooner or later. Granny and grandpa die, dogs die, cats die [...] all die like flies. So there's no point avoiding it'.[27]

Channel 4 was also crucial in sustaining the Children's Film Unit. While working as a secondary school English teacher at Forest Hill Comprehensive in London, Colin Finbow oversaw student productions of Ray Bradbury's *Something Wicked This Way Comes* (1972) and *The Custard Boys* (1979), which received a successful run at London's renowned ICA cinema. The Children's Film Unit was formally established in 1981 as a registered charity that solicited involvement from children aged 10 to 16. Volunteer children participated both as on-screen performers and behind-the-camera technicians. Films were shot during the schools' summer holidays, largely on location, with Finbow overseeing post-production. Generally between 60 and 90 minutes in length, they were shown on Channel 4, usually in mid-morning or early-afternoon slots, and were presented theatrically in specialised art houses and children's film festivals.

Finbow was not the first educator to move into filmmaking. Film education had been a popular pursuit in the 1930s, and during the 1970s school history teacher Terry Langman, based at Bishop Milner Comprehensive in Dudley, produced short historical films. But Finbow was unique in his desire to produce entertainment films. As he remarked in 1987, elucidating a crucial distinction from the work of the CFF,

> We are not making films for children, we are making films by children [...] Children tend to be more creative, and less inhibited. They can get their own ideas over here – a film we made about nuclear weapons pointed the finger at the people who are messing up our future. We are training the talent of tomorrow.[28]

The Unit's films became progressively more polished. *The Custard Boys* was funded entirely by Finbow with a budget of £600. The Unit's first official production, *Captain Stirrick* (1982), received £15,000 from Channel 4, and employed professional equipment and actors.[29]

In fact, the Unit's films *were* designed primarily for children, but also for young people up to the age of 16. As such, they were noticeably more 'adult' than typical CFF product. The horror film *Daemon*, one of the Unit's most accomplished productions, was fulsomely praised by author Kim Newman for providing 'a genuinely refreshing approach to the worn-out devil movie', for eschewing 'simplistic good/evil polarities', and for achieving 'more narrative surprises than most adult horror films'.[30] The Unit's output encompassed social realism (*The Custard Boys*), musicals (*Captain Stirrick*) and horror (*Dark Enemy*, 1984). *Daemon* is one of several supernatural-themed CFU films (cf. *Under the Bed*, 1988, and *Emily's Ghost*, 1992), and bears interesting comparison with the CFF's *Haunters of the Deep* (Andrew Bogle, 1984). Both are freed from didactic constraints, and both explore themes of adult abuse of children, focusing on the oft-unspoken social

From Thatcher to Blair: The Eighties and Nineties

evil of child labour during the nineteenth and early twentieth centuries. *Haunters of the Deep*'s apparition turns out to be the benign ghost of a boy killed while engaged in dangerous manual labour (i.e. mining), and the 'daemon' here is revealed as the ghost of an 8-year-old Victorian chimney sweep, Tom (Neil Walker). Tom's spirit became trapped when his master, in a callous attempt to hurry the child to finish his job, lit a fire beneath him and burned him alive.

Both films condemn the hypocrisy of a society that valorises childhood, yet treats individual children as commodities. Their child protagonists – who investigate and solve the mysteries that adults are content to ascribe to demonic possession – are invested in far more than their grown-up characters. Like other recent 'child possession' films, they articulate a sense of alterity, but nonetheless redirect their sense of 'otherness' from the otherworldly margins to the core of modern society. Benign adult individuals like *Daemon*'s child therapist Rachel (Susannah York), and *Haunters of the Deep*'s Captain Tregellis (Andrew Keir), are exceptions. Nick (Arnaud Clement), *Daemon*'s 11-year-old protagonist, is growing up without his parents (who are working in America but attempt to buy his affections with an expensive PC). He admits to being unhappy, but cannot explain why, despite lamenting the move to a new house and school. Rachel probably attributes the blisters and grazes on Nick's body – a result of his psychic link with Tom, who died in his house – to self-harming, a quotidian reality for many young people in modern society. School teacher Mr Crabb (Bert Parnaby), a self-proclaimed authority on demonic possession, is thoroughly misguided in his conviction that Nick is a conduit for evil forces.

The evil is more insidious and closer to home. Both films recognise that society's treatment of its most vulnerable members has progressed, but this is far from an age of enlightenment. Nick's sister has experienced bullying and has underwent therapy. Mr Crabb's obsession with occultism has inculcated a pervasive paranoia in his pupils, to the extent that a group of them – convinced that Nick is a daemon – plot to kill him. There is nonetheless a hopeful belief that relatively non-bigoted children represent a possible better future. In both *Haunters of Deep* and *Daemon*, the child protagonists lay the tormented spirits of their ghostly predecessors to rest, utilising skills both innate and learned. Where *Daemon* divagates from the CFF production is in its foregrounding of contemporary children's culture.

Doctor Who (1963–) posters are situated on Nick's bedroom wall, and a Mickey Mouse telephone – an artefact from a children's cultural tradition from which Nick is now graduating – is seen being dusted by the family's cleaner. The film acknowledges, though, that children's culture is an increasingly broad church by foregrounding illicit knowledge among its adolescent schoolchildren of *The Exorcist* (William Friedkin, 1973) and *The Omen* (Richard Donner, 1976), and pornographic videos.

The film openly acknowledges, without lingering over, the role of such material in the child's cultural experience. Between 1974 and 1980, the proportion of films rated 'X' by the BBFC ranged from 36 per cent to 50 per cent, while 'U' films declined from 13 per cent to 8 per cent.[31] In March 1984, a parliamentary inquiry into children's consumption of 'video nasties' – a generic term for violent and pornographic videos – alleged that 45 per cent of children between the ages of 7 and 16 had seen videos depicting 'sadistic sex and horrific violence'.[32] The report, based on a questionnaire completed by 7,000 children nationwide, found that horror films, such as *The Evil Dead* (Sam Raimi, 1981) and *Zombie Flesh Eaters* (Lucio Fulci, 1979), were most popular. Older children, it continued, were interested in 'occult' or 'pornographic' content, though it is hard to gauge what terms of reference the inquiry was using.[33] Such discourses reveal more about adult fears of the moral corruption of children than about the wholly predictable phenomenon of them viewing age-restricted material. More pertinent is the shifting definition of children's culture. Notably, the perennially violent *James Bond* films were straightforwardly considered 'family entertainment' by the time *A View to a Kill* (John Glen, 1985) was released.[34]

Dealing with complex and unidyllic social issues, CFU films reflect the experiences and desires of their makers, thereby rejecting the top-down model of children's culture imposed on young people. *Daemon* raises issues of alienation and depression among young people, while satirising the portentousness and moral binaries of supposedly more 'adult' films. 'Evil', such as it exists, is less an elemental and external force (as the schoolmaster Crabb believes it to be) than a byword for common, and distinctly human, traits of callousness and ignorance. Admittedly, it is impossible to tell which story elements are present at the behest of the young filmmakers as opposed to Finbow, who wrote the shooting script for all CFU productions. Farrah Anwar's review of *Hard Road* observes that:

From Thatcher to Blair: The Eighties and Nineties

> The input from the children [...] means that *Hard Road* is
> devoid of any cloying sentimentality – a hallmark of most chil-
> dren's films made by adults – and has enough faith in its audi-
> ence to allow a handful of mild expletives, an alcoholic party,
> and a celebration of high-speed racing to remain in the film
> without worrying about unhealthy influence.[35]

Yet, Anwar continues, one character 'seems to serve as a cipher for an
adult's awareness of innocence and loss', evincing a 'pessimism and world-
weariness' incongruent with 'the musings of a thirteen-year-old [...] kid'.[36]
Geoff Brown made a similar observation concerning *The Custard Boys*,
which worryingly 'distort[ed] the children's own views' with 'adults' preoccupations and rhetoric'.[37] Perhaps, given the realities of children's cultural
production, it is unrealistic to expect that any film will wholly be free of
'adult' drives and perspectives, but CFU productions remain unusual at
least in their *attempt* to be so.

Danny, the Champion of the World (Gavin Millar, 1989) is British family entertainment of a more traditional kind. Based on Roald Dahl's 1975
book, the film was shown on ITV on Boxing Day, 1989, after a limited theatrical release. Set in rural England, 1955, it centres on widowed William
Smith (Jeremy Irons) and his 9-year-old son, Danny (Samuel Irons), who
run a struggling petrol station and garage. The film develops a David and
Goliath dynamic between the Smiths and the *nouveau riche* landowner
Victor Hazell (Robbie Coltrane), whose attempts to establish a huge pheasant shoot in the area are being frustrated by their presence. Having failed
to entice Smith to sell, Hazell has him investigated by the social services
as a possible unfit parent, and then places a £100 bounty on his head. In
retaliation, Danny and his father sabotage Hazell's annual pheasant shoot
by feeding his birds drugged raisins and removing them from the estate,
humiliating him. It also transpires that Hazell's real agenda for buying the
Smiths' land is to pave the way for a new town, which Hazell insists is 'in
line with government policy' regarding urban planning. When the plan is
exposed, Hazell is discredited and the pastoral idyll is preserved.

The intimacy between father and son is one of the film's most appealing
aspects. Smith raises his son alone, home-schooling him – a decision partly
motivated by a selfish desire to keep Danny close after the death of his wife.
Smith's tender modes of address to Danny – 'my love', 'sweetheart' – reflect

217

his disregard for social codes disavowing effeminising tendencies between father and son. A World War II veteran, Smith has little use for macho posturing, even in his dealings with Hazell, whose exaggerated masculinity counterpoints his own understated toughness. Danny inherits his father's ethical integrity and resourcefulness as well as his physical likeness, representing the natural order of growth and renewal. Their simpatico relationship is deepened in performance by the fact that they are portrayed by real-life father and son, a rare felicity in a film which celebrates inter-generational reciprocity. While Hazell's villainy provides the traditional good vs. evil thematic, at its core the film is a rights-of-passage narrative. In a key sequence, Danny has to rescue his father, who has been caught poaching in Hazell's estate. Waking up in the middle of the night and seemingly intuiting that something is wrong, Danny clumsily drives his father's car into the nearby woods – narrowly evading a police car – to find him trapped in a gulley with a broken ankle. Danny throws his father a tow rope and hauls him out, driving them to safety before Hazell can apprehend them.

The following scene, which sees a helpless Mr Smith driven away in an ambulance while a tearful Danny stands watching, recognises an irrevocable shift in the balance of power and responsibility. Another important moment in Danny's maturation is when Smith notices the wounds on Danny's hand from a caning administered by the martinet schoolmaster, Captain Lancaster (Ronald Pickup). A furious Smith threatens to 'beat the living daylights' out of Lancaster, but Danny tearfully insists that: 'You've always taught me to fight my own battles. You've always said'. Smith, embracing Danny, penitently replies: 'I'm sorry, Danny. I'm sorry, I'm sorry. You're right. You're right. I'm all angry inside and when people get like that it just... Comes out'. In this regard, Danny appears an *improved* version of his father, able to respond to situations with greater temperance. This ascribes to a wider trend in Dahl's stories for children to possess greater wisdom than adults, who are often coded as sadistic or perverse. While Smith is a notable exception, there remains a sense that Danny will inherit his father's best traits and consciously repudiate his worst.

'Thank god for a children's film that parents, or indeed anybody, really can enjoy too', wrote the *Guardian*'s Derek Malcolm.[38] The *Observer*'s Philip French called the film 'an exquisite Ealing pastiche, an anarchic "small is beautiful" movie' and a family film in the sense of 'being a good family night out' and in 'treating England itself as a family'.[39] Members of the cast, too, clearly saw the film as a riposte to the excesses of North American family entertainment. Robbie Coltrane 'liked the idea of a film for children as well as adults, that wasn't either cynically produced as a device for marketing products, or just syrupy nostalgia'.[40] Implicit is the notion that British children's films are relatively free from corporate influence, embodying virtues of simplicity and authenticity. Coltrane's statement even suggests that the film is predicated on conscious, corrective rejection of such excess. The film's final scene – in which a crowd of British acting luminaries including Irons, Cyril Cusack, Michael Hordern and Lionel Jeffries doff their caps and proclaim 'hip hooray' to Danny – puts one in mind of France's much-vaunted 'cultural exception': an attempt to reassert national credentials through artistic expression in response to perceived North American hegemony. But this revanchism obscures the fact that the film – ironically, but hardly surprisingly given market conditions – was part-funded by the Disney Channel.

Branded Britishness

British cinema was in a wretched state at the start of the 1990s. A September 1990 report by the Policy Studies Institute found that investment in British film fell from £274 million in 1984 to £137 million in 1989, and that only television investment was keeping the industry afloat.[41] British screens and attendances had actually risen from their all-time low in 1984, but the recovery was misleading, because the primary stimulus for rising attendance had been imported Hollywood products, many of them family blockbusters in the *Star Wars* mould.[42] As Richard Linton argued in the *Guardian* in August 1992, 'Britain does not have the landscape or the climate to produce Hollywood-style films'; but to compete, 'British filmmakers need to learn the knack of appealing on both sides of the Atlantic [...] or tailoring their films to the American market'.[43] By the late 1990s, British cinema had revived somewhat, due to a series of factors: the international popularity of productions such as *Four Weddings and a Funeral* (Mike Newell, 1994), *Trainspotting* (Danny Boyle, 1996) and *The Full Monty* (Peter Cattaneo, 1997), which, alongside a favourable exchange rate, stimulated further Hollywood investment; greater government assistance, with tax breaks and National Lottery funding; and a more stable production base than in the 1980s, with the UK-based PolyGram investing more heavily in British blockbusters, and the formation of Film Four in 1998.

However, distribution problems remained. Of 114 British films produced in 1996, a mere third had attracted a distributor by 1998.[44] With *The Borrowers* (Peter Hewitt, 1997) and *Bean* (Mel Smith, 1997), Working Title, a subsidiary of PolyGram since 1989, moved purposely into production of higher-budget family films capable of attracting international distribution. Only four British films released in 1997 had more than 300 prints in global circulation: *The Borrowers* with 423, *Bean* with 398, *The Full Monty* with 378 and *Evita* (Alan Parker, 1996) with 373.[45] While the 'runaway' hits *Trainspotting* and *The Full Monty* represented an appealing image of small-scale Britishness conquering the world, for producers such as Working Title's Tim Bevan, international family audiences were an irresistible attraction. Bevan explained that 'With *Bean* and *The Borrowers* we wanted to start making family movies geared to the world market', noting that the 'ancillary' markets for such films – licensing, merchandising, and TV and home video sales – are 'huge'.[46]

Bean grossed $250 million from its estimated $18 million budget. The film is based on the ITV sitcom *Mr Bean* (1990–95), created by Rowan Atkinson and Richard Curtis. Clearly influenced by Jacques Tati's Monsieur Hulot, Bean (Atkinson) is an awkward, bumbling, idiot savant for whom things always work out despite his profound incompetence, inability to speak, and uncanny ability to wreak havoc wherever he treads. He is a lone figure without ties of friendship or family, who gives the impression of an innocent abroad, incapable of comprehending the intricacies of modern life. On other occasions, his behaviour is surprisingly petty, bordering on the malicious – perhaps a truer depiction of childhood than the innocent archetype handed down by the Romantics. The TV show's opening credit sequence coyly implies he may be heaven sent, perhaps even extra-terrestrial, showing him falling from the sky in a beam of light. Yet his tastes are peculiarly English. He walks around in a permanent state of formal dress, with shirt and tie and faded, grey tweed jacket, and even his cars are heavily associated with characteristic, if ersatz, British eccentricity: a 1970s British Leyland Mini, and the famously three-wheeled Reliant Regal.

Coinciding with the unexpected, but carefully stage-managed, resurgence of Great Britain ('Cool Britannia') as a global cultural brand, *Bean* capitalises on the pseudo-revanchist reassertion of British national identity fostered by successive governments – particularly Tony Blair's New Labour, which swept to power in May 1997. The triumphant return of James Bond with *GoldenEye* (Martin Campbell, 1995) after a six-year absence, the runaway success of *The Full Monty*, the London-based Austin Powers spy comedies (1997–2002), and the imminent publication of the first in J. K. Rowling's *Harry Potter* series (1997–2007), are all essentially interlinked by an aggressively confident self-image, superseding the prevailing introspection of Thatcher's Britain. This image is superficial and self-serving, but recognises the enduring cachet of British cultural symbols on the world stage.

Mr Bean was ripe for adaptation as a British family film with international appeal. While only 14 episodes were produced, it made an immediate impression in the UK, with audiences approaching 20 million. Apparently, the series was shown on more airlines than any other in-flight feature, and was sold to 94 countries worldwide.[47] Unencumbered by dialogue, *Mr Bean* won the prestigious Rose d'Or in 1990, and was later adapted into an animated series (2002–04). The character became a cult hero in Japan, where he was voted by graduates of the National Personnel Authority the boss they would most like to work for.[48] And in a 1999 international survey of 'educated young people' to find the best-known contemporary British 'artists', Mr Bean came fourth, behind Elton John, Hugh Grant and Kate Winslet, but ahead of the Beatles and Sean Connery.[49] Atkinson suggests that Mr Bean is perfect for audiences with 'intelligence but no education. That's why three-year-olds find it so easy and enjoyable to watch'.[50] It was reported that Atkinson, if he felt a joke was too sophisticated, would 'bring it back to the level of his ideal viewer, a nine-year-old boy'.[51]

There are obvious points of comparison with silent-era movie clowns, but while Chaplin is a victim of the surrounding world, Bean is a destructive force, and the surrounding world is *his* victim. He is a malicious sprite, wreaking chaos and calamity beneath a cloak of childishness, and his 'Englishness' is little more than a veneer masking his profound otherworldliness. However, while its television precursor often ended with a tragi-comic, melancholic flourish, in the film Bean eventually rights his wrongs. Having ruined the priceless, nineteenth-century painting, 'Whistler's Mother', by sneezing on it, then erasing half of the portrait with acetone in attempting to clean it, he breaks into the Los Angeles art gallery in the dead of night, and replaces the original canvas with a mass-produced copy. Then, forced to justify its importance to a room of art critics and reporters under the guise of an art historian from London's National Portrait Gallery, he bluffs his way through by arguing that the work is testament to Whistler's dedication to his elderly mother. In the process, he lauds the importance of family, which he has learned through his 'friendship' with the hapless curator David Langley (Peter MacNicol). Finally, having driven Langley's wife and children from the family home through his bizarre behaviour, Bean brings them back together by accidentally resuscitating teenager daughter Jennifer from a coma.

Much of the film's humour derives from familiar cultural misalignment. There are several obvious put-downs from the Americans in reference to English oddness and ugliness, yet, interestingly, the Americans ultimately come off rather worse. The fact that even Bean is capable of sending the LA audience into rapturous applause at the mere mention of the primacy of 'family' satirises the country's ostensible preference for superficial, emotive rhetoric and style over substance, and the various politicians who have ridden to power off the back of such vacuous demagoguery. This vignette recalls the simple-minded homilies of Peter Sellers's imbecilic gardener in *Being There* (Hal Ashby, 1979), which are mistaken for nuggets of deep profundity. Furthermore, although the Langleys eventually reconcile, and accept Bean, they only do so after he inadvertently revives Jennifer and salvages David's career. Hitherto, they had been quick to reject him – and even to abandon each other after a madcap period in his presence. Finally, there is an explicit, if humorous, allusion to American parochialism and xenophobia, with the wealthy General Newton (Burt Reynolds) explaining that he purchased 'Whistler's Mother' because 'I love my country, and I can't stand the idea of a bunch of "Frenchies" owning America's greatest painting'.

Aardman's *Wallace and Gromit* series (1989–2008) also rose from humble beginnings to become one of Britain's most profitable cultural exports. It began as a graduation project for animator Nick Park while he was a student at the National Film and Television School. The film, which was eventually completed by Park at Aardman, became the 23-minute *A Grand Day Out* (1989). It centres on amiably eccentric English inventor Wallace (voiced by Peter Sallis), who builds a rocket ship in the garage of his 1930s terrace with the help of his voiceless but anthropomorphised dog, Gromit. By the time the completed film was broadcast by BBC 1 on Christmas Day, 1989, Park and Aardman had already won acclaim with the Oscar-winning *Creature Comforts* (1989), in which stop-motion animated Plasticine animals discuss life in a zoo. *A Grand Day Out* uses the same technique of clay animation (aka 'Claymation'). The film was rapturously received by critics, and has been followed by three sequels, *The Wrong Trousers* (1993), *A Close Shave* (1995) and *A Matter of Loaf and Death* (2008), all written and directed by Park, and a feature film, produced in conjunction with DreamWorks, *Wallace & Gromit: The Curse of the Were-Rabbit* (Nick Park and Steve Box, 2005).

In conceiving the *Wallace and Gromit* films, Park 'tried to appeal to something in myself as an adult and at the same time appeal to what I wanted to see as a child'.[52] Their popularity might be ascribed to their fond evocation of small-scale 'Englishness', the skill and ingenuity of their composition, their deft verbal interactions, charmingly artisanal aesthetic, and central structuring incongruities. They juxtapose everyday events and situations with the extraordinary. Like Jim and Hilda Bloggs from *When the Wind Blows* (Jimmy Murakami, 1986), Wallace is a relic from a bygone age, but unlike the protagonists of that film, his parochialism is treated with undisguised affection. Eccentric and provincial (his Yorkshireman identity becoming more pronounced in subsequent films), he dresses old-fashioned, wearing a shirt and tie under a worn woollen pullover; he is softly-spoken and gentlemanly, but gauche; he is highly but unostentatiously intelligent, and lacks any trace of affectation.

Wallace's tastes, as with his appearance, are anachronistic. His home has no television, and unlike many late-twentieth century Brits, Wallace chooses not to holiday in warmer foreign climes, but rather prefers saltier, meat-and-potatoes recreation. His overriding predilection is for English cheese, pre-eminently the Yorkshire-produced Wensleydale (which received an enormous real-life sales boost). In *A Grand Day Out*, he hits on the idea of going 'somewhere where there's cheese!', then picks up a brochure ludicrously titled 'Cheese Holidays'. Wallace's perennial companion – and the films' second centre – is his dog, Gromit. Although voiceless, Gromit is highly competent. His face conveys a wide range of emotions, including glee, consternation, suspicion, anger, sorrow and affection, all communicated through the movements of his eyebrows. Gromit is the viewer's primary identification figure, retaining a measure of detachment from Wallace's frequent buffoonery and mad schemes, and his 'reaction shots', betraying his incredulity, exasperation and dismay, are not merely comic, but mirror the feelings of (what is imagined to be) the average viewer.

Much of the cultural specificity is in the painstakingly detailed visuals. Socio-cultural references throughout the series are manifold. Allusions to tea and cheese are widely acknowledged shorthand for English tradition and gentility, yet there are many other references that non-native audiences may miss. The day trip on which *A Grand Day Out* is predicated is particular to mid-twentieth century Britain, when new legal

Image 8.3 The cheese-obsessed inventor Wallace, and his anthropomorphised dog, Gromit

entitlements to paid holidays afforded working-class and middle-class families the opportunity for day trips. The mundanity of many of these 'days out', contrasted with the extraordinary excursion the protagonists enjoy here, is thus particularly attuned to British cultural memory, as are the brochures advertising unattractive caravan holidays and holiday camps that Wallace peruses in the opening scenes. Accoutrements such as deck chairs, beach balls and playing cards – all popular means of 'passing the time' during interminable holiday moments – sustain the milieu. Other culturally-specific references include Wallace's inability to discern whether the moon is made of Wensleydale or Stilton – English cheeses granted protected designation of origin by the European Union – and the packaging of Wallace's favourite brand of crackers resembling those produced by Irish manufacturer Jacob's since 1885. Many international fans of the series appear to view such allusions as an integral part of the films' appeal. Though unobtrusive, they are not extraneous. In animation, everything on the screen carries performative functions. One of the primary pleasures for adult audiences is the kind of cognitive play associated with puzzle-solving in identifying and interpreting such allusions. But unlike in many current US animated films, where multiple verbal exchanges are built around references to films or television shows and demand cultural literacy, in *Wallace and Gromit* recognition is rarely a prerequisite for understanding.

By the time *The Wrong Trousers* was shown on BBC 1 on Boxing Day 1993, Britain's reputation as the world leader in the field of animated shorts was firmly established. Four of the five nominations for Best Animated Short at the 1994 Oscars were British. But most were primarily adult-orientated. The *Wallace and Gromit* films are notable in combining critical acclaim with all-age popularity. *The Wrong Trousers* received the Academy Award (1994) for Best Animated Short Film and the BAFTA Award (1994) for Best Animated Film, and also won awards at film festivals in Hiroshima, Ottawa, Seattle, Tampere, Valladolid and Zagreb. Furthermore, the series had already attracted interest from the US. *The Wrong Trousers* was co-produced by CBS, and premiered in North America a week prior to its British broadcast. With the addition of former *Doctor Who* scriptwriter Bob Baker as co-writer, *The Wrong Trousers* embraces far more centrally genre parody and intertextuality. The title sequence recalls *A*

Grand Day Out, with a slow pan revealing an approximation of its home-made rocket ship forming the wallpaper pattern. The title arrives on the screen with a jagged font and melodramatic burst of music, consciously recalling Hollywood schlock horror movies of the 1950s. Moments later, Gromit is seen reading a paper with the headline, 'Moon Cheese Shares Soar', another unobtrusive gesture to the film's predecessor. But whereas *A Grand Day Out*'s storyline was comparatively rudimentary, *The Wrong Trousers* introduces new elements to the formula: a dastardly, if comically grotesque, antagonist; heightened dramatic tension; and a greater willingness to parade its cultural influences.

The film sees Wallace and Gromit foil a diamond robbery by Feathers McGraw, an arch-criminal penguin who has inveigled his way into their home as a tenant by posing as a chicken. Feathers's real agenda is to co-opt Wallace's new invention, Techno Trousers, to facilitate the diamond theft. A series of brilliant sight gags play on visual and/or logical absurdities. Examples include Gromit, annoyed with Wallace's inconsiderate behaviour (buying him only a dog collar for his birthday and cheerily asserting, 'You look like someone owns you, now!') sitting in an armchair, knitting; the conceit that Feathers McGraw can successfully masquerade as a chicken simply by placing a red rubber glove over his head, and Wallace's subsequent amazement ('Good grief – it's *you*!') when the penguin removes the disguise; Feathers's predilection for unbearably loud Hammond organ calypso music; his replacement of Gromit's bone-themed wallpaper with his own favoured fish theme; Gromit, spying on Feathers, cutting eye-shaped holes so he can see out of a cardboard box, and the penguin appearing to notice, before walking away, and a reverse-shot revealing Gromit's eyes perfectly aligning with those of a cartoon dog printed on the side of the box; Feathers installing a penguin-shaped cat-flap on the front door; and multiple isolated moments in Wallace's and Gromit's climactic pursuit of Feathers, who attempts to evade them on a model rail network that circulates the house, culminating in Feathers flying through the air and landing in an empty milk bottle held by Wallace, where he is captured.

A Close Shave, broadcast on Christmas Eve, 1995, was Aardman's final *Wallace and Gromit* short before branching into feature filmmaking. Again, it received almost universal acclaim, winning the Academy

From Thatcher to Blair: The Eighties and Nineties

Award for Best Animated Short (1996), BAFTA for Best Animation (1996), and numerous other plaudits. The *Observer's* Philip French deemed it 'Probably the most accomplished new work on TV this Christmas and the best piece of family entertainment', and the *Times'* Lynne Truss thought it 'Simply the finest thing on over Christmas'.[53] The film introduces another character, Shaun the Sheep, later the star of his own spin-off series for CBBC (2007–) and a feature-length film, *Shaun the Sheep Movie* (Richard Starzak and Mark Burton, 2015). Many of the film's set-pieces are conspicuous comic riffs on classic films. Gromit's sidecar, detached from Wallace's motorcycle, is revealed as a miniature gyroplane, evoking James Bond's *reductio near absurdum* gadgetry. The climactic fight scene between Wallace, Gromit, Shaun, and the villain-ous dog, Preston, consciously invokes *The Terminator* (James Cameron, 1984), with Preston unmasked as a psychotic 'cyberdog' with a steel exo-skeleton. Other gags are subtler. Gromit, falsely convicted and impris-oned, is seen reading *Crime and Punishment* by 'Fido Dogstoyevsky'; behind him, on the wall of the prison cell, 'Feathers Was Ere' can be seen scribbled on the wall, referencing *The Wrong Trousers'* penguin malefactor.

By this point, the franchise was a merchandising behemoth. Apparently a mere £150,000 of the film's reported £1.4 million budget was supplied by the BBC. The remainder was financed by the Corporation's commercial arm, BBC Worldwide, in expectation of returns from foreign sales, home video and merchandising.[54] As the *Sunday Times* observed:

> [Wallace and Gromit's] merchandising operation, set up to keep them in toast and tartan slippers, is extraordinary for a 30-minute film about a middle-aged bachelor and his tetchy dog – it's the kind of marketing machine that usually hangs on the coat-tails of commercial leviathans such as *The Lion King* and *Pocahontas*.[55]

Wallace and Gromit had become Britain's first global multimedia fam-ily franchise. Inevitably, Hollywood beckoned. According to Aardman's Michael Rose, the firm had rejected 95 offers from the US in 1995 alone.[56] 'The difficulties are over philosophy and creative control', explained Rose. 'Some of the contracts they presented us with read more like takeover bids'.[57] In December 1997, Aardman signed a five-film, $250 million distribution deal with DreamWorks, which was setting itself up as a rival to Disney in the field of animation. Studio head Jeffrey Katzenberg described Aardman as 'quite simply the best in the business'.[58]

The nature of family entertainment was rapidly evolving. Early-to-mid-1990s British/Hollywood co-productions, such as *The Secret Garden* (Agnieszka Holland, 1993), *Black Beauty* (Caroline Thompson, 1994) and *The Wind in the Willows* (Terry Jones, 1996), were predictably middle-brow. But the market had changed in two crucial regards. Firstly, children were being exposed to more 'mature' content. In August 1989, the BBFC introduced a new rating, '12', allowing children between the ages of 12 and 14 to see films previously restricted to over-15s.[59] Existing ratings were liberalising. Spielberg's *Jurassic Park* (1993) was rated 'PG', with the BBFC issuing a warning that: 'This film contains sequences which may be particularly disturbing to younger children or children of a sensitive disposition'.[60] According to December 1993 figures by the Broadcasters' Audience Research Board, the TV premiere of the '18'-rated horror film, *Child's Play 3* (Jack Bender, 1991), was watched by 532,000 viewers nationwide, of which 113,000 were aged under 15.[61] Notoriously, specific scenes in this film were apparently recreated by 9-year-old British schoolboys Robert Thompson and Jon Venables in their murder of the 3-year-old James Bulger in February 1993. In December 1996, the Broadcasting Standards Council published research alleging that a third of children aged 10 to 12 had viewed an '18'-rated film.[62] But according to outgoing BBFC director James Ferman in January 1999, adults are now more at risk from sex and violence on screen than children, who 'have learned to look after themselves'.[63]

Secondly, there was increasing recognition that adults are significant consumers of so-called children's media. As Docherty, Morrison and Tracey note, Lucas's *Star Wars* and Spielberg's *E.T.* (1982) had 'brought people to the cinema who had not been in years'.[64] In February 1996, *Guardian* columnist Ian Katz wrote of the increasing legitimacy of adults enjoying 'family films' without embarrassment.[65] The 'crossover' popularity of J. K. Rowling's *Harry Potter* fantasy series is a subject of considerable literature, and was a key element in the no-expense-spared approach to the subsequent film franchise. Rowling was determined that any film series retain the

'Britishness' of the novels, and sold the adaptation rights to a British firm, Heyday Films, in 1999. Heyday, in turn, formed a distribution deal with the Hollywood studio Warner Bros, and the resulting eight-film series, released over a 10-year period between 2001 and 2011, became the most profitable ever produced. Central to its appeal, as with Aardman's films, is its quintessential Britishness, fused with characteristically Hollywood strategies geared to mobilising cross-demographic audiences internationally.

9

Exporting Englishness

Since the turn of the century, *Harry Potter* has dominated not just the comparatively narrow field of British children's cinema, but also the wider international arenas of children's culture and family entertainment. Its enormous global popularity, sustained over seven novels (1997–2007) and eight films (2001–11), has played a major part in a broader recognition of the primacy of children's culture in the popular consciousness. For some critics, *Harry Potter* is a symptom of a lamentable 'infantilisation' of society and the commodification of childhood. Others praise its increasing maturity and narrative sophistication, while celebrating its ability to transform child consumers into avid readers. But it is generally agreed that *Harry Potter* is, essentially, 'British'; that its 'Britishness' is integral to its appeal; and that it presents a positive image of the nation. Self-image is inherently important in contemporary British children's cinema. The economic realities of international co-production necessitate that such films appeal to global audiences. It is scarcely surprising that *Harry Potter* and *Wallace and Gromit*, two of Britain's most lucrative cultural exports, have been utilised in international tourism campaigns.[1] Both support an attractive vision of heritage Britain that draws on recognisable landmarks and iconography, alongside nebulous values of decorum, antiquity and tradition.

Harry Potter's popularity has overshadowed the larger sphere of British children's cinema, but a similar commercial logic underpins Aardman's features (of which six have been released at the time of writing), as well as *Nanny McPhee* (Kirk Jones, 2005) and *Paddington* (Paul King, 2014). Equally, independent British children's film is still considered desirable. A 2012 report commissioned by the Department of Culture, Media and Sport found that, between 2008 and 2010, family films comprised 14 per cent of all major studio releases and 31 per cent of studio revenues in the UK, but that a mere 2 per cent of independent releases were family-orientated.[2] The report believed that 'there is significant growth potential in the UK for family films' and that the BFI should support the development of films 'for children and their parents or carers'.[3] The profitability of low-budget, 'independent' British family films such as *Nativity!* (Debbie Isitt, 2009), *Horrid Henry: The Movie* (Nick Moore, 2011), *Sir Billi* (Sascha Hartmann, 2012) and *Get Santa* (Christopher Smith, 2014) is still largely dependent on the domestic market. However, assertions of 'Britishness' derive from relations with the world-at-large. The image is almost always self-serving (the exception being hard-hitting 'child films' such as *The Selfish Giant* [Clio Barnard, 2013]), and is sourced from a diffuse combination of brand-based aesthetic associations and superficial ideological encodings, expressions of national identity (or seemingly benign nationalism), and 'otherness' in relation to feared US socio-cultural hegemony.

Harry Potter, Britishness and Contemporary Family Entertainment

There is much that may be said about *Harry Potter*, but my specific interest here is in the films' relationship with broader concepts of 'Englishness' and 'Britishness', and their placement within the cultural and commercial logic of contemporary family entertainment. J. K. Rowling's *Harry Potter* novels, published by the London-based Bloomsbury, have sold more than 400 million copies, making it the most profitable book series in history. The film series, as produced by the British firm, Heyday Films, is currently the second highest-grossing cinematic franchise ever, with a collective global box office of almost $8 billion. A nominally British entertainment franchise, then, is at the very centre of contemporary popular culture. The films closely follow Rowling's novels in centring on schoolboy wizard Harry Potter (Daniel Radcliffe). An orphan, unhappily raised in dull English suburbia by his aunt and uncle, the contemptible Dursleys, the 11-year-old Harry is unaware of his wizard heritage. Having reached admission age, he is enrolled at Hogwarts School of Witchcraft and Wizardry, as run by the benevolent Professor Dumbledore (Richard Harris and Michael Gambon). While *en route* to Hogwarts (having caught the Hogwarts Express steam train from Platform 9¾ at London King's Cross station), Harry meets Ron Weasley (Rupert Grint) and Hermione Granger (Emma Watson), who become his best friends. The larger narrative follows the three young protagonists from adolescence to adulthood over the course of their seven years at Hogwarts, and is framed by a developing struggle between Harry and the series' primary antagonist, Lord Voldemort (Richard Bremmer and Ralph Fiennes), a much-feared dark wizard who had tried and failed to kill Harry, having already killed his parents, when he was a baby.

On the surface level, much of *Harry Potter*'s fictional world is an assemblage of English symbols, iconography and archaisms. In common with the British Disney films discussed in Chapter 6, famous local landmarks are a kind of cinematic shorthand, signalling entry to the (associative upper-class) England of fantasy and make-believe rather than the (prosaic, working-to-middle-class) milieu of housing estates, tenements, tower

Image 9.1 The protagonists as they appear at the start of their journey in *Harry Potter and the Philosopher's Stone* (2001)

Exporting Englishness

blocks, suburban sprawl and rush hour. In particular, the first film in the series, *Harry Potter and the Philosopher's Stone* (Chris Columbus, 2001), ostentatiously showcases various locations in and around London, including London Bridge, the Palace of Westminster and 'Big Ben'. Other landmarks utilised include: Alnwick Castle; Gloucester Cathedral; Durham Cathedral; St. Pancras, King's Cross, York, Goathland and Pickering train stations; Christ Church College Oxford; Harrow School in Middlesex; Black Park in Buckinghamshire; and Fort William in the Scottish highlands. Such location filming presents the country in its most attractive guises. Hollywood movies, like most tourists, are largely unengaged with everyday realities behind the pleasing facade.

Harry Potter's world is steeped in ecclesiastical and academic detail. The CGI-created Hogwarts exterior owes something to gothic European architecture, but its interiors are quintessential British boarding school, redolent with splendour and privilege. Despite its magical milieu, Hogwarts strongly evokes classic English school fiction, such as *Tom Brown's Schooldays* (1857), eschewing more contemporary and socially-democratic representations, such as the BBC's *Grange Hill* (1978–2008). The clearly caste-based structures of wizard society, and Harry's pseudo-aristocratic bloodline, invoke the real-world global popularity of the British Royal Family. The fictional game, Quidditch, is a curious amalgam of football, rugby and polo, each of which are characteristically English pursuits lampooned for their eccentricity amongst American commentators. 'Englishness' is sustained by casting internationally-successful British actors such as Harris, Gambon, Fiennes, Maggie Smith, Alan Rickman, Gary Oldman, Helena Bonham Carter, John Hurt, John Cleese, and Julie Walters. That the films were shot in Britain, and produced by a British company, were among Rowling's stipulations when negotiating the adaptation rights. Chris Columbus, American director of the first two films in the series, has also spoken of his desire to evoke 'an entirely British world'.[4]

While suffused with local inflections, the *Potter* films nonetheless deal in universals such as friendship and family, maturation, and concepts of good and evil, as well as broadly-intelligible – and certainly transatlantic – socio-political currents such as classism, racism, internecine warfare, and terrorism (and the post-9/11 iconographies associated with it). Race and social class are constant presences in the *Harry Potter* films. Harry's

233

surrogate parents, the Dursleys, are very much *petit bourgeoisie*; it is appropriate that they live in a suburban cul-de-sac, for they are as parochial, self-regarding and directionless as Harry is bold, inquisitive and ambitious. The name of their street, Privet Drive, is redolent of dullness, conformity, and limited horizons. Harry's pseudo-aristocratic background suggests upper-class privilege and entitlement, perhaps even royalty, implied by the purity of his bloodline and repeated claims that he is born to greatness, both in his heritage and his future deeds. In contrast, Hermione is widely disparaged as a 'mudblood'; that is, as from a wizarding family that has interbred with humans. This offensive term is clearly established as a racial epithet, even if skin colour appears largely irrelevant (with dark-skinned pupils like Alfred Enoch's Dean Thomas and Luke Youngblood's Lee Jordan spared the racial prejudices familiar from our 'own' world).

The series' larger narrative draws explicitly and implicitly from British and US political concerns. A secondary plotline in *The Order of the Phoenix* (David Yates, 2007) is the Ministry of Magic's conviction that Dumbledore is spreading disinformation in asserting Voldemort's return in order to undermine the Ministry. In response, it installs a new Defence Against the Dark Arts professor, Dolores Umbridge (Imelda Staunton), at Hogwarts, in order to forcibly suppress the rumours. Outwardly a near-perfect simulacrum of a kindly, demure 1950s English housewife – with echoes of the early *Watch with Mother* (1953–75) BBC children's television presenters – her ruthless determination to expose non-existent conspirators recalls the McCarthy witch hunts of the 1950s, and also invites comparison with the treatment of Muslims in Western nations following the 9/11 terrorist attacks. In *The Half-Blood Prince* (Yates, 2009), the 9/11 allegory asserts itself with greater visual force, with the destruction of the London Millennium Bridge and one of the boutique shops in the magic precinct's Diagon Alley by Voldemort's forces. In the opening scene of *The Deathly Hallows – Part 1* (Yates, 2010), the Minister of Magic, Rufus Scrimgeour (Bill Nighy), intones: 'These are dark times, there is no denying. Our world has, perhaps, faced no greater threat than it does today'. The speech echoes rhetoric surrounding the War on Terror, the George W. Bushian concept of the 'Axis of Evil', and Western responses to subsequent atrocities in the years since release by organisations such as Isis. Portentous talk of 'dark times' has the capacity to resonate with almost any generation within any culture, but will particularly be familiar to citizens of the Western world, where political rhetoric and media coverage work to sustain and heighten fears of an invasive Other.

Conversely, the films' valorisation of family and friendship carries broader resonances. With Ron and Hermione (best friends/brother and sister), Robbie Coltrane's Hagrid (loveable, eccentric uncle), Gary Oldman's Sirius Black (nurturing father) and Dumbledore (kindly grandfather), the series constructs a surrogate family around Harry that inherits many of the roles and responsibilities of Harry's deceased parents. Friendship does not supersede family in such representations; rather, family is a mutable concept defined through common purpose and mutual intimacy instead of genetic inheritance (which is a potential source of conflict, as in Voldemort's crusade of ethnic cleansing). This wider definition of family embraces inclusiveness rather than social and racial insularity. It also opens the possibility of greater loss, as when Sirius's death in *The Order of the Phoenix* revives traumatic memories of Harry's parents' murder. However, family and friendship are repeatedly invoked as necessary defences against the world-at-large, as well as being celebrated for their own pleasures and comforts. This mutability also allows the possibility for new, and perhaps endlessly evolving, family forms.

The series' broad appeal also owes to the broad intelligibility of its overarching narrative. Like most children's stories, *Harry Potter* is concerned with maturation ('growing up') at least as much as elemental battles of good versus evil. The maturation narrative nonetheless unfolds with greater intricacy than the majority of child-orientated texts, with a succession of keynotes interspersed over the wider narrative. Ordinarily, one moment, or very few moments, symbolise the protagonist's coming-of-age. But the *Harry Potter* films – each one representing another school year, and hence another developmental stage – contain many, dispersed across its three primary characters. In the first film, Harry's winning the game of Quidditch for his house, Gryffindor, is such an instance, as is the first of his victories over Voldemort. Both are relatively low-key, perhaps in recognition that greater obstacles will be faced in later instalments. A need to conquer future worlds, as well as current ones, hangs over every film. In *The Philosopher's Stone*, for instance, Dumbledore's solemn admission to Harry that Voldemort will return is offset with the relatively minor victory of

235

Gryffindor in the Hogwarts house cup. The most significant aspect of this small triumph is its celebration of friendship and comradeship, with each of the three protagonists lauded by Dumbledore for some special, individual and mutually-complementary skill: Hermione's 'cool use of intellect', Ron's winning 'the best-played game of chess that Hogwarts has seen these many years', and Harry's 'pure nerve and outstanding courage'.

Later films introduce greater moral complexity, befitting their protagonists' graduation to higher forms of cognition and awareness. *The Chamber of Secrets* (Chris Columbus, 2002) reveals that Voldemort inadvertently transferred certain powers to Harry in his vain attempt to murder him as an infant, leaving Harry concerned that he may also have acquired Voldemort's evil disposition. Dumbledore explains that: 'It is not our abilities that show what we truly are. It is our choices'. This places emphasis squarely on individual agency, with morality representing a concerted choice. The implication is simultaneously disturbing and liberating, suggesting that ethics derive from rational choice rather than innate predisposition. It also eliminates simplistic moral certitudes, and affords supreme ethical authority to the individual. Characters such as Snape (Alan Rickman) are placed ambivalently between the moral certitudes of good and evil, serving as a reminder of contrary potentialities for corruption and salvation.

The films' repeated emphasis on the need to embrace change and accept loss reflects higher degrees of psychological complexity than that favoured by the most superficially uplifting family films. Voldemort's return in the closing stages of *The Goblet of Fire* (Mike Newell, 2005) leads to the death of the sympathetic Hogwarts student Cedric Diggory (Robert Pattinson). In his eulogy for Cedric, Dumbledore offers a unifying, humanistic affirmation of common human values and kinship ties between people who 'come from different places and speak in different tongues', and whose 'hearts beat as one'. But while such sentiments offer comfort and reassurance, they offer little protection against a world of manifold dangers. In the closing scenes, Hermione observes to Harry and Ron, 'Everything's going to change now, isn't it?' Harry moves to comfort her, but replies, simply, 'Yes'. The horrific events surrounding the return of Voldemort – transformed from a wizened baby into a fully-grown, spectral demonic force – are not wholly incongruous with the physical and psychological development of

236

the major characters, both evincing an almost Buddhist conviction that life depends on change and metamorphosis.

Points of tension in the 'growing up' process are also manifested in the friendship between Harry, Ron and Hermione. In *The Goblet of Fire*, incipient sexual awakenings alternate with adolescent feelings of inadequacy, fear of failure, and desire to assimilate and ascribe to standards of normalcy. Harry and Ron temporarily fall out (culminating in Ron dismissively telling Harry to 'piss off' and Harry retaliating by calling Ron 'a right foul git'). The occasion of the Hogwarts Yule Ball exerts all sorts of pressures as each of the characters seek dates for the dance. Harry (who observes that he would rather face a dragon than engage in this enervating game of courtship) and Ron end up settling for girls in whom they have little interest. Their assumptions that Hermione – whom they perceive as pre-sexual and undesirable – will have been as unsuccessful as them in the game of courtship prove untrue; she has been invited to the ball by a popular older boy. This situation provokes jealousy from both Harry and Ron, who begin to see Hermione as a sexual object. In *The Half-Blood Prince* (David Yates, 2009), a film that director Yates described as marking 'a real transition point between our cast as children and our cast as adults', all three take further tentative steps towards sexual maturity.[5] Hermione is devastated when Ron kisses another girl after triumphing at his Quidditch match, and Harry commiserates with Hermione when he sees Ron's sister Ginny (Bonnie Wright), to whom he has become attracted, in a fraught relationship with another boy. These soap opera-like subplots are primarily directed towards the tween and teen audiences – the contingent that made American soaps like *Dawson's Creek* (1998–2003) massively popular.

But there is a growing sense that what is imparted in schools, and, indeed, the overall experience of childhood itself, are insufficient preparation for the harsh realities of the 'real world'. As Harry tells a group of Hogwarts students who have come to learn dark arts defence from him:

> Facing this stuff in real life is not like school. In school, if you make a mistake, you can just try again tomorrow. But out there... When you're a second away from being murdered, or watching a friend die right before your eyes... You don't know what that's like.

The final four films purposely remove Harry's safety net. Just as old sureties have given way in the post-9/11 epoch, so genre conventions are subject to rewriting in accordance with shifting social standards, attitudes and ideologies. The deaths of Sirius Black in *The Order of the Phoenix* and Dumbledore in *The Half-Blood Prince* – characters whose goodness, bravery and ingenuity would, by established conventions of children's fiction, protect them from harm – are important in terms of Harry's individuation, and his coming-to-terms with the non-magical realities of the wider world; even Hogwarts itself is not impenetrable, and so new walls of defence, real or imagined, must be erected.

Another recurrent theme – one that contrasts sharply with the unimpeachable portrayal of representatives of adult authority in most family films – is that of coming to terms with the faults and frailties of the old order. Harry's father, it is revealed, bullied Snape as an adolescent, misusing his great powers. Harry's schoolboy nemesis, Draco Malfoy (Tom Felton), eventually rejects his heritage as a Death Eater, as does Snape. The latter is set up in the early films as a malign, untrustworthy figure, but his role in defeating Voldemort in the final instalment, *The Deathly Hallows – Part 2* (Yates, 2011), leads Harry to call him 'the bravest man I ever knew'. Conversely, Dumbledore is perhaps the films' supreme embodiment of moral authority, and the revelation that he planned Harry's death in order to defeat Voldemort is unsettling, though typical of the narrative strategies employed to discomfit and misdirect. Harry forgives Dumbledore, who appears one final time in a redemptive fantasy sequence in which he asks Harry not to pity the dead – himself, Snape, Sirius or his parents – but instead 'all those who live without love' (i.e. Voldemort and his followers).

Dressed in white robes, in a heaven-like surrounding preaching a message of forgiveness, Dumbledore's appearance invokes the Judeo-Christian God. His willingness to sacrifice his surrogate child, Harry, for the greater good, may allegorise the Almighty's sacrifice of Jesus on the Cross. His final message of peace and love is passed down, and channelled through, Harry, whose assimilation of these inherited virtues is signalled by his decision to destroy the all-conquering Elder Wand in compassionate recognition that power corrupts. The destruction of Hogwarts serves as a metaphor for the passing of childhood and the death of the child's world. The process of rebuilding starts at the end of the last film, but it is not for Harry, Ron or

Exporting Englishness

Hermione, but for the next generation of children. The final scenes show a grown-up Harry taking his own child to Kings Cross platform 9¾, suggesting that these Christian virtues do not abide *in* him, or rather, are *confined to him*. Rather, they are passed down in a hopeful extension of the series' broader valorisation of children and childhood as representing moral and spiritual newness and the possibility of growth and renewal. Tellingly, Harry names his son Albus Severus, after Dumbledore and Snape, rather than his own father.

The films thus engage in dialogue with the inherited conventions of children's cinema and family entertainment. It is harder to reach a definitive position on what they say about contemporary Britain. The films' thematic focus on family and friendship, war, religion, and extremism is broadly intelligible, so it is tempting to conclude that they deal in universals. Their cosmetic 'Englishness' scarcely negates such an interpretation. The films trade on established cultural stereotypes and surface pleasures (e.g. costume, architecture, accents, gentility, and overall milieu) that evoke a specific, occasionally ahistorical, set of cultural associations. These aspects are far removed from the everyday experiences of British people. However, it would be truer to suggest that the films develop a socio-political-cultural pluralism. The United States' cultural influence on modern Britain can be detected in many areas of narrative and production, ranging from idiom to the appropriation of classically Hollywood action-adventure structure and trappings (e.g. the focus on spectacle and sensorial appeal). More precisely, much of the detail of the battle between Harry and Voldemort (and their representatives) evokes the shock and awe of modern warfare and terrorism. As Fran Pheasant-Kelly persuasively argues, the iconography of 9/11 is mined, perhaps unconsciously, in various sequences depicting Voldemort's assault on the Muggle world.[6]

Yet there are more specific British allusions. Rowling has admitted that Minister of Magic Cornelius Fudge's refusal to acknowledge Voldemort's return invokes British Prime Minister Neville Chamberlain's denial of the Nazi threat. Fudge's successor's stoic, direct-to-camera address at the start of *The Deathly Hallows – Part 1*, articulating defiance against the dark forces threatening to plunge the world into chaos, might evoke Churchillian wartime rhetoric. The ghastly Dolores Umbridge's wholesale reforms to Hogwarts in *The Order of the Phoenix* point to the deleterious effects of conservative educational reform (specifically, the desired reintroduction of corporal punishment, and balancing security and liberty in the school environment). And the ongoing antagonism between Malfoy and Hermione, and later between Voldemort's 'pure-blood' movement and the 'mudbloods' contaminated by human inter-breeding, reflect ongoing tensions in British society between the working- and upper-classes, and, indeed, divisive racial tensions that show no sign of abating at the time of writing. However, many of these local socio-cultural currents are present only peripherally. The films may be comprehended and engaged with without knowledge of their allegorical resonances. For this reason, I do not think there is reason to divagate from the argument expounded in my previous book, *The Hollywood Family Film*, that in such films strong local markers are consciously contained. National specificities are not intelligible *only* to home-grown audiences. What *is* true, I think, is that such films increasingly invoke multi-cultural, multi-ethnic modes of representation. Can we legitimately say that the commodified Englishness of Hogwarts or the inescapable iconographies of 9/11 are legitimately *local* specificities, rather than transnational currencies that transcend borders of culture and language?

The *Harry Potter* films are situated within an international system of family entertainment, both industrially (via Warner Bros., a subsidiary of the multinational conglomerate Time Warner) and formally. The films evidence a willingness – as with much post-1960s Young Adult fiction – to deal with complex, 'adult' or 'challenging' themes without transgressing codes of acceptability at the level of the adolescent and young teenager. The attendance of pre-teenage children, however, *is* restricted (at least nominally) after the first three, 'PG'-rated films. A '12A' classification, which requires an adult to accompany children under the age of 12, was assigned to the last five entries in the series. As Mike Newell remarked of *The Goblet of Fire*, 'You can't keep making these films for little kids. It's clear that J. K. Rowling is not writing for little kids. She's moved on up, and you'd better do the same'.[7] David Yates later pointed to 'a higher tolerance for what we can present to the audience' in accordance with shifting sensibilities.[8] Yet codes of acceptability still exist. We need hardly imagine the level of dismay aroused if Ron, when telling Harry to 'piss off', had substituted a stronger four-letter word, or if Harry and Hermione's nude fantasy embrace in *The*

Deathly Hallows – Part 1 had not deployed special effects to disguise the actors' modesty.

The *Potter* films also challenge, to a point, conventions that child-orientated films uphold simple moral binaries. Dumbledore is ethically compromised by his willingness to sacrifice Harry in order to ensure Voldemort's death. Snape is redeemed for his killing of Dumbledore, and apparent betrayal of Harry and Hogwarts, when it emerges that he has been endangering himself by feigning allegiance to Voldemort. Redemption is an overarching theme throughout the films, but some measure of moral ambivalence survives the end credits. However, despite the series' much-trumpeted 'darkness', tragic interludes and many *longueurs*, a long-deferred 'happy ending' is still supplied in the final film's closing moments. A key distinction from aberrant, legitimately bleak films, such as *Tarka the Otter* (David Cobham, 1979), is that, in *Harry Potter*, a 'happy ending' – with all its emotive resonances – mediates against the narrative's disturbing aspects. As in many Spielberg films, emotional uplift is interspersed with (and heightened by) relief that a seemingly inevitable tragic or unpleasant ending has been averted. Admittedly, this relief is leavened with a burdensome acceptance of the tragic aspects in life, such as death, loss, and betrayal. But there is hope in the coda of the central trio's own children being dispatched to the restored Hogwarts, and even indulgent sentimentality in their survival, despite the apparent necessity that Harry must be sacrificed; in the rebuilding of the school (which, like Dumbledore's phoenix, rises from the ashes); in the vision of the protagonists' children; and, related, the emphasising of natural and narrative cyclicality, with the representatives of the new generation embarking on their first term at Hogwarts, as their parents did in *The Philosopher's Stone*. If *The Deathly Hallows* marks – even celebrates – the end of childhood, it scarcely represents the death of the children's film itself.

Just as Rowling's *Harry Potter* books vary between crossover and young adult fiction, so the film series fluctuates in its modes of address between the conventions of children's cinema and tween and teen movies. It is tempting to say that they graduate from children's film to teen film, but this would, I think, be a misreading. Many of the conventions of child- and family-orientated cinema continue to be upheld in the later films. Indeed, the obvious desire for the stories to grow deeper, more sophisticated and

Image 9.2 The child protagonists, advanced to adulthood at the climax of *Harry Potter and the Deathly Hallows – Part 2* (2011)

more mature is unavoidably tempered by the constraints of the milieu and by the requirement to keep the material suitable for pre-teen consumers. The benignly protective presence of surrogate parents Dumbledore and Hagrid quickly becomes dramatically constraining, and Rowling is forced to devise new ways of sidelining them. Voldemort constantly reappears towards the end of films, only to be defeated with relative ease, as demanded by conventions that disallow prolonged intensity or unpleasantness. Death and destruction of a scale commensurate with the apocalyptic mythology constructed around the character is scarcely permissible.

Ultimately, the *Harry Potter* films are moral fables. Rowling's novels follow a long tradition of British fantasy fiction similarly based on good vs. evil narratives (e.g. Tolkien, Lewis), but British children's cinema has largely eschewed them. Partly, this is because such narratives prevail most strongly in the fantastic mode, which, in its conventional stylistic excesses, has often proven beyond the modest resources of British producers. British cinematic conventions of realism and authenticity have also been inhibiting factors. *Harry Potter* reflects a different epoch, in which Hollywood values have become tightly interwoven in the fabric of mainstream British cinema. Fantasy, as Pheasant-Kelly observes, has become almost inextricably linked with post-2000 Hollywood live-action family films.[9] In a

2008 interview, Disney executive Mark Zoradi attributed this to the fact that: 'The fantasy genre travels exceptionally well, partly because there's nothing that makes it geographically unique [...] and its themes are pretty universal – good vs. evil, loyalty, the family sticking together'.[10]

The series' putative 'darkness' has become a tiresomely repetitive refrain in critical responses. But it seems necessary to differentiate between 'darkness' that is purely cosmetic and that which derives from theme and tone. The later films operate in a pseudo-gothic milieu and are consciously under-lit for purposes of heightening atmosphere. I suspect that some observers have conflated this purely aesthetic 'darkness' with their adult-orientated themes of maturation, loss and betrayal, so that the films are seen as 'darker' than perhaps they are. This is not to argue that 'darkness', however defined, does not progressively assert itself as the series unfolds, but rather that violent and disturbing aspects, moral ambiguities, and 'adult' thematic elements are heavily regulated, falling within the constraints of the 'PG' and '12A' ratings. In other words, they ascribe to the specifications and the limits that society – or its gatekeepers – places on entertainment for children and young people.

The Deathly Hallows – Part 2 was promoted, portentously, as being where 'it all ends'. However, although it marked the nominal conclusion of a 10-year film cycle, the *Harry Potter* franchise will continue for decades to come, barring some global apocalypse to rival Voldemort's return. More than any other 'family' entertainment property, with the possible exception of *Star Wars*, it epitomises the modern, synergistic multimedia franchise. It also delivered an important shot in the arm for the British film industry, supplying it with a world-class studio in Leavesden Studios in Hertfordshire, and advancing British expertise in special effects work. Following completion on *The Deathly Hallows – Part 2*, producer David Barron claimed that '*Harry Potter* created the UK effects industry as we know it', while visual effects supervisor Tim Burke observed that: 'Now we're recognised as the leading provider for visual effects in the world'.[11] On a narrative level, the influence of the *Harry Potter* films can also be seen in subsequent family adventure series with YA fiction elements, such as the *Hunger Games* (2012–). And Heyday, the small British company that produced the series in conjunction with Warner Bros., has gone on to make Hollywood-style action/adventure films, such as *Gravity* (Alfonso

243

Cuarón, 2013), as well the phenomenally successful Anglo-French production *Paddington*.

Aardman

Aardman, while maintaining its production of short films and animation for television, has moved purposely into feature films since the late 1990s. So far, it has produced six features: its distribution deal with DreamWorks yielded *Chicken Run* (Nick Park and Peter Lord, 2000), *Wallace & Gromit: The Curse of the Were-Rabbit* (Nick Park and Steve Box, 2005) and *Flushed Away* (Sam Fell and David Bowers, 2006); its subsequent partnership with Sony has produced *Arthur Christmas* (Sarah Smith, 2011) and *The Pirates! In an Adventure with Scientists!* (Peter Lord, 2012); *Shaun the Sheep Movie* (Richard Starzak and Mark Burton, 2015) was produced with the French company, StudioCanal. While all these films are co-productions with international firms, and as such are defined by their ability to transcend purely local appeal, authentic 'Britishness' remains the nebulous standard by which Aardman's features are routinely measured by critics in the UK.

Chicken Run remains Aardman's most successful film. Grossing approximately $225 million from a $45 million budget, it employs the studio's characteristic techniques of clay animation. The film centres on a group of anthropomorphised chickens who plan their escape from their farm when its owners, Mr and Mrs Tweedy (voiced by Tony Haygarth and Miranda Richardson), change their operation from egg-selling to the industrial manufacture of chicken pies. *Chicken Run* gives comic treatment to serious issues in its conceit of battery chickens desperately seeking escape from their short, wretched lives. There are obvious parallels with the Australian production, *Babe* (George Miller, 1995), in the anthropomorphism of animals treated as commodities, exempt from the relative privileges of domestication. As with *Babe*, *Chicken Run* was co-opted as a propaganda tool by activists campaigning for vegetarianism as the only conscionable recourse given the ethical implications of industrial farming practices.[12] However, *Chicken Run* presents another allegorical dimension in the farm's resemblance to a prisoner-of-war camp – perhaps even to a Nazi concentration camp, when Mrs Tweedy brings in advanced mechanised equipment to slaughter the chickens en masse. The final act appropriates the basic plot, as well as much of the iconography and emotive resonances, of *The Great Escape* (John Sturges, 1963), with the Yankee rooster Rocky (Mel Gibson), and the hens' unofficial leader, Ginger (Julia Sawalha), orchestrating the chickens' mass escape.

The narrative is punctuated by moments of brilliant, self-referential wit. For instance, when the elderly rooster, Fowler (Benjamin Whitrow), a Royal Air Force veteran, is called upon to pilot the aeroplane that carries the chickens to safety, he responds with astonishment: 'I can't fly this contraption!' He was in the RAF's 'Poultry division: we were the mascots…I'm a *chicken* – the Royal Air Force doesn't let chickens behind the controls of complex aircraft!' The joke deliberately disturbs the viewer's suspension of disbelief for comic effect with unexpected logical intervention, its humour deriving from recognition of the fact that, for narrative purposes, rationality must be suppressed. This dramatic *non sequitur* is followed by a moment of triumph, as Fowler pilots the craft faultlessly, proving that he is more than just an ineffectual gasbag. Indeed, a central theme is that of individuals transcending their apparent limitations and prevailing against the odds. Ginger fulfils her promise of leading the farm's population to safety, and Rocky overcomes his innate selfishness and rescues Ginger, joining the chickens in paradise. Their romance is fully realised in the closing scenes, in which a new generation of chickens are glimpsed. In this union between the British Ginger and the American Rocky (their cultural compatibility reinforced by Ginger's promise to teach him the quintessential English game, cricket), the film playfully alludes to the cultural (Anglo-American) crossovers it attempts to mine.

A key difference from the preceding *Wallace and Gromit* shorts is *Chicken Run*'s eschewal of narrative circularity. Those films ultimately uphold the status quo, returning their protagonists roughly to the point at which the films begin. *Chicken Run* is more centrally a packaged emotional experience. When the hens win their freedom by means of ingenuity and tenacity, constructing an aeroplane to transport them to a pastoral idyll far from the horrors of industrial farming (and mankind), the victory, and thus the emotive potential, is heightened commensurately. Furthermore, in following the narrative and emotional structures of a celebrated and iconic film (*The Great Escape*), *Chicken Run* is able to provide feel-good emotive uplift without wholly committing itself to the excessive sentimentality widely seen as the genre's Achilles heel. Yet despite these narrative appropriations, *Chicken Run* was still widely viewed by critics as a compromise between two cultural traditions. Suggestively, the *Los Angeles Times* ran a glossary of English colloquialisms to accompany the film's release.[13] While reviews on both sides of the Atlantic were largely favourable, cultural identity was a major preoccupation. The *Sunday Times*' Cosmo Landesman contended that: 'Beneath the surface of [the characters'] British quirkiness – lots of blinking and baring of bad teeth – these chicks are as bland as the homogenised heroes and heroines of American animation'.[14] The *Observer*'s Philip French, conversely, likened it to 'Sitting down to a home-cooked Sunday dinner of beef, Yorkshire pudding and home-grown potatoes after weeks of beautifully packaged meals from the microwave'.[15]

After this positive beginning, Aardman's partnership with DreamWorks turned sour with the release of *The Curse of the Were-Rabbit*. While it won the Oscar for Best Animated Feature (2006) and grossed $190 million, it failed to break even after costs. This is despite the fact that the film was rigorously tested with North American audiences, with UK-specific references strategically excised, and British accents, as Nick Park recalls, made 'more even and understandable, and more clear'.[16] DreamWorks co-founder Jeffrey Katzenberg oversaw development, although Park retained final control, and production was based at Aardman's Bristol studio, rather than in Burbank. The main departure from previous *Wallace and Gromit* films is that events are played out on a larger canvas. Much of the action is transposed from the provincial lower-middle class confines of West Wallaby Street to the higher social echelons of Lady Tottington's (Helena Bonham Carter) manor house, bringing associations of a globally-familiar British aristocracy.

There are many playful filmic allusions, most of them purposely intelligible to transatlantic audiences. The eponymous were-rabbit – a vegetable-obsessed amalgam of Wallace (Peter Sallis) and an ordinary rabbit – parodies Hollywood werewolf narratives, particularly the Lon Chaney Jr.-starred *The Wolf Man* (George Waggner, 1941). Iconography such as fog, shadows, and chiaroscuro lighting borrows from the milieu of 1930s/40s Universal horror movies. Wallace's Mind-o-Matic device, transmitting electrical energy directly to the brain, recalls Universal's *Frankenstein* (James Whale,

1931), and the Wallace/rabbit hybrid owes something to *The Fly* (David Cronenberg, 1986). While hunting the were-rabbit, Gromit turns on the car radio and is dismayed to hear Art Garfunkel's song 'Bright Eyes' from *Watership Down* (Martin Rosen, 1978). When Wallace transforms into a 10-foot-tall rabbit, he beats his chest in a Johnny Weissmuller-like Tarzan yell. And when, toward the end of the film, the towering were-rabbit seizes Lady Tottington in its hands, King Kong's famous embrace of Fay Wray is blatantly invoked.

The tendency in British critical responses to Anglo-American co-productions is to bemoan Hollywood's tampering with the artistic process. The assumption is that the British product is qualitatively superior, conceived through principles of artistry that are undermined by the creative interference of money-grabbing moguls. In the case of *The Curse of the Were-Rabbit*, however, minor interventions notwithstanding (e.g. the substituting 'marrow' for 'melon' in the final dub), DreamWorks remained comparatively hands-off. Indeed, the film's box office failure in the US was at least partially due to its English peculiarities. This is to understand 'English' in the sense of cultural identity, rather than brand-related surface details. The quaintness of Wallace and Gromit – 'Cool because they're not', as Nick Park hopefully put it – seems positively antiquated in comparison with the wise-cracking, dancing protagonists of Hollywood productions *Happy Feet* (George Miller, 2006) and *Kung Fu Panda* (John Stevenson and Mark Osborne, 2008), who are basically young hipsters disguised with fur and feather.[17] In contrast, *Wallace and Gromit*'s world is defiantly provincial, finding pleasures in mundane details and heroism in everyday activities. Park later observed that: 'Things we find funny, usually very British, self-deprecating humour, Americans don't do very much [...] They talk about losers. They find it sad in some way'.[18]

Ironically, DreamWorks may have regretted not taking a firmer hand in proceedings. DreamWorks' Kris Leslie's blunt post-release appraisal was that: 'We don't expect any significant earnings from this film in the future [...] It didn't achieve the consumer awareness that we'd hope for'.[19] *Flushed Away* – a CGI animation produced in Hollywood, albeit largely with British creative personnel – was released the following year, and proved another box office flop. The Aardman/DreamWorks partnership was subsequently dissolved, Katzenberg explaining that their 'business goals no longer support each other'.[20] US revenues were lower than anticipated, but tellingly the film was received far less positively in Britain. Whereas *The Curse of the Were-Rabbit* was described as 'defiantly, eccentrically, refreshingly English', *Flushed Away* was seen as inauthentic.[21] The *Guardian* identified 'Something irritatingly touristy and Hollywoodised about the London in which this film is set', and the *Times*, while admitting that it 'flies the flag for brand Britain' thought the tone 'more Piccadilly Circus than the quirky English-eccentric approach of previous features'.[22] North American trade paper *Variety* aptly described it as 'British drollery [...] fuelled by American aggression'.[23]

Flushed Away was the most notable casualty of what the *New York Times* called a 'glut of computer-animated movies', leading to 'too much sameness, with movie plots and characters looking increasingly alike'.[24] But in April 2007, Aardman signed another distribution deal with Sony – a partnership that still exists, at the time of writing. The aim, as Aardman's Stephen Moore admitted, is still 'to make movies for a global market' without compromising the company's essential Britishness, which founder David Sproxton described as its 'key strength'.[25] The commercial viability of this model is still uncertain. *Arthur Christmas*, Aardman's first Sony-distributed production, grossed approximately $150 million from a $100 million budget. This constituted a loss when costs are factored in. Some analysis of the revenue distribution is revealing. *Arthur Christmas* grossed almost as much (c. $30 million dollars) in Britain as from the far larger American (c. $45 million) market. Similarly, *The Pirates!* grossed a mere $30 million in the US, against almost $100 million worldwide. Many blockbusters earn approximately 50 per cent of their gross in North America. That *The Pirates!* only grossed in the region of 25 per cent of its overall receipts in America represents a significant underperformance, attributable perhaps to a combination of ineffective marketing strategies by the distributor, Universal, and Aardman's style failing to appeal to mass audiences in the United States. A similar pattern emerges with other Aardman features: overperformance in Britain, underperformance in North America, and solid grosses internationally – where animation is a reliable earner – which *may* be sufficient for modest profitability when ancillary revenues (e.g. licensing, home video) are taken into account.[26]

The Pirates!, in contrast to the CGI productions *Flushed Away* and *Arthur Christmas*, is actively *built around* its quintessential Britishness. A profusion of cultural markers and national registers are distilled into a 90-minute action-adventure format. Into the melting pot are famous historical figures (Queen Victoria, Charles Darwin), multiply-sourced fictional characters (the Pirates owe more to Stevenson's *Treasure Island* [1883] and Barrie's *Peter Pan* [1911] than to real-life equivalents such as Avery), geographical landmarks (Tower Bridge in the film's nocturnal Victorian London), English pop-rock (the 1970s punk anthems 'Swords of a Thousand Men' by Tenpole Tudor and 'London Calling' by The Clash; the 1990s Britpop anthem 'Alright', by Supergrass), early evolutionary theory (Charles and his monkey's remarked-upon resemblance to one another), merchandise (one of the pirates sports a Blue Peter badge, a relic from a long-running British children's TV show), and even foods (the Pirate Captain dunks a Custard Cream into his cup of tea).

In many respects, though, *The Pirates!* largely ascribes to the conventions of contemporary Hollywood animation. Like *Arthur Christmas*, it is a 3-D production, though its Claymation techniques differentiate it from the majority of films in a crowded marketplace. Fictional tropes are subject to comic subversion. For instance, the Pirate Captain (voiced by Hugh Grant) initially evokes bloodthirsty pirates such as Blackbeard, with his Georgian regalia, cutlass and 'luxuriant beard', but this image is subverted when we see him indulgently mothering his pet Dodo, Polly. A later sequence, in which the Captain bemoans his ineptitude and threatens to retire and make baby clothes for a living initially arouses pity, until Number Two (Martin Freeman) reminds him how much he enjoys running people through with his cutlass. Charles Darwin (David Tennant) is portrayed as a callow, untrustworthy cove unhealthily besotted with Queen Victoria (Imelda Staunton), and the Queen herself as a homicidal lunatic, secretly part of a covert international society predicated on eating endangered animals. In her intention to present Polly as the centrepiece of the feast aboard her steamboat, the QV1 (an obvious nod to the QE2), Queen Victoria is the villain of the piece; in the climactic confrontation with the Pirate Captain, she is transformed into a broadsword-wielding, kick-ass action figure. This new role requires viewers to divest themselves of the lingering image of the benign, if remote, real-world Empress of historical repute.

Image 9.3 Swashbuckling action comically realised in plasticine in Aardman's *The Pirates!* (2012)

These narrative strategies of disavowal and disorientation might be viewed as techniques of distanciation, because they preclude a coherent and rational engagement with the film's *fictional* world. They invite spectators (children as well as adults) to step back from proceedings, acknowledge the film's self-conscious artifice, and recognise that they are partaking of a universe of manifold absurdities. But in this wider sense, these strategies are not distancing but inclusive, assuming the audience is in on the joke. Audiences must be aware that subversion is taking place, and also be familiar with what is being subverted. Such films thus engage particularly with culturally-literate audiences. At their heart is an open-handed *bricolage*, an assemblage of disparate and multiply-sourced images, iconography, story elements and tropes. Such aspects are celebrated for their ingenuity and their provision of additional layers of narrative appeal that reward close observation and knowledge. As the *Guardian*'s Peter Bradshaw approvingly noted, 'Some people think you can improve children's minds by playing them Mozart. I think you could treble the IQ of any child, or indeed adult, by putting them in front of an Aardman project like this'.[27]

Despite the inescapable tone of ironic subversion, *The Pirates!* nevertheless adheres to the narrative conventions of the family-adventure movie in its central, if loose, good vs. evil antithesis, high action quotient (ironised, again, by the inherent absurdity of action manifested in clay figurines), and the happy ending. But even this ending – in which the pirates overcome Queen Victoria and save Polly, and the Captain is made Pirate of the Year – is ironically commented on. One of the Captain's crew observes, 'This is our most unexpectedly heart-warming adventure ever!', and then Number Two makes the unmanly comment, 'It's never been about the trophies or the treasure – it's about who you are inside', provoking the Captain's retort: 'I say, you're not a woman disguised as a man are you, Number Two?' In this exchange, the predictably pat moral is supplied, but immediately disavowed. This strategy of supplying, then retreating from, the classically Hollywood happy ending recurs in several Aardman films. It suggests a degree of discomfort with the wider convention, alongside a prevailing, if ambivalent, acknowledgement that it is necessary.

Aardman remains avowedly small-scale. In 2010, its overall turnover was £31.8 million, rising to £53.5 million in 2011. Its net profits in those years, however, were a mere £703,000 and £1.9 million, respectively.[28] Aardman must pursue funding and distribution partnerships and, thus, be prepared to broker artistic compromises. Such is the need to broaden its modes of appeal that, for some observers, its quintessential 'Britishness' is effaced or fatally compromised, reduced to tokenistic details (settings, accents, familiar plummy voices, and iconography). For instance, the *Independent*'s Nicholas Barber felt that *Arthur Christmas* was 'dazzlingly well done', but 'could easily have come from Pixar or DreamWorks'.[29] For North American consumers, the films apparently remain *too* British, not sufficiently rooted in the thematic and narrative structures of the genre's most popular current iterations (i.e., those produced by Disney and Pixar) or overly committed to their local cultural idiom. The result is an oddly 'stateless' mid-Atlanticism. That this is the case may be surprising to those who routinely assume that Britain has absorbed American cultural syntax to the extent that these national barriers are no longer relevant. A more pessimistic reading might posit that authentic, uncompromised British cultural expression is impossible due to the commercial politics of co-production.

Liminality in Contemporary British Children's Cinema

Harry Potter and Aardman represent an appealing upside to British children's cinema, but they are scarcely representative of broader industry conditions. In October 2003, the Children's Film and Television Foundation (CFTF) was awarded £900,000 by the National Lottery, the UK Film Council and the BBC to develop British children's films. CFTF chief executive Anna Home decried the practice of US studios optioning 'practically everything' from the stable of British children's fiction, adding that: 'Children's film is still not perceived as that exciting in Britain. British children are missing out culturally by existing on a diet of US films'.[30] The CFTF's low-budget production, *An Angel for May* (Harley Cokeliss, 2002), was serialised on ITV and won various international awards, but failed to secure a British theatrical release. At the time of writing, this is also true of the five CFTF projects under development. As film agent Nick Marston remarked in November 2005: 'For children's films to work, it does seem that you have to spend huge sums'.[31]

Nanny McPhee, a $25 million British-French-North American production that grossed $120 million internationally, is a pertinent example. Adapted by star Emma Thompson from Christianna Brand's *Nurse Matilda* series (1964–74), *Nanny McPhee* presents itself as a skewed take on *Mary Poppins* (Robert Stevenson, 1964), with Thompson's eponymous grotesque disciplinarian favouring the stick rather more than the carrot and using her magical abilities to impose order by force. Initially, Nanny McPhee appears as an elderly harridan, with disfiguring warts, melanomas and a huge, bulbous nose, dressed entirely in black, with a single tooth protruding, threateningly, over her lower lip. She slowly transforms into a more conventional image of English beauty as her ministrations succeed in reforming the children and reuniting the family. The other primary point of departure is the representation of Mr Brown's (Colin Firth) seven children, who – unlike Jane and Michael Banks – really *are* badly behaved, having repelled 17 nannies. Their unruly behaviour can be seen within a post-1960s representational framework in which degrees of misbehaviour are seen as normative, and even healthy. The children are also suffering, like their father, from the absence of their deceased mother. But Nanny McPhee cures them of their lewd vulgarity, as displayed when they try to befuddle her with profane false names: 'Oglington Fartworthy', 'Booger McHorsefanny', 'Knickers O'Muffin', 'Bum' and 'Poop'.

Despite its period setting, in its presentation of (and attitudes to) class, culture, manners and decorum, and family relations, *Nanny McPhee* is very much an artefact of early twenty-first century Britain. As with British children's films in their wider iterations, class is a domineering concern. Unceasingly polite, diffident Mr Brown is an upper-class, courtly Englishman in the classical mould. The egregiously grasping social-climber Mrs Quickly (Celia Imrie), who hopes to marry into money, is a stereotypically acquisitive 'commoner' who defers to the status of Aunt Adelaide (Angela Lansbury) – whom she addresses as 'Your Highness' – but ultimately holds her in contempt. But in marrying Mr Brown to the kindly scullery maid, Evangeline (Kelly Macdonald), the film subverts age-old barriers of class and status, to the extent that a scandalised Aunt Adelaide faints. The film delights in such transgression. There is little that is shocking about the children's lewdness, though certainly there would have been at the time the film is set, when the impeccable Jane and Michael Banks were the benchmark (if rarely the reality) for conduct among middle- or upper-class children. But the climax, in which the wedding descends into an orgy of cake and pie throwing, and sees the likes of Firth, Lansbury, Imrie, Imelda Staunton and Derek Jacobi delightedly covered in whipped cream, posits a structuring inversion of child-adult behavioural roles.

There is tacit acknowledgement, here, of the increasingly tenuous distinctions between childhood and adulthood, particularly in expressing primal impulse and emotion. There is supposed to be something liberating in the spectacle of distinguished adults engaged in childish play, and such sequences invite adult audiences to 'loosen up' – if not for their own sake, then for their children's. Ultimately, what saves the family is the father's and the children's new-found ability to transcend their socially-circumscribed identities. If Mr Brown's ultimate victory is his temporary infantilisation, the children's is their maturation. It is they who make the obvious match between their father and Evangeline, confirming their non-bigoted attitudes to social class, which gestures towards the pious hope of early twenty-first century egalitarianism. Having effected these transformations, Nanny McPhee is no longer required, and she departs. But the loss of her maternal presence is largely compensated by Evangeline's assumed position as wife and surrogate mother. While Mr Brown's initial single fatherhood – a family structure also, if less conspicuously, present in *MirrorMask* (Dave McKean, 2005) and *The Snowman and the Snowdog* (Hilary Audus, 2012) – allegorises contemporary changing family norms, *Nanny McPhee* ultimately embraces old orthodoxies in reasserting the primacy of the two-parent system.

Increasingly, British producers have turned to French companies such as Pathé and Canal+ for funding and distribution. *The Magic Roundabout* (Dave Borthwick et al., 2005) is an Anglo-French co-production, based on the vintage children's television show. *The Magic Roundabout* began in 1964 as a French series, *Le Manegé Enchanté*. The BBC thought the original series difficult to dub, so remade it as stop-motion animation, with five-minute original stories by Eric Thompson. It proved even more enduring than the French version, running from 1965 to 1977. Like the TV programme, the film – Britain's first CGI animated feature – was released with both English-language and French-language soundtracks. However, the US distributors took the unusual measure not only of redubbing the British voice cast with Hollywood actors (such as William H. Macy and Chevy Chase), but reworking the entire script to accommodate more pop referentiality. The re-titled film, *Doogal*, was disastrously received, but the key point is that its repackaging presupposes its inability to transcend its local specificities. We are accustomed to concepts of globalisation (and 'glocalisation'), but this example gives weight to the thesis that mass entertainment transcending national borders is largely a one-way process, negating the mutual reciprocity implied by such terms. That is, cultural products flow relatively unimpeded from the US to the world-at-large, but relatively few 'world' films find mainstream success in North America without major studio backing.

Nativity!, an ultra low-budget independent production, is virtually predicated on its anti-American 'Britishness'. The film centres on beleaguered primary school teacher Paul Maddens (Martin Freeman), who is charged with staging an elaborate Christmas school nativity to surpass that of a rival school. Maddens, standing as the adult audience's representative, views proceedings with a quizzical and ironic eye. But he develops a deepening affinity with his initially despised teaching assistant Mr Poppy

(Marc Wootton), an impulsive *idiot savant* who wins the trust and affection of the children and inspires them to their eventual nativity triumph. There are various allusions to deeper currents that are kept largely in the background, such as the school headmistress struggling to cope with the school's failures and seen crying alone in her office, and the subtext of the rival school being private, as opposed to Maddens's state-funded school, St. Bernadette's. These undercurrents are largely occluded by the feel-good emphases of the film's climax, a 25-minute improvised nativity performed in its entirety by untrained children, and heavily influenced, as Isitt readily concedes, by Disney's *High School Musical* (Kenny Ortega, 2006).

All three films in the *Nativity!* trilogy (2009–14) appropriate Hollywood narrative and representational strategies while actively setting themselves in opposition to North American cinema. They utilise actors with demonstrable box office pulling power, and follow Hollywood in compiling commercially-released soundtracks with big-name artists, thus manufacturing (or borrowing) a positive, feel-good vibe appealing jointly to children and their presumably reluctant parents. Moreover, the densely arranged ballads performed by the children in the defiantly non-traditional nativity are blatantly modelled on the Hollywood 'tween' musicals that Isitt discovered were most popular among her child actors.[32] Yet Britain symbolically trumps America. When Maddens's ex-girlfriend, Jennifer (Ashley Jensen), tries to persuade her Hollywood studio boss to film St. Bernadette's Christmas nativity, he asks what is so different to the thousands concurrently taking place across America. She is unable to provide a convincing answer, but the fact that she resigns from her job and returns to England to help stage the nativity points to ineffable virtues that cannot be found in the film's coldly alienating vision of Hollywood. Blighty can do cut-price 'feel-good' as well as anyone. It goes without saying that low-budget British family films must emphasise subtler virtues, just as British Everyman Maddens is ultimately preferred to Jennifer's flashier American boyfriend, Harrison (Matt Rippy). This dialectic between a small-scale, appealing Britishness, and superficially alluring, but disaffecting, America, recurs in multiple post-millennial British family films, reflecting the tightrope between appropriation and differentiation from the Hollywood norm.

What all these films both obscure and elucidate is the inherent instability of concepts of 'Britishness'. At the time of writing, the Union is at its most precarious in decades, if not centuries, with Scotland only narrowly electing not to leave Britain altogether in September 2014. Britain's position in Europe is similarly uncertain. Recent movements for Scottish and Welsh devolution, and greater devolved powers from Westminster to the English provinces, reveal an increasingly pluralistic, politically and culturally fragmented, and inherently decentralised nation. In 2003, Arthur Marwick observed that, such was the tendency towards regionalism, ' "English" could never again be used as a synonym for "British"'.[33] Concepts of British national identity endure, but we should be wary of actively pursuing an elusive and potentially undesirable 'Britishness'. As Andrew Higson wrote in the mid-1990s, 'I would rather call for a socialist cinema, or a green cinema, or a feminist cinema than for the renewal of British cinema'.[34] Heyday's *Paddington*, adapted from Michael Bond's stories centring on a young Peruvian bear who travels to England and is taken in by the kindly Brown family, cleverly articulates the dangers of withdrawing into an exclusivist or isolationist nationalism in the name of patriotism, mindful that such concepts may be co-opted for racist or xenophobic purposes. Many of the films discussed in this chapter embody a danger of a very different kind: that of commodifying local cultural tradition and reducing it to the most superficial meanings. How 'British' family films negotiate such difficulties are likely to define the evolution of the form in the years to come.

Conclusion

British children's films and family films are objects of affection and nostalgia for millions of people all over the world, many of whom will never have thought of them as serious cultural texts. They are, perhaps, the great under-addressed British film genres, and this neglect poses important questions. Are there overarching patterns in their long history? Do individual films and film cycles reside within a larger framework – a meta-system – from which broad patterns and meanings can be adduced? Do changes in narrative, form, and ideology outweigh the continuities that underpin the format? The answer to the first two questions must be a resounding 'yes'. The third is slightly more complex. At this point, it is useful to think of children's films and family films in terms of the semantic/syntactic approach to genre proposed by Tzvetan Todorov, and advocated by Fredric Jameson, Rick Altman and others.[1] Essentially, semantic aspects are those discernible on a surface reading; they include recurring character types, locations, sets, props, shots, lighting, music, mood and tone, camera set-ups, editing, and *mise-en-scène*. Most accounts of film genre gravitate towards semantic commonalities. For instance, *film noir* is characterised as much by lighting (chiaroscuro), character (detectives; femme fatales), setting (metropolitan criminal underworld), props (pistols; cigarettes) and mood (oppressive; downbeat) as by story type or political orientation. By contrast, syntactic aspects include overall narrative patterns and story structures, as well as the genre's ritual, cultural and ideological meanings.[2] The trouble with syntactic approaches to genre is that its characteristics are not as visible as semantic elements, and so often get overlooked.

Semantic approaches are most applicable to genres with instantly recognisable, relatively fixed iconographies, such as the western. They are also pertinent in relation to individual *sub-genres* and *cycles* within the broader categories of children's films and family films. There are recurrent settings, themes, character types and visual aesthetics in the children's adventure movie cycle of the 1930s and 1940s, the comedian comedies of the same period, the 1950s output of the Children's Film Foundation (CFF) under the direction of Mary Field, Disney's early-1950s cycle of British historical features, 1970s animal films, and Aardman's post-1990s Claymation animation. However, such commonality cannot be seen in children's films and family films as a whole, largely because semantic elements are heavily related to historically-bound questions of style and convention. For example, the chiaroscuro lighting of *Whistle Down the Wind* (Bryan Forbes, 1961) is rooted within the gritty British New Wave films of the period, and the vibrant colours of *Yellow Submarine* (George Dunning, 1968) reflect the mood of the 1967 Summer of Love. As with mainstream cinema more broadly, shot duration has reduced, the length of individual films has increased, and new technical potentialities have emerged. Limitations and advances in technology also impose their own requirements. Korda's great fantasy film, *The Thief of Bagdad* (Michael Powell et al., 1940), was pioneering in its use of Chroma key, a precursor to 'blue-screen' techniques. But the technical virtuosity of the *Harry Potter* films and some of the Aardman releases rests on costly post-1990s CGI.

Children's cinema in Britain and elsewhere is bound by expectations regarding what is suitable and appropriate for children's consumption, which values and norms ought to be upheld and which repudiated, and (particularly in commercial cinema) the representational elements that will draw audiences to the cinema. Stylistic principles, though, are fluid, and unlike in, say, the western or *film noir*, are rarely self-reflexively invoked. Aside from a broad, pre-1960s consensus that child-orientated films should maintain principles of basic film grammar (a school of thought that has since given way to acceptance of degrees of formal experimentalism),

Conclusion

there are very few semantic commonalities across the broad array of genres and sub-genres that operate within the overarching structures of child-orientated cinema. Conversely, syntactic aspects – narrative principles, ideological resonances, and cultural meanings – have remained relatively unchanged. Almost *all* British children's films and family films adhere to established conventions: reaffirming nation, family, friendship and community; foregrounding real or symbolic children; marginalising disruptive social elements, or engaging with them in order to defeat them; downplaying 'adult' themes and situations; and supplying storylines that negate ambiguity and work, ultimately, to uphold the social status quo, create emotional uplift and engender kinship.

Changes in culture and society continually impose modifications in how these aspects are communicated. Standards regarding what is deemed acceptable for children's consumption have shifted in conjunction with ongoing liberalising currents in Western society. The last five entries in the *Harry Potter* series received '12A' ratings, reflecting their stronger representations of violence, moral ambiguity, mild sexual content and occasional profanity. What might be called the 'adultification' of children's film reflects the commercial need to attract teenage and adult audiences, as well as a belief that children either no longer require stringent protection from such elements, or that attempting to impose such restrictions on them is futile given their ability to access knowledge, sights and sounds forbidden to previous generations through other means. Admittedly, the *Harry Potter* films pushed the boundaries of suitability for children. But the '12A' rating still allows young children to view such films in the company of their parents – a variation of the 'A' rating that the British Board of Film Classification introduced in 1913. A broader shift has occurred in relation to didactic elements, with pedagogy sublimated to pleasure. However, while the explicit didacticism of the early-period CFF films is no longer considered appropriate, moral patterns, as J. P. Mayer observed in 1946, are always present because films cannot be divorced from behavioural and psychological norms.[3]

More liberal attitudes to career women, 'unconventional' (i.e. non-nuclear) family types, and ethnic minorities are perceptible in recent productions. Yet the ratio of female to male child protagonists in British children's films remains extremely low, in spite of the popularity of girl-centred children's television shows, such as the BBC's long-running series, *The Story of Tracy Beaker* (2002–07). Non-white children were virtually unrepresented in British cinema until very recently; the Indian child-star Sabu was a notable, but isolated, exception, and his star persona embodied an exotically fetishised 'otherness' rather than assimilation. Children of the substantial British postwar diasporas were unable to see characters that related to their own ethnic and cultural identities. This has changed to a limited degree, with the multiethnic casting – albeit largely confined to supporting roles – of the *Harry Potter* film series. But it is necessary to look to less child-orientated films, such as Gurinder Chadha's *Bend It Like Beckham* (2002), to find non-white, female protagonists. In this regard, British children's cinema has, so far, failed to take the lead of contemporary children's and YA literature and television in actively working towards gender and racial equality. In this sense, popular cinema no doubt reproduces and reaffirms the inequalities of society-at-large; but it is also probable that pressures on producers to meet inherently conservative international expectations of 'heritage Britain' continue to mandate against sexual and racial egalitarianism.

In most regards, children's films and family films continue to uphold socially-prescribed values and modes of conduct: these include the primacy of family (usually nuclear, and thus paternalistic); supporting friends and treating others with respect and tolerance; acting with moral purpose, opposing criminals and other wrongdoers; and broadly upholding principles of state and civil society. Occasional deviations from these conventions can partly be attributed to a relative lack of narrative continuity across the tradition, and the absence of an industrial infrastructure that, in the Hollywood studio system, has served to regulate and standardise production. Historically, children's films have served various social purposes, namely to inculcate 'correct' moral and behavioural practice in youth, and the ritual function of engendering comradeship between groups of children, and kinship with other family members through a shared viewing experience. But numerous British commercial family films, particularly those released during the 1970s and 1980s (as discussed in Chapter 7), are characterised by bleakness and lack of sentiment. In such cases, the ritual imperative (bringing families together) may be unchanged, but the emotive function is radically different. Releases such as *Watership Down* (Martin

Conclusion

Rosen, 1978) and *Tarka the Otter* (David Cobham, 1979) represent a period in which a stratum of cinema and television challenged established conventions (even public information films were notoriously uncompromising), and when economic and social depression manifested in various overt and oblique ways in the culture of the period. However, these films also enter into dialogue with a more conventional image of family entertainment. Adapted from British children's fiction, they enunciate a parallel filmic tradition founded on less obvious pleasures than those offered by mainstream Hollywood. Such alterity could endure only in an industry that had lost touch with mass audiences, which lacked the resources to rival Hollywood, the means to undertake effective market research, and the mechanisms for international distribution.

British cinema is inextricably linked with that of North America. Hollywood's dominance of the British screen, established during the early days of the silent era, was never broken. Children's films in Britain have thus alternated between three positions in relation to Hollywood: competition (e.g. *The Thief of Bagdad*), differentiation (e.g. the CFF), and co-operation. *Chitty Chitty Bang Bang* (Ken Hughes, 1968), distributed by United Artists, and *Oliver!* (Carol Reed, 1968), distributed by Columbia, are precursors to contemporary Hollywood co-productions such as the *Harry Potter* series and the Aardman features. Another recent trend – the longevity of which is impossible to predict – is co-production with French studios, such as Canal+. The dominance of the post-1970s Hollywood family film model, heralded by George Lucas's *Star Wars* (1977), irrevocably altered British children's cinema. More precisely, the *children's film*, as represented by the Children's Film Foundation and the Children's Film Unit, was decisively superseded by the *family film*, a form whose inclusivity is predicated on commercial, not didactic, principles.

Local, small-scale and primarily child-orientated films gradually declined after the late 1970s. Since the turn of the century, funding and distribution partnerships with major transatlantic firms have virtually been a prerequisite for commercial release. This, in turn, has forced producers to relinquish the form's more whimsical, experimental, and pedagogic aspects in favour of a more overtly commercial style. In short, Hollywood's influence has imposed a new set of formal and industrial conventions on British cinema. This is not to deny that 'locally-produced' films continue to draw on British mores and idioms. With its barbed denunciation of xenophobia, the Anglo-French production, *Paddington* (Paul King, 2014), successfully engages with local and contemporary socio-political debates. However, in its narrative transparency, strategies of dual address, aggressive marketing techniques and ancillary revenue streams (particularly licensing deals), it closely ascribes to the Hollywood franchise model. Contemporary British family films are designed as constituents in broader multimedia franchises; they are no longer an end in themselves.

The seeming obsolescence of the 'unhappy ending' is a measure of the form's standardisation. Changing organisational structures (e.g. the conglomeration of various British studios, and long-term Hollywood distribution deals) – and, consequently, different consumer expectations – result in fewer deviations from the established model. The lyrical harshness of *The Snowman* (Dianne Jackson, 1982) was not just a reflection of Raymond Briggs's typically unsentimental view that children ought not to be protected from upsetting, potentially traumatic realities. Rather, it operated within a context in which greater expressive possibilities were open to filmmakers – particularly those willing to work on the margins of mainstream cinema. Individual sequences, or even entire films, illustrate the oppositional *potentiality* of British children's cinema: the unrelenting bleakness of Halas and Batchelor's animated adaptation of *Animal Farm* (1955); numerous instances of blasphemy in *Whistle Down the Wind*; the violent killing of the animal protagonists in *Ring of Bright Water* (Jack Couffer, 1969) and *Tarka the Otter*; the obfuscating symbolism of *The Boy Who Turned Yellow* (Michael Powell, 1972); the climactic death of the human protagonist in *The Belstone Fox* (James Hill, 1973) and the brutality of the scene where a pack of hounds is decimated by an oncoming train; the quixotic premise of *Bugsy Malone* (Alan Parker, 1976), with its cast of children situated in 1930s gangster film pastiche; the various bloody instances of animated rabbit slaughter in *Watership Down* and animal vivisection in *The Plague Dogs* (Martin Rosen, 1982); the black comic extermination of the child's parents in *Time Bandits* (Terry Gilliam, 1982); the plangent, elegiac final scene of *The Snowman*; and the slow succumbing of the elderly couple to radiation sickness in *When the Wind Blows* (Jimmy Murakami, 1986).

Admittedly, such instances cannot be taken as representative of British children's cinema in its broadest iterations. The comedian vehicles examined

Conclusion

in Chapter 2, the 1950s domestic comedies discussed in Chapter 5, and the blockbuster musicals of the 1960s analysed in Chapter 7 are all characterised by pleasurable formulaic structures. But it is a measure of how far things have changed that it is impossible to envision the 'oppositional' aspects noted above within a twenty-first century global family media marketplace. It is worth remembering that, with the exception of *Animal Farm* and *Time Bandits*, none of these films were big-budget Hollywood co-productions, and few of them were made for international export. Rather, they were small-scale, and largely restricted to British theatrical audiences. As such, their producers were availed greater creative latitude. It is not Hollywood 'cultural imperialism' that has reshaped post-1990s British children's cinema, but a necessary commercial pragmatism. Changes in taste and convention, in standards of acceptability (some of which are traced to current schools of psychological thought), and the composition of audiences, have also played their part in the evolution of the form.

The historical importance of children's cinema in Britain has, I hope, already been established. A slightly different question is that of the role of British children's films and family films in the nation's cultural memory. Hollywood family films such as *The Wizard of Oz* (Victor Fleming, 1939) and Disney's animated features form an indelible part of the cultural fabric of the nation. This is not generally the case with Britain's own tradition of child-orientated films. In the BFI's 1999 list of the top 100 British movies, as adjudged by industry figures and critics, only *The Railway Children* (Lionel Jeffries, 1970) is explicitly made for children.[4] In a subsequent list by the film magazine *Time Out*, the only family films to make the grade were *The Railway Children* and *Oliver!*[5] Cultural memory is affected and shaped by a multitude of factors, not just subjective quality. Contextual processes play a major part. Disney productions have remained visible due in part to semi-regular theatrical re-releases, television sales, merchandising, home video releases buoyed by expensive marketing campaigns, aggressive protectionism, and the relative prestige and influence of the studio and distributor. To a lesser degree, *Hue and Cry* (Charles Crichton, 1947) has benefited from being produced by Ealing, synonymous with British filmmaking wit and refinement.

However, many early British children's films that were seen as important at the time of release are now largely forgotten. This is especially

263

true of those that rarely, if ever, were exhibited to general audiences and had no post-theatrical afterlife, such as the CFF's *Bush Christmas* (Ralph Smart, 1947). As far as I can ascertain, *The Boy Who Turned Yellow* – perhaps the CFF's best-known production – has been broadcast on British national television only once (BBC1, 5.05–6.00pm, 22 December 1984). *Bush Christmas* has never been shown. In contrast, *The Railway Children*, first shown on BBC1 at 6.45pm on Christmas Eve, 1975, has been broadcast on more than 50 separate occasions, mostly by the main British terrestrial channels: BBC1, ITV and Channel 4. Unquestionably, *The Railway Children*'s status as the quintessential British family film has been forged, in part, from multiple repeats on television in family-friendly matinee and early evening slots.

Television broadcasts continue to offer useful insights into the films considered relevant to contemporary audiences. As ever, the peak period for the exhibition of family films in Britain is Christmas, when they fulfil the ritual function of affirming family and community and providing emotional uplift, and, from a commercial standpoint, when family audiences are most accessible. Over the 2014–15 and 2015–16 Christmas–New Year periods, the following British family films were broadcast on free-to-air TV:

2014–15: *Scrooge* (Brian Desmond Hurst, 1951); *A Hard Day's Night* (Richard Lester, 1964); *Mary Poppins* (Robert Stevenson, 1964); *One Million Years B.C.* (Don Chaffey, 1966); *Chitty Chitty Bang Bang*; *The Valley of Gwangi* (Jim O'Connolly, 1969); *Scrooge* (Ronald Neame, 1970); *One of Our Dinosaurs is Missing* (Robert Stevenson, 1975); *The Snowman*; *Legend* (Ridley Scott, 1985); *Father Christmas* (Dave Unwin, 1991); *Johnny English* (Peter Howitt, 2003); *Five Children and It* (John Stephenson, 2004); *Valiant* (Gary Chapman, 2005); *The Curse of the Were-Rabbit* and several *Wallace and Gromit* shorts (Nick Park and Steve Box, 2005); *Nanny McPhee* (Kirk Jones, 2005); *St. Trinian's* (Oliver Parker and Barnaby Thompson, 2007); *Arthur Christmas* (Sarah Smith, 2011); *Horrid Henry: The Movie* (Nick Moore, 2011); *The Snowman and the Snowdog* (Hilary Audus, 2012); *The Pirates! In an Adventure with Scientists!* (Peter Lord, 2012); and several of the *Harry Potter*, *James Bond* and *Carry On* films.

Conclusion

2015–16: *Oliver Twist* (David Lean, 1948); *Scrooge* (1951); *The Titfield Thunderbolt* (Charles Crichton, 1953); *Mysterious Island* (Cy Endfield, 1961); *Mary Poppins*; *An Elephant Called Slowly* (James Hill, 1969); *Scrooge* (1970); *Bedknobs and Broomsticks* (Robert Stevenson, 1971); *Dad's Army* (Norman Cohen, 1971); *Swallows and Amazons* (Claude Whatham, 1974); *The Land That Time Forgot* (Kevin Connor, 1975); *Clash of the Titans* (Desmond Davis, 1981); *The Snowman*; *The Secret Garden* (Agnieszka Holland, 1993); *The Borrowers* (Peter Hewitt, 1997); *Bean* (Mel Smith, 1997); *Chicken Run* (Nick Park and Peter Lord, 2000); *Five Children and It*; *The Curse of the Were-Rabbit*; *Flushed Away* (Sam Fell and David Bowers, 2006); *Nativity!* (Debbie Isitt, 2009); *Johnny English Reborn* (Oliver Parker, 2011); *The Snowman and the Snowdog*; *Horrid Henry: The Movie*; *Arthur Christmas*; *Nativity 2: Danger in the Manger!* (Debbie Isitt, 2012); *Shaun the Sheep Movie* (Richard Starzak and Mark Burton, 2015); and several *Carry On*, *St. Trinian's*, *Harry Potter* and *James Bond* films.

At first glance, these lists might suggest that British child-orientated films remain firmly in the public eye. In some cases this is true, but there are several important caveats. First, many of these films tend to be shown *only* at Christmas, or else are ghettoised to other family holiday periods, such as Easter. Second, there is a strong reliance on recent productions, with a general absence of pre-1960s films, and a complete absence of anything prior to 1948. Third, the emphasis is on fast-paced, action/adventure narratives, particularly fantasy and animation. Fourth, certain films (e.g. *Swallows and Amazons*, at 6.10am) were shown prohibitively early, and thus were inaccessible to most viewers. Fifth, and related, several films are clearly used as cheap schedule-fillers in 'graveyard' slots; predictably, only recent blockbusters releases, such as the *Harry Potter* and Aardman films, are afforded primetime viewing. Sixth – and this fact is not represented above – the ratio of British to Hollywood films is extremely low. British film-goers' ongoing preference for Hollywood family films over indigenous productions is thus reflected in current television programming policy. Finally, the emphasis, decisively, is on commercial 'family films' rather than non-commercial 'children's films'. This is hardly surprising: CFF films are only now receiving (costly, specialised) DVD releases courtesy of the BFI, while more child-orientated commercial productions, such as *Emil and the Detectives* (Milton Rosmer, 1935) and the *Just William* films (1940–48), have lapsed into near-absolute obscurity. Mainstream British television seldom recuperates forgotten films. Its (often commercially-mandated) function is to recapitulate cultural forms already in wide popular currency, particularly recent multimedia phenomena (e.g. *Harry Potter*) or films with an established place in the cultural imaginary (e.g. *Mary Poppins*). Unscientific though it is, this small sample adds weight to Terry Staples's claim to the ephemeral nature of British children's cinema.[6]

Of course, the selection of films above also reflects the changeability of the 'family audience'. When Russell T. Davies revived the BBC's long-running, family-orientated sci-fi series *Doctor Who* in 2005, he was told by a demographer that the family audience no longer exists, because 'children have television sets in their bedrooms and are embarrassed to be watching the same programmes as their parents'.[7] Sonia Livingstone has called this phenomenon 'bedroom culture'.[8] As she observes, 'a personalised media environment is taken for granted'; this constitutes a fundamental shift from previous generations, where television viewing was conducted almost exclusively in the living room.[5] A context in which a high proportion of children and adults have personal access to televisions, computers and smart phones with internet access, and various other electronic media, has obvious implications for the 'family audience'. The material profitability of family entertainment proves that such a demographic still exists, albeit perhaps as a more mutable entity that no longer meets the prototypical definition of the term (i.e. parents and children watching together).

There is a clear and pressing need for ethnographic audience research to reveal whether family viewing is still a common recreational activity, in conjunction with qualitative research that investigates what audiences do with their experiences of these films. Anecdotal evidence and a visual survey of audiences in multiplex cinemas suggests that contemporary family films such as *Paddington* are viewed by mixed audiences of younger children, teenagers, young adults and parents/guardians. This corresponds with marketing and distribution strategies, following rigorous audience testing, that function to broaden the audience base as much as possible. Such products demand interpretation within a broader international system of multimedia conglomeration. The commercial logic of

Conclusion

'family entertainment' requires that films transcend barriers of age, sex, class, nationality, race, religion and ethnicity in terms of their suitability and appeal. However, the feeling persists that the 'child audience' and the 'family audience' are not fixed entities, but individuals and groups that may be mobilised given the right conditions. This is also partially a matter of semantics. The 'child audience' clearly endures in some form, but it is no longer frequently alluded to in popular discourses (e.g. trade papers, journalistic criticism) as it was during the first half of the twentieth century. Rather, it has been subsumed within broader, overlapping categories such as the perennial (but ill-defined) 'family audience', 'youth audience' and 'kidult audience'.

The proliferation of the latter term, in particular, reinforces a popular truism that child-orientated films are no longer regarded exclusively, or even primarily, as belonging to children. Family films have repeatedly been credited in the new millennium with sustaining, or reinvigorating, Britain's moribund tradition of cinema-going. In December 2001, the *Daily Express* reported that 'the wizardry of *Harry Potter*' had boosted levels to their highest since the 1970s, with approximately 140 million attendances.[10] In November 2005, the *Daily Telegraph* observed, rather hyperbolically, that 'children's films' such as *Harry Potter* and *Nanny McPhee* 'are fuelling the boom at the box office as more Britons than ever before flock to the cinema'.[11] This success reflects the films' cross-demographic appeal, and adults' consumption of them has also widely been commented on. A 2001 survey found that *Harry Potter* characters were most recognised by people in the 25 to 35 age demographic, and a 2002 poll discovered that 90 per cent of parents regularly read to their children, a fact attributed to *Harry Potter*'s 'crossover' appeal.[12] These examples, in conjunction with the near-universal acclaim that has met the *Harry Potter* series and *Paddington*, confirm that adults partaking of such putatively child-orientated media is now a widely accepted phenomenon, no longer subject to stigmatisation. The twentieth-century disreputability of children's cinema, paradoxically situated against its self-avowed wholesomeness, has given way in the early twenty-first century to a general acceptance of its centrality in contemporary popular culture.

Notes

Introduction

1 Alan Lovell, 'British Cinema: The Known Cinema' in Robert Murphy, ed., *The British Cinema Book* (London: BFI Publishing, 2009), pp. 5–12.

2 Ibid.

3 See particularly Terry Staples, *All Pals Together: The Story of Children's Cinema* (Edinburgh: Edinburgh University Press, 1997), and, on the 1930s, Sarah J. Smith, *Children, Cinema and Censorship: From Dracula to the Dead End Kids* (London and New York: I.B.Tauris, 2005) and Jeffrey Richards, *The Age of the Dream Palace: Cinema and Society in 1930s Britain* (London and New York: I.B. Tauris, 2010 [1984]).

4 Many films discussed in this book were facilitated by North American production finance. Such films are still held to be 'British' if they were produced by British firms (as with Aardman's animated films and Heyday's *Harry Potter* series), and/or were filmed primarily in Britain with mainly British personnel (as with the Disney films examined in Chapter 6). Nonetheless, it should be acknowledged that the realities of international co-production are more fluid than terms like 'British cinema' or 'Hollywood cinema' imply.

5 Thomas Elsaesser, 'Images for Sale: The "New" British Cinema' in Lester D. Friedman, ed., *Fires Were Started: British Cinema and Thatcherism* (London: Wallflower Press, 2006), pp. 45–57 (p. 54).

6 Such a basic definition, it will be noticed, excludes productions which centre on children but are not aimed at a young audience, and may clearly be unsuitable for them. In British cinema, prominent 'child films' include Carol Reed's *The Fallen Idol* (1948) and *A Kid for Two Farthings* (1955), *Mandy* (Alexander Mackendrick, 1952), *Village of the Damned* (Wolf Rilla, 1960), *The Innocents* (Jack Clayton, 1961), *Kes* (Ken Loach, 1969), *The Boy in the Striped Pyjamas* (Mark Herman, 2008) and *The Selfish Giant* (Clio Barnard, 2013).

7 Cary Bazalgette and Terry Staples, 'Unshrinking the Kids: Children's Cinema and the "Family" Film' in Cary Bazalgette and David Buckingham, eds, *In Front of the Children: Screen Entertainment and Young Audiences* (London: BFI Publishing, 1995), pp. 92–108.

8 'Interview of Walt Disney and Cecil B. DeMille', 26 December 1938, in Kathy Merlock Jackson, ed., *Walt Disney: Conversations* (Jackson: University Press of Mississippi, 2006), pp. 13–14.

Notes to pages 5–15

9 Symbolic children, in this context, are understood as non-child figures in which 'childlike' attributes, such as innocence, goodness, unaffectedness, and a predilection for unfettered play, are invested, and in which child audiences can identify. In British cinema, symbolic children include 'childlike' grown-ups (particularly comedians, such as Norman Wisdom) and lovable animals (such as Rover, Digby or Gromit).

10 Smith, *Children, Cinema and Censorship*, pp. 125–26; Barbara Kesterton, 'The Social and Emotional Effects of the Recreational Film on Adolescents of Thirteen and Fourteen Years of Age in the West Bromwich Area', unpublished PhD thesis (University of Birmingham, 1948).

11 Readers are directed to 'The "Family" Film, and the Tensions between Popular and Academic Interpretations of Genre', *Trespassing Journal: An Online Journal of Trespassing Art, Science and Philosophy* (2), 2013, pp. 22–35.

12 Andrew Tudor, 'Genre' in Barry Keith Grant, ed., *Film Genre Reader III* (Austin, Texas: University of Texas Press, 2003), pp. 9–11.

Chapter 1: In the Beginning: Children and British Cinema in the Silent Era

1 Rachael Low with Roger Manvell, *The History of British Film 1896–1906* (London and New York: Routledge, 1997 [1948]), p. 15.

2 Ibid., p. 79.

3 Ibid., pp. 13–14.

4 Ibid., pp. 83–85.

5 Ibid., p. 37.

6 Rachael Low, *The History of British Film 1914–1918* (London and New York: Routledge, 1997 [1950]), p. 20.

7 Terry Staples, *All Pals Together: The Story of Children's Cinema* (Edinburgh: Edinburgh University Press, 1997), pp. 2–3.

8 Low, *The History of British Film 1896–1906*, p. 108.

9 Cecil M. Hepworth, *Came the Dawn: Memories of a Film Pioneer* (London: Phoenix House, 1951), pp. 66–67.

10 Ibid., p. 73.

11 Ibid., pp. 76–77.

12 Laraine Porter, 'From Slapstick to Satire: British Comedy Before 1930' in I. Q. Hunter and Laraine Porter, eds, *British Comedy Cinema* (London and New York: Routledge, 2012), pp. 18–37 (p. 21).

13 Ibid.

14 Rachael Low, *The History of the British Film 1906–1914* (London and New York: Routledge, 1997 [1950]), p. 181.

15 Low, *The History of British Film 1914–1918*, p. 176.

16 Staples, *All Pals Together*, p. 8.

269

Notes to pages 15–21

17 Jonathan Burrows, '"Our English Mary Pickford": Alma Taylor and Ambivalent British Stardom in the 1910s' in Bruce Babington, ed., *British Stars and Stardom: From Alma Taylor to Sean Connery* (Manchester: Manchester University Press, 2001), pp. 29–41 (p. 30).

18 Low, *The History of the British Film 1906–1914*, pp. 32–33.

19 Jeffrey Richards, *The Golden Age of Pantomime: Slapstick, Spectacle and Subversion in Victorian England* (London and New York: I.B.Tauris, 2015), pp. 41–42.

20 Low, *The History of the British Film 1906–1914*, p. 185.

21 *Cinema News and Property Gazette*, December 1912, p. 33.

22 Ibid., pp. 56–57.

23 'The Yuletide Pictures', *Cinema News and Property Gazette*, December 1912, p. 35.

24 Ibid.

25 Hepworth, *Came the Dawn*, p. 95.

26 Ibid., p. 185.

27 Low, *The History of the British Film 1914–1918*, p. 28.

28 Low, *The History of the British Film 1906–1914*, pp. 32–33.

29 Ibid.

30 Luke McKernan, '"Only the Screen was Silent...": Memories of Children's Cinema-Going in London before the First World War', *Film Studies*, no. 10 (Spring 2007), pp. 1–20 (p. 1).

31 *The Cinema: Its Present Position and Future Possibilities – Being the Report and Chief Evidence Taken by the Cinema Commission of Inquiry Instituted by the National Council of Public Morals* (London: Williams and Norgate, 1917), p. li.

32 Ibid., p. xxxi.

33 Low, *The History of the British Film 1914–1918*, p. 28.

34 'The Young Picturegoer', *Pictures and the Picturegoer*, 4 March 1916, p. 538.

35 *The Cinema: Its Present Position and Future Possibilities*, pp. 272–75.

36 Low, *The History of the British Film 1906–1914*, p. 17.

37 *The Cinema: Its Present Position and Future Possibilities*, pp. lviii–lix.

38 McKernan, '"Only the Screen was Silent...", p. 3.

39 Ibid.

40 Low, *The History of the British Film 1906–1914*, pp. 32–33.

41 Staples, *All Pals Together*, pp. 4–6.

42 Editorial, *The Manchester Guardian*, 13 January 1908, p. 6.

43 Jeffrey Richards and James C. Robertson, 'British Film Censorship' in Robert Murphy, ed., *The British Cinema Book* (London: BFI Publishing, 2009), pp. 67–77 (p. 67).

44 C. B., 'Cinema Shows' [Letters], *The Sunday Times*, 1 December 1912, p. 16.

45 Low, *The History of the British Film 1906–1914*, pp. 32–33.

270

Notes to pages 21–27

46 Sarah J. Smith, *Children, Cinema and Censorship: From Dracula to the Dead End Kids* (London and New York: I.B.Tauris, 2005), pp. 25–26.

47 Ibid., pp. 31–33.

48 Richards and Robertson, 'British Film Censorship', pp. 67–68.

49 Ibid., pp. 67–68.

50 Ibid.

51 Staples, *All Pals Together*, p. 10.

52 'Children and the Cinematograph', *The Times*, 23 January 1914, p. 7.

53 Ibid.

54 'Child and the Kinema: A New Movement for Reform', *The Manchester Guardian*, 28 May 1914, p. 5.

55 Ibid.

56 'Films for Children: A Women's Committee Suggested', *The Manchester Guardian*, 24 March 1914, p. 11.

57 'Correspondence – The Child and the Kinema', *The Manchester Guardian*, 9 June 1914, p. 7.

58 'The Future of the Cinema', *The Observer*, 10 November 1918, p. 3.

59 *The Cinema: Its Present Position and Future Possibilities*, pp. vii–viii.

60 Ibid., pp. lxxxix–xc.

61 Ibid., p. 217.

62 Ibid.

63 Ibid., p. 264.

64 Ibid.

65 Ibid., p. lx.

66 Ibid.

67 Smith, *Children, Cinema and Censorship*, pp. 26–28.

68 'A National Film Censorship', *The Times*, 1 October 1921, p. 8.

69 'Children and Cinema Theatres', *The Times*, 20 December 1922, p. 11.

70 'The New Film Censorship'.

71 Sydney W. Carroll, 'Cinemas and Children: Influence on the Young Mind, *The Sunday Times*, 9 January 1927, p. 9.

72 Ibid.

73 '"Dreadful" Films for Children', *The Manchester Guardian*, 31 December 1925, p. 10.

74 'The Child and the Kinema: An Introduction', *The Manchester Guardian*, 9 October 1925, p. 8.

75 Ibid.

76 Ibid.

77 'Film Matinees for Children', *The Times*, 13 May 1920, p. 14.

78 Carroll, 'Cinemas and Children'.

79 *Children, Cinema and Censorship*, p. 166.

Notes to pages 28–33

80 'British Film Quota', *The Manchester Guardian*, 5 February 1926, p. 12.
81 Staples, *All Pals Together*, p. 30.
82 Ibid, p. 30.
83 Walter Ashley, 'Standards of Film Censorship', *Sight and Sound*, Autumn 1932, pp. 68–69.
84 Ibid.
85 Ibid.
86 Ibid.
87 'Films Unsuitable for Children', *The Manchester Guardian*, 17 December 1929, p. 14.
88 'Children's Films: Impracticable to Have Special Category', *The Manchester Guardian*, 27 January 1930, p. 18.
89 Ibid.
90 Annette Kuhn, 'Children, "Horrific" Films', and Censorship in 1930s Britain', *The Historical Journal of Film, Radio and Television*, vol. 22, no. 2 (2002), pp. 197–202 (pp. 197–98).
91 'Films for "Adults Only"', *The Times*, 30 January 1931, p. 12.
92 Smith, *Children, Cinema and Censorship*, p. 65.
93 Kuhn, 'Children, "Horrific" Films', and Censorship in 1930s Britain', p. 198.
94 Staples, *All Pals Together*, p. 30.
95 Ibid., p. 33.
96 Ibid.
97 Quoted in Richard Ford, *Children in the Cinema* (London: George Allen & Unwin, 1939), pp. 4–5.
98 Smith, *Children, Cinema and Censorship*, pp. 69–71.
99 Ibid.
100 Ibid.
101 Ibid., pp. 72–73.
102 Seton Margrave, 'The Cinema Box Office Wonders Why', *The Daily Mail*, 1 March 1934, p. 10.

Chapter 2: The Children's Adventure Movie, 1930–60

1 The Children and Young Persons Act, 1933, effectively prohibited children under 12 from appearing in British films. The industry vehemently opposed this legislation, most notably before the Board of Trade's 1936 Departmental Committee on Cinematograph Films, where it was argued that: 'This restriction has proved very disadvantageous to British producers, and has resulted in their being unable to make many pictures of a very popular type which can be readily made abroad and shown without hindrance in this country' (*Minutes of Evidence*

Notes to pages 33–43

Taken Before the Departmental Committee on Cinematograph Films [London: Board of Trade, 1936], p. 39). The clause was not repealed until 1950, but an article in the *Manchester Guardian* (19 August 1935, p. 6) alleged that the restriction was routinely ignored in any case, with child actors 'smuggled' into studios. Hazel Ascot and Binkie Stuart were well underage. Apparently, no prosecutions over violations of the 1933 Act ever took place.

2 Sidney Bernstein's 1937 Film Questionnaire found that Temple ranked as the sixth most popular film star among 'general audiences', whilst numerous polls of children ranked her at number one. See 'The Bernstein Film Questionnaire 1946–7' report (London: 1947), p. 3.

3 Ewart Hodgson, 'Six New Films This Week', *The Daily Express*, 20 March 1933, p. 10.

4 'A Film Acted by Children', *The Manchester Guardian*, 18 March 1933, p. 7.

5 C. A. Lejeune, 'The Pictures: A Boys' Film', *The Observer*, 19 March 1933, p. 14.

6 Ibid.

7 Bryony Dixon, 'Emil and the Detectives: A Faithful Remake', *Emil and the Detectives* DVD liner notes (London: BFI, 2013), pp. 10–12.

8 Ibid.

9 'Emil and the Detectives', *Variety*, 27 February 1935, p. 26; Seton Margrave, 'The Gold-Digger Passes the Hollywood Censor', *The Daily Mail*, 20 May 1935, p. 20; 'Music and Drama', *The Yorkshire Post*, 23 July 1935, p. 5.

10 Gillian Lathey, '"What a Funny Name!": Cultural Transition in Versions of Erich Kästner's *Emil and the Detectives*' in Fiona M. Collins and Jeremy Ridgman, eds, *Turning the Page: Children's Literature in Performance and the Media* (Bern: Peter Lang, 2004), pp. 115–32 (p. 116).

11 Dixon, 'Emil and the Detectives: A Faithful Remake'.

12 Jeffrey Richards, 'Sabu, the Elephant Boy' in Noel Brown and Bruce Babington, eds, *Family Films in Global Cinema: The World Beyond Disney* (London and New York: I.B.Tauris, 2015), pp. 87–102 (p. 87).

13 Ibid., p. 88.

14 Ibid., p. 92.

15 'Jungle Friends Didn't Forget', *The Daily Mirror*, 21 June 1937, p. 5.

16 Reg Whitley, 'Thanks for the Beautiful Princess!', *The Daily Mirror*, 27 December 1940, p. 9; Seton Margrave, 'The Film for the Young in Heart', *The Daily Mail*, 20 December 1940, p. 4; Basil Wright, 'The Cinema', *The Spectator*, 26 December 1940, p. 11.

17 Quoted in Charles Drazin, *Korda: Britain's Only Movie Mogul* (London: I.B. Tauris, 2011), p. 211.

18 It is interesting, in terms of the film's symbolic nation-rebuilding, that *Hue and Cry* defied expectations that its appeal would largely be confined to London; it proved 'remarkably popular in the Midlands and the North'; see Reg Whitley, 'The Best Films of 1947', *The Daily Mirror*, 17 December 1947, p. 2.

273

Notes to pages 45–60

19 C. A. Lejeune, 'Bless Them All', *The Observer*, 23 February 1947, p. 2.
20 'Emil and the Detectives', *The Guardian*, 22 February 1947, p. 3.
21 As one might imagine, contemporary sources reveal *Hue and Cry* to have been highly popular among children; one 10-year-old boy interviewed for a 1947 Mass Observation report on children's Saturday morning cinema-going in Wickham Common went as far to describe it as 'the best film I have seen' ('Going to the Cinema on a Saturday Morning – A Further Report on Wickham Common Junior School', Mass Observation, July 1947, p. 4).
22 'A Week of British Films', *The Times*, 24 March 1958, p. 3.
23 'Revolution, War, and Aftermath', *The Manchester Guardian*, 8 April 1958, p. 3; Derek Granger, 'Men at Arms', *The Financial Times*, 24 March 1958, p. 8.
24 Dilys Powell, 'Eighteen Years Ago', *The Sunday Times*, 23 March 1958, p. 11; Granger, 'Men at Arms'.
25 'Val Guest' obituary, *The Independent*, 15 May 2006, unpaginated.
26 *The Advertiser* (Adelaide), 31 December 1954, p. 11.
27 Virginia Graham, 'The Cinema', *The Spectator*, 11 December 1953, p. 13; Reg Whitley, 'I Don't Mind a Chorus Girl Landing in my Lap!', *The Daily Mirror*, 19 February 1954, p. 2; 'Children in Command of New Film', *The Times*, 14 December 1954, p. 11; 'Entertainment Films', *Monthly Film Bulletin*, January 1954, pp. 4–5.
28 Virginia Graham, 'The Cinema', *The Spectator*, 2 January 1948, p. 16.
29 'Picture Theatres', *The Manchester Guardian*, 30 March 1948, p. 3.

Chapter 3: Family Entertainers: Formby, Hay, Lucan, Wisdom

1 Richard Ford, *Children in the Cinema* (London: George Allen & Unwin, 1939), p. 117.
2 Ibid., pp. 131–32.
3 Ibid., pp. 133–34.
4 Terry Staples, *All Pals Together: The Story of Children's Cinema* (Edinburgh: Edinburgh University Press, 1997), p. 73.
5 Ibid., p. 219.
6 C. A. Lejeune, 'Films to See', *Sight and Sound*, Autumn 1932, p. 89.
7 'Suburbs and Provinces', *The Observer*, 4 April 1937, p. 16; ' "Good Morning, Boys": Will Hay's New Film', *The Manchester Guardian*, 13 February 1937, p. 17.
8 'British Films: Paul Robeson and Will Hay', *The Manchester Guardian*, 30 October 1937, p. 16.
9 'Entertainment Films', *Monthly Film Bulletin*, November 1941, p. 145.
10 'Entertainment Films', *Monthly Film Bulletin*, December 1946, p. 167.

274

Notes to pages 60–81

11 'Entertainment Films', *Monthly Film Bulletin*, June 1941, p. 67.
12 See, for instance, Barbara Kesterton, 'The Social and Emotional Effects of the Recreational Film on Adolescents of Thirteen and Fourteen Years of Age in the West Bromwich Area', unpublished PhD thesis (University of Birmingham, 1948), pp. 125–26.
13 Tom Weaver, 'Richard Gordon on Mother Riley Meets the Vampire', *Science Fiction Confidential: Interviews with 23 Monsters Stars and Filmmakers* (Jefferson: McFarland, 2002), pp. 144–52.
14 'Music, Drama, and Films', *The Manchester Guardian*, 17 November 1934, p. 13.
15 'Relays from Pantomime Rehearsals', *The Manchester Guardian*, 29 November, 1935, p. 12.
16 Jeffrey Richards, *The Age of the Dream Palace: Cinema and Society in 1930s Britain* (London and New York: I.B.Tauris, 2010 [1984]), p. 192.
17 'Censoring a Sunday Concert', *The Manchester Guardian*, 4 January 1935, p. 5.
18 Richards, *The Age of the Dream Palace*, pp. 193, 196.
19 Weaver, 'Richard Gordon on Mother Riley Meets the Vampire'.
20 Richards, *The Age of the Dream Palace*, p. 298.
21 'The Film and Family Life', Mass Observation report, June 1944, p. 2.
22 'Picture Theatres', *The Manchester Guardian*, 14 March 1944, p. 3.
23 It is worth noting that the Royal Navy placed recruitment adverts in children's publications such as *Boy's Cinema* before the outbreak of war. One such advert reminded readers that 'Boys may now enter between the ages of 15 and 17½ years' (*Boy's Cinema*, 23 July 1938, p. 25).
24 'Popularity of British Comedy Films', *The Manchester Guardian*, 15 December 1954, p. 5.
25 'Entertainment Films', *Monthly Film Bulletin*, January 1954, p. 13.
26 'Adventure Film', *The Times*, 21 December 1953, p. 9.
27 'Picture Theatres', *The Manchester Guardian*, 5 January 1954, p. 3.
28 Grace Conway, 'Wisdom is a Treasure', *The Catholic Herald*, 9 September 1955, p. 8.

Chapter 4: J. Arthur Rank, Saturday Morning Cinema and the Children's Film Foundation

1 Sarah J. Smith, *Children, Cinema and Censorship: From Dracula to the Dead End Kids* (London and New York: I.B.Tauris, 2005), p. 142.
2 'At Your Local Cinema', *The Daily Mail*, 16 April 1934, p. 4.
3 William Farr, 'Films for Children', *Sight and Sound*, Winter 1934, pp. 162–64; 'News of the Quarter', *Sight and Sound*, Summer 1937, pp. 57–58.
4 'A Clean Screen', *Sight and Sound*, Summer 1936, p. 4; 'News of the Quarter'.
5 Farr, 'Films for Children'.

275

Notes to pages 81–85

6 'Films for Children', *The Yorkshire Post*, 8 May 1935, p. 8.
7 Richard Ford, 'Censorship and the Adolescent', *World Film News*, October 1938, pp. 261–63.
8 Richard Ford, *Children in the Cinema* (London: George Allen & Unwin, 1939), p. 23.
9 Ibid.
10 'Special Films for Children', *The Times*, 5 March 1932, p. 9.
11 'Children at the Pictures: An Interview with Miss M. Locket', *Sight and Sound*, Spring 1932, p. 27.
12 'Films for Children', *The Times*, 15 September 1936, p. 12.
13 Farr, 'Films for Children'.
14 Ibid.
15 'Films for Children', *Sight and Sound*, Summer 1936, pp. 1–2.
16 Ibid.
17 'Films for Children', *Sight and Sound*, Summer 1937, p. 60.
18 Ford, *Children in the Cinema*, pp. 7–8.
19 'Children and the Cinema', *Sight and Sound*, Autumn 1936, p. 77.
20 'Films for Children', *Sight and Sound*, Spring 1937, p. 2; 'Films for Children', *The Yorkshire Post*, 10 July 1937, p. 12.
21 'Films for Children', *Sight and Sound*, Summer 1937.
22 Ford, *Children in the Cinema*, pp. 9–10.
23 'Mickey Mouse Clubs', *The Observer*, 10 March 1940, p. 8.
24 Quoted in Terry Staples, *All Pals Together: The Story of Children's Cinema* (Edinburgh: Edinburgh University Press, 1997), p. 92.
25 Geoffrey Macnab, *J. Arthur Rank and the British Film Industry* (London and New York: Routledge, 1993), pp. 1–5.
26 Ibid., p. 149; Staples, *All Pals Together*, pp. 90–91.
27 Staples, *All Pals Together*, p. 91.
28 Mary Field, *Good Company: The Story of the Children's Entertainment Film Movement in Great Britain – 1943-1950* (London: Longmans Green and Co., 1952), p. 4.
29 Staples, *All Pals Together*, p. 97.
30 Ibid., p. 96.
31 Field, *Good Company*, p. 14.
32 Thomas Phillips, 'Children May Alter Whole Film Outlook', *The Observer*, 1 October 1944, p. 6.
33 Staples, *All Pals Together*, p. 118.
34 'Films for Children: Morals without Religion', *The Church Times*, 8 June 1945, p. 323.
35 Staples, *All Pals Together*, p. 124.
36 Michael Gareth Llewellyn, 'The Kind of Film for Children', *Sight and Sound*, Autumn 1945, pp. 77–79.

Notes to pages 85–90

37 Ibid.

38 'Films for the Child', *The Manchester Guardian*, 9 June 1947, p. 3.

39 Arthur Vesselo, 'The Quarter in Britain', *Sight and Sound*, Winter 1947, p. 136.

40 Arthur Vesselo, 'The Quarter in Britain', *Sight and Sound*, Autumn 1947, p. 121.

41 'A Film for Children', *The Times*, 23 May 1947, p. 6; Dilys Powell, 'Films of the Week', *The Sunday Times*, 25 May 1947, p. 2.

42 Henri Storck, *The Entertainment Film for Juvenile Audiences* (Paris: Unesco, 1950), pp. 93–95.

43 Arthur Vesselo, 'The Quarter in Britain', *Sight and Sound*, Spring 1948, p. 42.

44 Ella Jones, 'Films for Children', *The Daily Worker*, 2 February 1945, p. 2.

45 J. P. Mayer, *Sociology of Film* (London: Faber and Faber, 1946), pp. 52–54.

46 Ibid., p. 54.

47 'Films for Children: Entertainment as an Aid to Education', *The Times*, 5 January 1946, p. 5.

48 'Films for the Young', *The Times*, 10 January 1946, p. 5.

49 Ibid.

50 See 'Children's Cinema Clubs a Danger?', *The Manchester Guardian*, 28 November 1946, p. 6.

51 'Children in Cinemas: Committee to be Set Up', *The Times*, 2 July 1947, p. 4.

52 K. C. Wheare, *Report of the Committee on Children and the Cinema* (London: H. M. Stationary Office, 1950), p. 28.

53 Ibid., pp. 2, 78.

54 'Films for the Children', *The Manchester Guardian*, 2 June 1950, p. 5.

55 Staples, *All Pals Together*, pp. 133–34.

56 Storck, *The Entertainment Film for Juvenile Audiences*, p. 53.

57 Staples, *All Pals Together*, p. 179.

58 'Children's Films: Work of Foundation's First Year', *The Times*, 2 October 1952, p. 9.

59 Rowana Agajanian, '"Just for Kids?": Saturday Morning Cinema and Britain's Children's Film Foundation in the 1960s', *Historical Journal of Film, Radio and Television*, vol. 18, no. 3 (1998), pp. 395–409 (pp. 396–97).

60 Mary Field, 'Children's Taste in Films', *The Quarterly of Film, Radio and Television*, vol. 11, no. 1 (1956), pp. 14–23 (p. 21).

61 'The Bernstein Film Questionnaire 1946–7' Report (London: 1947), p. 18.

62 'For Better Films Banish Children from "Adult" Cinemas', *The Manchester Guardian*, 19 October 1949, p. 6.

63 Ibid.

64 'Going to the Cinema on a Saturday Morning', Mass Observation, July 1947, p. 6; Kathleen Box, 'The Cinema and the Public' (London: Central Office of Information, 1948), p. 6.

65 'Children's Films: Work of Foundation's First Year'.

66 Agajanian, 'Just for Kids?', p. 400.

Notes to pages 90–107

67 Mary Field, *Children and Films: A Study of Boys and Girls in the Cinema* (Dunfermline: Carnegie United Kingdom Trust, 1954), p. 3.
68 'Children's Films Abroad', *The Times*, 17 December 1952, p. 3.
69 'British Films for Children: Venice Film Awards', *The Times*, 24 August 1953, p. 10.
70 'British Films for Children: First American Award', *The Times*, 6 July 1955, p. 6.
71 Field, *Good Company*, p. 87.
72 Ibid., p. 86.
73 Ibid.
74 Ibid., p. 95.
75 Storck, *The Entertainment Film for Juvenile Audiences*, pp. 73–74.
76 Staples, *All Pals Together*, pp. 177–79.
77 Ibid., pp. 192–93.
78 'Catering for Children's Film Clubs', *The Guardian*, 18 May 1963, p. 12.
79 Staples, *All Pals Together*, p. 212.
80 Ibid.
81 *Saturday Morning Cinema: 25 years of Films for Children* (London: Children's Film Foundation, Ltd., 1969), p. 8.
82 Ibid.
83 Ibid., p. 6.
84 *Saturday Morning Cinema*, p. 8.
85 Ibid., p. 44.
86 Ibid., p. 7.
87 Ibid.
88 Ibid., pp. 50–51.
89 Staples, *All Pals Together*, p. 220.
90 Ibid., pp. 233–34.
91 Michael Powell, *Million Dollar Movie* (London: William Heinemann, 1992), pp. 536–39.
92 Richard Combs, 'The Boy Who Turned Yellow', *Monthly Film Bulletin*, October 1972, p. 208.
93 Peter Waymark, 'Growing Pains', *The Times*, 18 October 1972, p. 18.
94 Jonathan Rosenbaum, 'The Battle of Billy's Pond', *Monthly Film Bulletin*, April 1976, p. 75.
95 Margaret Hinxman, 'Delightful', *The Daily Mail*, 29 April 1977, p. 22.
96 Staples, *All Pals Together*, p. 240.
97 Robert Brown, 'Friend or Foe', *Monthly Film Bulletin*, May 1982, pp. 85–86.

Chapter 5: Happiest Days: British Cinema and the Family Audience in the Fifties

1 David Kynaston, *Family Britain: 1951–1957* (London: Bloomsbury, 2009).
2 Arthur Marwick, *British Society Since 1945* (London: Penguin, 2003).

Notes to pages 108–128

3 Cary Bazalgette and David Buckingham, 'Introduction: The Invisible Audience' in Cary Bazalgette and David Buckingham, eds, *In Front of the Children: Screen Entertainment and Young Audiences* (London: BFI Publishing, 1995), pp. 1–14 (p. 11).

4 Christine Geraghty, *British Cinema in the Fifties: Gender, Genre and the 'New Look'* (London and New York: Routledge, 2000), p. 133.

5 Kynaston, *Family Britain: 1951–1957*, p. 558.

6 Geraghty, *British Cinema in the Fifties*, p. 140.

7 Richard Hoggart, *The Uses of Literacy* (London: Penguin, 1992 [1957]), p. 51.

8 Marwick, *British Society Since 1945*, p. 44.

9 'Entertainment Films', *Monthly Film Bulletin*, December 1946, p. 166.

10 Jeffrey Richards, *Happiest Days: The Public Schools in English Fiction* (Manchester: Manchester University Press, 1988), pp. 58–60.

11 Tony Shaw, *British Cinema and the Cold War: The State, Propaganda and Consensus* (London and New York: I.B.Tauris, 2006), pp. 93–94.

12 Daniel J. Leab, *Orwell Subverted: The CIA and the Filming of Animal Farm* (Pennsylvania: The Pennsylvania State University Press, 2007), p. 112.

13 Ibid.

14 Leonard Mosley, 'Today I Hail the Disney of Britain', *The Daily Mirror*, 19 November 1954, p. 4.

15 '"Animal Farm" Shown in New York', *The Times*, 31 December 1954, p. 8.

16 Ibid.

17 Catherine de la Roche, 'Film Reviews – Animal Farm', *Sight and Sound*, Spring 1955, p. 196.

18 C. A. Lejeune, 'Pig Business', *The Observer*, 16 January 1955, p. 10.

19 'Animal Farm', *Kinematograph Weekly*, 13 January 1955, p. 13; Fred Majdalany, 'Their Animals Lack Characters', *The Daily Mail*, 12 January 1955, p. 3.

20 '"Animal Farm" in London', *The Times*, 12 January 1955, p. 7.

21 Ibid.

22 'Directors' Problems' [1938] in Sidney Gottlieb, ed., *Hitchcock on Hitchcock: Selected Writings and Interviews* (London: Faber and Faber, 1995), pp. 186–91.

23 'Duel in the Sun: What the Critics Say about It', *The Picture Post*, 7 June 1947, p. 24.

24 Jeffrey Richards and James C. Robertson, 'British Film Censorship' in Robert Murphy, ed., *The British Cinema Book* (London: BFI Publishing, 2009), pp. 67–77 (p. 72).

25 'Report on the "X"', *Sight and Sound*, January–March 1954, pp. 123–24; 153.

26 Ibid.

27 'Films in the "X" Class', *The Manchester Guardian*, 22 November 1952, p. 3.

28 'Report on the "X"'.

29 'The Cinema and the Child: Stricter Control Urged', *The Manchester Guardian*, 31 December 1953, p. 2.

279

Notes to pages 128–147

30 'Age and Time Limits Plan for Children at Cinemas', *The Manchester Guardian*, 6 May 1950, p. 7.
31 'Children at the Cinema: New Regulations Next Year', *The Manchester Guardian*, 4 October 1955, p. 2.
32 'More Film Fun', *The Manchester Guardian*, 12 May 1950, p. 6.
33 Ibid.
34 'How Goes the Enemy?', *Sight and Sound*, April–June 1954, p. 175.
35 'Entertainment Films', *Monthly Film Bulletin*, January 1960, pp. 2–3.

Chapter 6: Disney in Britain

1 Philip K. Scheur, 'Disney Animated by Flood of Films, Including All-Live "Treasure Island"', *The Los Angeles Times*, 5 June 1949, pp. D1, D8.
2 Velma West Sykes, 'Disney's "Treasure Island" (RKO) Wins August Blue Ribbon Award', *Boxoffice*, 9 September 1950, p. 28.
3 Paul Wells, *Animation: Genre and Authorship* (London: Wallflower, 2002), p. 77.
4 Ibid.
5 Michael Barrier, *The Animated Man: A Life of Walt Disney* (Berkeley: University of California Press, 2007), p. 222.
6 Ibid.
7 Ibid., p. 224.
8 'New Films in London', *The Manchester Guardian*, 24 June 1950, p. 5.
9 Dilys Powell, 'R. L. S. & Disney', *The Sunday Times*, 25 June 1950, p. 4.
10 Grace Conway, 'The Island That Must be Visited', *The Catholic Herald*, 30 June 1950, p. 3; Reg Whitley, 'Best Children's Film – For Grown-Ups!', *The Daily Mirror*, 23 June 1950, p. 4.
11 C. A. Lejeune, 'Bob's Your Uncle', *The Observer*, 25 June 1950, p. 6; 'Entertainment Films', *Monthly Film Bulletin*, July 1950, p. 103.
12 Raymond Williams, *The Country and the City* (Oxford: Oxford University Press, 1973), p. 2.
13 Ibid., p. 32.
14 'Entertainment Films', *Monthly Film Bulletin*, July 1953, p. 103.
15 Louis Berg, 'Walt Disney's Highland Fling', *The Los Angeles Times*, 27 December 1953, pp. H8–H9.
16 'Film of "Rob Roy"', *The Times*, 10 March 1953, p. 2.
17 Philip Hope-Wallace, 'The Royal Film Show – "Rob Roy" with Idealised Tartan Trimmings', *The Manchester Guardian*, 27 October 1953, p. 5; Grace Conway, 'A "Western" Over the Border', *The Catholic Herald*, 30 October 1953, p. 8.
18 Conway, 'A "Western" Over the Border'.
19 Colin McArthur, *Brigadoon, Braveheart and the Scots: Distortions of Scotland in Hollywood Cinema* (London and New York: I.B.Tauris, 2003), p. viii.

280

Notes to pages 148–162

20 'Films', *Boys' Life*, December 1966, p. 4.

21 Kevin J. Harty, 'Walt in Sherwood, or the Sheriff of Disneyland: Disney and the Film Legend of Robin Hood' in Tison Pugh and Susan Aronstein, eds, *The Disney Middle Age: A Fairy-Tale and Fantasy Past* (New York: Palgrave Macmillan, 2012), pp. 133–52.

22 Douglas Brode, *From Walt to Woodstock: How Disney Created the Counterculture* (Austin: University of Texas Press, 2004), p. 55.

23 Ibid., p. 63.

24 Steven Watts, *The Magic Kingdom: Walt Disney and the American Way of Life* (Missouri: University of Missouri Press, 1997), p. 291.

25 Ibid.

26 Ibid., p. 291.

27 Neil Smelser, 'The Victorian Family' in Robert N. Rapoport et al eds, *Families in Britain* (London: Routledge and Kegan Paul, 1982), pp. 59–74 (p. 59).

28 Ibid., p. 60; Ann Oakley, 'Conventional Families' in Robert N. Rapoport et al eds, *Families in Britain* (London: Routledge and Kegan Paul, 1982), pp. 123–37.

29 Landon Y. Jones, *Great Expectations: America and the Baby Boom Generation* (New York: Coward, McCann & Geohagan, 1980), p. 212.

30 Joel W. Finler, *The Hollywood Story* (London: Octopus Books, 1988), p. 277.

31 Muriel Nissel, 'Families and Social Chance Since the Second World War' in Robert N. Rapoport et al., eds, *Families in Britain* (London: Routledge and Kegan Paul, 1982), pp. 95–119 (p. 118).

32 Noel Brown, *The Hollywood Family Film: A History, from Shirley Temple to Harry Potter* (London and New York: I.B.Tauris, 2012), pp. 117–24.

33 Bruce Babington, 'Song, Narrative and the Mother's Voice: A Deepish Reading of Julie Andrews' in Bruce Babington, ed., *British Stars and Stardom: From Alma Taylor to Sean Connery* (Manchester: Manchester University Press, 2001), pp. 192–204.

34 Richard Schickel, *The Disney Version* (Chicago: Elephant Paperback, 1997 [1968], p. 304.

35 *Variety*, 9 August 1945, p. 13.

36 See Tom Wolfe, 'The "Me" Decade and the Third Great Awakening', *New York*, 23 August 1976, unpaginated.

37 While, at first glance, this is a more-than-respectable result, it was unusually low for Disney films of the period. Furthermore, like other late-1970s live-action Disney films, *Candleshoe* was comprehensively out-performed at the box office by *Star Wars* and other family blockbusters, and also grossed less than the low-budget British fantasy film, *Warlords of Atlantis* (Kevin Connor, 1978). See Justin Smith, 'Cinema Statistics, Box Office and Related Data' in Sue Harper and Justin Smith, eds, *British Film Culture in the 1970s: The Boundaries of Pleasure* (Edinburgh: Edinburgh University Press, 2012), pp. 261–74.

38 R. D. Laing, *Sanity, Madness and the Family* (London: Tavistock, 1964).

281

Notes to pages 163–169

39 Richard Combs, 'Bedknobs and Broomsticks', *Monthly Film Bulletin*, November 1971, p. 216.

40 Paul Wells, *Animation and America* (Edinburgh: Edinburgh University Press, 2002), p. 128.

Chapter 7: Summers of Love and Winters of Discontent: The Sixties and Seventies

1 David A. Cook, *Lost Illusions: American Cinema in the Shadow of Watergate and Vietnam, 1970–1979* (Berkeley, Los Angles and London: University of California Press, 2000), p. 9.

2 Peter Waymark, 'Growing Pains', *The Times*, 18 October 1972, p. 18.

3 'Striking Changes in Leisure Activities of Children', *The Guardian*, 11 May 1960, p. 5.

4 'Profile of the Cinema Audience', *The Guardian*, 21 March 1961, p. 18.

5 Ibid.

6 David Docherty, David Morrison and Michael Tracey, *The Last Picture Show?: Britain's Changing Film Audiences* (London: BFI Publishing, 1987), pp. 4, 29.

7 'Charles and Anne See Tough "A" Film', *The Daily Mirror*, 6 August 1960, p. 1.

8 Ibid.

9 '"Cannot Ban 'X' Films": Lord Morrison', *The Guardian*, 20 September 1962, p. 4.

10 Ibid.

11 '"X" Films Were Seen by Schoolboys', *The Guardian*, 9 March 1963, p. 4.

12 Ibid.

13 'Lure of the "X" Certificate', *The Guardian*, 15 October 1962, p. 17.

14 'Film Giants Step into Finance', *The Observer*, 19 April 1964, p. 8.

15 'Increase in British Films Financed by US Firms', *The Guardian*, 2 August 1966, p. 4.

16 Sarah Street, *British National Cinema*, 2nd edition (London and New York: Routledge, 2009), pp. 23–24.

17 'U.S. Domination of Film Market Worries British Producers', *The Times*, 13 July 1966, p. 16.

18 John Firehammer, 'The Beatles Are Pent-Up Prisoners of Their Own Notoriety in "A Hard Day's Night"', Popmatters.com, 10 July 2015. <http://www.popmatters.com/feature/192382-the-beatles-are-pent-up-prisoners-of-their-own-notoriety-in-a-hard-d/> [accessed 21/8/2015].

19 Paul Johnson, 'The Menace of Beatlemania', *The New Statesman*, 28 February 1964, unpaginated.

20 Geoffrey Nowell-Smith, 'A Hard Day's Night', *Sight and Sound*, Autumn 1964, pp. 196–97.

Notes to pages 169–180

21 'Entertainment Films', *Monthly Film Bulletin*, September 1965, p. 133.

22 Adrian Schober, "'Why Can't They Make Kids' Flicks Anymore": *Willy Wonka and the Chocolate Factory* and the Dual-Addressed Family Film' in Noel Brown and Bruce Babington, eds, *Family Films in Global Cinema: The World Beyond Disney* (London and New York: I.B.Tauris, 2015), pp. 53–68 (p. 68).

23 Nigel Gosling, 'Lessons at the Movies', *The Observer*, 28 July 1968, p. 21; Cecil Wilson, 'Dazzled by that Yellow Submarine', *The Daily Mail*, 17 July 1968, p. 10.

24 David Wilson, 'Yellow Submarine', *Monthly Film Bulletin*, September 1968, pp. 13–14.

25 Gavin Millar, 'Yellow Submarine', *Sight and Sound*, Autumn 1968, pp. 204–5.

26 Penelope Houston, *The Contemporary Cinema* (Middlesex: Penguin, 1963), p. 176.

27 Ernest Betts, 'Carol Reed Makes His First Musical Film After a Long Wait', *The Times*, 23 September 1968, p. 7.

28 Ibid.

29 Jan Dawson, 'Oliver!', *Monthly Film Bulletin*, November 1968, pp. 172–73.

30 'Win Your Own Chitty Chitty Bang Bang', *The Daily Express*, 4 November 1968, p. 7.

31 Donald Zec, 'The Sweet Yell of Success', *The Daily Mirror*, 28 November 1968, p. 7.

32 Ibid.

33 John Russell Taylor, 'Fairy Tales That Talk Down', *The Times*, 16 December 1968, p. 17.

34 Jan Dawson, 'Chitty Chitty Bang Bang', *Monthly Film Bulletin*, February 1969, pp. 24–25.

35 Richard Roud, 'Nannie Fodder', *The Guardian*, 17 December 1968, p. 6.

36 Donald Zec, 'The Hot Medium', *The Daily Mirror*, 16 October 1968, p. 7.

37 Ibid.

38 Ibid.

39 Neville Hunnings, 'In the Picture', *Sight and Sound*, Spring 1970, pp. 71–72.

40 Robert Head, 'Why Make an "X" Film When This Is the Draw?', *The Daily Mirror*, 25 September 1968, p. 25.

41 J. S. Stansby, 'Whatever Happened to the Nice Films?', *The Guardian*, 2 October 1968, p. 8.

42 Ibid.

43 'Film Chief Attacks "Filth"', *The Times*, 9 April 1969, p. 2.

44 Katherine Hadley, 'Striding On – the Pied Piper of Pinewood', *The Daily Express*, 26 June 1972, p. 6.

45 Donald Gomery, 'Always in Front of the Children', *The Daily Mirror*, 7 December 1972, p. 8.

46 Barry Norman, 'Sit Down Children and Let's Have a Lovely Cry', *The Daily Mail*, 7 December 1970, p. 6.

283

Notes to pages 181–200

47 Tom Hutchison, 'Lionel Jeffries', *The Guardian*, 24 December 1970, p. 8.

48 Merete Bates, 'Look, No Sex: Merete Bates on the Filming of "The Railway Children"', *The Guardian*, 4 June 1970, p. 10.

49 Ibid.

50 Anna Tims, 'How We Made… The Railway Children', *The Guardian*, 7 May 2013, p. 19.

51 Hutchison, 'Lionel Jeffries'; Bates, 'Look, No Sex'.

52 Terry Staples, *All Pals Together: The Story of Children's Cinema* (Edinburgh: Edinburgh University Press, 1997), p. 212.

53 Justin Smith, 'Cinema Statistics, Box Office and Related Data' in Sue Harper and Justin Smith, eds, *British Film Culture in the 1970s: The Boundaries of Pleasure* (Edinburgh: Edinburgh University Press, 2012), pp. 261–74.

54 Norman, 'Sit Down Children'.

55 Ian Christie, 'Smashing Adventure Just for Children', *The Daily Mirror*, 16 December 1970, p. 13.

56 Hadley, 'Striding on – the Pied Piper of Pinewood'.

57 Tom Milne, 'Truffaut's Wolf Boy', *The Observer*, 20 December 1970, p. 20; Freda Bruce Lockhart, 'Happy – Playing By the Railway', *The Catholic Herald*, 25 December 1970, p. 6.

58 'The Times Diary'; 'Peter Pan as a Film Musical', *The Times*, 18 January 1972, p. 8.

59 Alan Brien, 'Second Opinion', *The Sunday Times*, 6 June 1971, p. 24.

60 Brenda Davies, 'Cromwell', *Monthly Film Bulletin*, September 1970, pp. 179–80.

61 Russell Campbell, 'David Copperfield', *Monthly Film Bulletin*, February 1970, pp. 23–24.

62 Kenneth Jenour, '"Clean Up" Man Forbes Quits as Film Chief', *The Daily Mirror*, 26 March 1971, p. 14.

63 Dennis Barker, 'Alice in Studioland', *The Guardian*, 10 June 1972, p. 8.

64 'Frederic's Sentimental Education', *The Times*, 8 December 1972, p. 13.

65 See remarks to this extent in Henri Storck's Unesco report, *The Entertainment Film for Juvenile Audiences* (Paris: Unesco, 1950), pp. 73–74.

66 David Lewin, 'The Hound and his Best Friend…The Fox', *The Daily Mail*, 26 October 1973, pp. 6–7.

67 Paul Donovan and Douglas Thompson, 'Booming Bunnies', *The Daily Mail*, 17 October 1978, p. 24; Smith, 'Cinema Statistics, Box Office and Related Data'.

68 'Watership Down', BBFC Examiners' Report, 15 February 1978.

69 Glenys Roberts, 'The Rabbits of Warren Street', *The Times*, 19 October 1978, p. 11.

70 Ibid.

71 Ted Whitehead, 'Cinema', *The Spectator*, 20 October 1978, p. 30; Derek Malcolm, 'The Buck Stops Here', *The Guardian*, 19 October 1978, p. 12.

72 Roberts, 'The Rabbits of Warren Street'.

Notes to pages 200–210

73 'Interview of Walt Disney and Cecil B. DeMille', 26 December 1938, in Kathy Merlock Jackson, ed., *Walt Disney: Conversations* (Jackson: University Press of Mississippi, 2006), pp. 13–14.
74 For more on Harryhausen's films, see Noel Brown, *The Hollywood Family Film: A History, from Shirley Temple to Harry Potter* (London and New York: I.B. Tauris, 2012), chapter 5.
75 Stuart Husband, 'It Came from Los Angeles', *The Guardian*, 18 December 1995, p. B5.
76 Brown, *The Hollywood Family Film*, pp. 151–63.

Chapter 8: From Thatcher to Blair: The Eighties and Nineties

1 David Docherty, David Morrison and Michael Tracey, *The Last Picture Show?: Britain's Changing Film Audiences* (London: BFI Publishing, 1987), pp. 4, 29.
2 Penelope Houston, 'New Man at the NFFC', *Sight and Sound*, Spring 1979, pp. 70–73.
3 Ros Cranston, 'Ken Loach (1936–)' in *Black Jack* DVD liner notes (London: BFI, 2010), pp. 10–12.
4 Tim Pulleine, 'Black Jack', *Monthly Film Bulletin*, April 1980, pp. 65–66.
5 David Robinson, 'An Awesome Landscape of Distrust', *The Times*, 22 February 1980, p. 9.
6 David Wilson, 'Black Jack', *Sight and Sound*, Spring 1980, pp. 126–27.
7 Ibid.
8 Robert Sellers, *Very Naughty Boys: The Amazing True Story of HandMade Films* (London: Metro, 2003).
9 Watts, 'Michael Watts on *Time Bandits*'.
10 Ruth Inglis, 'Stand by for a Spot of That Zany Python Magic', *The Daily Express*, 26 June 1981, p. 26.
11 David Sterritt, 'Laughs and Deep Themes' in David Sterritt and Lucille Rhodes, eds, *Terry Gilliam: Interviews* (Mississippi: University Press of Mississippi, 2004), pp. 16–19.
12 Sellers, *Very Naughty Boys*.
13 Sterritt, 'Laughs and Deep Themes'.
14 Sellers, *Very Naughty Boys*.
15 Alan Brien, 'The Corrupt Charm of the Bourgeoisie', *The Sunday Times*, 19 July 1981, p. 40.
16 Philip French, 'The Ferocious Five', *The Observer*, 19 July 1981, p. 30.
17 'Tails of the Unexpected', *The Guardian*, 4 August 1988, p. 21.
18 Ibid.
19 Ibid.

Notes to pages 210–220

20 Allan Scott, 'The Witch Report', *The Guardian*, 7 June 1990, p. 25.

21 Tom Milne, 'The Witches', *Monthly Film Bulletin*, May 1990, pp. 146–47.

22 Marie Beardmore, *John Coates: The Man Who Built the Snowman* (New Barnet: John Libbey, 2012), pp. 83–84.

23 Jill McGreal, 'TVC, 1957–1997', *AWN.com*, vol. 1, no. 4. <http://www.awn.com/mag/issue1.4/articles/mcgreal1.4.html> [accessed 10/09/2015.]

24 Ibid.

25 Beardmore, *John Coates*, p. 87.

26 'On the Box', *The Guardian*, 15 December 1982, p. 10.

27 Benjamin Secher, 'Raymond Briggs: "I Don't Believe in Happy Endings"', *The Telegraph*, 24 December 2007, p. 24.

28 Charlotte Rastan, 'Psst! Wanna Make Movies?', *The Guardian*, 29 April 1987, p. 11.

29 Kathie Griffiths, 'Young Movie Makers', *The Sunday Times*, 10 January 1982, pp. 48–49.

30 Kim Newman, 'Daemon', *Monthly Film Bulletin*, August 1986, pp. 233–34; Kim Newman, 'Daemon (1985)', *The Encyclopaedia of Fantastic Film and Television*. <http://eofftv.com/kim_newman_archive/d/daemon_review.htm> [accessed 27/11/2014].

31 'X Films', *The Daily Express*, 10 December 1981, p. 17.

32 Gareth Parry, ' "Nearly Half" Children See Video Nasties', *The Guardian*, 8 March 1984, p. 4.

33 Ibid.

34 See, for instance, Philip French, 'Unshaken Again', *The Observer*, 16 June 1985, p. 19.

35 Farrar Anwar, 'Hard Road', *Monthly Film Bulletin*, October 1989, p. 302.

36 Ibid.

37 Geoff Brown, 'The Custard Boys', *Monthly Film Bulletin*, April 1980, p. 67.

38 Derek Malcolm, 'The Family at War', *The Guardian*, 27 July 1989, p. 21.

39 Philip French, 'Prisoners of Pretention', *The Observer*, 30 July 1989, p. 42.

40 Lindsay Mackie, 'Mr Big Turns Bad for the Boss', *The Guardian*, 26 July 1989, p. 20.

41 Nicholas de Jong, 'TV "Averts British Film Collapse"', *The Guardian*, 11 September 1990, p. 5.

42 Martin Linton, 'Camera, Lights, Inaction', *The Guardian*, 15 August 1992, p. 4.

43 Ibid.

44 Dan Glaister, 'Poor Distribution Deals Undermine British Film Boom', *The Guardian*, 15 May 1998, p. 9.

45 Ibid.

46 Sheila Johnston, 'Small But Perfectly Marketed', *The Times*, 3 December 1997, p. 35.

286

Notes to pages 221–231

47 Chris Blackhurst, 'Mr Bean Turns the Handle of Money-Making Machine', *The Independent*, 3 August 1997, p. 3.
48 Alex Brummer, 'Mr Bean: The Ultimate Boss, Say Japan's Civil Servants', *The Guardian*, 22 June 1998, p. 14.
49 Richard Brooks, 'Cool Britain Flops on the World Stage', *The Sunday Times*, 21 November 1999, p. 7.
50 Adam Sweeting, 'Has Bean, Will Travel', *The Guardian*, 21 July 1997, p. B6.
51 Blackhurst, 'Mr Bean Turns the Handle of Money-Making Machine'.
52 Dominic Murphy, 'Model Entertainer', *The Sunday Times*, 24 March 1991, p. 7.
53 Philip French, 'Wallace and Gromit in "A Close Shave"', *The Observer*, 17 December 1995, p. 182; Lynne Truss, 'Eeyore, Frank and Gromit, The Three Kings', *The Times*, 26 December 1995, p. 35.
54 Matthew Gwyther, 'Will Gromit Ever Be a Hollywood Puppet?', *The Sunday Times*, 17 December 1995, pp. 14–15.
55 Ibid.
56 Ibid.
57 Ibid.
58 Louise Jones, 'Gromit's Creators Mould a Deal with Spielberg', *The Daily Mail*, 29 October 1999, p. 39.
59 Sarah Boseley, 'New Grade for Mature Young at the Cinema', *The Guardian*, 29 July 1989, p. 6.
60 'Jurassic Park to Carry Special Warning', *The London Evening Standard*, 21 June 1993, p. 15.
61 Andrew Culf, '181,000 Children Saw Horror Film', *The Guardian*, 15 December 1993, p. 2.
62 Andrew Culf, 'Children's Diet of 18-Rated Films', *The Guardian*, 13 December 1996, p. 6.
63 Richard Brooks, 'Sex Films "Damaging to Adults"', *The Observer*, 10 January 1999, p. 5.
64 Docherty, Morrison and Tracey, *The Last Picture Show?*, p. 59.
65 Ian Katz, 'I've Got You, Babe, All to Myself', *The Guardian*, 15 February 1996, p. A10.

Chapter 9: Exporting Englishness

1 Joanne O'Connor, 'Wizard! Harry Saves Tour Industry', *The Observer*, 27 April 2003, p. E20; 'Wallace and Gromit in Tourism Campaign', *The Glasgow Herald*, 9 May 2013, p. 3.
2 'A Future for British Film: It Begins with the Audience…,' Film Policy Review Panel Report (London: Department for Culture, Media and Sport, 2012), p. 39.
3 Ibid.

Notes to pages 233–248

4 Helen O'Hara, 'Christopher Columbus Remembers Harry Potter', *Empire Online*. <http://www.empireonline.com/interviews/interview.asp?IID=1310> [accessed 20/10/2014].

5 Nicole Lampert, 'Sex, Drugs and Pottermania', *The Daily Mail*, 10 July 2009, unpaginated.

6 Fran Pheasant-Kelly, 'Dark Films for Dark Times: Spectacle, Reception and the Textual Resonances of the Contemporary Hollywood Fantasy Film' in Noel Brown and Bruce Babington, eds, *Family Films in Global Cinema: The World Beyond Disney* (London and New York: I.B.Tauris, 2015), pp. 239–55.

7 David Gritten, 'Film on Friday', *The Daily Telegraph*, 28 October 2005, p. 27.

8 Will Lawrence, 'Sex, Potions and Rock 'n' Roll', *The Daily Telegraph*, 3 July 2009, p. 29.

9 Pheasant-Kelly, 'Dark Films for Dark Times'.

10 Dave McNary, 'Fantasy World at O'Seas Wickets', *Variety*, 10 March 2008, p. 8.

11 Ryan Gilbey, 'Ten Years of Making Harry Potter Films, by Cast and Crew', *The Guardian*, 7 July 2011, unpaginated.

12 Paul McCann, 'Chicken Protest Run Out', *The Times*, 6 July 2000, p. 13.

13 Grace Bradbury, 'A Feather in Britain's Cap', *The Times*, 19 June 2000, unpaginated.

14 Cosmo Landesman, 'The Bantam Menace', *The Sunday Times*, 2 July 2000, p. 8.

15 Philip French, 'We'll Meet a Hen ...', *The Observer*, 2 July 2000, p. E11.

16 Mike Szymanski, 'Helena Bonham Carter Shows Off Her Acting Choppers for Director Nick Park in Wallace and Gromit', *Sci Fi Weekly*, 10 October 2005. <https://archive.is/soOP4> [accessed 30/9/2015].

17 Nigel Farndale, 'Wallace and Gromit: One Man and His Dog', *The Telegraph*, 18 December 2008, unpaginated.

18 Mike Wade, 'End is Nigh for Wallace and Gromit', *The Times*, 16 May 2014, p. 3.

19 Dan Sabbagh, 'Wallace & Gromit Film is a DreamWorks Loser', *The Times*, 11 March 2006, p. 64.

20 Tim Teeman, 'They Broke the Mould', *The Times*, 1 February 2007, p. 2.

21 Chris Tookey, 'Show Me the Bunny', *The Daily Mail*, 14 October 2005, unpaginated.

22 Peter Bradshaw, 'Flushed Away', *The Guardian*, 1 December 2006, p. 8; Wendy Ide, 'Flushed Away', *The Times*, 30 November 2006, p. 17.

23 Todd McCarthy, 'Flushed Away', *Variety*, 16 October 2006, p. 24.

24 Laura M. Holson, 'Is Th-Th-That All, Folks', *The New York Times*, 3 October 2006, p. C1.

25 Rebecca O'Connor, 'Aardman Refuses to Drop British Accent to make it in Movies', *The Times*, 3 April 2007, p. 43.

26 'Arthur Christmas', *Box Office Mojo*. <http://www.boxofficemojo.com/movies/?id=arthurchristmas.htm> [accessed 30/11/2015]; 'The Pirates! Band of Misfits', *Box Office Mojo*. <http://www.boxofficemojo.com/movies/?id=pirates12.htm> [accessed 30/11/2015].

288

Notes to pages 250–267

27 Peter Bradshaw, 'The Pirates! In an Adventure with Scientists', *The Guardian*, 29 March 2012, p. 15.

28 Matthew Goodman, 'Animated Accounts', *The Sunday Times*, 23 October 2011, p. 2.

29 Nicholas Barber, 'This Santa Can Find Everything in His Sack – Except a Decent Storyline', *The Independent*, 13 November 2011, p. 62.

30 Angelique Chrisafis, 'UK Bids to be Player in Films for Children', *The Guardian*, 11 October 2003, p. 7.

31 Amanda Craig, 'Hollywood-Style Endings for Some', *The Times*, 5 November 2005, p. 17.

32 Kevin Maher, 'The New Richard Curtis?', *The Times*, 21 November 2009, p. 5.

33 Arthur Marwick, *British Society Since 1945* (London: Penguin, 2003), p. 434.

34 Andrew Higson, *Waving the Flag: Constructing a Nation Cinema in Britain* (Oxford: Oxford University Press, 1995), p. 279.

Conclusion

1 Rick Altman, 'A Semantic/Syntactic Approach to Film Genre' in Barry Keith Grant, ed., *Film Genre Reader III* (Austin, Texas: University of Texas Press, 2003), pp. 27–41 (p. 31).

2 Ibid., pp. 31–32.

3 J. P. Mayer, *Sociology of Film* (London: Faber and Faber, 1946), p. 54.

4 'Best 100 British Films – Full List', *BBC News*, 23 September 1999. <http://news.bbc.co.uk/1/hi/entertainment/455170.stm> [accessed 24/11/2015].

5 'Time Out's 100 Best British Films', *Time Out*, February 2011. <http://www.time-out.com/london/film/time-outs-100-best-british-films> [accessed 24/11/2015].

6 Terry Staples, *All Pals Together: The Story of Children's Cinema* (Edinburgh: Edinburgh University Press, 1997), pp. 195–96.

7 Elizabeth Grice, 'The Timely Doctor Who Saves Family Audience', *The Daily Telegraph*, 21 May 2005, p. 9.

8 Sonia Livingstone, 'From Family Television to Bedroom Culture: Young People's Media at Home' in E. Devereux, ed., *Media Studies: Key issues and Debates* (London: Sage, 2007), pp. 302–21.

9 Ibid., p. 2.

10 Geoff Marsh, 'Now We're Harrying to the Movies', *The Daily Express*, 8 December 2001, p. 29.

11 Hugh Davies, 'Children's Films Help to Break Box-Office Record', *The Daily Telegraph*, 26 November 2005, p. 13.

12 Maev Kennedy, 'Blyton Gang Loses out to Harry Potter's Famous Five', *The Guardian*, 3 November 2001, p. 13; Rebecca Allison, 'Storytime Back with Kid-ult Books', *The Guardian*, 26 July 2002, p. 9.

Select Filmography

Adventures of Hal 5, The. Dir. Don Sharp. Children's Film Foundation: 1958.

Alice in Wonderland. Dir. Cecil Hepworth. Hepworth: 1903.

Alice's Adventures in Wonderland. Dir. William Sterling. Josef Shaftel Productions: 1972.

Animal Farm. Dirs. John Halas and Joy Batchelor. Associated British-Pathé: 1954.

Arthur Christmas. Dir. Sarah Smith. Aardman: 2011.

Battle for Billy's Pond, The. Dir. Harley Cokliss. Children's Film Foundation: 1976.

Bean. Dir. Mel Smith. Working Title: 1997.

Bedknobs and Broomsticks. Dir. Robert Stevenson. Disney: 1971.

Belles of St. Trinian's, The. Dir. Frank Launder. London Films: 1954.

Belstone Fox, The. Dir. James Hill. Rank: 1973.

Black Jack. Dir. Ken Loach. Kestrel Films: 1979.

Born Free. Dir. James Hill. Columbia: 1966.

Boy Who Turned Yellow, The. Dir. Michael Powell. Children's Film Foundation: 1972.

Boys will be Boys. Dir. William Beaudine. Gainsborough: 1935.

Bugsy Malone. Dir. Alan Parker. Goodtimes Enterprises: 1976.

Bush Christmas. Dir. Ralph Smart. Children's Entertainment Films: 1947.

Candleshoe. Dir. Norman Tokar. Disney: 1977.

Chicken Run. Dirs. Nick Park and Peter Lord. Aardman: 2000.

Chitty Chitty Bang Bang. Dir. Ken Hughes. Warfield Productions: 1968.

Close Shave, A. Dir. Nick Park. Aardman: 1995.

Cup Fever. Dir. David Bracknell. Children's Film Foundation: 1965.

Curse of the Were-Rabbit, The. Dirs. Nick Park and Steve Box. Aardman: 2005.

Custard Boys, The. Dir. Colin Finbow. Children's Film Unit: 1979.

Daemon. Dir. Colin Finbow. Children's Film Unit: 1985.

Daleks – Invasion Earth 2150 A.D. Dir. Gordon Flemyng. AARU Productions: 1966.

Danny, the Champion of the World. Dir. Gavin Millar. Thames Television: 1989.

Dick Barton at Bay. Dir. Godfrey Grayson. Hammer: 1950.

Dick Barton: Special Agent. Dir. Alfred J. Goulding. Hammer: 1948.

Dick Barton Strikes Back. Dir. Godfrey Grayson. Hammer: 1949.

Digby, the Biggest Dog in the World. Dir. Joseph McGrath. Walter Shenson Films: 1973.

Dr. Who and the Daleks. Dir. Gordon Flemyng. AARU Productions: 1965.

Elephant Boy. Dirs. Robert Flaherty and Zoltan Korda. London Films: 1937.

Select Filmography

Emil and the Detectives. Dir. Milton Rosmer. Richard Wainwright Pictures: 1935.

Father's Doing Fine. Dir. Henry Cass. Associated British: 1952.

Fighting Prince of Donegal, The. Dir. Michael O'Herlihy. Disney: 1966.

Flushed Away. Dirs. Sam Fell and David Bowers. Aardman: 2006.

Ghost of St. Michael's, The. Dir. Marcel Varnel. Ealing: 1941.

Glitterball, The. Dir. Harley Cokliss. Children's Film Foundation: 1977.

Go Kart Go. Dir. Jan Darnley-Smith. Children's Film Foundation: 1964.

Good Morning, Boys. Dir. Marcel Varnel. Gainsborough: 1937.

Grand Day Out, A. Dir. Nick Park. Aardman: 1989.

Greyfriars Bobby. Dir. Don Chaffey. Disney: 1961.

Happiest Days of Your Life, The. Dir. Frank Launder. Individual Pictures: 1950.

Hard Day's Night, A. Dir. Richard Lester. United Artists: 1964.

Harry Potter and the Chamber of Secrets. Dir. Chris Columbus: Warner Bros.: 2002.

Harry Potter and the Deathly Hallows – Part 1. Dir. David Yates. Warner Bros.: 2010.

Harry Potter and the Deathly Hallows – Part 2. Dir. David Yates. Warner Bros.: 2011.

Harry Potter and the Goblet of Fire. Dir. Mike Newell. Warner Bros.: 2005.

Harry Potter and the Half-Blood Prince. Dir. David Yates. Warner Bros.: 2009.

Harry Potter and the Order of the Phoenix. Dir. David Yates. Warner Bros.: 2007.

Harry Potter and the Philosopher's Stone. Dir. Chris Columbus. Warner Bros.: 2001.

Harry Potter and the Prisoner of Azkaban. Dir. Alfonso Cuarón. Warner Bros.: 2004.

Haunters of the Deep. Dir. Andrew Bogle. Children's Film Foundation: 1984.

Horrid Henry: The Movie. Dir. Nick Moore. Vertigo Films: 2011.

Hue and Cry. Dir. Charles Crichton. Ealing: 1947.

Innocent Sinners. Dir. Philip Leacock. Rank: 1958.

Jason and the Argonauts. Dir. John Gilling. Columbia: 1963.

Just William. Dir. Graham Cutts. Associated British: 1940.

Just William's Luck. Dir. Val Guest. Alliance: 1948.

Kes. Dir Ken Loach. Woodfall Film: 1969.

Kidnapped. Dir. Robert Stevenson. Disney: 1960.

Kidnappers, The. Dir. Philip Leacock. Group Film Productions: 1953.

Land that Time Forgot, The. Dir. Kevin Connor. Amicus: 1975.

Magic Roundabout, The. Dir. Dave Borthwick et al. Pathé: 2005.

Mary Poppins. Dir. Robert Stevenson. Disney: 1964.

Mr Drake's Duck. Dir. Val Guest. Douglas Fairbanks Productions: 1951.

Nanny McPhee. Dir. Kirk Jones. Universal: 2005.

Nativity! Dir. Debbie Isitt. E1 Entertainment: 2009.

No Kidding. Dir. Gerald Thomas. Peter Rogers Productions: 1961.

No Limit. Dir. Monty Banks. Associated Talking Pictures: 1935.

Off the Dole. Dir. Arthur Mertz. Mancunian Film: 1935.

Oh, Mr Porter! Dir. Marcel Varnel, 1937. Gainsborough: 1937.

Old Mother Riley in Paris. Dir. Oswald Mitchell. Butcher's Film Service: 1938.

Select Filmography

Old Mother Riley Meets the Vampire. Dir. John Gilling. Renown: 1952.

Oliver! Dir. Carol Reed. Romulus Films: 1968.

On the Run. Dir. Pat Jackson. Children's Film Foundation: 1968.

One of Our Dinosaurs is Missing. Dir. Robert Stevenson. Disney: 1975.

Paddington. Dir. Paul King. Studio Canal: 2014.

Pirates! In an Adventure with Scientists!, The. Dir. Peter Lord. Aardman: 2012.

Railway Children, The. Dir. Lionel Jeffries. EMI: 1970.

Raising a Riot. Dir. Wendy Toye. London Films: 1955.

Rescued by Rover. Dir. Cecil Hepworth. Hepworth: 1905.

Ring of Bright Water. Dir. Jack Couffer. Rank: 1969.

Rob Roy, The Highland Rogue. Dir. Harold French. Disney: 1953.

Runaway Railway. Dir. Jan Darnley-Smith. Children's Film Foundation: 1965.

Run Wild, Run Free. Dir. Richard Sarafian. Irving Allen Productions: 1969.

Sammy's Super T-Shirt. Dir. Jeremy Summers. Children's Film Foundation: 1978.

Scrooge. Dir. Brian Desmond Hurst. Renown: 1951.

Secret Garden, The. Dir. Agnieszka Holland. Warner Bros.: 1993.

Shaun the Sheep Movie. Dirs. Richard Starzak and Mark Burton. Aardman: 2015.

Smiley. Dir. Anthony Kimmins. London Films: 1956.

Snowman, The. Dir. Dianne Jackson. TVC: 1982.

Spanish Gardener, The. Dir. Philip Leacock. Rank: 1956.

Story of Robin Hood and His Merrie Men, The. Dir. Ken Annakin. Disney: 1952.

Swallows and Amazons. Dir. Claude Whatham. Anglo-EMI: 1974.

Sword and the Rose, The. Dir. Ken Annakin. Disney: 1953.

Tales of Beatrix Potter, The. Dir. Reginald Mills. EMI: 1971.

Tarka the Otter. Dir. David Cobham. Tor Films Limited: 1979.

Thief of Bagdad, The. Dir. Michael Powell et al. London Films: 1940.

Time Bandits. Dir. Terry Gilliam. HandMade Films: 1981.

Tom Brown's Schooldays. Dir. Gordon Parry. Talisman Productions: 1951.

Treasure Island. Dir. Byron Haskin. Disney: 1950.

Trouble in Store. Dir. John Paddy Carstairs. Two Cities Films: 1953.

Vice Versa. Dir. Peter Ustinov. Two Cities Films: 1948.

Watership Down. Dir. Martin Rosen. Cinema International: 1978.

When Dinosaurs Ruled the Earth. Dir. Val Guest. Hammer: 1970.

When the Wind Blows. Dir. Jimmy Murakami. TVC: 1986.

Whistle Down the Wind. Dir. Bryan Forbes. Allied Films: 1961.

William Comes to Town. Dir. Val Guest. Diadem Films: 1949.

Witches, The. Dir. Nicholas Roeg. Warner Bros.: 1990.

Wrong Trousers, The. Dir. Nick Park. Aardman: 1993.

Yellow Submarine. Dir. George Dunning. Apple Corps: 1968.

Select Bibliography

Agajanian, Rowana. "'Just for Kids?'": Saturday Morning Cinema and Britain's Children's Film Foundation in the 1960s', *Historical Journal of Film, Radio and Television*, vol. 18, no. 3 (1998), pp. 395–409.

An Investigation Conducted into the Influence of the Film on School Children and Adolescents in the City (Edinburgh: Edinburgh Cinema Enquiry, 1933).

Barclay, J. B. *Children's Film Tastes* (Edinburgh: Scottish Education Film Association, 1956).

Bauchard, Philippe. *The Child Audience: A Report on Press, Film and Radio for Children* (Paris: Unesco, 1952).

Bazalgette, Cary and Terry Staples. 'Unshrinking the Kids: Children's Cinema and the Family Film' in Cary Bazalgette and David Buckingham, eds, *In Front of the Children* (London: BFI Publishing, 1995), pp. 92–108.

Brown, Noel. *The Hollywood Family Film: A History, from Shirley Temple to Harry Potter* (London and New York: I.B.Tauris, 2012).

——. 'The "Family" Film, and the Tensions between Popular and Academic Interpretations of Genre', *Trespassing Journal: An Online Journal of Trespassing Art, Science and Philosophy*, no. 2 (2013), pp. 22–35.

——. '"Family" Entertainment and Contemporary Hollywood Cinema', *Scope: An Online Journal of Film and Television Studies*, no. 25 (2013).

——. '"A New Movie-Going Public": 1930s Hollywood and the Emergence of the "Family" Film', *The Historical Journal of Film, Radio and Television*, vol. 33, no. 1 (2013), pp. 1–23.

——. '*The Railway Children* and Other Stories: Lionel Jeffries and British Family Films in the 1970s' in Noel Brown and Bruce Babington, eds, *Family Films in Global Cinema: The World Beyond Disney* (London and New York: I.B.Tauris, 2015), pp. 120–36.

——. 'The Feel-Good Film: A Case Study in Contemporary Genre Classification', *Quarterly Review of Film and Video*, vol. 32 (3), 2015, pp. 269–86.

——. *Contemporary Hollywood Animation* (Edinburgh: Edinburgh University Press, forthcoming).

Brown, Noel and Bruce Babington, eds, *Family Films in Global Cinema: The World Beyond Disney* (London and New York: I.B.Tauris, 2015).

Select Bibliography

——. 'Introduction: Children's Films and Family Films' in Noel Brown and Bruce Babington, eds, *Family Films in Global Cinema: The World Beyond Disney* (London and New York: I.B.Tauris, 2015), pp. 1–16.

Buckingham, David et al. *Children's Television in Britain: History, Discourse and Policy* (London: BFI Publishing, 1999).

Children and the Cinema (Middlesbrough: Head Teachers' Association, 1946).

Docherty, David, David Morrison and Michael Tracey. *The Last Picture Show: Britain's Changing Film Audience* (London: BFI Publishing, 1987).

Field, Mary. *Good Company: The Story of the Children's Entertainment Film Movement in Great Britain – 1943-1950* (London: Longmans Green and Co., 1952).

——. *Children and Films: A Study of Boys and Girls in the Cinema* (Dunfermline: Carnegie United Kingdom Trust, 1954).

——. 'Children's Taste in Films', *The Quarterly of Film, Radio and Television*, vol. 11, no. 1 (1956), pp. 14–23.

Ford, Richard. *Children in the Cinema* (London: George Allen & Unwin, 1939).

Going to the Cinema on a Saturday Morning – A Further Report on Wickham Common Junior School, Mass Observation, July 1947.

Kesterton, Barbara. 'The Social and Emotional Effects of the Recreational Film on Adolescents of Thirteen and Fourteen Years of Age in the West Bromwich Area'. Unpublished PhD thesis (University of Birmingham, 1948).

Krämer, Peter. '"The Best Disney Film Disney Never Made": Children's Films and The Family Audience in American Cinema since the 1960s' in Steve Neale, ed., *Genre and Contemporary Hollywood* (London: BFI Publishing, 2002), pp. 185–200.

Kuhn, Annette. *An Everyday Magic: Cinema and Cultural Memory* (London and New York: I.B.Tauris, 2002).

——. 'Children, "Horrific" Films', and Censorship in 1930s Britain', *The Historical Journal of Film, Radio and Television*, vol. 22, no. 2 (2002), pp. 197–202.

Kynaston, David. *Family Britain, 1951-57* (London: Bloomsbury, 2009).

Low, Rachael. *The History of the British Film 1914-1918* (London and New York: Routledge, 1997 [1950]).

Low, Rachael with Roger Manvell. *The History of the British Film 1896-1906* (London and New York: Routledge, 1997 [1948]).

McKernan, Luke. '"Only the Screen was Silent…": Memories of Children's Cinema-Going in London before the First World War', *Film Studies*, no. 10 (Spring 2007), pp. 1–20.

Macnab, Geoffrey. *J. Arthur Rank and the British Film Industry* (London and New York: Routledge, 1993).

Mayer, J. P. *Sociology of Film* (London: Faber and Faber, 1946).

Select Bibliography

Miller, Emanuel. *Report on the Bernstein Children's Film Questionnaire* (London: Granada, 1947).

Parnaby, Mary C. and Maurice T. Woodhouse, *Children's Cinema Clubs: Report* (London: British Film Institute, 1947).

Rapoport, Robert N. et al., eds, *Families in Britain* (London: Routledge and Kegan Paul, 1982).

Richards, Jeffrey. *The Age of the Dream Palace* (London and New York: I.B.Tauris, 2010 [1984]).

Richards, Jeffrey and James C. Robertson. 'British Film Censorship' in Robert Murphy, ed., *The British Cinema Book* (London: BFI Publishing, 2009), pp. 67–77.

Saturday Morning Cinema: Twenty-Five years of Films for Children (London: Children's Film Foundation, Ltd., 1969).

Smith, Sarah J. *Children, Cinema and Censorship: From Dracula to the Dead End Kids* (London and New York: I.B.Tauris, 2005).

Staples, Terry. *All Pals Together: The Story of Children's Cinema* (Edinburgh: Edinburgh University Press, 1997).

Storck, Henri. *The Entertainment Film for Juvenile Audiences* (Paris: Unesco, 1950).

The Cinema: Its Present Position and Future Possibilities – Being the Report and Chief Evidence Taken by the Cinema Commission of Inquiry Instituted by the National Council of Public Morals (London: Williams and Norgate, 1917).

Wheare, K. C. *Report of the Committee on Children and the Cinema* (London: H. M. Stationary Office, 1950).

Index

101 Dalmatians (1961) 163
5,000 Fingers of Dr T, The 186
9/11 234, 238, 240

Aardman 9, 204, 212, 222–29, 231,
    244–51, 252, 258,
    261, 265, 268
Abbott and Costello 94
Abbott and Costello Meet
    Frankenstein 74
ABC (cinema chain) 83, 89
ABC Minors Club 83
ABPC *see* Associated British Picture
    Corporation
Adventures of Deadwood Dick, The 14
Adventures of Hal 5, The 92
Adventures of Huckleberry Finn, The 37
Ah, Wilderness! 49
AIP (film studio) 201
Alice in Wonderland (1903) 11
Alice in Wonderland (1951) 163
Alice's Adventures in Wonderland
    (1972) 185, 186–87
Allen of Hurtwood, Lady 84–85
Amazing Mr Blunden, The 184
Amicus 201
An Alligator Named Daisy 107
An Angel for May 252
An Elephant Called Slowly 168
Andrews, Julie 154, 180
Andy Hardy (series) 41, 76
Andy Pandy 185

Animal Farm (1954) 123–26, 198, 200,
    262, 263
animal film (genre) 152–53,
    167–68, 188–200, 258
Arabian Adventure 201
Aristotle 156
Arthur Christmas 244, 248,
    249, 251
As You Like It 143
Ascot, Hazel 36, 38, 67, 273
Askey, Arthur 69, 70, 77, 78
Associated British Picture Corporation
    (ABPC) 180
At the Earth's Core 201
Atkinson, Rowan 221
Attlee, Clement 107
Austin Powers
    (series) 221

Babe 244
Back to the Future 207
Balcon, Sir Michael 166
Balfour, Betty 60
Baron, David 243
Bart, Lionel 173, 174, 175
Bartholomew, Freddie 174
Battle for Billy's Pond, The 101–2,
    103
Baxter, John 1, 35, 73
Baxter! 184, 186
BBC *see* British Broadcasting
    Corporation

Index

BBFC *see* British Board of Film Classification

Bean 220–22

Beatles (film series) 164, 168–72

Bedknobs and Broomsticks 137, 138, 151, 157–59

Bell, Oscar 83

Bell-Bottom George 71–72

Belles of St. Trinian's, The 74, 107, 112–13

Belstone Fox, The 188, 189, 192, 193–95, 262

Ben-Hur 165

Bend It Like Beckham 260

Bernstein, Sidney 27, 82, 89

BFG, The (1989) 211

BFI *see* British Film Institute

Birkenhead Vigilance Committee (1931) 29

Birmingham Cinema Enquiry Committee (1931) 29

Black Beauty (1907) 14

Black Beauty (1971) 188

Black Beauty (1994) 228

Black Jack 204–6, 207, 211

Blair, Tony 221

Blue Murder at St. Trinian's 122

Blyton, Enid 91

Booth, James 57

Boots! Boots! 61

Born Free 2, 167, 168, 188–90

Borrowers, The (1997) 220

Boy and the Bridge, The 35

Boy in the Striped Pyjamas, The 268

Boy Who Stole a Million, The 35

Boy Who Turned Yellow, The 2, 99–101, 262, 264

Boys will be Boys 60, 64–65

Brazil 207, 209

Briggs, Raymond 212–13, 262

Briggs Family, The 49

British Board of Film Classification (BBFC) 6, 21–22, 25, 28–29, 81, 127, 128, 179, 198–99, 216, 228, 259

British Broadcasting Corporation (BBC) 51, 60, 85, 103, 104, 107, 227, 260

British Film Institute (BFI) 6, 82–83, 85, 184, 231, 263

British Film Production Fund *see* Eady Levy

British Instructional Films 84

British Lion (studio) 166

Brown, Joe E. 82

Bugsy Malone 2, 119, 186, 187–88, 205, 211, 262

Burke, Tim 243

Bush Christmas 86, 264

Call Me Bwana 167

Call of the Wild (1973) 188

Candleshoe 137, 138, 151, 159–62, 281

Captain Nemo and the Underwater City 168, 201

Captain Stirrick 214

Carroll, Lewis 171

Carry On (series) 77, 79, 121, 122, 164

Carry on Camping 122

Carry on Teacher 121

CEF *see* Children's Entertainment Films

censorship 6, 7, 21–22, 28–29, 165–66, 179–80, 198–99, 240–41, 259

'12' rating 228

'12A' rating 240, 243, 259

'18' rating 228

297

Index

censorship (*Cont*)
'A' rating 21, 25, 28–29, 30, 80–81, 131, 165–66, 199, 202, 259
'AA' rating 179–80
'H' rating 30, 126
'PG' rating 228, 243
'U' rating 21, 25, 29, 81, 165–66, 174, 198, 202, 216
'X' rating 99, 126–28, 130, 165–66, 179–80, 216
Central Intelligence Agency (CIA) 123–24
CFF *see* Children's Film Foundation
CFU *see* Children's Film Unit
Challenge for Robin Hood, A 167
Channel 4, 204, 211–14
Chaplin, Charlie 15, 76, 94, 221
Chicken Run 2, 153, 244–46
'child films' 268
Child and the Killer, The 35
Child Welfare Commission (League of Nations) 82
Child's Play 3 228
children
  as audiences 4–5, 17–19, 108, 165
  as performers 272–73
Children's Act (1908), The 20
Children's Entertainment Films (CEF) 1, 6, 8, 80, 85–88, 90, 104
children's film (genre) 2–3, 5–8, 90–91, 201–2, 207–10, 241–43, 257–60
Children's Film Department (CFD) 84–85, 88
Children's Film and Television Foundation (CFTF) *see* Children's Film Foundation
children's film festivals 6
Children's Film Foundation (CFF) 1, 2, 5, 6, 7, 8, 35, 44, 55, 56,

80–105, 106, 128, 129, 133, 182, 183, 204, 214–16, 252, 258, 261, 264, 265
  attitude to authority 90–91, 96–97, 101, 102
  'New Look' programme 94
  representation of adults 90–92, 96–97
  representation of children 91–92, 95–98
Children's Film Society, India (CFSI) 104
Children's Film Unit (CFU) 204, 213–17, 261
children's matinees 12, 19–21, 26, 27, 59, 81–83, 89–90, 93, 99, 100, 201
Chips 34
Chitty Chitty Bang Bang 2, 167, 173, 175–79, 180, 261
Christmas Carol, A (1843) 151
Cinderella (1899) 10
Cinderella (1912) 14
Cinderella (1979) 211
Cinderella and the Fairy Godmother (1898) 11
Cinema: Its Present Position and Future Possibilities, The 17–19, 23–24
Cinematograph Act 20, 21
Cinematograph Exhibitors' Association of Great Britain and Ireland (CEA) 23, 30
Clash of the Titans 201
class 90, 93, 94, 154, 182–83, 233–34, 240
Close Encounters of the Third Kind 162, 202
Close Shave, A 223, 226–27
Coates, John 212
Columbus, Chris 233

298

Index

Confessions series 121

Connor, Kevin 201, 202

Coogan, Jackie 174

Cosgrove Hall 211

Crazy Gang, The 57

Creature Comforts 223

Creatures the World Forgot 201

Crockett, Davy 150

Crompton, Richmal 50–51

Cromwell 185

Cup Fever 96–97, 101

Curse of Frankenstein, The 131

Custard Boys, The 213, 214, 217

Daemon 214–16

Dahl, Roald 209, 210, 217

Daleks – Invasion Earth 2150 A.D.
185, 188

Disney (company) 6, 46, 114–15,
124–25, 126, 137–63, 195, 198,
200, 219, 258, 263, 281

Disney, Walt 5, 41, 139, 140, 146, 148,
149–50, 200

Divided Heart, The 106

Doctor in the House 74

Doctor in the House (series) 77

Doctor Who 201, 216, 225, 266

Dog and the Diamonds, The 90

Doll's Revenge, The 14

Dracula (1931) 30

Dracula (1958) 131

Dr. Who and the Daleks 167, 201

DreamWorks 223, 227–28,
244, 246, 247–48

Duck Soup 75

Duel in the Sun 127

Digby, the Biggest Dog in the World
167, 201

Danny, the Champion of the World
(1989) 217–19

Dark, John 201, 202

Dark Enemy 214

David Copperfield (1913) 15

David Copperfield (1970) 185

Davies, Russell T. 266

Davis, John 87, 99, 180

Dead End Kids 43

Death of a Salesman 127

Deutsch, Oscar 83

Devil Girl from Mars 130

Diamonds on Wheels 137

Dick Barton at Bay 130

Dick Barton – Special Agent (radio)
51, 129–30

Dick Barton: Special Agent
(film) 129–30

Dick Barton Strikes Back 130

Dickens, Charles 173–74, 185

Did'ums 14

Eady Levy 89, 104,
204

Ealing Studios 263

Early Bird, The 78–79

East of Eden 124

Easy Rider 179

Edelmann, Heinz 170

Edinburgh Cinema Enquiry
Committee (1933) 29

Educational Kinematograph
Association 23

Elephant Boy 34, 39

EMI Films 180, 184,
185, 201

Emil and the Detectives (1931), 31,
32–33, 42, 43, 45

Emil and the Detectives (1935) 7,
32–38, 40, 48, 49, 51, 69, 106, 266

299

Index

Emil and the Detectives (theatre) 34–35
Emily's Ghost 214
Escapade 54
Escape From the Dark 137
E.T. The Extra-Terrestrial 103, 162, 228
Evil Dead, The 216
Exorcist, The 216
Expresso Bongo 131

fairy tale (genre) 11
Fallen Idol, The 35, 182, 268
family audience 1, 8, 12, 16, 79,
    106–7, 127–29, 166–67,
    266–67
family film (genre) 3, 4, 5–8,
    241–43, 257–60
  happy ending, the 5, 48, 124,
    197–200, 209, 210,
    241, 251, 262
  in Hollywood 3, 70, 103, 178, 202,
    228–29, 243, 249–50
fantasy (genre) 11, 167–68,
    200–3, 242–43
Farr, William 82
Father Christmas 212
Father's Doing Fine 107, 115–16, 123
Ferman, James 228
Ferry across the Mersey 167
Field, Mary 84, 86, 89–91, 258
Fields, Gracie 59, 70, 78
Fighting Prince of Donegal, The 137,
    138, 143, 148–50
Finbow, Colin 213–14, 216
Finders Keepers 167
First Men in the Moon (1964) 167, 201
Five on a Treasure Island (1957) 91–92
Flaherty, Robert 39
Flushed Away 244, 247–48

Fool of the World and the Flying Ship,
    The 211
Forbes, Bryan 1, 180–81, 184, 185
Formby, George 4, 8, 57–58, 59, 61, 69,
    70, 71–72, 75, 76, 78, 187
Frankenstein (1931) 30
French Mistress, A 121
Freud, Sigmund 69
Friend or Foe 104
Front-Line Kids 34
Full Monty, The 220, 221

Gardener with Hose, or The
    Mischievous Boy 11
Garnett, Tony 205, 206
Gaumont (cinema chain) 83, 84,
    87, 88, 89
G-B Animation 88
Geddes, Henry 94, 99
Get Santa 231
Ghost of a Chance, A 101
Ghost of St. Michael's, The 66, 71
Ghost Train, The 71
Gilliam, Terry 1, 207–9
Glitterball, The 103
Go Kart Go 95, 98
Godfather, The 162
Golden Voyage of Sinbad, The 201
GoldenEye 221
Gone with the Wind 129
Good Morning, Boys 60, 66–67
Goodbye, Mr Chips (1969) 167
Goons, The 169
Goose Steps Out, The 71
Granada (cinema chain) 27, 83
Granadiers 83
Grand Day Out, A 223–25
Grand Escapade, The 34

300

Index

Grange Hill 104, 233
Granpa 212
Gravity 243
Great Escape, The 245
Great Expectations (1946) 122
Greyfriars Bobby 137, 138, 151–53
Guest, Val 1, 35, 50–51, 52
Guinea Pig, The 110

Halas and Batchelor 123–26, 211, 262
Hammer (studio) 51, 129–31
Handley, Tommy 60, 76
HandMade Films 207
Happiest Days of Your Life, The 107–8, 109, 110–12, 113, 115
Hard Day's Night, A 167, 168–69
Hard Road 216–17
Harris, S. W. 81, 82, 127
Harrison, George 207
Harry Potter
  book series 221, 230, 231
  film series 2, 6, 8, 9, 104, 153, 228–29, 230–44, 252, 258, 259, 261, 265, 266, 267, 268
  Harry Potter and the Chamber of Secrets 153, 236
  Harry Potter and the Deathly Hallows – Part 1 234, 239
  Harry Potter and the Deathly Hallows – Part 2 238–39, 243
  Harry Potter and the Goblet of Fire 236–37, 240
  Harry Potter and the Half-Blood Prince 234, 237–38
  Harry Potter and the Order of the Phoenix 234, 235, 238, 239–40
  Harry Potter and the Philosopher's Stone 153, 231, 235–36

Harryhausen, Ray 131, 201
Haunters of the Deep 104, 214–15
Hay, Will 8, 57–58, 59, 63–67, 73, 75, 77, 110
Hays, Will 28
Heidi (1880) 56
Hello, Dolly! 179
Help! 167, 169
Henson, Jim 209
Hepworth, Cecil 1, 11, 12–14, 15, 16, 152
Heyday Films 228–29, 231, 243–44, 268
High School Musical 255
Hitchcock, Alfred 126–27
Hoffman 185
Home, Anna 252
Hook 207
Horrid Henry: The Movie 231
Hue and Cry 1, 34, 35, 42–45, 46, 47, 48, 51, 54, 56, 69, 86, 108, 109, 111, 113, 263, 273, 274
Huggetts film series 49, 114
Hulbert, Jack 82
Hunger Games (film series) 243

Impossible Voyage, The (*Voyage à travers l'impossible*) 10
Indiana Jones (series) 200
Inn for Trouble 167
Innocent Sinners 35, 42, 45–48, 54
Innocents, The 268
It's Great to be Young! 129
It's That Man Again 60
Ivanhoe 122, 123

J. Arthur Rank Organisation (JARO) 83–88, 166, 180

301

Index

Jack's The Boy 60
Jackson, Dianne 212
Jackson, Pat 1, 95
James Bond (film series) 6, 164, 167, 175, 216, 221, 227
Jason and the Argonauts 167, 201
Jean's Plan 85
Jeffries, Lionel 180–84
Johnny on the Run 90
Jones, Buck 59, 82
Jules Verne's Rocket to the Moon 168, 201
Jungle Book, The (1942) 39
Jungle Book, The (1967) 163
Jurassic Park 228
Just William (1940) 34, 48, 49–50, 51
Just William (film series) 67, 106, 266
Just William's Luck 35, 48, 50–53, 56

Kamen, Kay 6
Katzenberg, Jeffrey 227–28, 246
Katzman, Sam 131
Kes 193, 268
Kid for Two Farthings, A 182, 268
Kidnapped (1960) 137, 138, 143, 146–47, 149, 150
Kidnappers, The 1, 35, 48, 54–56
'kidult' 69, 202, 210, 266, 267
Korda, Alexander 35, 39, 41, 42, 138, 258

La Ronde 127
Land that Time Forgot, The 201, 202
Langley, Noel 122–23
Langman, Terry 214
Lassie 152, 195
Laurel and Hardy 57, 59, 94
Leacock, Philip 1, 35, 54
Lean, David 140

Lear, Edward 171
Lee, Sir Sidney 23
Les Quatre cent coups 132
Let it Be 167
Lieutenant Rose (series) 14–15
Life With Father 154
Life With the Lyons 107, 114
Lion at World's End, The 188
Little Ballerina, The 85–86
Little Caesar 187
Little Women 29
Living Free 188
Lloyd, Harold 82
Loach, Ken 1, 205–6
London County Council Education Committee (1932) 29–30
Loneliness of the Long Distance Runner, The 131
Look Back in Anger 131
Lucan, Arthur 57–58, 70, 74, 75, 76, 77, 78
Lugosi, Bela 74
Lumière brothers 10, 11

McShane, Kitty 58, 68
Magic Roundabout, The (2005) 254
Magic Sword, The 11
Man Who Haunted Himself, The 185
Mandy 35, 106, 268
Manvell, Roger 89–90
Marx Brothers, The 75
Mary Poppins 137, 138, 151–58, 167, 252, 266
matinees *see* children's matinees
Matter of Loaf and Death, A 223
Mayer, J. P. 87, 88
Maynard, Ken 59
Meet Me in St. Louis 51, 116, 154

302

Index

Méliès, Georges 10, 11

Men of Sherwood Forest 130

Mickey Mouse Club 83

Midnight Cowboy 179

Midshipman Easy 82

Midsummer Night's Dream, A 143

Miller, Emanuel 82

Miller, Mandy 118–19

Miller, Max 57, 79

Million Dollar Duck, The 114–15

MirrorMask 254

Moffatt, Graham 64

Monster of Highgate Ponds, The 92

Monty Python 207

Mr Bean 220–21

Mr Drake's Duck 107, 114–15

Much too Shy 63

Muffin the Mule 185

Mummy, The (1959) 131

My Fair Lady (1964) 167

Mysterious Island (1961) 167, 201

Nanny McPhee 231, 252–54, 267

National Advisory Council (Children's Entertainment Films) 84–85, 88

National Council of Public Morals (NCPM) 17–19, 23–24

National Film Finance Corporation (NFFC) 164, 166, 204, 205

Nativity! 231, 254–55

Newell, Mike 1, 240

No Kidding 107, 120–21, 167

No Limit 62

Nothing Venture 35

Nyman, K. A. 82

O'Brien, Denis 207, 209

O'Connor, T. P. 21, 24

Odeon (cinema chain) 83, 84, 87, 88, 89

Off the Dole 60, 62–63

Oh, Mr Porter! 60, 63

Old Mac 168

Old Mother Riley 8, 58, 59, 61, 68–69, 70, 73–74

Old Mother Riley in Business 70

Old Mother Riley Joins Up 70

Old Mother Riley Meets the Vampire 60, 70, 73–74

Old Mother Riley, MP 70

Old Mother Riley in Paris 70

Old Mother Riley's Circus 60

Old Mother Riley's Ghosts 73

Old Mother Riley's New Venture 70

Old Yeller 152

Oliver Twist (1838) 173–74

Oliver Twist (1912) 15

Oliver Twist (1948) 122

Oliver! 2, 8, 153, 167, 173–75, 179, 185, 261, 263

Omen, The 216

On Moonlight Bay 49

On the Run 98

On the Waterfront 188

One of Our Dinosaurs is Missing 137

One Million Years B.C. 167, 201

One Way Pendulum 167

Orwell, George 123, 125

Our New Errand Boy 14

Paddington 2, 231, 244, 256, 262, 266, 267

Palin, Michael 207, 209

pantomime films 15–16

Paper Moon 162

303

Index

Park, Nick 222–23, 246, 247
Parker, Alan 1, 211
Pathé 254
Paul, R. W. 11
Peeping Tom 99
People that Time Forgot 201
Peter Pan (1953) 163
Pickford, Mary 15, 187
Pickwick Papers, The 122, 123
Pied Piper of Hamelin, The 211
Pirates! In an Adventure with Scientists!, The 244, 248, 249–51
Pixar (studio) 200
Plague Dogs, The 262
Plato 156
Poil de Carotte 48
PolyGram 220
Pop Gear 167
Powell, Michael 1, 99–100
Pressburger, Emeric 32, 99, 100
Prince and the Pauper, The 174
Prisoner of Zenda, The 122, 123
Production Code (Hollywood) 28–29, 30

Quatermass Xperiment, The 130
Quo Vadis 127

race 94, 98, 233–34, 240, 260
Radnitz, Robert B. 54
Railway Children, The 2, 4, 159, 180–84, 185, 186, 263, 264
Raising a Riot 107, 118–20
Rank, J. Arthur 1, 35, 80, 83–88
Rashomon 127
ratings, film *see* censorship
Red Balloon, The (*Le Ballon Rouge*) 48
Redford, George A. 21
Reed, Carol 1, 140, 173, 182, 268

Reed, John 124
Rescued by Rover 13–14
Richard, Cliff 131, 167
Rin Tin Tin 82, 152, 195
Ring of Bright Water 168, 188, 190–92, 262
River, The 48
Rob Roy, The Highland Rogue 137, 138, 143, 144–46, 149–50
Robin Hood (1973) 163
Rochemont, Louis de 123
Rock Around the Clock 131
Rock You Sinners 131
Roeg, Nicholas 1, 209–11
Room at the Top 131
Rose, Michael 227
Rosen, Martin 198–99
Rowling, J. K. 228, 239, 240, 242
Rowson, Simon 82
Ruddigore 126, 167
Run Wild, Run Free 168, 188, 192–93
Runaway Railway 96–98
Rutherford, Margaret 74, 77

Sabotage 67
Sabu 38–40, 138, 260
Saint's Return, The 130
Sammy's Super T-Shirt 102–3
Sandy the Seal 188
Saturday Night and Sunday Morning 131
Saving Mr Banks 153
Scarlet Blade, The 167
science-fiction (genre) 11, 167–68, 200–3
Scrooge (1935) 82
Scrooge (1951) 122, 123
Secret Garden, The (1993) 228
Selfish Giant, The 231, 268

Index

Shaun the Sheep Movie 227, 244
Sheffield Juvenile Organisations
Committee (1932) 29
Shortt, Edward 29
Sinbad and the Eye of the Tiger 201
Sir Billi 231
Slave Girls 201
Smiley 35, 86
Smith, G. A. 11
Snow White and the Seven Dwarfs
60, 138
Snowball 35
Snowman, The 2, 211–13, 262
Snowman and the Snowdog, The 254
Soiuzmultfilm 104
Something Wicked This Way Comes
(1972) 213
Sony 244, 248
Sound of Music, The 167
Spanish Gardener, The 54, 116–18
Spock, Benjamin 120
Sprinkler Sprinkled, The (*L'Arroseur
arrosé*) 10, 11
Square Peg, The 75, 78
St. Trinian's (series) 65, 72, 108, 109,
110, 115, 119, 120, 121
Star Wars 103, 132, 159, 162, 202, 207,
228, 261, 281
Star! 179
Stars on Parade 68
Steptoe and Son 68
Stevenson, Robert Louis 139
*Story of Robin Hood and His Merrie
Men, The* 137, 138, 140,
141–43, 144
Story of Tracy Beaker, The 260
Stranger from Venus 130
Stuart, Binkie 36, 38, 59, 67, 273
StudioCanal 244

Subotsky, Milton 131, 201
Summer Holiday 131, 167
Superman 162
Swallows and Amazons (1974) 185, 265
Swiss Family Robinson 137, 150, 153
Sword and the Rose, The 137, 138,
143–44, 150

Tales of Beatrix Potter, The
(1971) 184–85
Tarka the Otter (1979) 188, 195–97,
241, 261, 262
Taste of Honey, A 131
Taylor, Alma 14, 32
teen film 5, 107, 129, 130–32, 201–2
television (in relation to chil-
dren's cinema) 104, 107, 185,
211–19, 264–66
Temple, Shirley 15, 31, 33, 36, 38, 55,
59, 174, 273
Terrornauts, The 201
Terry on the Fence 104
Thatcher, Margaret 204, 206, 221
They Came from Beyond Space 168, 201
Thief of Bagdad, The (1940) 1, 34, 35,
39, 40–42, 56, 258, 261
Thief of Baghdad, The (1979) 201
Those Kids From Town 34
*Those Magnificent Men in Their Flying
Machines* 167
Three Lives of Thomasina, The 137
Three Stooges, The 57
Thunderbird 6 167
Thunderbirds are Go 167
Tilly the Tomboy 14, 15
Time Bandits 2, 205, 207–9, 211,
262, 263
Tom Brown's School Days (1951) 107–8,
110, 123

305

Index

Tom Jones (1963) 166

Tom Sawyer (1876) 86

Tom Tom Topia 60

Tom's Ride 84

Tommy Steele Story, The 131

Toto and the Poachers 92

Treasure Island (1950) 122, 137, 138–41, 144, 149

Tremain, Johnny 150

Trevelyan, John 179

'trick' films 11

Trip to the Moon, A (Le Voyage dans la lune) 10

Trouble in Store 74–76, 77, 78

Tudor Rose 82

Turned Out Nice Again 60

'tween' Audience 5

Twice Upon a Time 107

TVC 211–12

Tyrell, Lord 81

Under the Bed 214

Unidentified Flying Oddball 137

Vice Versa (1948) 107–9, 115

View to a Kill, A 216

Village of the Damned 268

Voyage of the 'Arctic', or How Captain Kettle Discovered the North Pole 11

Voyage of Peter Joe, The 85

Wainwright, Richard 32–34

Wallace and Gromit (franchise) 6, 222–29, 230, 245, 246–48

Wallace & Gromit: The Curse of the Were-Rabbit 2, 223, 244, 246–48

Warlords of Atlantis 201, 281

Warner Bros. 229, 240

Watch with Mother 234

Water Babies, The (1978) 184

Watership Down 2, 124, 125, 188, 195, 197–200, 260–61, 262

Watkins, Arthur 127

Wheare, K. C. 87–88

Wheare Report, The 87–88, 128, 129

When Dinosaurs Ruled the Earth 201, 202

When the Wind Blows 124, 125, 223, 262

Whistle Down the Wind 2, 132–36, 258, 262

White, Chrissie 14, 32

Wilkinson, Joseph Brooke 21, 24

William Comes to Town 35, 48, 53–54

Williamson, James 11

Wind in the Willows, The (1983) 211

Wind in the Willows, The (1996) 228

Wisdom, Norman 8, 57–58, 69, 74–79

Witches, The 2, 209–11

Withers, Jane 59

Wizard of Oz, The 40, 123, 138, 207, 263

Wombling Free 184

Woodstock 179

Working Title 220

Wrong Trousers, The 223, 225–26

Yellow Submarine 2, 167, 169–72, 175, 258

Young Ones, The 131, 167

youth culture 110, 115, 126–32, 153–54, 179

youth film *see* teen film

Zombie Flesh Eaters 216

Zoo Baby 168

Zulu 166

CPSIA information can be obtained
at www.ICGtesting.com
Printed in the USA
LVHW022033230721
693495LV00019B/1459